REPRINTS OF ECONOMIC CLASSICS

EUROPE: THE WORLD'S BANKER
1870–1914

EUROPE
THE WORLD'S BANKER
1870-1914

AN ACCOUNT OF
EUROPEAN FOREIGN INVESTMENT
AND THE CONNECTION OF
WORLD FINANCE WITH DIPLOMACY
BEFORE THE WAR

BY

HERBERT FEIS

With an Introduction by
CHARLES P. HOWLAND

AND WITH A
NEW INTRODUCTION BY THE AUTHOR

PUBLISHED FOR THE COUNCIL ON FOREIGN RELATIONS

REPRINTS OF ECONOMIC CLASSICS

Augustus M. Kelley, Bookseller
New York 1964

Printed in the United States of America.

TO
EDWIN F. GAY
TEACHER AND FRIEND

COUNCIL ON FOREIGN RELATIONS

The Council on Foreign Relations is a non-profit institution devoted to study of the international aspects of American political, economic, and strategic problems. It takes no stand, expressed or implied, on American policy.

The authors of books published under the auspices of the Council are responsible for their statements of fact and expressions of opinion. The Council is responsible only for determining that they should be presented to the public.

1964 INTRODUCTION

The reissuance of this study of the connections between world finance and diplomacy before the First World War leads me to glance back over the shoulder of history. A scanning of the vicissitudes that have occurred during the thirty years or so since it was published may turn up some useful hints for our times.

The era of great private foreign investment by the British, French and Germans recounted in these pages came to an end during the First World War. The British were compelled to dispose of most of their immense overseas investment to pay the expenses of the war; the only valuable portion retained were shares in oil companies, gold and other metal mines, and rubber plantations. The great sums lent by the French to foreign governments, especially that of Czarist Russia, were all lost; but investments in the French colonies, the Suez Canal and Latin America remained intact. What fragments of the German foreign investment not ruined by the war were requisitioned by the victors.

The competitive efforts of each of these countries to enlist its capital in the source of its national diplomacy proved futile. It was a symptom rather than a primary cause of the antagonistic relations between the powers and nationalities of Europe. But it intensified rather than soothed the rivalries which ended in lethal strife.

Stunned and impoverished, these three great financial centers were not able to resume their foreign lending and investment on its former scale. British groups managed to finance some alluring ventures in the Commonwealth and Empire and in Middle Eastern oil, and the French slowly expanded their investment in their colonies—but hardly more.

American private capitalists took over their former role as bankers to the world. In their sprouting self-confidence they were disposed to try to clean up the rubble of the war and put the world on its feet again. Most Americans were opposed, as the outcome of the national argument about joining the League of Nations proved, to share in the anxieties and risks of en-

forcing peace. But American dollars were made available. Individuals, banks, business corporations all vied with one another
in risking their capital abroad in pursuit of the large anticipated returns. All were made careless by the rapid rise in their
paper fortunes, resulting from the great surge in value of stocks
and real estate. Foreign governments, corporations and banks
bid temptingly for loans. American industry in a similarly
bold mood plunged into new enterprises in every continent.

During this decade of the nineteen-twenties (the decade now
remembered by many only through the personal chronicles of
Joyce, Hemingway, Scott Fitzgerald and Gertrude Stein, which
leave the impression that the world centered around Sylvia
Beach's Bookshop) the American government smiled upon this
overflow of American private capital into foreign lands, while
seeking discreetly to insure that its loans or ventures did not
contravene American diplomacy. It used its power to debar
our former associates in the First World War from American
financial markets, to compel them to sign agreements to repay
what they had borrowed from the American government during
and just after the end of the war. Concurrently, it refused to
make any other government loans to foreign authorities. All
three administrations in office before 1933—those of Presidents
Harding, Coolidge and Hoover—steadfastly maintained the
stand expounded by Secretary of State Hughes in 1923, "It is
not the policy of our government to make loans to other governments, and the needed capital if it is supplied at all, must
be furnished by public organizations."

The outflowing tide of American private capital during this
decade did assist the war-damaged and socially disturbed
countries of Western Europe to crawl back towards health. It
soothed temporarily some of the discords left by the war and
the peace treaties. But these beneficial results vanished, as,
after 1929, the economic depression deepened and monetary disorder—verging on panic—developed. This accentuated, and
was accentuated by the political turmoil and disorder in
Europe and the Far East. The financial institutions of Central
Europe, to which American banks had loaned so much of their

liquid funds, collapsed. Almost all governments in Europe and Latin America ceased to pay interest on their debts. Many of the foreign enterprises owned by Americans ceased to pay dividends.

Consequently, both as a financial venture and as an agent of diplomacy, these exuberant foreign forays of American capital were adjudged to have been a foolish mistake. The sense of obligation to assist in the material improvement of other countries was drowned in the swell of our own troubles. The idea that our financial power should be used to aid our national diplomacy or improve the prospects of peace subsided as the United States tried to isolate itself against the storms lowering over Europe and the Far East.

Consequently, during the next decade of the nineteen thirties, few new foreign loans were made by private American investors; and the expansion of American enterprise abroad slowed down except in a few countries such as Canada and Australia, deemed to be safe and stable, and some ventures in the development of natural resources—mainly in oil and mines.

The American government began to provide credits to assist American exports. But the Roosevelt administration continued to refuse to consider other types of financial assistance to foreign governments or enterprises. Thus it passed up the chance to use our productive power to influence the course of events in Europe and the Far East. Had it, during the thirties, lent or given Great Britain, France, China and their associates, sums equivalent to those provided later under the Marshall Plan, this might have made the difference between peace and war. For these opponents of the Axis would then have been able—had they chosen to do so—to enlarge their industrial capacity and military forces, and stand up earlier and more firmly and confidently against Mussolini and Hitler. But would they have done so unless the United States, while aiding them financially, also gave a promise to join them if war should ensue? Probably not.

Since the end of the Second World War the mutations in the nature of international finance and in its connection with diplomacy have been even more extensive and deep. At last the American government allowed the unpaid inter-governmental debts of the First World War to lapse into oblivion. Having helped to finance the war effort of its Allies in the Second World War through Lend-Lease, it recognized the necessity of providing resources for relief and reconstruction thereafter. It made to them and many other governments which lacked means to pay for essential imports, gifts, and grants, in ascending amounts.

The next vigorous steps along this route were taken when Congress, in response to President Truman's urgent appeal that the United States must prove that freedom was not synonymous with poverty, voted large grants in aid for Greece where a civil war against the Communists was going on, and for Turkey, part of whose territory the Soviet Union was trying to grab. Soon thereafter it sponsored that largest and most sustained cooperative effort—The Marshall Plan. Then, in his Inaugural Address in 1949, President Truman declared that ''We must embark on a bold new program for making the benefits of our scientific advances and industrial progress available for the improvement and growth of undeveloped areas.''

Thus step by step American financial power was put to work in the service of our foreign policy—to end distress and stagnation, especially in Europe—and ward off political and social disorder and the menace of Communism.

During the subsequent years the American program of foreign aid conducted by the American government became global. In some form and amount loans and technical assistance were extended to almost four score foreign countries. The scope of our dispensations was widened to embrace every element of national life and every kind of activity which affected the prospect of economic growth and of political stability and friendship. For experience induced the sobering conclusion that most of the presently poor peoples, even given much financial aid, would not progress unless all the arteries of their national life were regenerated.

To a few countries assaulted or seriously threatened by

Communism, the loans and grants of the American government were disproportionately great, particularly Turkey and Greece, South Korea, Taiwan, India, Pakistan and Vietnam. The Philippines were similarly rewarded because of their previous relation to the United States and their valiant stand during the war.

While the needs of these areas were receiving generous attention in Washington, those of the Latin American countries were being neglected. Suddenly the United States became aware that many of their people were concluding that we were indifferent to their welfare and were turning against us and toward Communism. Therefore, the American government created special banking institutions to assist them, and accepted continuing responsibility of doing so under the auspices of the Alliance for Progress.

Besides these programs, directly linked with our national foreign policies, the American government provided a large fraction of the resources available to the United Nations to sustain its efforts to keep the peace and give economic aid to its poorer members.

During these same two post-war decades American and European private foreign investment also revived. But purchases of foreign securities by individual investors and institutions remained comparatively small, and confined to those originating in the economically advanced countries such as Japan, Germany, Canada and Australia. However, American enterprises established thousands of branch or subsidiary plants in manufactures, the extractive industries (particularly oil and the metal ores), and some branches of agriculture, such as sugar and rubber.

While these changes in the source, scope and nature of international finance were occurring, earlier evaluations of the benefits accruing to the dispensers of capital and technical assistance and to the recipients were being brought into question.

During 1870-1914 when European capital was penetrating all the primitive, backward, unsettled, unexplored areas of the globe, almost all commentators were sure that the expansive activity was mutually beneficial. The investing nations would secure income; the nations in which the investments were made would secure the benefits of advanced productive enterprise—deemed to be humanly ''civilizing'' as well as economically stimulating.

True, even then, there were a few dissenters among the Western professional observers, such as J. A. Hobson and H. N. Brailsford. Their criticisms focused on the episodes where the pursuit of private gains were connected either as a cause or pretext for the extension of imperial control over weaker peoples. They strove to arouse opinion by stressing the instances in which financial activities were implicated in the dangerous rivalries between the European powers for colonies, wealth and spheres of influence. By their dissections and admonitions they sought to check the further extension of colonialism, and break the associations between international finance and frictional international politics. But even as they did so, these protestants stayed intellectually in the capitalist camp.

However, other treatises were being written which were inspired by hatred of capitalism and the wish to bring about revolution. These Marxian-Communist commentaries averred that national financial and trade rivalries, compelled by a frantic need to keep the capitalist system going, were the main cause of war. They construed the spread of imperialist control as viciously oppressive. They argued that the profits derived from foreign investments were exorbitant, and gained by exhausting the natural resources of the underdeveloped countries and keeping their workers down.

These denunciations of the foreign engagements of private capitalists were given liturgical sanction in the pronouncements of Lenin and other proponents and admirers of the arisen Union of Soviet Socialist Republics. In the years between the two wars their treatises were studied by many of the young men who became the political leaders of their countries after the Second World War. The impressions made by them merged with and nourished the demand for independence and the excited flare-up of nationalism.

And even though the relations between affluent and poor countries are now essentially different than they were in the earlier era, and even though almost all the former colonies are now free, such evaluations still are having an important impact. Communist authorities and sympathizers continue to reiterate their validity. For by doing so, they often discourage recourse by poor countries to the western capitalist democracies for aid and sustain opposition to western private initiatives. They rejoice in, rather than lament, the harm done to the prospects of the poorer countries to better their lot.

As a consequence of the attitude thus fostered, many of the poorer countries, especially the newly independent ones, are determined to retain public and national control over resources and basic industries even though they have not the means or knowledge to develop them. Some debar private foreign capital from these fields of production or impose unacceptable restraints. Thus their chance of securing the needed means depends more and more on what they can procure as loans or grants from the governments of the wealthier countries or the international financial institutions.

Of recent years many of them have come to believe they are entitled to the aid of the American government on their own terms; and that the United States has a moral obligation to provide it—as an act of justice, not of generosity. Even as they demand help, they continue to fear the intrusion of the foreigners who give it. They insist that aid be given "without strings"; that the foreign suppliers of capital and technical assistance should not try to sustain any significant connection between their contributions and their diplomacy. In short, their craving to emerge from poverty consorts uneasily with the over-excited gush of nationalism, residual fears that foreigners will again manage to secure control of their national life, and resentment at the difference between their condition and that of the foreigners to whom they appeal for help.

The common wish to restrain Communism has caused the affluent western capitalist (semi-socialist) governments to co-operate in the making of foreign loans and grants rather than to rival one another. None are seeking special exclusive spheres of profit or financial opportunity. They have formed a joint committee, whose assignment it is to coordinate their foreign aid activities. Through it the American government has been trying to induce others to provide more aid so that its relative share of the expense be lessened.

Concurrently, the scores of countries which have accepted the developing designation as "undeveloped"—through no acknowledged fault of their own—have been flocking together in order to make their claim for greater assistance on their own terms more effective. They have just secured approval by the Assembly of the United Nations for a constitution of a new organization whose prime duty it will be to assist them in this effort. The Soviet Union and its associates, of course, are endorsing their complaints against the capitalist countries and urging them to unite in their demands and to use all means to cause the West to give into them. Communist spokesmen will continue to do so in the expectation that the resistance and refusal of the wealthy capitalist countries will arouse resentment and alienate those whose claims may be rejected or reduced.

In pursuing this course the Soviet government is not apparently deterred by the probability that impoverished countries will also ask more of it. For despite its fiasco in China, it still seems to be confident of its skill in turning whatever aid it provides foreign countries to its own advantage, or in any case to the disadvantage of the capitalist countries.

Whether or not this organization of the "undeveloped" countries will work harmoniously with other multi-national institutions who provide capital and technical assistance or clash with them, time alone will tell. It will be most regrettable if the poorer countries, in their urgent efforts to get more financial or more favorable trade treatment, upset the several important existing organizations which are striving to serve these same ends. Together these have been gradually creating a new alignment of connections between world finance and diplomacy. The congeries of agencies and committees which

function under the auspices of the United Nations, in which all
its members are represented, have striven hard and done much
in the way of technical aid and guidance in all fields of national
life. The International Bank of Reconstruction and Development, however, has been able to give far greater financial assistance to large economic undertakings. For its disposable
capital is many times greater, and since the Communist countries are not members, it is not riven by division. Recently the
Bank, through an affiliated institution, has been extending its
operations on far easier terms into areas of productive promise
that could not currently pay for themselves.

Several other significant multi-national organizations engaged in similar activities are acquiring independent renown
and notice. Among them are the Development Assistance Committee (DAC), the Organization for Economic·Cooperation
and Development (OECD), the Alliance for Progress in Latin
America, the Inter-American Development Bank, and the
Colombo Plan for Cooperative Economic Development in South
and Southeast Asia.

All of these multi-national agencies would like to direct their
planning and employ their capital and expert knowledge, without having to take account of any considerations save those
affecting the economic growth and social advancement of their
members. That is, by free choice, under happier circumstances,
they would prefer to supersede all connections between finance
and *national* diplomacy by a single clear and tingling line of
relationship *to the whole* community of nations. But because
up to now they have operated in the shadow of the cold war,
and because their main contributors and sources of funds are
the Western capitalist democracies, they have thought it prudent not to ignore the diplomatic desires of their mentors. Even
so, the help of these institutions is preferred by many governments to that of national aid agencies or foreign private
capitalist groups.

I will end this brief scanning of the vicissitudes and mutations in the connections between finance and diplomacy that
have occurred since the period of which I wrote in EUROPE:

THE WORLD'S BANKER, by an observation as true now as in the past; a lesson of experience that must he heeded by all countries—the Western capitalist countries, the Communist countries, the impoverished nations in all hemispheres which may strive to remain aloof from both or flirt with both diplomatically. It is that the competitive use of capital by political antagonists may—or may not—extend the time in which they may find the terms on which they can live more trustfully and peacefully with one another. But it can do no more. All the great resources, technical knowledge and energies of the contestants will not in the end permanently benefit any country— the providers or the recipients—unless one and all govern their conduct and their treatment of each other by mutual restraint, toleration and renunciation of the will to dominate. The contribution which international finance can make to either economic progress or international amity cannot be substantially greater than what the nations, individually and collectively, merit by their behavior.

These thoughts, written down as a supplementary introduction to the reissue of this book, have taken on a somber tone. But there are signs that enough nations are taking this truism to heart to constrain those few which are still ruled by hostility or bent on imposing their will and way of life on others. Until this is a proven fact, not merely a hopeful, wishful surmise, the Western democracies must continue to devote vast sums to maintenance of strong military forces. If expenditures for this purpose should be reduced by world accord, and a substantial part of the savings employed in aiding poorer countries, the whole international scene would become more tranquil and buoyant. Should this transpire, the links of connection between international finance and national diplomacy will evolve into a more unified and reliable system than that of yesterday and today.

June, 1964

HERBERT FEIS
York, Maine

INTRODUCTION

THIS important contribution to economic history traces the outward flow of European surplus capital from 1870 until the war of 1914–18 caused waste and destruction again to usurp the place of creation and thrift. The first aim of the author is that of the economist, namely, to give a tableau of the way in which British, French, and German savings were employed in loans to governments, in financing railways, harbor developments and other public works, in exploring and exploiting the resources of colonies and of undeveloped states or areas, in building railways in India and Africa.

On this purely economic side there were well-marked national characteristics. British capital favored an economic development that would produce the revenue for debt-service or dividends rather than loans to governments or government guaranties, to supply constructive talent and management, to stay with the enterprise and to make it "earn its own keep." Other types of investment of course there were—emissions of loans of foreign governments, of the bonds of American and Argentine railways, and so on—but relatively the British investment emphasis was on control and management.

The volume of this total foreign investment was enormous, rising from the annual investing of £1,700,000 in the five-year period 1875–79—the period of world-wide financial depression and contraction—to the annual investing of £185,000,000 in the four-year period 1910–13, when the annual foreign investment equaled approximately one-half the national savings. At this time the total foreign investment amounted to about four billion pounds, or one-quarter of the national wealth, and produced one-tenth of the national income.* It seems to have

---

* As Mr. Feis points out, the disproportion is accounted for by the fact that national income includes the return for all forms of productive labor.

been about equally divided between investments within
and those without the empire. Obviously it created a pre-
ponderating interest that the world should be orderly and
peaceful.

French conditions were different. Social habits had determined a life of patient toil, a desire for an unlaborious
old age, small families and a stationary population, remaining at home, finding "warmth of assurance in patiently accumulated sums"—in financial terms, a lending
rather than an adventuring people. The amount of foreign investment was much less than the English—in the
1909–13 period perhaps $250,000,000 a year as against
a British average foreign investment of $900,000,000 in
the same period; a total in 1914 of about $9,000,000,000
or one-sixth of the national wealth, as against the British
$20,000,000,000, or one-fourth of the British wealth.

But it is the character of the French investment that
differentiates it sharply from the British. For the French
there were practically no opportunities for the development of regions colonized by their own people, opportunities to build, to manage, and to profit by the dividends
on ownership-management. The investment was that of a
lender, who relies upon the general solvency of the borrower rather than upon the success of the enterprise. The
first result of this type of lending is the capitalist who is
much less concerned as to the use made of his money than
if he were the entrepreneur who must earn his dividends.
The second result is that until the approach of the borrower's bankruptcy is apparent, the lender, confident in
the borrower's general ability to pay, sees ulterior political
purposes that can be accomplished through a loan without too great risk to the security of the investment.

This French idea of using the savings of the citizens
for political purposes is in direct line of descent from the
ideas of Colbert, Louis XIV's Prime Minister. The French
Revolution, which broke the continuity of the domestic
political system of France, exerted little effect on the re-

lation between state policy and economics. As in the time
of Colbert, policy between 1870 and 1914 was directed
primarily by two sets of conditions and desires. French
industry was lagging in its growth behind that of rival
states; French foreign investment must serve to aid it.
French political destiny was being worked out from day
to day in a world that included enemies; French foreign
investment was seeking forces by which the destiny of
France might be made a safe, perhaps a triumphant one.
French capital and enterprise, in greater measure than
either English or German capital, "was shaping political
alignments—making the fortunes of a new day." The
French bankers, even the ordinary French investors, were
dealers in "Affaires."

These financial studies constitute a major contribution
to the problem of the causation of the World War, disin-
tegrate Article 231 of the Treaty of Versailles which imposes sole "war-guilt" on Germany and perpetuates the
myth of a planned and deliberate aggression against a
peace-loving world. Nothing, of course, can cleanse the
scutcheon of the Dual Monarchy from the blot of having
put the match to the powder magazine, or relieve the German Reich from the responsibility of having in July, 1914,
backed an ally in dealing a vendetta blow, blind to the
frightful aftermath; but as for the deeper causes of the
War these financial studies underpin the conclusion of
Lowes Dickinson, "that the War was caused by the system
of international anarchy involved in alliances, armaments,
and secret diplomacy," and show how that system called
to its aid the financial strength of the counter-intriguing
nations.

The Franco-Russian connection was not more iniquitous than other such alliances, but it is more easily traced
and more spectacular in the essential cultural and institu-
tional antitheses that existed between the ramshackle au-
tocratic government of Russia, heading blindly for the
abyss, and the thrifty egalitarian close-knit French re-

public. The France of republicanism, liberty, and equality, was gradually harnessed to decaying Russian imperialism, oppression, and corruption; and French peasants of the blue blouse, French shopkeepers of the black coat, bowed their backs, pinched their household budgets, and hoarded their francs with the effect of enabling Russian despotism to resist the pressure of the Duma for constitutionalism and a peaceful revolution. A common hatred and fear of the common neighbor bound these antitheses together and themselves became a factor in bringing on the cataclysm against which they were intended to protect.

This is not to blame a France which had suffered from such master-intrigue and master-preparation for the war of 1870 as Bismarck's. Indeed, it was the later intrigue of Bismarck in the financial field, seeking by a refusal of credit to Russia to bring her into humiliating subservience to Germany that first threw Russia into the arms of France. The first Russian loan, 500,000,000 francs, was floated on the Paris Bourse in December, 1888, after the approval of both governments, and was quickly followed by one of 700,000,000 francs and another of 1,200,000,-000. French financial help to Russia, once begun, increased rapidly as the Czardom brought its Danaïdean jar to be continually refilled at the inexhaustible French spring. In 1902 French investments in Russia were approximately 7,000,000 francs and by 1914 had become 11,300,000,000 francs, about one-quarter of the whole French foreign investment; over 9,000,000,000 francs of French-owned Russian securities were obligations of the Russian Government. The distribution in France was extraordinary; after the war the Property Office established by the French Government "received some 1,600,000 individual declarations from owners of Russian securities."

The huge French investment in Russia came to be guided almost exclusively "by the stir of political arrangements"; the weaker Russia became in her financial and domestic affairs, the higher price did she put on her mili-

tary friendship, until, as may sometimes happen, the ulterior purpose of the borrowing endangered the financial
interest of the lender. About 37 per cent of the Russian
railways were built primarily for political and military,
not economic, reasons. Isvolsky in 1911 boasted of the way
in which he had forced the French Government to subordinate the financial interests of the French banks to the
needs of the dynasty and the strategic requirements of the
far-stretching military fronts of Russia.

The Franco-Russian illustration has been selected, I
repeat to avoid misunderstanding, because the red military
entries are so conspicuous among the plain black-and-
white entries of humdrum finance, but not because the
case was otherwise with the Central Powers. Germany, too,
was throwing gold and the sword into the same scale, and
in the various phases of the Moroccan controversy backed
German enterprise with a resolution which shifted questions from the terrain of finance to that of irreducible
prestige,* and with a recklessness which enlarged the universal fears and set camp against camp in prepared array.

The chapter on the Balkan railways shows how financial
interests were entangled in the web of politics and nationalism, each financial maneuver contributing to the
suspicions and antagonism that brought on the Balkan
wars and thereby the cataclysm that began at Sarajevo.
The chapter on Japan's financing, on the other hand,
leads out of the atmosphere of constant intrigue, and by
coincidence of the period studied with that of Japan's own
phenomenal expansion, gives the financial side of the
drama of Japanese development from a local to a first-
rank power.

The illustrative material selected in this introduction
only indicates the illuminating mass of facts which the
author has brought together from a great variety of

---

* "Vital interests and national honor" is the American euphemism for
the will to dominate.

sources and many archives. The book presents the major
episodes of the financial contribution to the war-drift
without moralizings, but the author is by no means ob-
livious of the implications of the facts presented; these
are so ordered that they might well serve as material for
a philosophical inquiry into the relation between man's
organized acquisitiveness and the political anarchy of a
world of stubborn "sovereignties." The export of capital
raises profound questions both in the economic and in the
political spheres, which bring us, as the author says,
"close to questioning the whole of modern history, its
motives, dominant national ideals, new industrial life and
methods."

The volume is published under the auspices of the
Council on Foreign Relations, which has undertaken to
bring out occasional special studies in addition to its annual *Survey of American Foreign Relations* and *Political
Handbook of the World;* it follows H. Foster Bain's study
of *Ores and Industry in the Far East* and James W.
Angell's work on *The Recovery of Germany.*

Charles P. Howland,

New York   *Director of Research*
  July, 1930.   *Council on Foreign Relations.*

PREFACE

WHEN in the stillness of some distant, uninhabited valley the steam shovels and pneumatic drills pound out the path for steel rails and the locomotive, a drama of new life is begun. Human power is applying itself to an intricate creation. One world is destroyed, another founded.

Before the World War the capital of western Europe was impelling forward this drama of change upon a limitless stage. Through the savings of a few countries the power of industrial civilization was carried from its first home to all other lands; the world of machines, of organized, time-consuming production, of large-scale exchange, of numbers, extended itself. The financial journals stand as birth registers of the continuous union of capital, technical skill, and purposeful planning of the capital-accumulating countries, and the resources and labor of the rest of the hemisphere. Western Europe, through its spared accumulations of capital, impregnated all other regions with the growing cells of its civilization. The economic and political arrangements of the world were thereby permanently changed.

To study the main trend of this migration of capital, to measure and record it, was the original purpose of this volume. But preliminary study soon revealed that its connections with the political and diplomatic events of pre-war days were numerous and important. The world from which the capital moved was made up of highly ambitious, competitive national states. The regions to which it moved varied enormously in the character of their peoples, their powers of self-government, their ability to put borrowed capital to good use, their political strength. The place of many of these regions in the political arrangement of the world was, even then, in the balance. Their transactions with foreign capital often settled the outcome. In short, the financial transactions between western Europe and other areas were an important element in political affairs. They became all the more important because the official circles of lending countries gradually came to envisage the foreign investments of their citizens, not as private financial transactions, but as one of the instruments through which national destiny was achieved. Financial force was often used to buy or build political friendship or alliance, was often lent or withheld in accordance with political calculations.

The lines of political division in pre-war Europe, the situations which were created and which led ultimately to the War, can be understood only by taking account of the borrowing-lending relations which existed. On the other hand, the action of capital, seeking return, can be understood only by taking account of the national influences to which it was subject. The volume, it is hoped, reveals the strength of the tendency of capital to move over national boundary lines in search for opportunity, and at the same time amply illustrates the special risks, controls, and pressures to which such capital movement has been subject.

These are the reasons for believing a study of lending and borrowing relations in the pre-war years worth undertaking. But additional point may be given to the effort by the fact that the United States has taken its place with western Europe in supplying capital to other lands. It has become, and will remain, a great, perhaps the greatest, center from which the revolutionizing force of accumulated capital and machine technique will travel outward. The account which follows proves, I think, that a capital-lending country should possess a policy, or at least a carefully defined attitude, toward this process of foreign investment and the situations it creates. Some instruction may be in the record of policy and experience of pre-war Europe.

The great dimensions of the matters which I have attempted to study may help to excuse the shortcomings of the result. Within the covers of one volume it has been impossible to give attention to many of the aspects of this course of capital movement which are of greatest interest to economists and international lawyers: to cite a few in the economic sphere, the operation of the financial mechanism by which the capital is transferred from lender to borrower, the effect of such transfers on trade balances and prices; or to cite one in the legal sphere, the consequences of the spread of the doctrine within borrowing countries that those who invest capital within their borders must accept the same status as domestic capitalists. It has also been impossible to traverse the whole area of lending and borrowing. Only the capital investments made by the British, the French, and the Germans, with the concomitant government activity, are included: the ventures of the Dutch, the Belgians, and the Swiss, as much as they deserve consideration as part of the historic process, could not be adequately reviewed without virtually doubling the task and the consequent number of pages.

So much for the pretensions and limitations of this volume. For assistance given I am heavily indebted to many individuals and groups. The necessary study in Europe was undertaken with the aid of a fellowship award of the Guggenheim Foundation. The Graduate School of the University of Cincinnati also made some grants for the work. The advice and encouragement of Professor F. W. Taussig greatly helped me to plan the study. The critical reading of the manuscript by Professor William R. Langer and Professor Parker T. Moon enabled me to understand and partly to correct its faults. Among those who aided me by giving information or putting material at my disposal I take the liberty of mentioning, as grateful acknowledgment, M. Cousin, of the Association Nationale des Porteurs Français des Valeurs Mobilières; M. De Mouy, formerly of Lazard Frères, Paris; M. Masson, Director of the Crédit Lyonnais; M. Joseph Caillaux, formerly Prime Minister and Minister of Finance of France; M. Fernand Faure, Editor of the *Revue Politique et*

Parlementaire; H. G. Hawtrey, Esq.,˙ of the British Treasury; B. I. G. Lloyd, Esq., of the British Board of Trade; Hartley Withers, Esq.; Walter T. Layton, Esq., Editor of the *Economist;* Douglas Reid, Esq., of the Council of Foreign Bondholders; Sir Josiah Stamp; Sir George Paish; Sir Alexander Kleinwort; Henry M. Andrews, Esq., of J. H. Schröder, London; Herr Ernst Kahn, of Lazard Speyer-Ellissen of Frankfort. To the authorities and staff of the École des Sciences Politiques, the London School of Economics, and the New York Public Library, I owe thanks for unfailing courtesy and aid.

H. F.

New York
 June, 1930.

TABLE OF CONTENTS

PAGE

New Introduction by the Author ix

Introduction, by CHARLES P. HOWLAND xix

Preface xxv

PART I

THE RECORD OF CAPITAL MOVEMENT

Chapter

I. British Foreign Investment 3

    The greatest free financial force 3
    The geographical spread of the investment 17
    The character of the investment 26

II. French Foreign Investment 33

    The world of saving and the world of lending 33
    The rôle of the French banks 39
    The growth of the foreign investment 43
    Where the investment was made 49
    The character of the investment 57

III. German Foreign Investment 60

    Two needs for every mark 60
    The German great banks and their allies 62
    The growth of the investment 68
    The zones of investment 73
    The character of the investment 78

PART II

RELATIONS BETWEEN FINANCE AND GOVERN-MENT IN THE LENDING COUNTRIES

IV. Finance and Government in Great Britain 83

    Legal freedom and informal intercourse 83
    The adjustment of financial and political policy 88
    The colonial stocks act 92

The Government's concern with foreign oppor-
tunities for British capital and enterprise   95
The Palmerston circular and subsequent policy   102
The investors endeavor to help themselves   113
Concluding observations   117

V. Finance and Government in France   118
The texts   118
Supervision for economic ends   122
The search for political advantage   133
Favor for the colonies   142
The Government's part in securing concessions   144
Government protection of foreign investment   146
The organization of the investors   154
Some general observations   156

VI. Finance and Government in Germany   160
The growth of a doctrine   160
Means and methods   163
The actual exercise of government influence   169
Government aid in securing concessions   176
German capital and the colonies   181
The protection of the foreign investment   183
Concluding observations   186

PART III

STUDIES IN LENDING AND BORROWING

VII. Introduction   191
VIII. Nonintercourse between France and
the Central Powers   196
The ban against German securities   196
Austria-Hungary: the ending of a financial friend-
ship   201

IX. The Financing of Imperial Russia   210
The largest borrower in Europe   210
French capital serves the Alliance   212

The German Government intervenes 224
Upon accord, British investment follows 229

X. The Financing of Italy by Rival Alliances 235

XI. The Financing of Portugal—a Debtor with a Noble Past 243

Default follows upon default 243
Attention turns to the Portuguese colonies 247

XII. The Financing of the Balkan States 258

Serbia is assisted to rise 262
Creditors' control in Serbia 266
The development of Roumania 268
The financing of Bulgarian ambitions 272
The French Government vacillates 275
The German Government wins 279
Creditors' control in Bulgaria 283
Financing Greece's national career 284
Creditors' control in Greece 289

XIII. The Financing of the Balkan Railways 293

Across the Turkish provinces from Constantinople to Vienna 293
The Oriental railways live amid trouble 298
From the Danube to the Adriatic 302
The Balkan wars bring fresh troubles 304
International ownership is proposed 306
Sarajevo—the original terminus of the line 310

XIV. The Turkish Empire and European Investors 313

Between war and bankruptcy 313
The rôle of the powers—Germany 318
The rôle of the powers—France 320
The rôle of the powers—Great Britain 330

To protect the bondholders—the Ottoman public
debt administration 332

XV. The Financing of Railroads in Asiatic Turkey 342

The railway progresses toward Bagdad 342
The project of internationalization fails 348
German capital goes as far as it can 353
Opportunity is divided by spheres 355

XVI. The Financing of Persia: Between Two Imperial Ambitions 361

The Shah mortgages his domains to travel in Europe 361
Lending is controlled 365
Russia and Great Britain divide the field 366
The Trans-Persian railway project 379

XVII. Finance and Fate in North Africa 382

1. THE FINANCING OF EGYPT 382
The Khedive goes bankrupt 383
The creditors take control 384
The British take charge 390
2. THE FINANCING OF MOROCCO 397
France bargains for a free hand 399
Germany demands international control 404
France pushes ahead 407
On the verge of war 412

XVIII. Japan Is Helped To Become a Great Power 422

XIX. The Financing of the Chinese Government 430

The Chinese Government and the Powers 430
The financing of government needs 435
A note on the consortium 455
A note on the maritime customs administration 459

Concluding Observations—By Way of Apostrophe 463

PART I
THE RECORD OF CAPITAL MOVEMENT

CHAPTER I

BRITISH FOREIGN INVESTMENT

THE GREATEST FREE FINANCIAL FORCE

BEFORE the war, in the gray and smoke-encrusted lanes and alleys close by the Bank of England, there converged the greatest free financial force in the world. The London financial market derived its strength from great wealth, diversity, experience, world connections—all directed by a sober yet daring energy. The great wealth had enlarged itself gradually through the pioneering organization of machine industry, through the conduct of commerce throughout the world, and the development of the resources of distant areas. Out of the past there came, and grew more aggravated with the course of industrial change, the marked inequality of wealth and income which bred many of the bitter antagonisms of the day. At the top of the pyramid of wealth there rested a substantial group whose great income and investing power was one of the revolutionary forces of the world.[1] In 1914, according to the best available estimates, the annual income of the British people was in the neighborhood of 11 billions of dollars; and of this total approximately 1.8 billions were saved.[2] These savings, available

---

[1] See essay on "The Distribution of Capital" in H. Clay's *The Problem of Industrial Relations* (London, 1929), especially Table III, p. 291. In 1912 two-thirds of the accumulated capital in England and Wales were in estates of 5,000 pounds or more—these being in number less than one-tenth of the total number of estates. In these larger estates stocks and bonds were the chief component.

[2] Some of the expert estimates of annual savings (millions of pounds) follow:

	Savings	Source
1911	320	(Bowley and Stamp)
1911	330	(Pigou)
1913	380	(*Economist,* Oct. 10, 1925)
1913	350–400	(Report of Committee on National Debt and Taxation, 1927)

for capital expenditure of some kind, were mainly in the possession of those whose field of business and personal interests extended far beyond the British Isles.

For many decades back the natural resources and industrial operations of the British Isles had not offered as great opportunities for gain—differences of risk and circumstance considered—as had those of foreign lands.[3] Unobstructed by law, invited especially by lands to which the British people were spreading, solicited and directed by able young Englishmen, who in large numbers sought their fortunes in developing the resources of young countries, much of these savings found employment abroad. They took the whole of the outside world as the field of opportunity—and in so doing propelled that outside world into the stream of history along which Europe moved. In the early decades of the nineteenth century Great Britain was virtually the only important source of capital for those countries which lay outside of the circle of western Europe. During the century, with the quickened travel of ships and trains, the dispatch of the cables, the cheapened mails and daily press, and the greater movement of peoples, all capital acquired greater mobility. British capital remained the quickest and freest to move. But even in far-distant countries it met a strengthening competition. For as the capital resources of France, Ger-

[3] Statistical verification of this judgment is difficult. R. A. Lehfeldt's studies, *Journal of the Royal Statistical Society,* January, 1913, and *Economic Journal,* March, 1914, calculated the actual yields obtained by the holders of large issues (900,000 pounds or over) of fixed interest-bearing securities, covering about half the British investment. He took into account the consequences of default. The average return, 1898–1910, obtained on colonial and dominion securities was higher than that obtained on home securities of the same type by 0.2 per cent; the yield on foreign issues was 1 per cent higher. Between 1900 and 1913 the rise in return on all classes was well over 1 per cent indicating the strain that prevailed in all European money markets in the later period. This calculation is based on the assumption that the securities were purchased at their original public offering price and continuously held.

many, Belgium, Switzerland, and Holland (once the world's financier) grew more adequate, the sphere of their investment activity steadily expanded.

The volume of British investment and its cumulative additions remained the greatest, its distribution the widest, its undertakings the most substantial. London was the center of a financial empire, more international, more extensive in its variety, than even the political empire of which it was the capital. In the sphere of financial interest and calculation, distance lost its meaning; along all lines of latitude and longitude British capital worked its way; though, and here we interject an observation given repeated illustration in succeeding chapters, national boundary lines often were effective barriers. By the turn of the twentieth century approximately one-half of the current British savings was being invested abroad. The names of foreign lands and ventures vibrated unceasingly in the shadowy dimness of the London Stock Exchange, and the financial journals gave a panorama of the world's strivings in factory, mine, and field. Most men of property held some foreign securities—even though they were of the lords who stuck to the land. Premier Baldwin in a speech delivered in a full Parliament on July 1, 1926, marked the exceptional character of those who would not invest abroad. Accused by his opponents of having been partisan in the recent coal strike because of his ownership of the Baldwin Iron Works, he presented that ownership as a mark of pride, not of shame, for he had steadily refused to invest outside of Great Britain.

The movement of British capital to other lands was one of the shaping forces of Great Britain's economic structure and political destiny—steadily turning men's thoughts outward, making its own chains of connection, of cause and effect. Whether it was beneficial from the national and international points of view, whether it was excessive and left important matters at home neglected for lack of social direction—to these and many similar questions no certain answers can yet be returned. A margin of doubt remains for future history and study to resolve. General analytical reasoning upon its direct economic effects and observations of British economic history on the whole yields a favorable estimation, but cannot deal with all sides of the questions it presents. The subject remains unexhausted even when such analysis and observation have had their say.[4] Prevailing judgment tends to agree with that recently passed by an expert committee of the party that was in power while the greatest capital movements were taking place: "that in the Railway Age, the development of foreign and colonial railway systems abroad out

---

[4] Because of the many-sidedness of these effects, the difficulties of isolating them, the many forms of foreign investment, and the huge variety of circumstances which have attended such movements, no simple satisfactory set of judgments, even of the general deductive kind, can be framed. For an interesting criticism of the practice of leaving the distribution of British savings between home and foreign investment to the judgment of private financial institutions and banks, see *Britain's Industrial Future*, being the "Report of the Liberal Industrial Inquiry" (London, 1928). The literature on the subject is large, but little of it contains much substance. Throughout the British literature there is a steady bent toward favorable judgment of its economic effects. The most systematic analysis in that language is C. K. Hobson, *The Export of Capital* (London, 1914). Marshall, Bowley, Keynes, and Taussig, by their successive contributions, have opened up a promising new basis of judgment, by the study of changes in the "terms of trade." J. Viner's *Canada's Balance on International Indebtedness, 1900–1913* (Cambridge, 1924) is an outstanding example of an inductive study of *some* of the economic changes wrought by capital movement between countries. J. W. Angell's *The Theory of International Prices* (Cambridge, 1926) traces out lucidly many of the intricate theoretical issues raised by the subject, and carries speculation forward. The novelty of the French literature is mainly in its controversy, which refers primarily to the French situation. The German literature is disappointingly empty of new ideas, despite the complex reasoning which often appears in it, and gives the appearance of a new system. Of the analyses known to me, A. Sartorius Von Waltershausen, *Das Volkswirtschäftliche System der Kapital-Anlage in Auslande* (Berlin, 1907), and W. Zollinger, *Die Bilanz der Internationalen Weltübertragungen* (Jena, 1914) are the most interesting.

of British capital, when British materials, British savings, and British engineering enterprise were opening up the world for the supply of food and raw materials, was greatly in the interest of this country as well as of the world."[5]

Half a hundred types of financial institutions played a part in the process of investment of British capital.[6] The huge commercial banks, where most checking accounts were kept, which financed commodity movements throughout the world, were the greatest source of credit; yet they played but an indirect part in the security issue business. Alongside of them stood the banks, public and private, of the British Dominions. These, growing to power, kept establishments in London to employ their funds, to share in the profits of trade financing, to handle governmental financial affairs. Such were the Commonwealth Bank of Australia, the Imperial Bank of India, the National Bank of South Africa, and the Bank of Montreal. In London, too, met the directing boards of many of the British banks which operated in foreign lands. Such were, for example, the Hong Kong and Shanghai Bank, the Chartered Bank of India, Australia and China, the London and River Plate Bank, the Anglo-Egyptian Bank, and the London and Hanseatic. Through all these British capital was applied to the financing of foreign commerce, and the discovery and sustenance of commercial opportunity abroad. In addition, by their loans and purchases, they supported the security market and facilitated security operations. But with a few notable exceptions, such as the Hong Kong and Shanghai Bank, these institutions did not share actively in the spread of foreign securities among the British people. Their chief concern was with short-time financing, not with the placing of capital in

[5] *Britain's Industrial Future, op. cit.,* p. 110.

[6] F. Lavington, *The English Capital Market* (London, 1921), and B. D. Nash, *Investment Banking in England* (New York, 1924).

long-term ventures or securities. That was left to another
group of financial houses. Thereby no such concentration
of capital and credit resources occurred, no such dominance over the investment judgment of the ordinary bank
depositor arose, as happened in France and Germany.

At the head of the issue houses, and until well into the
nineteenth century, dominating the business, there were
powerful private banks, such as the Rothschilds, Barings,
Brown Shipley, Glyn Mills and Currie, and Schröders,
commanding resources sufficient for any promising demand. By tradition the partners of these houses abstained,
with rare exceptions, from holding places on the boards
of industrial enterprises; only here and there among the
directorates of investment trusts and insurance companies
were they to be found. Important as they were in the sale
of securities, they did not furnish leadership to British enterprise or control it. Besides these large and conservative
private banks (their conservatism did not prevent heavy
losses and the issue of securities which went into default),
which on the whole undertook only the issue of government and railway bonds, there was a considerable group
of smaller private banks. They, along with acceptance
houses and issuing brokers, handled many of the smaller
government and railway loans and much of the colonial
borrowing, and frequently undertook the issue of industrial securities. More numerous still were the financial,
land and investment companies engaged in promoting
and underwriting. These differed greatly among themselves. Some were primarily promotion companies; others
retained permanent interests in the properties they sponsored. Some carried on a varied activity; others spe-
cialized, for example, in Australian real estate, in tin
mines, in rubber, in tea or coffee plantations. It was this
group of companies, more than any other, which found
capital and management for pioneer enterprises. Offering
steady support to all were the investment trusts, grown

powerful through a combination of daring faith and careful judgment—absorbing, in particular, a large part of the loans of the governments and enterprises of the American continent.

Such were the different types of organizations which carried out the issuance of new securities, and the presentation of the securities to the investing public. To extend their reach, or to divide their risk, many other institutions were admitted to a share in the process, specializing in some part of it: as underwriters (a large and miscellaneous group including banks, investment trusts, insurance companies, etc.) ; as brokers who lent their names and carried out the technical formalities; as bankers who aided the sale. Within each group of organizations and between them constant change went on; combinations formed and parted; new forces came to the front, and old ones faded. The death of the head of the house could reduce the activity of the Rothschilds; an Argentine panic could submerge the Barings for a time; the discovery of gold fields could create new fortunes and new financial powers in Rhodes, Beit, Barnato, and Eckstein; the management of Egyptian banks and land companies could enrich a Sir Ernest Cassel and make him friend and financial intimate of the ruling monarch.

This was the market for "money," the agency through which financial support was bought and sold. To its bartering, scheming, and developing was attracted a large part of the saving of the British people. To this market you might come with a collection of treaties bearing the smeared symbols of an African chief, a survey map of properties located in India, suitable for tea-growing, a concession for a power plant in some South American town, the prospectus of a new bond issue of the Erie Railroad, and find some door open to you, some dim office where your treaties, maps, concessions, and prospectuses would be taken as familiar chances. Here stayed the representatives and agents of the British dominions and colonies, to arrange for the borrowing of their countries.[7] Here foreign governments sent their finance ministers, foreign railroads their executives or banking representatives, foreign mining syndicates their founders. Between the larger institutions some agreements existed, especially as regards government loans, based on some arrangement for dividing the business, or on habitual practices of working together, or on tacit recognition of place and privilege. But the market for securities, once issued, was free and broad. The Stock Exchange, through which virtually all the trading in foreign securities took place, regulated its own affairs without official supervision—except such as was embodied in the general "company" laws. The individual investor went to the market through his broker. The investment trusts supplied stability and cool judgment to the movement of investment affairs.

Though in the factories and banks of the lending country, and over the land of the borrowing country, the effects of foreign lending and borrowing are immediately felt, though their outcome becomes visible to the eye in the form of new railroad lines, new electric light systems in remote towns, new uniforms for armies, they leave behind no easily computable public record. Of that ever changing world of debts and balances, only approximate estimates can be made, only rough sketch maps. Such are the figures that can be given of the extent to which British capital went abroad from 1870 on, such the indications of the fields of its activity. The average new investment abroad

[7] The Secretary of State for British India acted as agent for British India; the Crown agents, appointed by the Secretary of State for the Colonies acted for almost 50 non-self-governing colonies; the Bank of England for New Zealand, Transvaal and Queensland, the Bank of Montreal for Canada and most of the Canadian provinces, the Bank of Adelaide for South Australia, and the London County and Westminster Bank for the other Australian states. These governments also had brokers who arranged for the underwriting of their loans.

of British capital during short periods from 1870 to 1914 was as follows:

BRITISH FOREIGN INVESTMENT
(of long-term or permanent character)[8]

Annual average of period	*Amount (millions of pounds)*
1870–74	61.0
1875–79	1.7
1880–84	23.9
1885–89	61.1
1890–94	45.6
1894–99	26.8
1900–1904	21.3
1904–9	109.5
1910–13	185.0

Plainly the movement of British capital into the outer world was no regular and uninterrupted trend. Resting, as it did, upon individual calculation, it rose and fell, was active or inactive, according to the multitude of conditions which determined the investors' judgment. The movement of interest rates, the state of business at home and abroad, the financial condition of borrowing governments, the shock of losses experienced, the lure of newly discovered opportunities abroad, wars and rumors of war—these are but a few of the matters which decided the volume of investment abroad at any one time.

The persisting financial stringency and fear which followed the world-wide panic of 1873 caused the movement of new capital abroad to fall off to almost nothing. Slowly in the eighties it resumed, reaching unprecedented volume toward the end of the decade under the impetus of the continued decline of interest yields upon domestic securities.

[8] This table is derived from the figures given by Hobson, *op. cit.,* p. 204. Some technical shortcomings of Mr. Hobson's computations are pointed out by Sir Josiah Stamp, *British Incomes and Property* (London, 1920), pp. 234–236, which, however, do not invalidate them. The fact that they rest upon the annual estimates of the British balance of indebtedness of the Board of Trade, which contain many doubtful figures, introduces more serious qualifying doubts. But they cannot be improved upon; other published estimates are little more than guesses.

British capital headed, then, especially toward Australia, Canada, South America, and the United States, which were in the sweep of rapid, boom-like development, and to South Africa after the diamond and gold discoveries. So were the preferences formed, the new choices of risk decided upon. In the decades of the nineties disillusionment and hesitation succeeded. The fortune-making effort of the United States collapsed into the panic of 1893, and half of the American railroad system was in bankruptcy. The Argentine Government was forced to suspend payment on its huge foreign debt which was mainly held in Great Britain; many of the other Latin-American governments either went into default or seemingly faced that prospect.[9] On the continent, the Portuguese and Greek governments reduced their interest payments; the finances of Spain and Serbia wavered. Drought in Australia brought heavy loss to the land and development companies; many of the South African mining companies were not fulfilling the promises of their promoters. Yet before the end of the nineties British investors were again rushing forward to buy the shares of the joint-stock and exploration companies formed to operate in Africa and in new regions of Australia. The movement of British capital outward had been resumed before the South African War cut it short.

Upon the termination of that conflict and the gradual restoration of British financial affairs to a more normal state, the movement took on fuller volume, and grew almost without interruption to 1914. One of the contributing causes of this increased movement was probably the hope of escaping the consequences of new social legislation and increased taxes. Changing political relations took British capital into countries from which it had previously

[9] *Economist,* March 23, 1895, calculated, for example, that the securities of North and South America listed on the London Stock Exchange had depreciated 125.3 million pounds sterling during the preceding five years.

abstained—Japan, Russia, and Turkey. But more important than these causes in producing a great growth in
foreign investment was the fact that during the 1900–
1914 period those distant lands to which the capital had
been going in earlier periods, seemed to have overcome the
risks and crashes of their first growth. Now in the greater
stability and greater order of their development, they
needed still more capital than before and offered surer return. Or—the idea presents itself in alternative form—it
was as though many regions of the world in which British
capital had invested itself had come to fit themselves better
for that investment, learning from pioneer failures. In
their use of capital they were tending to resemble more
and more the land from which the capital came. Though
the capital accumulations of some of these regions were
growing fast, their need for foreign capital seemed
greater, too.[10] In spite of the deferring influence of financial stringency, losses, war, and the like, there comes
to the observer of this process of British capital investment a sense that the great increase in investment that
occurred after 1900 had been prepared by the earlier investment. Conditions were created which made the borrowing regions more safely penetrable, capable of using more
capital well; while, on the other hand, the increasing income received by British investors from their steadily
mounting total of foreign investment facilitated the making of greater new investment without financial or monetary strain.

Though the volume of new investment fluctuated, the

[10] The available amount of American capital was increasing at a
prodigious rate, yet the British investment in the United States was
never greater than in 1913. The same fact was true of Canada, though
American investment there was beginning to grow substantially before
the war; Australia showed the same tendencies. Even British India was
beginning to accumulate some capital and there was a tendency for more
and more of the rupee debt registered in India to be held by natives of
India. C. N. Vakil, *Financial Developments of Modern India* (London,
1924), Appendix, p. 20.

total of British foreign ownership and the income therefrom steadily augmented, and its place in the economic
system in which the British people lived became ever more
important. The flow of British income from ownership,
as from commerce, moved with events in all corners of the
world. To the owners of foreign railway securities, the
rainfall in western Canada, a strike of the locomotive
engineers on American railways, a change in the political
administration in Brazil, became of consequence. To the
participant in rubber plantations in the Far East, the
building of new automobile factories in Detroit became
of interest. To the financier of foreign governments, the
levying of a new tax in Japan might have significance. The
satisfactory operation of the British economic system became more and more fully linked with the satisfactory
development of the rest of the world.

To measure accurately the growing importance of foreign investment in the British economy is a task that balks
statistical effort. But some rough degree of precision may
be given to the fact. By 1914 the total foreign ownership
of the British was in the neighborhood of 4 billion pounds,
and thus composed substantially over a quarter of the
total national wealth (estimated by Sir Josiah Stamp at
14.3 billions of pounds).[11] Its rate of growth had been

[11] Stamp, *op. cit.*, pp. 404–405. Hobson, *op. cit.*, p. 207, gives the following estimate of British capital invested in the United Kingdom and
abroad—in millions of pounds:

Year	Capital in United Kingdom	Capital abroad	Total
1885	8,735	1,302	10,037
1895	9,063	1,600	10,663
1905	11,009	2,025	13,036
1909	11,654	2,332	13,986

and remarks that these "figures support the view that, although foreign
investments have increased at a greater percentage rate than domestic
capital, yet the growth absolutely has been more rapid in capital invested at home than in capital invested abroad." The computations of
total capital are those given in the *Economist,* November 25, 1911, compiled in accordance with Sir Robert Giffen's method, and are subject to
a very substantial margin of error. The figures for capital invested

substantially faster than that of the capital wealth of the country. In the years immediately preceding the war approximately one-half of the British savings was taking the form of increased ownership abroad—about 185 out of 350–400 millions of pounds saved on the average during the years 1910–13.

The income received from foreign investment multiplied itself three or four times during the three decades preceding 1914, while the total national income scarcely doubled. In the early eighties income from abroad was hardly more than 50 million, but by 1913–14 it was in excess of 200 millions of pounds; while total national income increased from something over 1,200 millions of pounds to about 2,250 millions of pounds.[12] The great

abroad are much too low. Furthermore the progression of the total of capital investment abroad does not accord with the figures given elsewhere in Hobson, *op. cit.*, p. 204. L. H. Jenks, *The Migration of British Capital to 1875* (New York, 1927), p. 335, estimates British foreign ownership in 1875 to have been about 1.2 billion pounds. Of all recent estimates of total British investment abroad those of Sir George Paish, "Great Britain's Investment in Other Lands," *Jour. Royal Stat. Soc.*, September, 1909, January, 1911, and *Statist Supplement,* February 14, 1914, command the most respect, though the author does not make his methods of valuation as clear as might be desired. Part of the total was arrived at by capitalizing income, part by inspection of reports and balance sheets to ascertain paid-up capital, and part by taking the issue price of securities. The estimates are "gross," i.e., they make no allowance for foreign capital invested in Great Britain. The totals given of approximately three billion pounds (1907) and four billion pounds (1913) include a rough allowance for "direct" investment of 300 million pounds, which, as his colleagues of the Statistical Society pointed out, was only a guess, albeit an expert one. "Direct" investment is presumably that not leaving traces in the form of a security issue; the forms of such investment are extremely numerous. All valuations of capital goods or capital resources are difficult and somewhat arbitrary; they may be made on any one or several of a variety of bases or "principles." Valuations of foreign investment are apt to be particularly difficult and arbitrary. The figures given here and similar figures given elsewhere in the text must be taken merely as rough indications; usually they represent either "original actual investment" or "nominal value." A long technical essay might be written on this subject—instead of a footnote.

[12] These figures for income from abroad are drawn from Hobson, *op. cit.*, those for the later years being substantiated by Paish, *op. cit.*,

growth in income from abroad came partly from the
growth of the investment, partly from the increased yield
of previous ventures then improving their condition (as,
for example, the Argentine and American railways were),
partly from the almost complete absence of default on
government bonds as contrasted with earlier periods.
While in the eighties only about 4 per cent of the national income was being drawn from ownership abroad,
by 1903 it had risen to 7 per cent, and at the outbreak of
the war did not fall far short of 10 per cent. When it is
remembered that this is entirely an income from ownership, while the estimates of national income include the
return for all forms of labor, its importance as a source
of new capital becomes evident. The equipment of British
industry and the social structure of the country was growing increasingly dependent upon the peaceful prosperity
of the rest of the world.

During some periods the amount of new foreign investment was substantially greater than that of the income
received from ownership abroad; in other periods it was
substantially smaller. The former fluctuated hugely, the
latter was a rather steady growth ascending with unusual

and the *Board of Trade Journal,* January 31, 1924, p. 152. The estimates
of total national income for the earlier period are by R. Giffen and L.
Levi as given in Stamp, *op. cit.,* chap. xii; those from the later years are
from A. L. Bowley, *Division of the Product of Industry* (London, 1919).
In the following table figures deduced from diverse sources are brought
into comparison:

(*Millions of pounds*)

Year	Income from foreign ownership	Total national income
1883	50 (Hobson)	1,370 (Giffen)
1891	100 (Hobson)	1,600 (Bowley)
1903	115 (Hobson)	1,750 (Giffen)
1907	140 (Hobson)	1,945 (Bowley revised)
	153 (Paish)	2,030 (Report of Census of Production)
1913	210 (*Board of Trade Journal*)	2,250 (Stamp & Bowley)
	205 (Stamp & Bowley)	2,300 (*Economist,* October 10, 1925)

rapidity after 1900. In all but two periods, during the late eighties, and in the years immediately preceding the war, the new investment was less than the income received from foreign investments previously made. The investment was producing the whole of the means for its further extension. But during these two periods the contrary was the case; other sources of savings were drawn upon.

THE GEOGRAPHICAL SPREAD OF THE INVESTMENT

THERE were few governments in the world to which the English people did not make a loan, few corners in which some enterprise was not financed from London. The spread of English commerce, the almost universal range of the British-owned foreign banks, the huge extension of the colonial domain made it natural that British foreign investment should be widely scattered. Despite the strength of the main currents of foreign investment, this diversity was sustained—recording both the enduring character of the British financial connections, and the readiness with which British capital entered newly penetrated countries and the "pioneer belts." The market was capacious enough to take care of the large loans of powerful governments. Its financial organizations were supple enough, commanded organizing ability and technical competence enough to face novelty of problem and strangeness of environment.

In 1870 British capital was already playing a lessening part in the financing of the countries on the European continent. All the governments of Europe had earlier sought its help. The governments of Spain, Portugal, and Greece had been among the earliest and most disappointing borrowers; the rulers of the many states which later formed the German Empire, Austria, Hungary, and the Scandinavian countries, had often found aid in London; Russian and Turkish bonds were widely held. In addition to this financing of governments, the British people had supplied, during the early and middle part of the century, the enterprise of the neighboring continent. Not only capital was sent out to the mainland, but industrial knowledge, directing experience, machinery, and skilled workmen as well. In Austria, Rhenish Germany, Italy, Spain, Roumania, and Belgium, British capital had helped to finance the early railroad building, and English contractors had carried through the construction. English capital and enterprise had pushed through the first important railway in France, from Paris to Rouen—inaugurating nearly twenty years of Anglo-French coöperation in railroad construction.[13] Almost up to 1914, an interesting reminder of this early participation was to be found in the presence of a British representative on the Board of Directors of the Compagnie de L'Ouest.

In the closing decades of the nineteenth century the British holdings of continental securities declined rather than the contrary. France attained financial sufficiency—became an important lending country, in fact—and Germany moved in the same direction; the yield on their securities fell, while the perilous possibilities of continental politics grew no less. The financial situation of the Russian Government did not give assurance, while throughout the Middle and Far East its forward thrust collided with the British. From the middle seventies on, British investors were selling their "Russians." The continuous borrowing of the Spanish Government, its partial default in 1872 and perpetual approach to a repetition of that necessity, caused its securities to be sold to the continental markets; in similar fashion the Portuguese Government likewise moved from one default to another and shook the British faith. After the Turkish bankruptcy in 1876, the London market tended to refrain

[13] See Jenks, *op. cit.*, chaps. v and vi. "Thus," he writes by way of summary, "Great Britain stood in much the same relation to most of the regions of Europe around 1850 that Europe and the United States bore to the Orient and South America a half century later."

from further reliance upon the credit of that country—
despite the existence of an International Debt Administration. Of the loans of the Balkan governments it took
only a small fractional share. The chastening influence of
losses suffered, the risks and uncertainties from which the
financial and political outlook of the continental governments were never free, made the British investor obdurate
to their requests. Furthermore, while those circumstances
which had invited and stimulated the operations of British capital and enterprise on the continent continued to
diminish, French, German, Belgian, and Swiss capital accumulations grew more adequate and their industrial
competence greater. In construction work, in industrial
organization, in technical knowledge, the independent
capabilities of these countries came to rival England's.
Thus Paris and Berlin became the borrowing centers for
sovereigns of eastern and southeastern Europe. It was left
mainly to the French and German banks, industrialists,
and engineers to carry the machine equipment of the industrial age throughout those regions. The British contractors and their supporters took up new chances in
British India, South America, the plains of Canada and
Australia, the United States, and the reaches of Africa.

British capital was turning in greater measure to what
seemed to computing minds more attractive opportunities,
and to national sentiment more desirable employments.
These lay, above all, in the young and agricultural countries largely peopled by the British race. The populations
of these countries, their farmers, miners, and builders, were
on the march, and impetuously following upon the fringe
of settlement railroads were being laid across vast areas.
British capital entered into the movement, providing, in
the late eighties especially, unprecedented sums for railroad building, land settlement schemes, construction and
mine operation. The same eager breaking open of new
areas was going on in Argentina, the same headlong pushing forward of the railroad tracks, and here too British

capital was willing to risk itself in the new effort. Hardly
smaller were the loan requirements of British India,
chiefly for railroad construction. During this period, also,
a multitude of enterprising companies were alluring the
British investor with the glint of the riches of Africa.
Within twenty years of the discovery of gold a full 100
millions of pounds were contributed by British savings to
pursue the quest. Inland from a dozen points along the
African coast railroad systems were headed toward the
interior. Great chartered companies, and smaller promotion groups, found capital for the work of exploration,
for cultivation, railroad building, mining.

These were the chief occupations of British capital
during the last decades of the nineteenth century. For a
while at the end of the period they came to a halt in
temporary, balked disappointment.[14] The rapid extension
of agricultural production brought falling food prices
and financial distress in the newly opened areas. The
speculative land and mining booms ended in a violent
smash, especially in Australia. Many of the railroad systems of the United States, financially mismanaged and
plunged into headlong competition, ceased payment on
their bonds. Economic and financial maladjustment in
Argentina ended in default upon all the securities of that
government; while revolution and currency troubles in
Brazil seemed to make further losses of the same sort inevitable. Repeatedly throughout the century investors in
South American lands had seen their calculations defeated
by such defaults, yet with a faith that was to be justified
later on they continued to finance their development. In
the midst of the disappointment the *Economist* reflected
that "South American investments have for half a century

[14] Illustrative of the proportions assumed by the boom, was the fact
that the market value of shares of Transvaal gold mines and exploration companies was in September, 1895, about 215 million pounds, of
which less than 20 per cent was in dividend-paying properties. By December, 1895, the market value had fallen to 143 millions.

been a thorn in the flesh of the British investors, and it is, perhaps, because we have become so accustomed to the infliction that the country has, time after time, shown its readiness to increase the sore."[15] For a time, prolonged almost to a decade by the Boer wars, British capital movements to these new lands were of much smaller proportions, until people and · governments recuperated, improved the organization of their economic life, and European needs for foodstuffs and raw materials caught up to the new production.

Then in the succeeding years of the twentieth century when the outward flow of British capital grew greater than ever before, it was to these same countries that the largest volume went. The credit of the Argentine and Brazilian governments became firmly and completely restored. In these two countries alone the British in the seven years from 1907 to 1914 risked over a billion dollars. Canada and Australia between 1900 and 1914 almost doubled their railway mileage, calling upon British investors for most of the needed funds. British India did not lag behind. The firm establishment of the gold standard in the United States, the gradual emergence of its railways from bankruptcy and the passage of the improved railway legislation, its vast industrial growth, all invited the resumption of British investment. The formation of the South African Union ushered in a period of economic advancement there.

But in this period British capital also moved in substantial amounts into distant lands where previously its connections had been slight. The outlines of the British financial empire again expanded. The new recognition of the competence of the Japanese people and government, and the concert of British and Japanese policy in the Far East inaugurated by the alliance of 1902, was followed by the increased sale of Japanese securities in Lon-

15 August 20, 1892.

don. By 1914 the British holdings of these securities exceeded sixty millions of pounds. A substantially equal amount of Russian securities were purchased in the years before the war. The 1907 Anglo-Russian agreement brought to an end thirty years of refusal on the part of British investors; the deepening intimacy of the two governments, drawn together by France, quickened the perception of the opportunities offered in the Russian industrial and mining fields. In China, too, the British investment grew. Throughout the tropics—especially in the recently acquired tropical colonies of Africa—private companies devoted growing sums to the cultivation of tropical products. The British Government, hitherto grudging, devoted generous sums for the development of these colonies, and began to give its guaranty to their loans.[16] The government of the tropical colonies began to appear in the London market to finance the extending range of economic functions they were taking upon themselves. For with the exception of some of the railways of British India, Nyassaland and Rhodesia, the railways in the British tropical possessions were built and operated by the colonial governments.

The following table gives roughly the distribution of British foreign investment, as it was in December, 1913:

[16] L. C. A. Knowles, *The Economic Development of the British Empire* (London, 1924), pp. 98 *et seq.*

LONG-TERM PUBLICLY ISSUED BRITISH CAPITAL INVESTMENT IN OTHER LANDS[17]

Within the empire	Millions of pounds	Outside the empire	Millions of pounds
Canada and New-foundland	514.9[18]	The United States	754.6
Australia and New Zealand	416.4[19]	Argentina	319.6
South Africa	370.2	Brazil	148.0
West Africa	37.3	Mexico	99.0
India and Ceylon	378.8[20]	Chile	61.0
Straits Settlements	27.3	Uruguay	36.1
British North Borneo	5.8	Peru	34.2
Hong Kong	3.1	Cuba	33.2
Other colonies	26.2	Remainder Latin-America	25.5
	1,780.0	Total Latin-America	756.6
		Russia	110.0[21]
		Spain	19.0
		Italy	12.5
		Portugal	8.1
		France	8.0
		Germany	6.4
		Austria	8.0
		Denmark	11.0
		Balkan States	17.0
		Rest of Europe	18.6
		Total Europe	218.6
		Egypt	44.9
		Turkey	24.0[22]
		China	43.9
		Japan	62.8
		Rest of foreign world	77.9
		Total	1,983.3
		Grand Total	3,763.3

[17] Adapted with modifications from Paish's table in the *Statist Supplement*, February 14, 1914. The totals do not include investment in the shipping industry.

[18] For a review of the estimates made of investment in Canada, see Viner, *op. cit.*, chap. vi.

[19] See materials presented to the Dominions Royal Commission, *Minutes of Evidence Taken in Australia* (Cmd. 7171, 1913), p. 272.

[20] Compare F. Howard, *India and the Gold Standard* (London, 1911), chap. v.

[21] Paish, *op. cit.*, gives for investment in Russia only 66.7 million

To this total must be added that investment which took place privately, without the intercession of the public "money" market—an amount estimated to be not less than 300 millions of pounds. But the means are lacking for assigning in detail the geographical distribution of this part of British foreign ownership; more than half was in the British Empire.

In substantially equal parts, British capital seems to have sought the other parts of the empire, and the outside world of foreign states. That so nearly half selected the lands of the empire is primarily accounted for by the huge spread of the imperial domains, the variety of their resources, the fertility of the most important units. There was, besides, a general faith, which survived the occasional shocks received, in the orderly economic development of lands under British rule and in their freedom from political disturbance. Furthermore, there was a general approval bestowed upon investment in the empire which gave the act a faint touch of virtue; the economic strengthening of the rest of the empire through the capital of the home country conveyed a promise of greater domestic political security and commercial benefit. By the inclusion of the securities of the colonial and dominion governments in the list of "trustee" securities, by the passage of the Colonial Stocks Act of 1900, this favoring sentiment was turned into effective practice.

From the times of Queen Elizabeth, English invest-

pounds. But this is too low. According to H. G. Moulton and L. Pasvolsky, *Russian Debts and Reconstruction* (New York, 1924), pp. 17–21, British holdings of Russian government debt were approximately 56 million pounds (converting at 9.5 rubles to the pound). According to the computation of L. J. Lewery, *Foreign Capital Investments in Russian Industries and Commerce* (Bureau of Foreign and Domestic Commerce, Miscellaneous Series, No. 124, Washington, 1923), p. 15, British capital in Russian industries amounted to about 48 million pounds (at same conversion rate). There was besides investment in various other securities guaranteed by the government and in municipal loans.

[22] Paish's estimate, *op. cit.*, of 18.7 million pounds was certainly too small.

ment in the United States had been substantial. Taking all the centuries together, this country was the greatest foreign field of financial adventure for the British capitalist. Our wars had embargoed his capital, our statesmen had criticized it, our state repudiations had embittered it, and our panics had scared it. At times the total fell rather than rose, and certainly its proportionate part in the available American capital resources fell. Yet the volume of British capital invested in this country was probably never greater than 1913—well over a third of the whole British investment outside the empire. The three-quarters of a billion pounds sterling was scattered over the United States, invested in our municipal and state bonds, in our largest railway systems, industrial plants, and public utility enterprises. The earlier investment in the land and cattle companies of Texas, Arkansas, Dakotas, and the rest of our earlier frontier regions had been mainly liquidated. The full variety of British holdings was revealed during the war, when the British Treasury appealed to the investors to loan or sell their American securities to the government.[23] In the list of those obtained by the Treasury there are 1421 different "dollar" bond issues alone (including a handful of Canadian issues) and 389 different American stocks. Railroad bonds predominated in the bond list. Of the stocks a substantial proportion were the "preferred" issues. The largest holdings were in the railway systems and the United States Steel Corporation.

The British investor was sending his capital where there was the growth of youth, and where the land was yielding riches to the initial application of human labor and technical skill. Thus, with patient disregard for early disappointments, the resources and the extending settlement of the Latin-American countries were nurtured. Four

---

[23] *Report of the Dollars Securities Committee* (House of Commons Document 212, 1919).

times as much British capital was employed in these countries at the outbreak of the war as in the financing of the
governments and enterprise on the European continent.

The sums invested on the continent were probably no
greater than they had been a half-century before. That
separation from affairs on the continent, which proved
untenable in the realm of political policy, was in the investment sphere substantially realized.

THE CHARACTER OF THE INVESTMENT

IN the earlier periods of British foreign finance the governmental loan business held first place. The great private banks had made their fame and fortune by the distribution of securities of foreign sovereign states. But of
the total British foreign investment, as it stood before
the war, only a quarter was in the form of loans contracted
by governmental bodies—national, state, and municipal.
The rest was employed in private economic ventures. This
division does not give an accurate indication of the part
applied to direct economic purposes. For, of the 1,100
millions of pounds of government borrowing outstanding
in London, much over half was used for such matters as
railroad construction, municipal public utilities, roads,
and harbor works. Such was certainly true of the borrowing of the governments of British India, Canada, Australia, South Africa, and Argentina, for example.[24] After
the defaults of the eighties the market was not responsive
to the invitations of spending governments, unless it was
felt that there was in its domain fresh vitality or important resources awaiting the steam shovel, the locomotive,
the plow, or the mining shaft.

[24] For example, G. H. Knibbs, Dominions Royal Commission, *Minutes
of Evidence Taken in Australia* (Cmd. 7171, 1913), pp. 292–295, estimated
that out of the Australian and New Zealand government loans to the
aggregate of 275.5 million pounds up to June 1912, 168.1 were expended
for railroads and tramways, and much of the rest for enterprises often
operated for public profit.

In the following table the employments entered by British capital are grouped in a few main fields, as of December, 1913:

FIELDS OF EMPLOYMENT OF CAPITAL PUBLICLY INVESTED IN OTHER LANDS[25]

	Millions of pounds	
Loans to national and state governments		
Dominion and colonial	675.5	
Foreign	297.0	
Total		972.5
Loans to municipal governments		152.5
Railway securities		
Dominions and colonies	306.4	
British India	140.8	
United States	616.6	
Other foreign countries	467.2	
Total		1,531.0
Mines		272.8
Financial, land and investment companies		244.2
Iron, coal, and steel industries		35.2
Commercial establishments and industrial plants		155.3
Banks		72.9
Electric light and power industries		27.3
Telegraph and telephone systems		43.7
Tramways		77.8
Gas and waterworks		29.2
Canals and docks		7.1
Oil industry		40.6
Rubber industry		41.0
Tea and coffee industry		22.4
Nitrate industry		11.7
Breweries		18.0
Miscellaneous		8.1
Total		3,763.3

It was for the railroad and mining fields that British capital and enterprise felt the strongest attraction and displayed the greatest aptitude. By far the greatest part of the investment in railways was in the form of bonds issued by the railway enterprise or government, or in pre-

[25] Adapted with modifications from the tables of Paish, *op. cit.* The investment in shipping is excluded, except for a minor item.

ferred stock; holdings of common stock were small. In some of the railway ventures, British participation went no further than the provision of all or part of the capital. Such was the case of the investment in American, Russian, Australian, and Canadian railroads. True, even in these ventures a representative of the supporting financiers was now and again to be found on the board of directors.

In other ventures the financing groups were given a share in the control of construction and operation, as in the case of various railways built in China and some of the British colonies. In still other ventures an outright concession was obtained, giving the financing group full control of operation, as in the case of railways built in Mexico, Argentina, Brazil, Rhodesia, British India, and Turkey. A very usual arrangement for the exercise of this control was the creation of two boards of directors, one meeting in the foreign country and giving representation to local interests, one meeting in London and representing mainly the bond and stock owners. The degree to which the London boards attempted actually to share in the management of the property varied greatly in different instances. Usually they acted merely as agencies by which the actual managers kept in touch with British manufacturers, the banks and stock exchanges and the Foreign Office; sometimes they served as recruiting agencies for the European personnel. In the main, their chief preoccupations were the selection of the heads of the actual management, and the safeguarding of the general financial position of the company. Still, even this moderate exercise of control from abroad was challenged with increasing frequency by the governments through whose territories the railways ran. What they wanted was the capital and the right to use it as they pleased, whether they were competent or not. In the financing of the Chinese railways, the question was always one of the most difficult to settle. In British India the demand that the London boards be abolished increased in firmness. In the Latin-American countries, however, the arrangement worked, up to 1914, without serious hitch and to the common benefit.

Almost all of the mine properties financed by British capital were held under British control and management. The British were the great explorers for minerals in the pre-war world. American mining interests and financiers limited their sphere to the resources of the United States, Canada, and a few neighboring Latin-American states, especially Mexico. The gold and diamond mines of South Africa and West Africa were almost entirely under British management; these made up over half the British investment underground. In the copper mines of Africa and of South America, they shared ownership with the French, the Belgians, and the Americans. Most of the tin mines of the Malay States and Bolivia were held in British possession. The English and Scotch mining engineers and mine managers ran, besides, many mining enterprises held under other ownership, as American oil operators and drilling crews do now.

The investment in oil-producing areas was scattered in Persia, Turkey, Russia, Roumania, the Dutch East Indies, and Mexico. It was small compared to the investment that has been made subsequently. These properties, like the rubber plantations laid out in the Malay States, the coffee and tea plantations in India, Africa, and Latin-America, operated under British management. Many of these investments, like those made in mines and land, were of the order which did not become fully productive until several years after the capital was originally raised. Such, in fact, was a characteristic of the British investment. Conducting their affairs with order, the participants waited with faith and patience for the ground to yield its riches or the country to grow. The supreme instance of that faith and patience was the South African Chartered Company, which continued to be able to secure new capital for twenty years after its creation though it never paid a dividend.

With the spread of empire and the ever increasing mer-
chandise traffic between the British Isles and the other
parts of the world, the British-owned banks abroad grew
in number and in strength. The volume of their nominal
paid-up capital was hardly more than a third of the market
value commanded by their securities—so steadily profitable were their operations and so substantial their surpluses. Their cash dividends ranged commonly from 10
to 20 per cent. Because of the widespread use of the
pound sterling to discharge international debts, and the
trust inspired by their record, there fell to these banks not
only the business of financing trade back and forth from
the British Isles, but also much of the trade between and
within other countries. In the regions where the technique
of trade financing was little developed, and the means
therefor small, or where the necessary business experience
and probity were lacking, or where the fluctuations of the
local currency gave special place to the stable English
pound, they found their greatest opportunity—in the Far
and Near East, in British India, Egypt, and the African
colonies, and throughout Latin-America. On the continent
of Europe, too, they were not without importance, though
tending to withdraw before the competition of the German and French banks.[26] Outside of the continent there
was virtually no competition until the decade of the
eighties. Thereafter the German and French systems of

[26] Most of the British banks on the continent were launched before
1870 in the era when the Crédit Mobilier was pressing forward with its
career of industrial financing. "Banks abound whose familiar names in
every variety suggest the one pervading fact of the marriage of British
capital with foreign demand. There is the Anglo-Austrian Bank, the
Anglo-Italian Bank, the Anglo-Egyptian Bank. There is the English
and Swedish Bank; there is the British and California Bank; there is the
London and Hamburg Continental Exchange Bank; there is the London
and Brazilian Bank, the London Buenos Ayres and River Plate Bank;
and one bank wishing to outstrip all other banks in the ambition of
its title, calls itself the European Bank." Viscount Goschen, "Seven Per
Cent," *Edinburgh Review,* January, 1865.

foreign banks began to duplicate the spread of their operations except in regions under the British flag.

From 1870 until after 1900, British investment in commercial enterprise and industrial manufactures abroad grew but little. In these fields the domestic capital of growing nations like the United States tended to resent the competition of foreign capital; while on the other hand it was not always easy to win financial support in Great Britain for ventures which might compete with the production and export trade of home industry. Besides, undertakings in the industrial fields were risky, difficult to manage well from a distance. Their success depended upon a thorough understanding of the local market and its changes. Greater adaptability and knowledge of special conditions were needed than in most other branches of financial enterprise. Too, most commercial and industrial operations were in that earliest period organized on a smaller scale than railway, public utility, and mining operations—more an affair for partnerships than for large corporations. But, in the decade before the war, British investments in these fields extended—created jute mills, cotton factories, engineering works in British India, iron and steel and paper mills in Canada and in Russia, tobacco companies and department stores in Argentina. "It would appear," as Hobson has said, "that the obstacles in the way of successful foreign investment in manufacturing (were) being overcome."[27] Improved communications and the progress of standardization probably diminished the risk.

This summary analysis can give but a poor notion of the actual variety of British private enterprise abroad. There are few branches of profit-making activity in which to large or small degree it did not venture. Strong risks, bad climates, isolation, did not deter the English promoter and organizer; young men were willing to risk their careers where capital was willing to risk the losses or gains. Still,

27 Hobson, *op. cit.*, pp. 159–160.

contrary to the usual idea, the major portion of the British investment was in the form of securities yielding a
fixed return.[28] Almost all of the large public issues for
governments and public works were in that form, and in
these the major portion of the investment was amassed.
Among the smaller issues, those of a million pounds or
less, common shares were more frequently sold, taken up
first by promotion and investment companies, then later
sold to the public. It was these promoting groups, the
investment trusts, the smaller private bankers who accepted most of the initial entrepreneur risks rather than
the general public. Still to this rule there were notable exceptions, as in the case of the South African gold mines
and the Chartered Companies. The shares passed on to the
public were often those whose prospects the promoting or
financing groups held in doubt. Despite its mistakes, however, that public by and large shared in the gains of foreign investment. The British capital that went abroad
prospered, though its owners often needed a more than
usual share of patience. That they possessed.

[28] R. A. Lehfeldt, *Jour. Royal Stat. Soc.*, January, 1913, p. 199.

CHAPTER II

FRENCH FOREIGN INVESTMENT

THE WORLD OF SAVING AND THE WORLD OF LENDING

THE French people paid the five billion francs indemnity which was imposed upon them as a consequence of their defeat by Prussia, mainly out of the interest proceeds and sales of their previous foreign investment. Hardly had the last payment been met in August, 1873, when the outward movement of capital was resumed. During the succeeding half-century Paris came to rival London in the volume of capital made available to foreign borrowers. In particular it became the center in which the drama of financing the other governments of continental Europe was played out. Capacious, stable, and with prevailing interest rates lower than elsewhere, the French capital market was, for some types of borrowing, the most attractive of all. From 1875 to 1914 the average annual official rate of discount in Paris never rose as high as 4 per cent; for most of the period it hung close to 3 per cent; in the late nineties it fell to 2 per cent; by 1914 it had climbed to 4. These were the lowest rates in the world.

It is not in the rapidly enriching returns of new industrial mastery nor in the resources of imperial domains that the source of the loaned capital is to be found, but in a combination of less spectacular conditions. These were the variety and steady operation of the French economic system, the cheerful industry and almost impassioned economy of the French people (both these had the quality of art in them, somehow), and the attraction which the land held for foreign peoples. Until 1890, especially, French industry grew very slowly, and even thereafter it utilized much less machine and power equipment than that of Great Britain or Germany. The tradition and instinct ran toward individual design rather than mass production. "France remained to the end a home of artistic trades, of ateliers, of small workshops, many of which used no power."[1] This type of industry made less call upon the savings of the people than did the other type, though also providing a smaller volume of production from which savings might be made. Again, in the development of the industries whose life was drawn from recent scientific discovery, the chemical and electrical industries, France moved more slowly than its neighbors. Hence, its people were not called upon to finance a vast and rapid transition to the more complicated industrial system which rests on these industries. But with their own technique, with their preference for the modest-sized establishment, the individual workbench, the French worked with a zeal that fell little short of genius.

The factories and workshops occupied fewer of the people than in the other states of Western Europe, the farms and pastures more.[2] Hence France lived largely upon itself, felt less urgent need of foreign products, tended to draw gold unto itself, to have a relaxed credit situation. In the villages, towns, and small cities of the provinces, there was little pecuniary display, little luxury, much sobriety of living, cautiousness in spending, economy often described as "pinching meanness" by the French authors. Social habits changed but little. Family ties were strong. Through days of laborious application and self-denial the French family, of the cities as well as the provinces and farms, nourished the will and determination to save, found warmth of assurance in patiently accumulated sums. If circumstances favored, the head of

[1] J. H. Clapham, *Economic Development of France and Germany, 1815–1914* (Cambridge, 1921), p. 258.

[2] In 1878, 67 per cent of the French people lived in communes whose "chef lieu" contained less than 2,000 inhabitants; in 1911 this had been reduced to 55.9 per cent—a smaller shift than was occurring in any of the lending countries of Europe or even in the United States.

the family planned for the closing years of life, secure in the income of these accumulations—a *rentier,* enjoying the limited but steady receipts of his collection of slowly acquired bonds. This desire for security, for a period in which life could be enjoyed without labor, was among the influences which kept French families small, and the population stationary.

The pace and nature of French economic organization tended to favor a comparatively even distribution of wealth, a widespread holding of small properties and small savings. The registers kept of the holders of French Government and railway securities, of depositors in savings banks, of inheritances, all combine to show the presence of millions of small savers, of perhaps, in 1914, ten million in a country of about forty million population.[3] The inheritance laws, which required a division of the property among the heirs, assured the wide distribution of landed and other "real" property. Despite some moderately large fortunes, chiefly in and about Paris, the capital which France had to invest abroad was diffused very widely among its people. The total income and the per capita annual income were small compared to that of the United States—less than two hundred dollars per person in 1913. Yet always a substantial part of this annual income was turned into the channels of savings. Two to three billion francs (then their gold value was 5.18 francs to the dollar) were saved each year during the closing decades of the nineteenth century, even though during much of this period the countryside suffered from depression, industrial development was slow, and the losses suffered at the hands of bad debtors large.[4] During the years of the twentieth

[3] A. Neymarck, *Finances Contemporaines* (Paris, 1911), VII, 129.

[4] There are wide differences in the various estimates of French pre-war savings, owing partly to the differences of meaning attached to the term by different students, partly to the use of different methods of computation. The most consecutive studies are those of R. Pupin, *La Richesse de la France devant la Guerre* (Paris, 1916), and *La Richesse Privée et Finances Françaises* (Paris, 1919), which used the method

century this fund of savings grew, reached four, then five billion francs each year.

Much of the saving sought the liquidity, the presumed safety, of investment in securities. French industry did not call for it all, and could not then offer as high returns as did foreign petitioners—even when judgment was passed upon relative risk.[5] The unexplored natural resources of the country were small. The rate of traffic growth did not appear to justify the thorough reconstruction of railway lines for greater power, speed, volume, or economy. New lines of manufacture developed, new techniques of invention and operation were accepted, but less rapidly than in foreign industrial centers. There was no swift, incessant recasting of the fixed capital plant of the country. For what capital extensions and improvements many of the French industries, such as the textile industries, undertook, they were self-sufficient, able to finance themselves without fresh public appeal to the investors. The virtually stationary population made urban construc-

of measuring the growth of wealth, making allowance for price changes. According to his computations the annual savings were:

Average 1875–93   2   billion francs
Average 1903–11   3.5 billion francs after allowing for losses.

By 1911 the annual savings were something over 4.5 billions. In his later study the annual average for 1911–14 is put at something over 5.0 billion francs per year. These calculations are close to those of C. Rist, *Revue de Paris*, December 1, 1915, and of J. Lescure, *L'Épargne en France* (Paris, 1914).

[5] Indication of the difference of return in comparable French and foreign securities at different periods is found in the computations of Pupin, *La Richesse de la France devant la Guerre*, p. 59:

Year	Per cent French securities	Per cent foreign securities
1878	4.12	5.50
1903	3.13	4.20
1911	3.40	4.62

These calculations are based on the same assumptions as were used in figuring the return on British investment. M. Thery at the meeting of the Société d'Économie Politique Nationale, April 18, 1900, estimated that the yield of French listed securities during 1897–99 was 3.21 per cent, of foreign 4.28 per cent, on their market values.

tion and development less urgent than elsewhere. Nor was there a constant utilization of the stream of savings by the national government for its public purposes; its borrowings were small between 1890 and 1910.[6] The communes and municipalities borrowed by direct contact with state-controlled institutions such as the Crédit Foncier, and Caisse des Dépôts et Consignations. Hence from these sources the volume of securities offered the investor was comparatively small. The rate of return on the bonds of the French governmental bodies and of the stronger French industrial enterprises fell continually till the middle of the nineties. Thereafter they rose somewhat but still offered narrow hopes to savers who were arduously building an annuity for their later years. The French *rente* yielded, by way of illustration, less than 3 per cent during the period of lowest interest rates in the nineties, not much more than $3\frac{1}{4}$ per cent in the years of higher interest rates before the war.

From the outer world better paying offers and proposals came and French savings accepted them. Other governments, whose credit seemed to shine bright, made Paris the focus of their financial plans. They came to the French investor for the means of meeting the deficits which their own taxpayers would not or could not meet. Out of the small black purse of the French bourgeois, the Russian monarchy could draw the substance for its monumental plans, the Austro-Hungarian Empire equip itself with railroads, banks, and factories, the Turkish Sultan spend without accounts, Italy endure the anxieties of the first years of unification, the small Balkan states establish their national existence. Besides, the French banks

---

[6] The Crédit Lyonnais in its annual report for 1909 estimated that from 1892 to 1908 the public loans of the government, state, cities, and colonies had been:

In France	1.9 billion francs
In Germany	13.6 billion francs
In Great Britain	14.4 billion francs

and syndicates drew French savings after them to the promising opportunities of lands not able to finance or construct the stone and steel foundations of modern industrial organization. Railroads, bridges, ports, gas and power works in Russia, Turkey, and Latin-America were built, the shovels were set to dig a canal across the narrow strip of Panama. Or, attracted by some glimpse of sudden fortune, some private decision, the man of capital would reach out to purchase on a foreign stock exchange shares in a South African gold mine or the growing Royal Dutch Petroleum Company or the Canadian Pacific Railroad.

The small French investor grew accustomed to the purchase of foreign securities. His first funds went into the bonds of the French Government or French railways; as the hoard increased a Russian bond would usually follow, its annual coupon rate a little higher; then as the increase in savings continued, he added a wider variety of foreign holdings, still better paying. The current offerings in the later years resembled, in their exotic composition, the students at the French universities and the visitors on the Paris boulevards. French finance had the same thriving, cosmopolite activity as the rest of Paris business, the same tolerance and indulgence for difference and weakness, the same disposition to strike a bargain with these qualities. In the diversity of its connections and transactions, its willingness to deal with all comers, its zest for strangeness, the Paris market surpassed London and Berlin. The world of saving was a sober, stationary, provincial one, of plain black suits, gray aprons and stiff bombazines. The world of investing was a mixed, transactional, Parisian one bringing together the figures of finance, public affairs, and journalism with the borrowing representatives of the races of the continent, of the Latin-American states, of the whole circle of the Mediterranean coast. For these, or many of them, Paris was the financial capital, as it was the intellectual and culinary one—a place toward which it was easy to become a debtor. Paris took in their securities as it did their presences.

THE banking mechanism through which these foreign securities were distributed into the possession of millions of Frenchmen, centered in Paris. Practically all of the larger loans were arranged through the agency of one or more of a small group of powerful banking houses. During the earlier part of the century a few great private banks had held complete sway of the security business. Of these private banks the Paris house of Rothschild was the head, whose participation had been indispensable to any foreign loan of the first magnitude. The houses of Hottinguer, Vernes, Mallet, Mirabaud, De Neuflize, were among the less wealthy but highly respected institutions of the same type, known as a group as the Haute Banque. It was with these banks that sovereigns dealt. But even before 1870 their part in the direction of French capital investment had greatly declined in the face of the competition of new types of banks. These had a broader power of attracting popular savings, a disposition to push forward business whose risks frightened the private banking houses which had not limited liability and which managed their own fortunes. The important part played by the Rothschild firm in bringing out the loans required to pay the German indemnity was almost the last sign of past supremacy given by private banking circles. The defaults of many of the foreign governments whose securities they had introduced, of Spain and Portugal and Greece, the irritations caused by Austria and Italy to the holders of their bonds, had shown their fallibility, thinned the somber aura of their reputation. But the private banks remained, right up to 1914, solid and important among the security-issuing houses. From them came part of the capital and

directing ownership of the newer institutions. Rarely did
they make any large independent offerings. But their
capital power remained great and their coöperation remained necessary to the other issuing syndicates for they
continued to administer many of the large private fortunes. Besides the great Paris firms that have been mentioned, were a large number of smaller banks in Paris and
the provinces, playing a similar part, but often more spe-
cialized, more given to handling smaller ventures, more
apt to keep permanent place in the enterprises which they
financed.

The newer banks were corporate institutions with
limited liability, and with widely diffused ownership. Two
groups were recognized among them, the Banques D'Affaires and the Banques de Dépôts—the Industrial Banks
and the Deposit Banks.[7] Of the first group the ill-fated
Crédit Mobilier, formed in 1852 to challenge the dominance of the Rothschilds, was the forerunner. For fifteen
years this pioneer carried forward with cumulative capital
burdens and immobilized assets, an ambitious program of
financing and controlling industrial enterprise, then
smashed—leaving its example to be corrected by successors. These came, doing the same business of promotion,
financing, and issue. A few survived and became powerful
in deciding the uses of French capital. Oldest and strongest of all was the Banque de Paris et Pays Bas. The
Banque de L'Union Parisienne, the revived Crédit Mobilier, the Banque Française pour le Commerce et L'Industrie stood out among the others. These Industrial
Banks had large share capitals, and a small number of
wealthy depositors and clients, chief among which were the
companies they organized, financed, and sometimes controlled. Each looked largely to the foreign field. They had

[7] See E. Kaufmann, *La Banque en France* (Paris, 1914), E. Baldy,
Les Banques d'Affaires en France (Paris, 1922), H. Collas, *La Banque
de Paris et des Pays Bas* (Dijon, 1908).

the capacity and daring to undertake government loans which other markets were reluctant to risk and often provided the impulse to foreign industrial developments from which investors of other lands turned or asked a higher price. Each held in its portfolio the shares of other banks located abroad in whose control it shared; each founded foreign branches. The subordinate institutions of the Banque de Paris et Pays Bas alone make a formidable list; they were the center of important financial enterprises in Russia, China, Bulgaria, Japan, Morocco, Roumania, Italy, Mexico, Belgium, Holland, and Switzerland. So, too, with the other Industrial Banks.

Of almost every large investment operation on the continent of Europe involving foreign financing these banks were a part, and usually a partner. Between themselves, and with the Deposit Banks, there existed a large measure of accord and coöperation. Occasional rivalries did not seriously modify mutual consideration for each other's special fields of operation, and did not deter the combination of strength for large ventures.[8] Upon the Deposit Banks, these Industrial Banks leaned heavily for aid in the sale of the loans they brought to Paris. For their powers of sale to the public were below the pace and energy of their numerous operations. Consortiums were formed which at their greatest included all the powerful units of the two groups.

It was through the Deposit Banks that the scattered savings of the French were most effectively reached. Four possessed hundreds of branches which extended to every corner of the land—the Crédit Lyonnais, the Comptoir Nationale D'Escompte, the Société Générale and the Crédit Industriel et Commercial. Warned by early experience they had turned their energies primarily to the conduct of

[8] Evidence of M. Ullman, Director of the Comptoir D'Escompte, in *Interviews on the Banking and Currency Systems of England, Scotland, France, etc.* (National Monetary Commission, Washington, 1910).

a regular banking business in short-time credit, in money transfers, in self-liquidating commercial financing. But gradually, through their branches, their crowds of depositors who welcomed advice, their traveling security salesmen, a vast business in securities was carried on over their counters, while any great immobilization of capital was avoided. Government securities were the favorite medium of this trade. Now and again the Deposit Banks arranged the issues themselves, dealt directly with the borrower and bought the loan outright, or on option, as did the Crédit Lyonnais with the Russian Government. But far more often the loan was arranged and underwritten by the Industrial Banks, and the Deposit Banks participated in the selling syndicate, or sold merely on commission. Equipped with a knowledge of the state of their customer's account, acquainted through local representatives, the recommendations of these banks amounted to a sale.[9] So effective was their distributing power, especially that of the Crédit Lyonnais, that large issues of securities could be disposed without public offering, by direct sale to their customers over the counter.

Such were the main elements in the financial organization through which a substantial part of French savings found employment. That so much of it found employment abroad rather than within France, is, in the controversial literature of the subject, laid up to the character of this banking system rather than to the general conditions of French life and industry.[10] It was charged that the banking system exploited the passivity, prejudices, and con-

[9] Evidence of Baron Brincard, Director of the Crédit Lyonnais, in *Interviews on the Banking and Currency Systems of England, Scotland, France, etc., op. cit.*

[10] This controversy was extraordinarily widespread. Its leaders wrote under pseudonyms. Lysis led the attack; his criticisms were republished in a large volume, *Politique et Finance d'Avant-Guerre* (Paris, 1920). Testis led the defense, *Le Rôle des Établissements de Crédit en France* (Paris, 1907).

servation of the French people, rather than stimulated
their industry, their inventive genius, their organizing
capacities. If, the argument continued, that had not been
so, the capital would have found better occupation within
the country. This judgment made a major influence of
what was a subsidiary one, a first cause of what was a
secondary one. Still when due allowance is made for ex-
aggeration, an element of truth remains in the opinion.
Those institutions which dominated the security market
favored, because of their liquidity and the ease of placement and of profit, the larger security issues, especially
those of governments. They did not concern themselves
primarily with the foundation and continued supervision
of industrial enterprises; they issued bonds rather than
stocks. Even the Industrial Banks tended to end their
connection with the enterprises they financed, unlike the
German Great Banks. The banking system facilitated the
contented and routine ways of French economic life. It
did not through determined leadership impart to industry
a drive toward constant improvement, toward "efficiency"
and technical change. Whether any special duty of "leadership" rests upon the banking system of a country,
whether France was not more fortunate and content in
its actual *régime* than it would have been with a more
intensified industrial life—these are questions that must
be left for others to resolve.

THE GROWTH OF THE FOREIGN INVESTMENT

In the current chronicles the outward movement of French
capital is registered and remarked with varied detail—
notes of loan arrangements concluded, enterprises begun,
securities admitted to trading on the stock exchange, conversations with foreign governments, ups and downs of
price. But still, as in the case of the British foreign investment, it remains impossible to make certain and precise measurements of the movement.

From what material exists the following table is drawn:

FRENCH FOREIGN INVESTMENT

(of long-term or permanent character)[11]

Annual average of period	Amount (millions of francs)
1871–75	Very little
1876–80	−50 to +50
1881–85	None or very little
1886–90	443–533
1891–96	519–619
1897–1902	1,157–1,257
1903–8	1,359–1,459
1909–13	1,239–1,339

For fifteen years after the conclusion of the Franco-Prussian War, as the table indicates, French foreign investment grew hardly at all. In the decades of the fifties and sixties France had been a venturesome foreign investor on a large scale. The sovereigns of Italy, Spain, Austria, Hungary, and Portugal, among others, went into debt to the French people. Stimulated by the example of the British, French contractors, engineers, bankers, and diplomats, had united their efforts to construct railways in these lands. De Lesseps had started the Suez Canal in 1859 and completed it by 1869. French syndicates operated gas works, mines, tramways, banks, in a dozen countries. In 1869 there were officially listed on the Paris

[11] This table is taken, with some modifications, from H. G. Moulton and C. Lewis, *The French Debt Problem* (New York, 1925). Derived as it is from a study of the other elements in the French balance of international indebtedness, this table is more guardedly and correctly entitled by its authors "Net Income Available for Foreign Investment." On the whole this table fits well with various other estimates (made from tax returns or other sources). The figures given by Moulton and Lewis in their original tables, however, for 1876–80, are −50 to +50; for 1881–85, −102 to −2; from which it would follow that the total French foreign investment declined during this period. While that is possible, it is unlikely; the estimates made by Neymarck for 1880 and 1890 tend to show a small increase, *Bulletin de L'Institut International de Statistique,* 1913, Vol. XX, Part II, p. 1406. For the years just prior to the war other competent estimates give higher totals than those presented, e.g., Pupin, *La Richesse Privée et Finances Françaises,* p. 25, puts the new investment of 1912 at 2,233 million francs, for 1913 at 1,895 million francs.

Bourse 109 foreign securities, of which about one-half were the bonds of foreign governments.

All this activity was interrupted by the war with Prussia, the defeat, the period of financial mobilization to meet indemnity payments. All available liquid capital was needed for that latter purpose. The yield of the French Government securities went up to 6 per cent. Some of the stock of foreign securities previously acquired were sold to purchase those by which the indemnity was met. During the next few years many foreign governments came to borrow, and the private banks and industrial banks launched their enterprises in and out of Europe—railroads and mines in Spain, Austria, Turkey, and Russia, banks in Egypt, Mexico, Haiti, and the Balkans, nickel in Caledonia, guano in Peru, the canal at Panama. But each vigorous resumption of foreign investment was cut short by shock and loss. Panic spread from Germany in 1873. During the middle seventies, the bonds of the Egyptian and Turkish governments, on whose weak credit the French investors had wagered huge sums, went into default, as did those of various Latin-American states and American railroads. The seventies had seen the foundation of the new Industrial Banks with large capital, widely held; the eighties witnessed their difficulties and, of most, the end. L'Union Générale, most enterprising of these promotion and flotation banks, sought glory with too great a speed and failed, leaving great loss behind, and the memories of a frenzied boom. This parade of mistakes and losses, for a time, caused French investors to withdraw from doubtful commitments abroad—till the falling interest rate in France roused them again to seek high return in South African gold mines and the building of a canal across Panama. The banking and other failures of this period did not permanently turn either the savers or the banks aside from foreign investment. But now increased emphasis was put upon liquidity of assets. The Deposit Banks would handle only securities easily distributed, the Industrial Banks bent in the same direction. The bonds of governments seemed best to meet their need of safety and liquidity, and in the same preference the investors joined.

The late eighties saw the revival of foreign lending on a larger scale, and in the nineties it rose to double the volume of any previous period. Russian deficits and Russian railroads were financed without stint after the formation of the Alliance. New and strengthened Industrial Banks were forming strong connections throughout the continent. The difficulties created in London by the Baring failure opened the way to new ventures throughout Latin-America. In Argentina, Brazil, and Mexico, French capital grew important in the financing of the public authorities, the railways, banks, mines, and mortgage companies. This increased sweep of foreign investment was sustained up to 1914, despite the upward trend of interest rates in France which began in 1898. While the public securities of the European creditor countries fell in value, those of governments previously deemed poor risks, improved. The bonds of the governments of Argentina, Brazil, Mexico, Italy, and Japan, increased in market value, yet continued to offer higher yields than domestic securities. Failures and defaults had fallen off, and the market forgot old fears, while those countries which relied mainly on French capital appeared no nearer self-sufficiency. Each year the new foreign investment exceeded substantially a billion gold francs.

It was to Paris primarily that all the belligerents of the Balkan wars looked for the means of consolidating the indebtedness left by the war, of organizing newly acquired territory, of building larger armaments against the next conflict. It was on the same market that Russia primarily leaned, on which the Austro-Hungarian governments would have liked to lean. Toward its fulness Japan and China became increasingly attracted. Upon Paris these demands converged in the two years just prior to 1914, while all the money markets of Europe were under strain and interest rates were leaping. The French Government stood guard over the nation's savings, so that they might be exchanged for favor or privilege, and the banks resembled embassies. All the while the carefully matured hopes of millions of small *rentiers* became more and more dependent upon the maintenance of peace throughout the continent.

How the gross foreign ownership of the French people grew is shown in the following table:

TOTAL FRENCH FOREIGN INVESTMENT[12]

Year	Amount (billions of francs)
1870	12–14
1880	15
1890	20
1900	28
1905	34
1910	40
1912	42
1914	45

The more than triple growth within the period surveyed far outran the growth of the total capital wealth of the country. In 1914, that 45 billion francs of foreign ownership was not far short of one-sixth of the total national wealth (which was around 300 billion francs), while in

[12] This is drawn from a number of estimates, particularly that of Leon Say for 1870, Neymarck and Thery for intermediate years, and Colson for 1914. The totals I have given are "gross," i.e., no deduction is made for foreign holdings of French securities; they include investment in the French colonies.

[13] These are only approximate proportions. The following table of estimates made by various French authorities is not corrected for differences of method or scope, as the necessary facts are lacking. All these estimates are of total wealth of the French people, in billions of francs:

1878	209 (Pupin)	1906–8	220 (Stamp)
1883	220 (Pupin)	1908	287 (Thery)
1893	251 (Pupin)	1911	285 (Pupin)
1899	229 (Colson)	1913	302 (Colson)
1902–3	200 (P. Leroy-Beaulieu)	1914	295 (Stamp)

1885 it had been, perhaps, one-twelfth.[13] During the thirty years before the war, around a third of the increase in French wealth was in the extension of French ownership of properties outside of France and in the growing volume of debts owed by foreign governments.

During the same three decades the national income increased by little more than half, while that derived from foreign loans and investments tripled. In the early eighties the average annual income from such loans and investments was well short of 600 million francs, and in the early nineties about 700 millions; by 1914 it had grown to exceed 1900, perhaps 2,000 million francs.[14] While it made up perhaps 2 per cent of the total national income in 1885, it had risen to about 4 per cent in 1900, and at the outbreak of the war was almost 6 per cent. Again in weighing these figures it must be recalled that the estimates of national income include the return from all forms of labor, while that from abroad is entirely drawn from ownership. This income was the growing margin from which new savings were most easily made, the source of supply on which French industry and government might draw by bidding, the flow of payments which drew

14 In the following tables estimates are given of income derived from foreign investment taken chiefly from Moulton and Lewis, *op. cit.*, and total national income taken from various authorities:

Annual Average	Income from foreign investment (Millions of francs)	Years	Total French income (Billions of francs)
1876–80	500–600	1878	21.9 (Pupin)
1881–85	480–580	1892	29–30 (Thery)
1886–90	515–615	1893	24 (Moulton & Lewis)
1891–96	640–740	1889–1901	26.2 (Colson)
1897–1902	915–1,015	1903	27.8 (Colson)
1903–8	1,315–1,415	1913	32–35 (Rist)
1909–13	1,705–1,805	1914	37.5 (Stamp)

The estimates of income from abroad are net, after deduction of amount due foreigners on French securities. For the later years especially they are lower than those given by other authorities, e.g., Pupin, Felix, Meynial and Colson, whose figures range from 1,900 to 2,300 million francs for 1913–14.

gold into France and made possible that steady low interest rate from which French commerce benefited.

During all periods, save perhaps a few years at the beginning of the century, the return from previously made foreign loans and investment exceeded the current new investment. The rapid rise in the volume of income received was in part the natural result of the increased investment, in part the outcome of the higher bond yields that prevailed throughout the world, in part due to the extension of a larger volume of French lending to countries whose securities paid comparatively high interest, as, for example, Latin-American states. Up to the middle nineties the proceeds of the foreign lending were eaten up by losses, or used to supplement the yield of a depressed agriculture and stationary industry. Thereafter they were mainly lent abroad again. Increasingly foreign chancelleries looked to the black-coated Frenchman in his shop or office, the industrious peasant on his farm, to solve their problems; increasingly French commerce looked to them for orders; the Foreign Office took them into account in the operations of give and take which made up diplomacy.

WHERE THE INVESTMENT WAS MADE

THOUGH it spread in later years to the distant continents and the newly grown countries, the main field of intercourse and of enterprise of French capital was in the near-by regions which were penetrated by its banks, its instruction, and its culture. France, as it always has done, lived and traded primarily within Europe and along the Mediterranean shores. In none of those broad and fertile outside areas which were being most zestfully and vigorously developed by white men, save in a few Latin-American countries, were there large and influential groups of French people who would naturally draw upon French capital to finance their plans. For they were primarily Anglo-Saxon lands, and drew their technical help and financial collaboration from Great Britain and the United

States. Within them, no political influence was to be acquired by such investment, and no strong congenial ties of history, taste, or outlook, gave comfort or attraction. French foreign lending was not dominated by careful, objective measurement of economic opportunity. Guided and often controlled by government and the opinions of the financial institutions, it was swayed by antipathies and sympathies, traditional, emotional, political. These bound it to the countries of the Latins and Slavs. To retrace the history of French foreign lending would be, as a French writer had said, almost equivalent to writing the history of French political sympathies, rapprochements, vague dreams of influence, alliances in arms.[15]

The approximate division of French fortune in outside lands, at the beginning of the century and the outbreak of the war, is given in the following table.[16]

[15] Lecture of M. Aupetit in *Les Grands Marchés Financiers* (Paris, 1912).

[16] For the estimates of the earlier years the article by R. G. Levy, "La Fortune Mobilière de la France à l'Étranger," *Revue des Deux Mondes,* March 15, 1897, and the official estimate made by the French Government as of 1902, *Bulletin de Statistique et de Législation Comparée,* October, 1902, were of value, though the latter is unreliable. For the estimates of the later years the tables of Neymarck in *French Savings and their Influence* (U. S. National Monetary Commission, 1910), and Moulton and Lewis, *op. cit.,* were consulted. In the latter study the estimate of French investment in Roumania, Austria-Hungary, Spain and Portugal is substantially greater than that indicated by other sources, and means of measurement; on the other hand the figures given for the Latin-American countries and for the United States and Canada appear to be underestimates. Information regarding French investment in Russia and Austria-Hungary as of 1914 is given by the reports of the official offices established to register them. A good analysis of French investment in Russia based on this material, by L. Martin, is to be found in the *Revue Politique et Parlementaire,* February, 1921. For the estimates of investment in Latin-America use was made of the record of current issues and the study by F. M. Halsey, *Investments in Latin-America* (U. S. Department of Commerce, Special Agents Series, No. 169, Washington, 1918). Of all the Latin-American countries, French capital sought Mexico and Argentina in greatest volume. In the *Économiste Européen,* January 30, 1914, details are given of the French investment in Mexico. The tables in the text are estimates of investments at nominal value in terms of gold francs. The actual market value

GEOGRAPHICAL DISTRIBUTION OF FRENCH FOREIGN
LONG-TERM INVESTMENT

(Billions of francs)

1900		1914	
Russia	7.0	Russia	11.3
Turkey (in Asia and Europe)	2.0	Turkey (in Asia and Europe)	3.3
Spain and Portugal	4.5	Spain and Portugal	3.9
Austria-Hungary	2.5	Austria-Hungary	2.2
Balkan states	0.7	Balkan states	2.5
Italy	1.4	Italy	1.3
Switzerland, Belgium, and Netherlands	1.0	Switzerland, Belgium, and Netherlands	1.5
Rest of Europe	0.8	Rest of Europe	1.5
Total Europe	19.9	Total Europe	27.5
French colonies	1.5	French colonies	4.0
Egypt, Suez, and South Africa	3.0	Egypt, Suez, and South Africa	3.3
United States and Canada	0.8	United States, Canada, and Australia	2.0
Latin-America	2.0	Latin-America	6.0
Asia	0.8	Asia	2.2
Grand Total	28.0	Grand Total	45.0

It will be seen that Europe remained up to the war the
chief field of employment of French capital abroad,
despite the acquisition of a large colonial domain, the
opening up of fertile continents, and the extension of
French commerce and political interest throughout Asia.

The loans to the Russian Government and the private
investments made within that country grew unceasingly
from the formation of the Alliance. Deprived temporarily
of both British and German support, Russia in the years
immediately after 1887 not only met all its current needs
in Paris, but converted at lower rates issues outstanding
elsewhere. The government and the banks threw their

was much less in some cases, e.g., Portuguese bonds, much more in others,
e.g., the Suez Canal shares. The tables do not include investment in shipping. The best established computation of colonial investment in the
pre-war period is that of G. Martin, *Les Problèmes du Crédit en France*
(Paris, 1919).

combined effort behind the successive flotations, defended
Russian credit, and made place for Russian securities
second only to that possessed by those of the French Government. Since the Alliance was the foundation on which
French diplomatic effort was built, this demand had to be
met—favor was given for favor. This movement of capital
was sustained besides by a sense of vast, hardly exploited
agricultural and mineral riches of Russia, the giant character of the economic life that might arise therein, once
it was properly managed. Of the total French investment
in Russia something over a billion and a half francs were
put into private enterprise; the rest represented the purchase of securities directly or indirectly guaranteed by
some branch of the government, issued for general governmental purposes, for railroads, for mortgage banks, for
the municipalities. From the eighties French capital had
set about the creation of iron and steel works, and the
total investment in them grew to about 400 million francs.
They remained largely under French technical as well as
financial control, were connected with the metallurgical
plants in France, and were dependent upon the Russian
Government for their profit—derived from railway and
war materials.[17] The total French investment in Russia
made up a quarter of all French ownership abroad; it was
a still greater share of the foreign securities owned by the
smaller capitalists.[18]

Toward the realms of the Turkish Empire French
capital had early been drawn, by historic and religious
tradition. Upon both the Sultan of Turkey and the Khedive of Egypt the Paris market bestowed the right to
borrow up to the cold dawn of bankruptcy, gambling upon
its ability to protect the investment against the final event.

---

[17] L. J. Lewery, *Foreign Capital Investments in Russian Industries
and Commerce* (Bureau of Foreign and Domestic Commerce, Miscellaneous Series, No. 124, Washington, 1914), p. 9.

[18] See E. Thery, "Les Valeurs Mobilières en France," *Congrès Internationale des Valeurs Mobilières* (Paris, 1900), who gives the results of
an examination of 1,032 portfolios left at the Banque de France.

Large sums of capital were provided, besides, for railway and public works construction throughout that disunited, faltering empire. French financial enterprise built and operated lighthouses and docks in the waters of the Mediterranean, the Black and the Red Seas, and the Persian Gulf. In the consortium formed in 1911 to operate the transport and electricity enterprises of Constantinople, it was preponderant; the operation of the gas works and construction of sewers in that city was under its direction. In some other Turkish cities its part was hardly less prominent, while throughout several provinces it held contracts for road construction and transport enterprises. Something over half a billion francs of capital were invested in the railways under French direction. In land companies and mortgage companies, in coal, silver, manganese and copper mines, French capital was engaged. By concessions obtained between 1910 and 1914 the prospective field of French enterprises was vastly extended. It was French capital above all, which was financing economic change in the Near East.

In the Balkan states, which rose out of the former European provinces of Turkey, French capital also entered in volume, especially after 1890. Of all foreign capital it was most willing to support the hopes and plans of these small countries, most entangled in their fortunes. To Paris each government turned to finance the railway construction that was to fructify its territories, to equip its armies in the fields, to repair the damages of war. After their requests had been screened through the wires of the Foreign Offices, the banks and the people bought the bonds, maintaining a hope of continued peace in the Balkans. They were encouraged by the stubborn capacity shown by these governments to pay their debts even in the midst of trouble. In the railway plans of these countries, and in their banks, French investment became dominant.

Spain and Portugal were among the earliest and heaviest borrowers in France—made welcome by a racial kinship, and in the days of the Empire, by the religious and political sympathies between the reigning families. But toward the close of the nineteenth century, French ownership of their debt tended to decline rather than the contrary. The bondholders were forced to accept repeated reductions of principal or interest. For long periods the Paris market was closed to their further borrowing. With the financial and economic recovery in Spain that followed the war with the United States, the Spaniards gradually bought back part of the internal and external debt held in Paris. Portugal, which faced the loss of her colonies as the price of further borrowing, managed without it. Neither country invited or gave great assurance to private enterprise financed abroad. The French investment in Italy tended, too, to decline during the period of our interest. Political differences divided the two countries and kept the Paris market closed for many years. During the years prior to the war, French financial enterprise was again taking up new ventures in Italy; but on the other hand, the Italians were repatriating their external government debt. The amount of French capital invested in Austria-Hungary was reduced somewhat by similar withdrawal. The Dual Empire owed some of its important railways to the interest of the French investor, and had found in France a ready market for its securities. The French industrial banks, especially L'Union Générale, had carried forward many branches of industrial and mining enterprise. But as the alliances on the continent grew more sharply edged and as antagonism between Russia and Austria-Hungary became defined, the movement of French capital almost ceased.

In the early financing of the Latin-American Republics, French finance took little part. But in the two decades before the war growing attraction was felt for the railway and other opportunities perceived in these lands, and faith grew in the credit of the governments. French opinion became impregnated with a sense of racial and intellectual kinship to these peoples, and they, in turn, looked to France for their education and their pleasure. French banking syndicates began to compete successfully for Latin-American concessions and loans. A substantial investment in the government bonds of Argentina and Brazil accumulated, and French participation in railway finance extended. The port works of important Brazilian coastal cities were the product of French enterprise. In Mexico, the French became large holders of the public debt, and the most important investors in commercial and mortgage banks. In all three countries and the rest of Latin-America there were numerous smaller, public utility, commercial, manufacturing, banking, and mining companies financed from Paris. It was in the Latin-American republics that French investment was growing most rapidly toward 1914, and not a negligible part of it was in the form of shares, not bonds.

Of American securities few were listed on the Paris Bourse. The tax arrangements and various legal requirements of the two countries contributed to keep their number small. Chief among those of which sizeable amounts were held in France were the bonds of the American railway systems, bought mainly in 1906 and thereafter; especially the bonds of the Pennsylvania, the New York, New Haven, and Hartford, the Big Four, the Central Pacific and the St. Louis and San Francisco.

Though favored by colonial legislation which reserved opportunity for French capital, and by official institutions, the investment in the colonies before the war was comparatively small, something over four billion francs— about a tenth of the total foreign holdings.[19] In this figure are included the colonial government loans not offered to the public, but bought directly by the Caisse Nationale

[19] The legislation of the colonies reserved for French subjects or companies under French law the mining resources; the railways were similarly reserved for or built by French capital. H. Paulin, *L'Outillage Économique des Colonies Françaises* (Paris, 1911).

des Retraites pour la Vieillesse and the Crédit Foncier de France. Of the total investment two-thirds were placed in the North African colonies, Algeria, Tunis, and Morocco (where the Banque de Paris et Pays Bas was most active), and most of the rest in Indo-China. That the spacious regions brought under the French flag attracted no more capital is attributable to diverse conditions. The colonial governments were fumbling in their efforts to develop their domains. The home government was preoccupied with continental plans and politics. Railroad construction went forward less vigorously than in the corresponding British areas. French private enterprise suffered many losses in their early ventures and grew afraid. Even into the North African colonies the French migration was small, and into the other colonies it was almost negligible. The colonists took mainly to farming; they organized few enterprises of large enough dimension to win the attention of the financial syndicates of Paris. In the tropical regions, curiously enough, little capital was engaged in the production of raw materials. The concession *régime* in the French Congo worked poorly, and in Indo-China the private enterprises which undertook raw material production were comparatively few.[20] It was left to the war to bring home freshly both to the colonial administration and industrial enterprises what a rich field these colonial areas were for the application of capital.

The French investment in the colonies, in Latin-America, Russia, Turkey, China, and elsewhere was making available new resources for its industry and that of the rest of the world, and bringing these regions into the circle of world exchange. Of these objects French commercial and industrial circles were conscious. But a still broader consciousness existed that the French investment was sustaining French prestige, political position and purposes. In the making over of the economic organization of the

[20] See J. Chailley, *Économiste Français*, March 31, 1917.

world, French capital and enterprise, despite much technical genius, a gift for planning and unsurpassed workmanship, was playing less part than English, or German capital. But in greater measure than either of these, it was shaping political alignments—making the fortunes of a new day. The French bankers, even the ordinary French investors, were dealers in "Affaires," not merely computers of interest, or surveyors of new countries.

THE CHARACTER OF THE INVESTMENT

THE employments to which French foreign investment were put cannot be measured with sufficient precision to justify their presentation in statistical form. A great portion, well over half, was represented by loans to foreign governments, whose ultimate disposition of the borrowed funds cannot be checked or assigned. Paris kept its gates open more widely than any other money market to the governments whose treasuries were perpetually empty, whose expenditure was determined autocratically, whose national vitality seemed corrupted and declining, such as Spain, Portugal, Turkey, Egypt, Morocco. It kept its gates open, also, for the governments of Europe which were still struggling with the difficulties of the first stages of national existence or development, living in their ambitions beyond the resources of their tax systems—Italy (in earlier days), Russia, and the Balkan states.

This selection of doubtful risks was partly a matter of circumstances, partly of faith, partly of policy. The circumstances lay in the past losses and new caution of the banks in undertaking industrial ventures abroad, the lack of industrial organization competent to carry out such projects in great number, and the preference of the small investors. The faith was a characteristic of French temperament—their imaginative, though stay-at-home, interest and response to the exotic, their acceptance of difference, weakness, and difficulty as natural. M. Paul

Leroy-Beaulieu, a close observer of French investment, has remarked: "I do not believe there are more venturesome capitalists on earth than the small and average French capitalists. Offer them railroad or canal shares, I will not say on the moon, which is too well known, but on Mars or Saturn, and you will find some subscribers." But there was, besides, in all this lending to governments of weak credit, an element of policy. It was in their domains, through their weakness sometimes, that French power might be extended; it was because of the urgency of their needs that alliances might be assured, friendships encouraged by financial aid—or so it was thought. Mingled with all these elements was the attraction of the high return promised to a people of small savings.

Despite the prevalence of government securities among the foreign holdings of the French, despite the fact that much of this was wasted, or spent for purposes of strategy and war, it still is true that much more than half, perhaps as much as three-quarters, of the total French investment served a direct economic purpose. Much of the government borrowings were used to build railroads, ports, to found banks and to improve cities. Virtually all the investment in private enterprise served similar purposes. In Russia, Turkey, Austria-Hungary, China, the Balkans, and the colonies, railroads were financed, bridges, ports, power plants, local public utilities built. The operators of copper mines of Spain and Africa, the coal mines of Turkey, gold mines of Africa, sulphur deposits of Italy, and silver mines of Mexico drew support from French speculative capital. Agriculture and agricultural production in a dozen countries were financed by the land banks (Crédit Fonciers), whose bonds were sold in France and whose directing committees resided there. French-owned commercial banks operated in most of the countries of Europe, throughout North Africa and the other French colonies, in Turkey and the Near East. In manufacturing enterprises the investment was small—the chief of them being in metallurgical and textile plants in Russia.

The earlier failures of the Industrial Banks confirmed for several decades a preference for securities of fixed return, bonds of government or of private enterprise. Besides, the French tax system tended to deter strong foreign industrial concerns from seeking official listing for their shares. Still after the turn of the century, the spirit of venturesomeness showed itself again. Large amounts of savings turned to stock of such companies as the Royal Dutch Shell, the Rio Tinto Copper Company, American railroads, rubber plantations, gold mines.[21] Banking institutions and industrial circles organized to improve their power to manage foreign enterprises. Before the war signs were visible of a closer coördination of effort between banks and French industry along the path of the arrangements prevailing in Germany. French opinion was tending to seek the presumed advantage to industry, the investor, and the state from the actual direction of business enterprise abroad. It was not completely satisfied with the rôle of universal banker to foreign governments.

[21] An indication of the drift toward securities of variable returns is given by the statistics of issues on the Official Stock Exchange. In January, 1900, of 273 listed issues but 58 were of variable returns; in January, 1912, the number had increased to 120 out of a total of 464.

CHAPTER III

GERMAN FOREIGN INVESTMENT

TWO NEEDS FOR EVERY MARK

GERMANY has gone into history as a poor country. Voltaire prophesied that it was a region condemned to eternal poverty. The beginning of the nineteenth century witnessed a land broken up into a multitude of small states, entirely rural except for some few commercial centers and seacoast towns of great renown. By the end of the century the industrial organization of a unified Germany had taken massive form. Its foreign commerce was rivaling that of the British. Its highly concentrated banking system was finding the means not only to finance the impulsion of industry at home, but also to implant offshoots abroad.

From 1870 to 1914 the domestic demands for the capital available in Germany were numerous and urgent, and all foreign borrowers had to face the competition of these demands. Within this period German population grew from about forty millions to not far short of seventy millions; a vast mechanized industry, leading Europe in its applications of electrical power and chemical science, was built up; the greatest coal fields on the continent were equipped; a powerful merchant marine launched on all the oceans; the cities grew famed for the public works and services by which their doubling population was provided for; the imperial and state governments extended the range of their civil duties, bore the cost of social legislation, and supported great military establishments on land and sea. All these enterprises and projects required capital sums that increased with the changes in industrial technique and the course of public affairs. Within Germany, before 1870, the available amount of liquid capital was small. The official discount rates were often a full point above the British and French, and the charges for advances on securities were seldom below 5 per cent. It is rather surprising that German capital moved abroad at all in view of these conditions, and note should be taken of the fact that even while substantial sums were being invested abroad the German market was borrowing on short-time account. The English and French banks extended short-period loans, both directly and in the form of acceptance credit. The volume of these short-period loans was probably greater before 1900 than thereafter, and after the Moroccan crisis of 1911 it was kept within still narrower limits.

Thus German foreign investment did not primarily rest upon the existence of a large, inactive *rentier* group seeking diversity and return which domestic securities could not afford—though the savings of such people figured in the total. The investment was stimulated and maintained rather by the initiative of the German banks and industries. They recognized that Germany must participate in the financing of certain areas into which German commerce was trying to expand. It was carried forward sometimes against an unfavorable current by the Government as an investment in German commercial and political aspirations. The capital was found for foreign loans and enterprises whenever a commercial gain seemed at stake, a political hope or purpose in question.

Irregularly, a part of German savings found its way abroad. In some periods, the early seventies and middle eighties in particular, more than one-tenth, perhaps as much as one-fifth of the savings of the country made a choice of foreign employment. But that movement did not grow with the volume of savings in the nineties and after the turn of the century. From 1900 to 1914 less than one-tenth, rather than more, of current savings went abroad despite the appeal of undeveloped lands, the exertion of the Government in behalf of foreign enterprise, the great

growth of the overseas banking system and commerce.[1]
Investors and banks alike in this later period found the
strongest attraction and duty in the strengthening combinations of their own industries and in the demands of
their home governments. Only foreign governments or enterprise with special claims or special promise received
support from German finance which, conscious of its limitations, strove constantly to concert itself with French,
British, at times American finance. Even against this relatively small outward flow of capital opposition smoldered
and sometimes flared up. The agriculturists and socialists
turned the forces of their criticism against the great banks
who were its agents. Partly because of that opposition but
primarily because of the fact that every mark they could
command was being bid for by other urgent bidders within
the country, the banks often stood aside from promising
foreign loans and investment projects. The Berlin market
never possessed the broad availability, the cumulative
volume of free resources on which foreign lenders depend,
that existed in London and Paris.

THE GERMAN GREAT BANKS AND THEIR ALLIES

OF much of the investment, the banks were more than
agent. They were the controlling owner or proprietary
representative. The rise and character of the German
Great Banks are familiar economic history. In 1872 there
were about 130 deposit banks in Germany; by 1914 almost all the liquid savings and credit resources were con-

[1] This is as precise as I dare be in these estimates because of the
great margin of doubt surrounding all available estimates both of German foreign investment, and even more so of German savings. The best
known estimate is that of K. Helfferich, *Germany's Economic Progress
and National Wealth, 1888–1913* (New York, 1914), who calculated the
average annual increment of German-earned wealth from 1896 to 1912
to be between 8 and 8.5 billion marks; with unearned increment included (i.e., without making allowance for price change), these totals
were raised to 9.5–10.5. The annual increase was, according to his further estimate, perhaps 6 to 7 billion marks at the start of the period,
10 billion marks or more in 1912 and 1913.

centrated in the hands of about a dozen banks. Four of these greatly surpassed the rest in capital resources and in the volume of their varied business, the Deutsche Bank, the Diskonto-Gesellschaft, the Dresdner Bank, and the Darmstädter Bank—the 4 D's, as they were called. In second rank came the Commerz Bank, the National Bank für Deutschland, the Berliner Handelsgesellschaft, the Schaffhausen'schr Bankverein. Each of these had numerous and scattered branches and conducted diverse fields of banking. They were at once furnishers of short- and long-time commercial credit (clearing house banks), acceptance houses, security originators, and promoting syndicates.

From the time of their creation they brought the securities of foreign governments upon the German market. Possessed of large capitals, which they continued to increase, commanding all needed varieties of expert knowledge and judgment, their support and guidance were behind the development of the great German corporate enterprises which expanded abroad. When there were new lines to be established for the Hamburg American line or Norddeutscher Lloyd, concessions to be developed in Shantung or Asia Minor, a colonial chartered company to be sustained, submarine cables to be laid, petroleum companies in Roumania to be combined and strengthened, it was these banks that stepped forward, or were called forward to respond to the opportunity. Always in their vaults there was a great volume of securities, not yet distributed to the general investing public, or held to secure representation or control of direction. The holders of shares in a German bank were participating in an investment trust (among other things), which held mainly German securities, but many foreign securities besides. The risks arising from immobilization of resources the banks met not only through their large capital and their retention of control, but by shifting many of them to subsidiary companies especially founded for the purpose.

The effort of each, the interests held by each, extended in many directions. The Deutsche Bank took the lead, for example, in securing financial support for virtually all the German enterprises which combined into a network of power in Turkey. Its representatives wielded control over the Bagdad and Anatolian railways in Asiatic Turkey, the Oriental railways in European Turkey, over the Port Company at Haida-Pasha, the Tramways Company at Constantinople, to name only outstanding ventures. They were to be found as well on the boards of banks operating in South America, on that of the Electric Lighting Company in St. Petersburg, on those of Roumanian oil companies, on the Barcelona Electricity Company—to give a notion of the dispersion. The officials of the Diskonto-Gesellschaft, to give further illustration, could be found on the governing boards of railways in Venezuela, China, German East Africa, Austria-Hungary, Belgium, and Argentina, on banks in Italy, Roumania, Bulgaria, South America.

Among these banks a vigorous competition existed for the accounts of depositors, or new business connections within Germany. But in their financing negotiations and relationships with the established highly integrated enterprises within Germany, with foreign governments and other foreign lenders, the rule was division or combination rather than competition. Each had its established connections which were observed by the others, or, as expressed by an official of the Dresdner Bank, "While it is the desire and endeavour of each bank to build up its business, it must be recognized that each institution has more or less its own field of operation, which is in a large measure respected by the other banks."[2] Thus, the leader-

2 Evidence of Herr Schuster and Herr Nathan, Directors of the Dresdner Bank, *Interviews on the Banking and Currency Systems of England, Scotland, France, etc.*, pp. 404–405; J. Riesser, *The German Great Banks and Their Concentration* (National Monetary Commission, Washington, 1911), pp. 407 *et seq.*, enumerates the stable groupings.

ship of the Deutsche Bank in Turkey was not challenged. In Russian railroad loans, in Roumanian finance and Brazilian (in combination with Rothschild), negotiations were left to the Diskonto-Gesellschaft. For Austro-Hungarian financing the Darmstädter Bank (working with Rothschild) was granted the front place. Around each of these Great Banks clustered diverse banking groups of lesser importance, helping to distribute the securities brought to the German market by the larger institutions. Often for large or unusually risky issues joint consortiums were formed among all of the syndicates.

The private banks, which had conducted foreign financing long before the corporate institutions were created, retained up to 1914 much importance—especially the houses of Bleichröder, Mendelssohn, Speyer, Warburg, and Rothschild. The private banks had made Frankfort an important financial center before Berlin had grown into a great capital. They had furnished much of the family wealth and financial talent for many leading private banks of London, New York, and Paris; the banks of the Rothschilds, the Speyers, the Schröders, the Seligmans, Barings, and Huth—all to some degree or other sprang from the counting houses along the river Main. Their own wealth, and that of their selected clients, had become smaller only in comparison not in actual sum. They were large purchasers on foreign stock exchanges. Their financial connections abroad were excellent. It was through their agency, for example, that American and Mexican railway securities were mainly brought into Germany. An indication of the importance retained by Frankfort—chiefly because of the weight of these private banks —is to be seen in the fact that at the end of 1912 there were listed on the Frankfort Stock Exchange 439 security issues not listed in Berlin.[3] But gradually these private

[3] O. Wormser, *Die Frankfurter Börse* (Tubingen, 1919), Table XII. Of these, 180 were railway bonds, mainly Austro-Hungarian, Russian, and American; 124 were government loans, largely those of Austria-Hungary and the Balkan states; 27 were railway stocks.

banks became subordinate to their Great Banks. Some were bought up. The rest could not undertake by themselves business of the first magnitude.

Both in their negotiation of foreign securities and in their provision of short-time credit to German enterprise abroad the German Great Banks worked in large measure through the system of overseas branches, subsidiaries, and partnerships, which they established. These banking institutions located abroad were in themselves an important form of capital investment. Some of them were the creation of one of the Great Banks acting alone; others were created by the joint action of several of the Great Banks. They were established primarily to take advantage of the profit to be gained from financing German overseas commerce. Ordinarily they were located where German commerce was developed, or where it was believed that development might follow bold financial aid. The Great Banks, interested in domestic industry in so many ways, calculated upon the gains of banking and the gains to German industry, and thus plunged into competition with the British overseas banks. Though some transient ventures were engaged in earlier, the establishment of the German overseas banking system really began in 1886 with the establishment of the Deutsche Überseeische Bank in South America. The era of greatest expansion centered around 1905–6.[4] By 1914 strong, many branched institutions operated throughout South America with lesser extension in Central America, Turkey, Egypt, the Far East, the Balkans, and the German African colonies.[5]

[4] During these years alone the following institutions were founded or bought by the large German banks—Deutsche Ostafrikanische Bank, Deutsche Afrika Bank, Banque d'Orient (Athens), Mamorosch Blank & Co., Banque de Crédit (Sofia), Mexikanische Bank für Handel und Industrie, Deutsche Orientbank, Deutsche Zentral-Amerika Bank, Deutsche Südamerikanische Bank, Amerika Bank.

[5] This system of foreign banks growing more rapidly than those of the British and French created enmity in British financial and commercial circles. Their every move was watched with mingled fear and dislike. It is not easy to understand why they were taken to be such a

The Great Banks and the private banks, with the stock exchanges, made up the financial organization through which the foreign investment was made. The depositors of each of the Great Banks ran into the many thousands and these ordinarily purchased the securities recommended or offered to them. The large German industrial organizations financed and directed by the Great Banks could also be counted upon to follow banking lead. The banks sometimes disposed of foreign securities by direct sale to their depositors or affiliated institutions, without seeking listing. But the more usual method of issue was by general public offering through syndicates and listing on the stock exchanges.[6] Over both the admission of securities to trading on the exchanges and upon the course of trading, the Great Banks exercised much influence. The orders to buy and sell accumulated in their hands. Upon the floor of the exchanges they had a great number of representatives. Thus through capital power, their initiative in the creation of enterprise, their affiliations, their great number of depositors and clients, their part in stock exchange trading, these banks decided in the main the course of German investment in securities. Yet individual investors retained more independence of judgment than in France. The financial journals were better informed and more honest. The private banks retained greater power. The German Great Banks could not lead German savings into gambling adventures with foreign governments as easily as could

portentous menace. Among the reasons, however, it may be supposed that the following played a part: (1) the British had more or less accustomed themselves to conditions of semi-monopoly; (2) the banks were so closely connected with the German Great Banks; (3) they, like their parent banks, were prepared to handle all kinds of business; (4) they made easy terms to acquire place against their rivals.

[6] The Great Banks ordinarily bought the securities and distributed them with the aid of smaller banks by public offering and through the Berlin Stock Exchange. By means of advertising and house-to-house solicitation smaller security dealers sold to the public a substantial volume of unlisted securities or of securities listed on foreign stock exchanges.

the French. They had not the experience in directing financial activities toward the unmeasured natural resources of new countries that belonged to the British. German investment leadership was more informed, vigorous, and conscientious than the French, more dominant, but also more circumscribed than the British.

THE GROWTH OF THE INVESTMENT

THE early seventies witnessed the introduction of many new foreign securities on the German exchanges. For the triumph of the war, followed by the receipt of indemnity payments and the establishment of the gold standard placed a new and unwonted plenitude of liquid funds in the capital market. An industrial boom of unbalanced proportions took place. The German investors were attracted to the securities of the Austro-Hungarian, Russian, Turkish, Greek, Roumanian, and Portuguese governments among others. They increased their purchases of American railway securities, taking an interest in the extending systems of the American west and northwest. This new foreign investment was more widely distributed than that of earlier years, which had been held largely by the private banks and their wealthy clients. A fresh excitement and variety characterized the security markets. In 1873 the crash of the industrial boom brought the emission of foreign securities (as well as domestic) to an abrupt end. Throughout the decade of the seventies the losses, the immobilizations, and discouragement of this crisis cast their shadow over German security markets. The rate of expansion of German industry fell off. Capital was scarce. It is possible that in these years the resale by German capitalists of foreign securities previously bought exceeded the new purchases. In 1883, after the outward movement of capital had again begun, Schmoller estimated that German foreign investment was only between 4 and 5 million marks.

During the eighties the employment of German capital in foreign securities was resumed with fresh zest and in growing amount. Certainly the volume of foreign investment was in this decade greater—in relation to the total national income (and perhaps even in actual amount)—than during any other decade. German industry had overcome its difficulties, and German trade was fast expanding. It was a period of easy money and of falling interest rates throughout Europe. The rate of interest on German government loans was reduced, the German railroads were nationalized. The investors were seeking higher returns, and in response to the opportunity the banks provided securities, issued by the Balkan states, by Turkey, Russia, Spain, and Portugal (two issues of the City of Lisbon, two issues of Portuguese railway bonds and one of the Portuguese Government). Many of these new investments were of doubtful quality. The stronger foreign governments tended to favor the London and Paris money markets where their connections were of older standing and the available financial terms better. In 1887 Bismarck, alarmed, protested to the House of Bleichröder over the volume of foreign investment. Not long after the first defaults occurred. But the high tide of the foreign security issues came between 1887 and 1890. Heavy purchases of Argentine securities were made. At Bismarck's behest financial assistance was repeatedly extended to the Italian Government. The Deutsche Bank earned the Anatolian Railway Concession by a loan to the Turkish Government. The securities of the Venezuelan and Mexican governments made their first appearance in the German market. In Berlin there was flushed speculation in the shares of gold mines and the Panama Canal.

A harvest of disappointment followed. In all the defaults of the times the German investors found themselves involved.[7] Not least important as a source of loss were

---

[7] See V. W. Christians, *Die Deutschen Emissionshäuser und Ihre Emissionen* (Berlin, 1893). The *Geschichte der Frankfurter Zeitung* (Frankfort, 1911), pp. 594 *et seq.*, describes the popular reaction.

the numerous failures of the American railways; that of
the Northern Pacific was particularly felt. As early as
1884 the *Frankfurter Zeitung* had proposed that governmental supervision of railway finances should be made
a condition for admission of American railway securities
to listing on the German stock exchanges. The *Nord-
deutsche Zeitung* now asked for the expulsion of all these
securities.[8] According to Schmoller's estimate German
losses in foreign investment between 1885 and 1893 could
not have fallen far short of a billion marks—about one-
tenth of the total investment.[9]

But by 1894 the damages suffered through these defaults were in part repaired, in part forgotten. The amaz-
ing success of the chemical and electrical industries gave
a fresh impulse to security operations. New foreign borrowing was again contracted within Germany, by Austria-
Hungary, Turkey, the Balkans, by China, and the South
American states. The German overseas banking system
was being expanded at a rapid pace. Still on the net balance the outward movement of capital was not very large
—perhaps an average annual investment of 500–600 million marks from 1894 to 1900. For the German banks and
private capitalists during this period tended to dispose of
their holdings of Russian, Italian, and Spanish government securities. Shifts in political allegiance had caused
friendship toward these countries to dim, and had cast
shadows of fright over the continental situation.

The new century opened amidst great industrial activity, but with high interest rates and a crowded capital
market. These conditions tended to prevail up to 1914—
interrupted by one major and one minor crisis period. The
volume of new foreign investment tended at first to increase, and to extend to new areas. A larger part of the
foreign investment of these years went overseas than in
previous years, a smaller part to continental borrowers.

8 *Geschichte der Frankfurter Zeitung*, p. 583.
9 *Economist*, October 20, 1894.

A larger share went for the financing of industrial and banking enterprise under German control. Investment in the German colonies, hitherto almost negligible, grew. In all these fields the selection of issues by the banks and investors became more rigorous.

In the years immediately preceding the outbreak of the war the rate of new foreign investment again tended to decline.[10] The domestic demand, governmental and private, for available capital supplies was unrelaxed. The German banks were constant seekers of credit in other financial markets. Interest rates were decidedly higher than in Paris and London. The maintenance cost of Germany's expanding army and navy, the extension of German industry, the demands of the cities, tended to shut foreign borrowers out of the German market.

For measurement of the total German foreign investment we are dependent upon estimates, made from time to time by a variety of methods. The following figures can be taken only as a rough approximation of the truth.[11] The mark was then worth 4.2 to the dollar.

Year	Billions of marks
1883	5
1893	10–13
1905	15–18
1914	22–25

The average annual growth of investment during the twenty years before the war approximated 600 million

[10] German writers appear to agree on this. Computations of the balance of payments tend to support this view. See, for example, H. G. Moulton and C. McGuire, *Germany's Capacity to Pay* (New York, 1923), pp. 26–33.

[11] The material is lacking for year-to-year measurement. The figures given in the table in the text are for the total gross ownership, i.e., no deduction has been made for foreign investment in Germany by foreigners. They include the investment in overseas banks and in the German colonies, but not the investment in shipping. After studying the investment country by country, I would set 25 million marks as the highest total within the range of possibility. In Moulton and McGuire, *op. cit.*, Appendix A, a list of estimates for different years will be found.

marks, including the investment in overseas banks. It remained but a minor fraction of total German wealth, growing in about the same proportion as the total, and representing in 1914 in the neighborhood of one-fifteenth of the total German wealth.[12] It was an even smaller part of the current income of the country. During the closing years of the eighties when foreign securities were favored in eager calculations, perhaps as much as 5 per cent of the total income of the nation was so invested. But this was a peak. In the years following 1900 when the foreign borrowers were appealing in greater numbers to the German money market, it is likely that the amount of income so diverted did not much exceed 3 per cent. When after 1911 domestic demands became more urgent certainly no more than 2 per cent of the total income was turned to earn revenue abroad.[13]

The income received from these foreign employments of capital made up between 3 per cent and 4 per cent of the total national income up to 1900; thereafter it tended to fall to about 3 per cent. In the years when the volume of new foreign investments was high, it exceeded the income received from those previously made; in years when the German bankers and investors lent little to foreign borrowers, it fell below the income currently received. From 1911 to 1914 the latter situation prevailed. The

[12] These calculations are derived from J. C. Stamp, "Wealth and Income of the Chief Powers" in *Current Problems in Finance and Government* (London, 1924), p. 332, as revision of the computations made by Karl Helfferich.

[13] The calculations of total income relied on for the statements in the text are, in billions of marks:

Year	Amount	Author
1895	25.0	Schmoller
1896	21.5	Helfferich
1907	27–30	Riesser
1913	42	Colson
1914	44	Stamp's revision of Helfferich

German economic and financial system was using part of
the revenue of its foreign investments to pay for the growing volume of goods brought from abroad—for raw materials needed to keep huge factories at work, and foodstuffs, raised abroad, relished by a working population
whose wages were increasing.

THE ZONES OF INVESTMENT

ECONOMIC, financial, and political considerations mingled
in the processes which determined the selection of fields of
foreign investment by German capital. No fixed and dominant affiliations narrowed down the direction of its flow
to a few definite areas. Up to almost the end of the nineteenth century it moved mainly toward near-by states,
especially those on its eastern frontiers. The governments of these countries then were bound to Germany by
friendly alliance or by fear of the national power demonstrated in the war with France. They needed German
capital for the exploitation of their resources, German
technical knowledge and organizing capacity. From them
Germany drew raw materials, to them she sold manufactured products. This was the natural area of extension of
German financial enterprise.

But even before the nineteenth century was over financial and political influences were restraining the process in some of the directions it had previously taken and
were stimulating it in others; and these influences continued to be active up to 1914. French capital was more
freely and cheaply available for European borrowers;
French savers showed less anxiety regarding the solvency
of badly governed states. At the same time, German commercial interests and political aims began to extend to
many other parts of the globe. Colonies were acquired in
Africa and on the Asian Continent. The growing countries
of Latin-America appeared to be an open area for German finance and trade, certain to increase in importance

as their populations increased and modern productive technique was applied to their resources. The girth and rapid development of the United States, of Canada and the other British dominions, tempted with their opportunities. German foreign investment scattered more widely, pursued more aims at once.

The measurement of its distribution must be faulty—the following figures are only rough approximations.

GEOGRAPHICAL DISTRIBUTION OF GERMAN LONG-TERM
FOREIGN INVESTMENT 1914[14]

(Billions of marks)

Europe		*Outside of Europe*	
Austria-Hungary	3.0	Africa (including German colonies)	2.0
Russia	1.8		
Balkan countries	1.7	Asia (including German colonies)	1.0
Turkey (including Asiatic Turkey)	1.8	United States and Canada	3.7
France and Great Britain	1.3	Latin-America	3.8
Spain and Portugal	1.7	Other areas	0.5
Rest of Europe	1.2		
	12.5		11.0

Somewhat over half the total foreign investment, in 1914, was in the European Continent, including Turkey as a European state. Of the bond investment, probably as much as two-thirds was in this region.[15] German capital held many securities of the Austro-Hungarian governments. It had helped to build the Austrian railways, and had intimate connections in all fields of banking and industry. Yet it is possible that in the years before the war German investment declined rather than the contrary, as the pressure upon German capital resources increased. The investment in France and Great Britain represented

[14] The material for this table was drawn from a large variety of sources, mentioned in later chapters where the financing of various areas is discussed.

[15] Compare the analysis in F. Lenz, "Wesen und Struktur des Deutschen Kapital-Exports vor 1914," *Weltwirtschaftliches Archiv,* July, 1922.

attempts to supplement or extend German business activity. Iron ore supplies were sought. Branches of German chemical, metallurgical, and electrical plants were established to operate in markets more effectively reached thereby. Branch banks and trading companies working with German commercial interests were founded.

Of the investment in the Balkan states, almost half of the total was in Roumania, some in government securities, the rest in oil and industrial properties, timberlands, and banks. Up to the defaults of the nineties Germany had been the chief financial support of the other Balkan governments, but thereafter this investment was hardly enlarged. Investment in private enterprises in these countries grew, but not without discouragement and opposition. In Russia, likewise, it was in the decades before the nineties that German purchases of government securities mounted most rapidly. Thereafter, till 1914, the stock exchanges were closed to new listings of Russian government securities with the exception of a few issues favored by temporary political circumstance. German enterprising capital, too, was checked in its efforts at extension in Russia, but substantial amounts were engaged in metallurgical and machine-making works, banks, public utilities, power plants, and the electrochemical industry.[16] During the eighties and early nineties German capital became heavily interested in Italian government securities, and put much besides in banks, in electrical, metallurgical, and shipping industries. But later on many of the government securities were sold, and the participations in industrial enterprise extended only slowly and against

[16] According to the computations given by L. J. Lewery, *Foreign Capital Investment in Russian Industries* (Bureau of Foreign and Domestic Commerce, Miscellaneous Series, No. 124, Washington, 1923), p. 7, the German investment in Russian industry and commerce was 317 million rubles (not including commercial undertakings), of which 72 were in financial institutions, 55 in municipal public utilities, 48 in mining and metallurgy, 78 in metal and machine-making plants, 30 in chemical factories.

unfriendliness. The holdings of Spanish and Portuguese securities were not added to after early disappointments. In the small neighboring states, Switzerland, Holland, Belgium, German industrial enterprise and capital were more thoroughly at home, and German capital was active in half a hundred fields. But it was in Turkey, during these later years, that the accumulation of German capital was most notable. It extended its purchases of government securities, and found even under difficult circumstances the means of carrying along the Bagdad railway project, engaged in port construction, in local public utility and other enterprise. Such was the panorama of German investment in Europe.

Of the investment overseas the largest share was in the American continents. Securities of many American and Canadian railways had long enjoyed an active market on the German stock exchanges. German capital built branch factories in lines of industry in which they were preeminent, created establishments to utilize chemical and metallurgical patents and formulas; numerous trading concerns established themselves.[17] The investment in Latin-American countries was scattered and took many forms. During the years after 1900 a reception was given to the government bonds of almost all the Latin-American

[17] *Report of the U. S. Alien Property Custodian,* February 15, 1919 (Washington, 1919), contains a detailed list of the securities owned, and the enterprises in which Germans held an interest before American entry into the war. The list includes the ownership of German citizens then resident in the United States. Important among the security holdings were the stocks and bonds of the Baltimore & Ohio and Pennsylvania railroads, the United States Steel and American Telephone & Telegraph. The amount invested in stocks exceeded that invested in bonds. One interesting feature of the stock holdings is the number of stocks of "unknown and undetermined value." These were chiefly oil and mining stocks; apparently the promoters of the West found a good field in Germany. The total value of the property, including patent rights, in the hands of the Custodian, was set at 566.7 million dollars. But because of the circumstances of sale, the condition of valuation, the lack of distinction between enemy aliens of different nationalities, etc., this total must be taken only as a general indication.

states, of Argentina, Brazil, Mexico, Chile, Venezuela, and others, and even to the provincial and municipal loans of these countries. A coördinated and profitable system of banks was built up south of the Panama Canal. A number of port works and public utilities was financed and operated under German direction. In contrast to the activity of British capital, the railway ventures undertaken were few; a small part in Mexican and Argentine railway financing, a small line in Brazil, trouble-making lines in Venezuela, unexecuted plans in Guatemala—these made up the German financial interests in this field. British and American financial and construction enterprise enjoyed a preference over German right up to 1914; only second choices were left. A favored form of enterprise was that for the conduct of export and import trade. Some investment was made in mortgage banks and plantations.

Of the investment in Asia, only that in China was of importance. German capital participated in most of the general loans of the Chinese Government. In Shantung it undertook, by itself, the financing of railroads and mines; a share was taken in other railway borrowing. The number of German business houses in the Far East increased.

The capital invested in African territories outside of the German colonies exceeded that placed in the German colonies. The interest in South African gold mines and railways antedated the Boer War. That in Egyptian government securities also went back to an early period. The purchases of Moroccan bonds, the investment in public utility and mining enterprises, grew before the establishment of the French protectorate, but never was great in total. Within the German African colonies, investment was small before 1907, consisting largely of that in trading and plantation companies, some of which possessed imperial charters. Heavy losses were suffered by these companies in their first efforts, and the German Government and Great Banks had to come to their rescue repeatedly. After 1906 investing interest in colonial enter-

prises increased. Railroad building was carried forward
vigorously with the direct financial aid of the German
Government in all four of the colonies in Africa; three
roads of penetration were headed toward the Congo. Mining and exploration companies overcame their first difficulties and were finding it easier to raise capital for extending operations.

In this scattering of German investments, despite the
intrusion of political circumstance, there was a bent
toward those investments which would produce an economic development beneficial to German industry and
commerce. By loans to governments of countries with
promising economic futures, German finance might win
place which would indirectly yield opportunity to German
industry and commerce. By the creation of banks, the
establishment of branch factories, the building of railways, the same purposes would be served. The whole
operation of the German economic system, between 1870
and 1914, became increasingly dependent upon the development of foreign markets for German goods. Thereby
only could the expansion of the German heavy industries
be sustained, the raw materials necessary for that expansion secured, the rapidly growing working population be
kept in employment with an improving level of life. The
banks weighed these considerations against the needs of
domestic industrial establishments and the demands of the
government.

THE CHARACTER OF THE INVESTMENT

DESPITE a prevailing conception to the contrary, substantially more than half of the foreign investment was in
fixed interest-bearing securities, especially the bonds of
foreign governments.[18] A large part of the investment of

---

[18] According to the calculation of H. Zickert, *Die Kapital-Anlage in
Ausländischen Wertpapieren* (Berlin, 1911), pp. 39–40, 56.8 per cent of
all foreign securities listed on the German Stock Exchange in 1910 were
fixed interest-bearing.

variable return was not in the hands of individual investors but of the Great Banks. They in many different fields bore the main financial risk of new enterprise; even after the enterprises were established they tended to keep stock in their possession when disposing of fixed interest-bearing securities.

Next to government securities, it was in railway securities that most German capital was invested. Some of these securities represented merely outside investment without banking participation in control, as in the case of the American, Canadian, Mexican, and Russian railways. Other railway investments were accompanied by complete or partial control of the property as, for example, in the railways of the German colonies, of Venezuela, of Shantung, of the Oriental, Anatolian, and Bagdad railways in Turkish territory. The investment in other public utilities was comparatively small and widely scattered, those in Turkey, in Russia, in the Balkans, and South America being most important. The sum so invested was probably exceeded by the amount devoted to the establishment of branch industrial factories. The great establishments (Allgemeine Elektricitäts Gesellschaft, Siemens and Schuckert) had plants in Austria-Hungary, Russia, Italy, Spain, and elsewhere, to make and instal electrical equipment. Electrochemical works were established in Russia, Austria-Hungary, Spain, Sweden, Norway, and Switzerland. In the development of mining properties comparatively little capital was invested. Shares were taken in the gold mines of south Africa; iron ore properties were sought in Europe and Africa; colonial enterprises were developed in Shantung and southwest Africa. But the Germans had little experience in the mining field, and left it chiefly to the British and Americans. In oil-bearing properties the important investment was in Roumania, where six large companies were grouped under the financial direction of the Deutsche Bank and Diskonto-Gesellschaft.

These, along with the interest in foreign banks, commercial and mortgage, plantation companies, and trading companies, were the forms which German loans and investments took. As the era from 1870 to 1914 moved to its end, there was a growing reluctance to supply capital for the needs of foreign governments. There was a growing determination that some visible advantage should be obtained for German commerce and industry from the foreign investment of capital of which, it was felt, the German Government and industry had constant need.

PART II

RELATIONS BETWEEN FINANCE AND GOVERNMENT IN THE LENDING COUNTRIES

CHAPTER IV

FINANCE AND GOVERNMENT IN GREAT BRITAIN

LEGAL FREEDOM AND INFORMAL INTERCOURSE

BRITISH loans and investments in foreign lands first attained substantial volume in that same era —the first half of the nineteenth century—in which British industry and commerce found their growth by supplying the rest of the world. Like those who carried on industry and trade for their own profit, those who had capital to invest, and those whose business it was to deal in investments claimed the right to carry on their activities without government hindrance and control. Their affairs, they argued, were best run, judged both by their own interest and by national interest, without government interference. To this *laissez faire* argument official opinion subscribed. Such a view was natural in the country which did not impose legal reserve requirements for banks, which permitted gold to enter or pass out without control, which left to private individuals the direction of the Bank of England, and which allowed the Stock Exchange, as a private institution, to manage itself. Thus the government attempted no formal regulation of capital investment, except to prevent fraud and to prevent activities judged socially unwholesome. As the capacity of the London money market grew, as London became the center where the world's commerce and development was financed, banking circles came to regard their freedom as essential to the maintenance of their dominance. The power to act without the complications of official formality, without having to weigh considerations outside of those inherent in every financial deal, was considered to be one of the secrets of supremacy. Freedom of capital movement, too, fitted naturally with the free-trade commercial policy of the country, and was supported by the same arguments as supported this commercial policy.

That under this *régime* of freedom so large a part of the available British capital sought occupation abroad, provoked little serious doubt of its wisdom. For the chief industries of the country came to rely increasingly upon their foreign commerce. The investment of British capital abroad was regarded as bringing additional sustenance to that commerce. If it created foreign competition—but it was seen that for the most part it avoided opportunities where it might—there was confidence that the competition might be met. Since most entered fields such as railroad construction, mines, shipping, land development and the like, the return, in the form of orders for British industry, was direct and evident. Furthermore, a large part of the capital which went abroad was serving to develop lands owned by Englishmen, part of the Empire, of a far scattered, yet felt to be integral, whole. Thus there was much less of that undertone of criticism of foreign investment on economic grounds by commercial and industrial circles than existed in other lending countries. As for the agricultural interests, they were too weak to make a divergent opinion effective, even if they entertained one. Little opposition existed to the movement abroad of British capital either because of the volume this movement attained, or because of its economic results. Save in exceptional instances where some British interest, usually political, seemed to be threatened, there was little wish for formal official interference.[1]

---

[1] Of course there were a few scattered critics among the socialists and advocates of imperial unity. The most capable critical analysis of the political and economic results of British foreign lending, written by a lifelong opponent of the extension of European power over backward countries, is J. A. Hobson's *Imperialism* (London, 1902). This is, however, not a plea for government regulation of foreign investment, but an argument against the use of governmental power in support of investors in backward countries.

This attitude was agreeable to the cabinets which succeeded each other in office; they did not wish to have to concern themselves regularly with the process. Numerous official documents bear witness to the reluctance of the government to introduce itself into this field either to check an investment operation or to call upon banking institutions to render assistance to some governmental purpose. Such was the general tradition and official policy. The government tended—as far as ordinary practice went—to treat the financial institutions as a separate independent power, rather than as a subordinate one. The chief reason was explained in 1914 by Sir Edward Grey, as Secretary of State for Foreign Affairs, in describing this policy.

British financiers run their business quite independent of politics, and, if we attempt to interfere, they naturally consider that we come under some obligation. If they do some particular thing, either in granting or withholding a loan, to oblige the Foreign Office, then, of course, we come under some obligation, and I do not think that it is a desirable system. It is much better that we should leave them to deal with these matters of loans. I do not say that there are no cases in which loans have a political character and in which financiers come to the Foreign Office and ask if there is any objection to them. But generally speaking, and especially in South America, these are things in which the Foreign Office does not interfere.[2]

In keeping with this policy, communication between the government and the financial institutions was irregular, a matter of informal choice, indirect, and unrevealed. In a variety of ways suggestions passed back and forth between the financial world and the government, subtle indications of each other's judgment. For the absence of any formal official requirement that the government be

[2] *Parliamentary Debates, House of Commons,* 5th ser., LXIV, 1448–1449.

consulted before the emission of foreign loans did not
mean that there was no interchange between the government and those who engaged in the loan business. The
course of foreign investment was pointed in unofficial intercourse between those who shaped the country's political
and financial behavior. Without being compelled to do so,
as Sir Edward Grey explained, financial groups contem-
plating an issue which might affect some official purpose
often sought to inform themselves of official opinion. This
the government might refuse, often did refuse, to indicate;
or it might choose an indirect method of making it known.
But if and when it was discerned these financial groups
ordinarily took serious heed. Banking groups, alert as is
their wont, were guided by some brief public intimation, a
speech in the House of Commons or at a political dinner,
or suggestion passed through the press. For such information was often of vital importance in gauging the security
of the investment. Then, even outside of the particular
transaction in question, they could ill afford to offend.
Some groups, more closely connected with the government financially or personally, or more desirous of official
favor and recognition, sought guidance far more frequently than others; some never entered into communication with the government.

In the Bank of England there existed a useful medium
between the banks and the government. As banker for the
state, it was in touch with the Treasury, and less directly
with the Board of Trade and with the Foreign Office. The
meeting of its Board of Governors brought together representatives of large investment houses; through them a
government policy could easily be conveyed. Financial
institutions outside this group were in business relations
with the Bank of England, and could hear echoes of official desire. Often the bank's approval of contemplated
issues was definitely asked especially when the state of the
money market made it possibly inadvisable to issue foreign

loans. To the informed mind the action of the bank in regard to the discount rate and the sale or purchase of bills and securities, itself conveyed an indication of official wishes which financial considerations made it prudent to regard.

The habits and structure of British society, too, contributed to foster a natural harmony of action. In the small circles of power, financial power was united with political power, and held mainly the same ideas. Partners of the important issue houses sat in the House of Commons or among the Lords, where they were in easy touch with the Ministry. In clubs, country week-ends, shooting parties, Sir Ernest Cassel, Lord Rothschild or Lord Revelstoke could learn the official mind and reveal their own; there was ample opportunity to discuss the wisdom or needs of the moment. The smallness of England, the concentration in the same circle of those possessing influence or prestige, the responsiveness to group opinion which ruled, the personal honesty and discretion of English officialdom, the acceptance by the financial world of a high standard of honor—all these combined to make it easier to understand the freedom left to private judgment.

But various broader circumstances of Great Britain's position among the nations of the world contributed to make the operation of this policy sufficient and effective. British foreign policy kept itself aloof from many of the quarrels and agitations of European politics. It had no important direct aims on the continent of Europe except the maintenance of peace, and, incidentally thereto, the balance of power. For these it felt no need to take a part in many of those fierce and obscure struggles for influence which engaged the continental powers. The important objects of British policy, to be defended or advanced, lay outside the continent. When these were touched, the British Government renounced its attitude of nonintercourse between itself and the financial forces of the country.

When these came into issue, all prepossessions were laid aside.

Again, the British position bred a large-mindedness, an assurance, in which it grew easier to trust to the unrestrained actions of private enterprise, to forego calling upon its aid or pushing it forward against its intention. Early in possession of a great empire which offered vast opportunity to British commerce and influence, not feeling an acute need for additional colonies or regions of influence, it dispensed with certain tactics used by Germany and France. An accumulated experience showed, and continued to show, that the manifold connections and activities of British commerce and finance achieved for Great Britain in their freedom a vigorous expansion.

THE ADJUSTMENT OF FINANCIAL AND POLITICAL POLICY

WHETHER these be the true explanations of the fact, or whether it was plainly and simply a matter of financial calculation, it is beyond question that the main course of British foreign investment was in accord with the main national purposes. The feelings and decisions of the investors showed substantial identity with those of the government in power. Capital went primarily to those lands from the development of which the British people hoped for benefit—in the way of new sources of raw materials and foodstuffs, new markets. Likewise, it entered chiefly those types of employment which brought benefit, in the form of orders, to British industry. Most freely and in greatest volume it moved to countries under the British flag and to the United States—within the circle, that is, of established political friendship. From countries toward which antipathy existed it abstained, quick to detect the beat of the war-drum, no matter how muffled and distant, in the rhythm of relations. As in the decade before the war that beat grew louder and more insistent throughout Europe, British judgment showed a growing mistrust of ventures anywhere on the continent.

A striking illustration of the accord that existed between national policy and investment activity is given by the attitude shown toward opportunity in Russia. During the eighties and nineties, until 1906 in fact, while Great Britain and Russia opposed each other's forward movement in China, Afghanistan, Thibet, and Persia, British investors and banks abstained almost entirely from additional Russian loans or investments. Toward Japan the London loan market was, on the contrary, responsive. In 1901–2, while the British-Japanese alliance was being worked out, and all the continental money markets refused or hesitated, Japan found ready support in London. During the Russian-Japanese war, only Japanese war loans were bought. But as matters in dispute between the British and Russian governments began to move toward settlement, British capital began to move toward Russia. Not long before the publication of the 1907 understanding, a large Russian government loan was contracted in London for the first time in several decades. In the following years, as the political intimacy ripened, many emissions of Russian government and municipal loans followed. British capital and enterprise began to operate Russian mines and oil fields, found banks, and build factories. A similar modulation of investment activity to official attitude and political circumstances tended to show itself throughout the field.

In not a few instances of importance, however, no such adaptation of banking action to official wont or need occurred. Banking firms, whether out of ignorance, indifference or disagreement, transacted loans which interfered with the fulfilment of some government intention. Then the government took steps to make its will known, and to enforce it. The most spectacular of such interventions were called forth by loans to countries where financial transactions formed the channels through which political tides ran—as in Turkey, China, and Persia.

After many previously given indications of interest,

and after drawing the banks into the negotiations, the British Government in 1903 withdrew its support from the project to build a trunk line across Turkey, from Constantinople to the Persian Gulf—the Bagdad railway plan. Simultaneously those British banks that had arranged to participate in the financing and operation of the line, withdrew. Whether the bankers, frightened by the opposition shown in the press and Parliament, withdrew even before the announcement of the final decision of the government or in deference to this decision remains in some obscurity—as the account given in a later chapter indicates. But for the next decade it was the opposition of the government to the project which prevented the entry of British capital. British banks, consistently though with reluctance, rejected proposals that were made to them. At least once, the Foreign Office intervened in financial negotiations with Turkey, which had no direct bearing upon the Bagdad railway project. In 1910, Sir Ernest Cassel, head of the newly founded National Bank of Turkey and friend of King Edward, was induced to withdraw from a loan for the Turkish Government arranged in coöperation with the Deutsche Bank.

Twice, to give further illustrations more fully presented later, the British Government felt itself compelled to intervene in the loan negotiations with China-checking British banks whose activities hindered the consortium which had official support. To enforce its purpose the government did not hesitate to threaten the Chinese Government, and to indicate its serious displeasure to the interloping banks.

It was also to make another government conform to its will that the British Foreign Office introduced itself into loan negotiations between Persia and British bankers. By their agreement of 1907 Russia and Great Britain had divided Persia into spheres of influence, of operation for their capital and enterprise. The Nationalist party in the Persian Assembly took this agreement to portend the loss of Persian independence. Hence when during 1909–10, the two governments asked in return for direct financial aid, that a partly European commission be appointed to supervise the expenditure of the borrowed funds, that seven Frenchmen be employed in executive posts in the Ministry of Finance, and that they be given prior right to build railways, the National Assembly refused to borrow and endeavored to contract a loan with private bankers. Three times the British Government appears to have acted to constrain British financial institutions from responding. In 1909, just as the British and Russian governments were making joint proposals to the Persian Government, the arrival of word that a British firm had been offered an option on a Persian loan by a continental group, the International Oriental Syndicate, caused the Foreign Office to take swift action to compel the arrangement to fail. Again in April, 1910, the British Government joined the French in an action of the same kind. Some months later still, Seligman & Company of London offered Persia a loan, part of which was to be used to pay off the advances received from the Imperial Bank of Persia and to remove the lien held upon the customs of South Persia—the British sphere of influence. The Imperial Bank of Persia had been founded with the approving patronage and support of the British Government, and through it loans and advances had been made to the spendthrift Shah before his overthrow. By arguments of a nature unrevealed, the Foreign Office persuaded or compelled the Seligman firm to withdraw from the transaction.

In these instances (and subsequent chapters contain many more), the incompatibility between a privately arranged investment and the span of some imperial interest caused the government to interpose itself. Of such interventions some probably remain unrevealed, for they were conducted under strict rules of secrecy, were kept within the locked chambers of the minds of diplomatic officials

and bankers. No good, it was judged, could come from re-
vealing official purposes to the outer world, to other European governments, to states which might regard the
conduct of the government as an unfriendly act. A difficulty overcome, an object achieved quietly, seemed
doubly achieved. These were the prime reasons for the
maintenance of secrecy; and in many cases, good reasons
they were. But the government ordinarily chose to explain
it as a matter of obligation to the private interests concerned. Thus Lord Lansdowne, Secretary of State for
Foreign Affairs, defended his refusal (March 5, 1903)
to lay before the House of Lords the correspondence which
preceded the decision in regard to the Bagdad railway.

. . . These communications were . . . of the most confidential character. Now I am under the impression that the
occasions upon which the British Government finds itself in
such confidential communication with the representatives of
that great organism which we are in the habit of describing
as the City, are of rare occurrence—probably much rarer
than in any other country in the world. But I do say that
when those occasions arise, and when those confidential communications take place, it should be on the clearest possible
understanding that the confidence which is given and received is respected from beginning to end, and I think that
we should ill requite the manner in which the gentlemen to
whom I have referred have approached this question if we
were to offer any encouragement to the idea that we should
lay before Parliament or in any way give to the public the
documents, or the purport of the conversations, that passed
between us.[3]

THE COLONIAL STOCKS ACT

THESE interventions were affairs of the moment, bred by
special circumstance, and directed to precise ends. But in
one way the movement of British capital was affected per-

[3] *Parl. Debates, House of Lords,* 4th ser., CXXI, 1343–1344.

sistently by standing government policy, by the standing law of the land. British capital was directed toward the British dominions and colonies by the Colonial Stocks Act.

By this act, as revised in 1900, the securities, duly registered in the United Kingdom, of the British colonial and dominion governments which observed the applicable Treasury orders, were made eligible for inclusion among "Trustee Securities."[4] The loans of the Indian Government had been previously so privileged as their issue was subject to the control of the British Parliament. By acquiring "trustee" status, securities became purchasable by trust bodies and institutions whose choice was restricted closely and whose security holdings were considerable. This provided a strong market for colonial and dominion bonds within which the bonds of foreign governments could not compete. In addition the safeguards imposed by the Treasury orders augmented the confidence felt by investors.

In accordance with the duty assigned by the Colonial Stocks Act (Section 2), the British Treasury prescribed the conditions of eligibility to be observed by the borrowing governments. First, the colony (or dominion) had to provide by legislation for the payment out of its revenues of the sums which might become payable to the investors under any judgment, decree, rule, or order of a court in the United Kingdom. Second, the borrowing government had to satisfy the Treasury that adequate funds, as and when required, would be made available to meet any such decisions. Third, the borrowing government had to place on record a formal expression of their opinion that any of its legislation "which appears to the Imperial Government to alter any of the provisions affecting the security to the injury of the investor, or to involve a departure from the original security contract, should properly be disavowed."

4 The question is discussed in the *Report of the Departmental Committee Appointed to Consider the Investment of Trust Funds in Colonial Inscribed Stocks* (C6278, 1890–1891).

In establishing the preference conferred by this legislation Great Britain was moved by diverse considerations.
To promote the economic development of the colonies and
dominions recommended itself both on political and economic grounds. These were the natural political allies of
the government, the natural area of operation for British
industry and commerce. A trust in consanguinity, in British qualities transplanted abroad, bred the conviction that
they were the safest outside fields of investment and so,
wisely favored. Then, too, there was the assurance that a
substantial part of such borrowing would be expended in
the United Kingdom. For under the British colonial regulations, the borrowing of the colonies not possessing responsible self-government was arranged through Crown
Agents. These officials were resident in London, and appointed by the Secretary of State for the Colonies. Into
their care was given the purchasing of colonial governments in foreign markets.[5] In the offices of these agents
were drawn the specifications for colonial railways, harbor
works, public utility plants, and the contracts for materials signed. For the foreign purchases of British India,
whose loans had to be authorized by Parliament, the same
system was operated through the office of the Secretary
of State for India. In 1923 it was stated by the Under-
Secretary of State for India that in the past 95 per cent
of the borrowed funds spent abroad by the Indian Government had been devoted to purchases in the United Kingdom.[6] The self-governing dominions, the largest borrow-

[5] For information as to these regulations and their operation, see the
Regulations for His Majesty's Colonial Service, the *Dispatch from the
Secretary of State for the Colonies to Governors of all colonies not possessing responsible government, etc., February 26, 1904,* and especially
the *Minutes of Evidence, Committee of Enquiry into the Organisation of
the Crown Agents Office* (Cd. 4474, 1909).

[6] On the occasion of a debate in the House of Commons, July 17, 1923,
over the proposal to insert in an East India Loans Bill "provided that
at least seventy-five per cent of any such sum, or sums, so raised be expended in Great Britain." In this connection see also the *Resolution of
the Legislative Assembly of India, 1921,* advocating purchases "in the
cheapest markets."

ers, similarly retained financial and purchasing agents in London. But they were of their own selection, and the home governments used their discretion entirely in deciding to what extent purchases should be made through them. These arrangements created a sentiment favorable to colonial and dominion loans, especially in the industrial circles which could foresee a direct benefit to be obtained. The accepted belief that foreign investment always must stimulate foreign sales after all, rested upon abstract, complex reasoning. In the case of colonial and dominion loans the fact became self-evident. Thus opinion in industrial circles supported the preference conferred by the Colonial Stocks Act.

THE GOVERNMENT'S CONCERN WITH FOREIGN OPPORTUNITIES FOR BRITISH CAPITAL AND ENTERPRISE

THOSE who directed the foreign affairs of Great Britain between 1870 and 1914 desired uninterrupted friendly relations with outside powers. Thus they were inclined to eschew fields of action which multiplied disputes with other countries without bringing great benefit. The vicissitudes of British capital and enterprise in search of opportunity abroad often fell, or seemed to fall, in that class. The underlying wish of the government—to be detected in phrases, gestures, unexplained actions of omission or commission, not in formal utterances—was that this hunt for opportunity should engage the Foreign Office as infrequently as possible. The importance of the operations of British capital abroad was not underestimated, once the philosophy and calculus of empire were generally accepted. But a place achieved solely through private effort and arrangement was doubly valued, for it involved the government in no rivalries, no difficult and uncomfortable negotiations. "The Honorable Member asked me what laurels I had on my brow with regard to railway concessions," Sir Edward Grey, the Secretary of State for Foreign Affairs, informed the House of Commons on

July 10, 1914, "I would much rather if when we get commercial concessions, that they were given with the goodwill of foreign countries from which they were obtained and not by diplomatic pressure. And that is one of the reasons why, if I had laurels, I would much rather not wear them on my brow but put them in my pocket."[7]

This was the traditional official attitude, inherited from the early nineteenth century, tinged by the training and outlook of those circles which bred most of the political leaders. But as the century bore to its close, this natural inclination, attitude, yielded to the shaping forces of the time. As highly organized industry and commerce attained a steadily growing part in deciding Great Britain's political course, the demand increased that the government use the power of the state to aid British industry to secure openings and contracts abroad; and in response to the demand, the government yielded.

The important European lending countries, moved either by that same age-long zeal for an extension of their rule that carried Alexander and Caesar across the known world, or by some compulsory tendency of their national economies—the question of basic moving force cannot be settled here—were seeking to assume dominion over foreign regions, or when that seemed unobtainable, preferred or exclusive opportunity. But the political morals of the time did not countenance the outright use of force, which, in addition, was apt to be costly. Diplomacy discovered that its ends might be realized by alliance with private capital and enterprise. In many countries the people were wholly unhabituated and unable to construct and manage, by themselves, a machine and power industry. The political units under which they lived were obsolescent, and their loyalties local and undeveloped. Their government organization was incapable of planning industrial development, of managing relations with outside capital equitably and

7 *Parl. Debates, House of Commons*, 5th ser., LXIV, 1442.

firmly. To aid private capital and enterprise in a world in which such ambitions were active, and such conditions prevailed, became an important activity of government, whatever the nature of the country's aims.

Despite the traditional dislike of mingling in the negotiations of private business, and of complicating relations with other powers, the British Government undertook to give such aid. Sir Edward Grey clearly explained in answer to members of the House of Commons who were accusing him of laxity (July 10, 1914),

. . . I regard it as our duty, wherever *bona fide* British capital is forthcoming in any part of the world, and is applying for concessions to which there are no valid political objections, that we should give it the utmost support we can and endeavor to convince the foreign government concerned that it is to its interest as well as to our own to give the concessions for railways and so forth to British firms who carry them out at reasonable prices and in the best possible way.[8]

This aid was extended wherever some major aspect of British foreign policy seemed vitally affected, and the natural forces of competition could not be trusted to produce an equitable or desired outcome.

The exertions of the government adapted themselves to the strength and character of other governments, and to the ruling political relationships which existed in different areas. Where strong and orderly governments existed, which might resent any display of pressure—as in the larger Latin-American countries, Japan, Spain, and the

---

[8] *Ibid.*, p. 1445. Still the government was criticized by groups which found government aid unsatisfactory compared to that extended by other governments. Thus, an influential member of the House, recounting episodes in which the Foreign Office showed itself unwilling to interfere, "I was told the Foreign Office could not interfere in matters like that. Other Foreign Offices do interfere; they recognize, and why should we not recognize as we are the greatest of commercial countries, what other Foreign Offices recognize, that the advancement of the commerce of their country is the chief aim for which they exist. Why do we not acknowledge that?" Sir J. D. Rees, *ibid.*, pp. 1408–1409.

Scandinavian countries—government action rarely went beyond friendly recommendation, promotion of British interest where it was apparent that a common interest would be served. In the smaller states of Latin-America, where governments were often in the hands of self-enriching groups, and the play of wits and force rather than normal competitive considerations shaped decisions, government representation became more pointed. But here the existence of the Monroe Doctrine and American policies were restraining influences. Twice, in fact, in deference to American wishes, the British Government seems to have actually induced British enterprise to withdraw from rivalry with American in regions in which the United States asserted a special interest. British oil interests were persuaded to cease their effort to extend oil concessions in Colombia and in Mexico by tactics objectionable to the American Government.[9] From the conflicts of influence in Eastern and Southeastern Europe the British Government tended to stand aside; it was inclined to leave this field of opportunity to the financial groups of France and Germany, Belgium, and Switzerland.

It was in the undeveloped, disorganized Chinese Empire, in the lands on the road to India, Turkey, Persia, and Egypt, and in the continent of Africa that the government stepped to the fore, strove with, by, and for British private groups. Sometimes this effort had no other object than helping an English group to secure equitable consideration. Sometimes it was bent on having a field of opportunity set aside for British capital and enterprise. Sometimes it was guarding a political front or acquiring new dominions. Always the government retained freedom to act in accordance with its best judgment. But that judgment was shaped by a recognition that the initiative of these groups was building up Great Britain's power in

[9] *Life and Letters of Walter H. Page* (New York, 1922), I, 181, 217, 225, 227. *The Intimate Papers of Colonel House* (New York, 1926), I, 194, 199, 202.

disputed regions; and these groups, themselves, through their influence in Parliament and outside had much weight in deciding the course pursued.

By way of indication, some of the major interventions of the British Government—more fully presented in subsequent chapters—may be touched upon. From the territorial partition of China, British commerce had more to fear than hope. British policy gave support to the maintenance of Chinese unity in rather cautious and intermittent fashion (as was required by the alliance with Japan, and, after 1906–7, by the growing friendship with Russia). Its aims in intervening the British Government phrased for itself as "redressing the balance of power" in China, and "retaining equal opportunities for trade and enterprise." Between 1896 and 1898 the field of British intentions was marked out. By direct ultimatum in 1898, the Chinese Government, which had already yielded to the demands of other governments, was forced to assign to British groups concessions for railways traversing ten provinces and to promise that it would not alienate the Yangtse Valley region to any other power. In later years, by skilful negotiations with other European governments, by patient support of British banks in troubled dealings with the Chinese Government, these rights were turned into actual opportunities, guarded against the invasion of other governments or capitalist groups, and augmented. The willingness of the government was indicated by Lord Lansdowne, on June 16, 1903, in concluding a speech on Chinese affairs. ". . . I may say that the noble Earl may depend upon it that the associations which represent British interests in the matter of railway construction in China will certainly receive from His Majesty's Government a backing which I hope will bear comparison with that received by the representatives of other countries."[10] So, too, negotiating force and shelter was supplied to British interests which engaged in mining in China.

[10] *Parl. Debates, House of Lords,* 4th ser., CXXIII, 1048.

To establish British influence and interests in Persia and the lands of the Turkish Empire, the same type of assertive activity was undertaken by the government. In the poor and distant land of Persia, no hope of serious economic gain stimulated official action. Major aspects of imperial policy were deemed at stake—the prevention of Russian expansion toward India, the fear lest some alien interest would build a railway to the Indian frontier, the determination to maintain political dominance in the region of the Persian Gulf. For these reasons, the resources of the Persian Government must not be pledged to other lenders than British. Railroad and navigation concessions in South Persia must be in British hands. No powerful group of foreign nationality must be permitted to establish itself there. The British Government induced, and when conditions demanded, coerced the Persian Government to put these matters in British hands. An additional purpose appeared with the discovery of oil in Persia. Lord Fisher had already made up his mind that the battleship of the future would be fueled by oil, and the supplies of Persia appeared as the answer to a suddenly realized need.

In Turkey, too, the government was moved more decisively by political considerations, than by a sense of the importance of opportunity to British capitalists. Active the British Ambassador was in making place for his compatriots, but less ardent and assiduous than his rivals, less driven on by an excited government. British financiers were permitted to reduce their interest in Turkish railways. The successes of French and German syndicates and negotiators were witnessed without much anxiety. But the British Government kept its attention riveted upon those parts of Turkey, alien control of which was considered dangerous to the imperial scheme—Bagdad and the regions south to the Persian Gulf. Here British commerce was nourished, the claims of British navigation companies urged, the advancing project of the Bagdad railway stopped. In those negotiations of 1911–14, which prom-

ised at the time to settle the division of opportunity in
Turkey among the powers—these aims were vindicated.

Africa, its precious metals, its offerings of all the resources of tropical and temperate zones, its untraversed
reaches waiting the track-layer and the locomotive, attracted British youth and enterprise to its unexplored
chances. In this continent where new political dominions
could be secured by trafficking with some native chief,
where concessions could be turned into political constitu-
tions, where colonial boundaries were uncertain and rich
regions were under the control of minor powers like Portugal and Belgium, each action of private enterprise became an element in political arrangement. In these facts
the British Government needed no instruction. But outside
of Egypt and South Africa, the British Government
sought, at first, no additions to its responsibilities. It was
not eager to undertake expenditure and military action
to acquire new domains, rich as they might prove to be.
But its citizens, its Rhodes, Jamesons, Taubmans, Mac-
kinnons, and Lugards and the financial groups that followed their daring lead had momentum of their own; they
would drag the British Empire after them, and they did.
Thus the historian of the economic development of the
British Empire has observed that

it has been the function of the British Chartered Companies
to go in front of the nation and discover and organize a
trade. Sooner or later this trade brings the company into
conflict with foreigners or with native rulers, and the Crown
has to intervene whether in the interests of its own people,
or that of the natives, or to preserve order.[11]

In occupied regions like the Boer Republics, in neglected
colonial areas like Mozambique, in native highlands like

[11] L. C. A. Knowles, *The Economic Development of the British Overseas Empire* (London, 1924), p. 261. See the contemporary comments of
the *Economist,* October 26, 1889, on "The New Sovereign Company" which
is described thus: "merely agents bound to take the advice of the Secretary of State."

Rhodesia, in the jungles of East Africa, and the tropical interior of the Nile, the government found itself occupied with the affairs of the adventurers and capitalists. It moved slowly, often without clear recognition of what it was achieving, deciding its course by circumstance—yet with a stubborn will, once a situation shaped itself, to support the British advantages. The Colonial Office was geared to forces stronger than itself. Government and private enterprise became often part of one mechanism driven by the forces of geographical discovery, industrial technique, and nationalistic feeling.

THE PALMERSTON CIRCULAR AND SUBSEQUENT POLICY

A LOAN to a foreign government is an act of faith; the financing of an enterprise in a foreign land is hardly less so. For the foreign government, because of misfortune, miscalculation or merely bad intention, may refuse to meet the obligation of its debt. Or it may pursue policies, become involved in difficulties, pass legislation injurious to the pecuniary interest of foreign investors who have undertaken an enterprise within its domains. In all such situations there are no established legal institutions with authority to pass judgment upon the rights of the parties, the just course to be pursued. Governments usually claim that their behavior toward their creditors, and the treatment accorded any private interest within their borders, are matters within their sovereign jurisdiction for which they cannot be brought to book except by their grace and consent. Thus with grievance real or fancied, the foreign investor may find himself without adequate legal recourse against the state through whom loss has been suffered. To strengthen himself in negotiation with the foreign government it is natural that he should turn to his fellow investors, form protective associations, and to his own government asking that action be taken in his behalf. With a foreign investment so great and scattered as the British,

with a lending world so willing to take long risks against
a promised high return, and a borrowing world inclined
to take its debts lightly, the British Foreign Office became
a seat of supplication.

The changing shades of British policy in the early part
of the nineteenth century have been summed up in a sentence, "What had been an embarrassment to Castlereagh,
a subject to be virtuously shunned for Canning, was ap-
pearing to Palmerston as an opportunity and as a right
to be employed with discretion, and was foreshadowed as
a possible national duty."[12] That Prime Minister, Palmerston, put strikingly into words what, during the rest
of the century, not only in Great Britain but in other lending countries, was held to be the only reasonable and practical position for a government to take. The doctrine
which he enunciated created an expectation that dishonest
governments could not count on too much forbearance,
that on the other hand too imprudent investors could not
count on aid. It was sufficiently broad to permit the British Government to justify any course it chose to take,
sufficiently flexible to permit the measurement of advantage in each situation. This doctrine and even many of
the phrases with which it was expressed in the famous circular letter was first set forth by Palmerston in a reply
delivered in Parliament to the demand that the government intervene in behalf of the holders of bonds of the
Spanish Government. Not long afterward these views
were more formally phrased and communicated to the governments concerned by circular letter. Two main paragraphs conveyed the substance of policy.[13]

As some misconception appears to exist in some of those
states with regard to the just right of Her Majesty's Government to interfere with authoritatively, if it should think

[12] L. H. Jenks, *The Migration of British Capital to 1875*, p. 125.

[13] Circular addressed by Viscount Palmerston, presented to the House
of Commons, March 2, 1849. *State Papers British and Foreign*, XLII,
385.

fit to do so, in support of those claims, I have to inform you
as the Representative of Her Majesty in one of the states
against which British subjects have such claims, that it is
for the British Government entirely a question of international right, whether they should or should not make this
matter the subject of diplomatic negotiations. If the question
is to be considered simply in its bearing upon international
right, there can be no doubt whatever of the perfect right
which the Government of every country possesses to take up,
as a matter of diplomatic negotiation, any well-founded
complaint which any of its subjects may prefer against the
Government of another country, or any wrong which from
such foreign Government those subjects may have sustained;
and if the Government of one country is entitled to demand
redress for any one individual among its subjects who may
have a just but unsatisfied pecuniary claim upon the Government of another country, the right so to require redress
cannot be diminished merely because the extent of the wrong
is increased, and because instead of their being only one individual claiming a comparatively small sum, there are a
great number of individuals to whom a very large amount is
due.

It is simply therefore a question of discretion with the
British Government whether this matter should or should
not be taken up by diplomatic negotiation and the decision
of that question of discretion turns entirely upon British and
domestic considerations.

In the exercise of its discretion the British Government
showed no particular zeal in resorting to action. It was
difficult to maintain good relations with a foreign government while dunning it, and good relations especially with
other large states were important. Against more forceful
action there were still more forceful objections. Yet a
great capital-lending country like Great Britain, it was
reasoned, could ill afford to permit losses to be imposed
upon its investors with impunity; such a policy would in

itself stimulate further mistreatment. Swayed between political and financial considerations, the government now resisted, now yielded to the pressure of the interested parties. The outlook of the Ministry in power, the course of domestic politics, the allies that injured bondholders could find—all these might, and sometimes did, enter to turn events. Small wonder then that the record shows a fitful, hesitant, policy, a tendency now to drift with events, now to act with sternness, now to evade. So there is no simple formula by which the government's behavior can be summarized. Among its features were a careful concern for the political consequences of policy, and occasional readiness to take notice of situations not because of their financial importance but because they afforded an opportunity of achieving a desired political end.

On the whole, the resolution not to intervene was maintained during the decade of the seventies, which brought grief to those who had sought high interest in financing lax governments. Spain, and a dozen Latin-American states went into default. Italy imposed vexatious restrictions upon the payment of its bond coupons. Greece had to be argued into resuming payment on its long outstanding debt. The bonds of seven states of the American union still remained in neglect. Egypt and Turkey, bankrupt, ceased payment on their vast debt. Yet in all cases except Turkey and Egypt, the government left the burden of negotiation with the debtors to the bondholders who were, it is true, united in association, backed by punitive powers of the stock exchange, guided and given standing by the diplomatic and consular agents abroad. In Guatemala and Colombia, for example, Her Majesty's Minister Resident, and Consul and *Chargé D'Affaires*, were authorized to act as agent for the bondholders, and collectors of the sums due them.

So immediate had been the default of some of the small Latin-American borrowers (Honduras, Guatemala, Paraguay, Santo Domingo, and Costa Rica), so obviously squandered were their borrowings, so marked by manipulations were the issues in default that Parliament undertook an investigation of the episodes.[14] This financing, the Parliamentary Committee found, had been marked by reckless disregard by the borrower, misuse of the loan proceeds, commissions so usurious that no honest borrower would submit to them, collusion between government representatives and issuers, and falsification of the market to dispose of the bonds. Innocent subscribers bore the losses. Irresponsible governments faced in the future rapidly mounting claims which destroyed their borrowing power and made them the focus of intrigue and dispute. Still the committee rejected proposals that control should be exercised over the issue of foreign loans. Such a course would give false security and increase the government's obligation to take measures against defaulting debtors. The evil, it stated, could be lessened by proper action of the stock exchange, by changes in the company laws to compel the publication of full and honest prospectuses and provide recourse against false statements and wilful omissions. The negotiations between the bondholders, and the borrowing governments concerned, dragged out for another quarter century and more before they were settled.

One Latin-American default of the same period illustrates well how the policy pursued by the British Government might fluctuate. When in 1876 the Committee of Peruvian Bondholders asked the Foreign Minister to apprise the British Minister at Lima that the committee was a responsible body, the Earl of Derby refused. When shortly thereafter the committee appealed again, asserting that the security pledged to them under an agreement with the Peruvian Government was being turned over to French creditors, they were informed,

. . . Her Majesty's Government cannot depart from the policy of declining to interfere diplomatically in regard to

[14] *Report from the Select Committee on Loans to Foreign States* (1875).

foreign loans; but Lord Derby is willing to instruct her Majesty's Minister in Peru to assist unofficially any agent or representative of the bondholders in bringing their case before the Peruvian Government.[15]

But if the Peruvian Government could discern the unofficial character of the exertions of the British Minister, the reader of the pertinent Blue Books cannot. Not many months had elapsed, in fact, before the British Foreign Secretary was discussing the question with the Peruvian Government, and giving his opinion of proposals made. By 1879 the Marquess of Salisbury, who had succeeded to office, had assumed the whole burden of protection against the duplicity of a distracted Peruvian Cabinet. Still despite repeated disappointment, no threat of force was made. With war and revolution, Peru's financial condition grew worse, not better, after 1879. But British official efforts ceased; the really distressed government was not pushed. A new agreement was not reached till 1890.[16] When in the nineties, under the new settlement, the bondholders found themselves again in dispute with the Peruvian Government, the British Government refused to interfere.

The suspension of payment on their huge debt by Turkey and Egypt, in 1875–76, created situations which drew the British Government to participate in the establishment of international control over the first, and to assume dictation of the government in the second. With the other great nations of Europe, the British Government signed a declaration at the Congress of Berlin, which Turkey heeded in creating an international debt administration to administer the revenues assigned to the foreign debt. While the bondholders were discussing terms of settlement and control with the Turkish Government, and after the

15 For this episode, see the papers issued by the Foreign Office, *Peru No. 2 (1877)*, *Peru No. 1 (1882)*.

16 For its terms, see *Statesman's Year Book* (1921).

control administration was established, the British Government proved itself willing to give firm, though moderate assistance.

In Egypt, Great Britain finally took control of the government. While the disagreements and disturbances which led to the assumption of control had their origins in debt default, while the wish to aid its investors prompted interference in the settlement of Egyptian affairs, considerations of another character explain the final extension of that interference. A detailed analysis of the course of events must be left to a subsequent chapter. The ambitions of imperial policy, the wish to safeguard the Suez Canal, and the preoccupation of the Gladstone Cabinet, combined to provide the bondholders with unusually vigorous protection, and ultimately to secure their investment by British control.

Toward the Latin-American defaults of later years, and they continued to outnumber all others, an equanimity was in general shown, fitfully interrupted by brusque threat or intervention when patience no longer held. The most serious of these defaults, the suspension of payments by Argentina in 1891, was left to be settled by agreement between the government and the bondholders. Against precedent, the negotiations were carried on under the auspices of the Bank of England. That institution, however, declared itself not responsible for the proceedings or outcome. Its interest was in sustaining the London money market under the shock of the default and the failure of Baring Brothers which followed. Smaller Latin-American states, however, were made to feel the strength of the British will, to face old debts and claims. Of these interventions the one in Venezuela was the most startling. A dozen issues divided the British and Venezuelan governments, defaulted government bonds, unpaid contract claims, reparations for property seized or damaged in civil war, and matters more indisputably in the realm of government concern—ship seizures and delays. To offers of arbitration the Venezuelan Government replied that most of these were matters for its own courts; it would submit a few to diplomatic discussion if Venezuelan counter-claims were admitted at the same time. Germany and Italy were likewise embroiled in dispute. The three European countries joined in the presentation of ultimatums and the use of armed force. In Parliament, which had not been given explanatory papers before action, Lord Lansdowne emphasized the personal injury done to British subjects, the affront to English sovereignty, rather than the direct pecuniary claims—though the collection of these, too, he defended. In this episode the government had swung full circle; the whole force of the state had been put behind the foreign investor. Before the final act indignation arose in Great Britain and the United States. If this was the "discretion" of the government, the feeling ran, it had not been wisely used. Throughout Latin-America doc-trines were framed in opposition to the forcible collection of pecuniary claims. A new responsibility was presented to the American upholders of the Monroe Doctrine. There-after Europe could, by proper planning, collect its debts through the United States.

On occasion subsequently, Great Britain showed a dis-position to use forceful pressure, when necessary, to collect a debt or claim in the Caribbean region. Haiti was forced by ultimatum to compensate a British subject for prop-erty damage suffered in revolution.[17] Guatemala in 1913 was induced by the appearance of a battleship to restore to the service of loans held by British investors, coffee du-ties alienated in favor of newer creditors.[18] In Honduras and Mexico during 1910–14 unusually assiduous and aggressive British officials made their compatriots' claims a leading duty. Still, when in July, 1914, Sir Edward Grey was urged in Parliament to interfere with the flota-

[17] *American Journal of International Law,* 1914, p. 623.
[18] *Economist,* September 8, 1917, and *Foreign Relations of the United States,* 1913.

tion of a projected Brazilian loan, till various outstanding claims were settled, a refusal was returned. "British financiers," his answer ran, "have to make their own arrangements with the Brazilian Government, and, if they choose to bring out a loan, if it is to their advantage to do so, we cannot go to them and ask them to withhold bringing out the loan until we have got some claims settled in which they have no particular interest themselves."[19] The matter was left to friendly intercession. So ran the variations of official discretion in regard to Latin-America. Frequently, it must be remarked, the Foreign Office watched with apparent indifference losses suffered by British investors in railway ventures scattered throughout this region, in which the burden of loss was attributed to the action of the foreign authorities. There was scarcely a Latin-American country which did not contribute some episode of this kind to the annals of the stock exchange.[20]

By defaults occurring on the continent of Europe, the government's attention was no less frequently engaged in these decades. Greece in 1893 reduced interest payments on its external debt. Great Britain, like the other powers, went no further than friendly remonstrance. But it undertook a study of the situation since proposals of international financial control were in the air.[21] Then, when Greece issued defeated from war with Turkey in 1898, its finances more disorganized, and needing foreign financial

[19] *Parl. Debates, House of Commons,* 5th ser., LXIV, 1448–1449.

[20] For a partisan but amusing account of failing ventures in the Latin-American railway field, see H. A. Bromberger, *Les Chemins de Fer Exotiques* (Paris, 1913).

[21] As indicative of the opinion, critical of government intervention in such situations, take the comment of the *Economist,* April 22, 1893, on this action. "In sending Major Law to Athens to investigate and report officially upon the financial condition of Greece our government made a mistake which it is to be hoped will not be repeated. It is no part of the business of our Foreign Office to audit the accounts of other nations and certify as to their solvency or insolvency, and if it goes beyond its province, and attempts anything of the kind it is certain ultimately to have cause to regret the imprudence."

aid, Great Britain joined the other powers in establishing international supervision of the revenues pledged to foreign debt. On the occasion of the serious Portugal default of 1892, the government left the matter to be settled by the action of the Bondholders' Committee and the Stock Exchange, despite the maneuvers of the French and German governments. Any plan of international financial control would have admitted Germany and France into the direction of Portuguese affairs, an outcome not desired, it may be surmised. The bondholders' agitation was not permitted to create a situation whereby Portuguese colonies neighboring the South African colonies might be placed under international jurisdiction. During the same decade of the nineties, Spain did not live strictly up to the terms of its external loan obligations, but the difficulty was left to private groups to manage.

Of the remaining instances of British Government action in support of its investors that taken in behalf of the British investors in the Boer Republics of South Africa was most sustained and important in the result. Here the British Government, after long contemplation and doubt, undertook the direct support of an organized British group, controlling a vast investment, against a small republic which was moved by hatred and fear of losing its supremacy. Purposes, incommensurate with each other, stifling sympathy which breeds compromise, were at issue. On the one side, the excited desire of thousands of foreign newcomers who were risking life and fortune in pursuit of the fabulous wealth of the diamond and gold fields; on the other, the impassioned determination of pioneer farmers of a different race that the land they ruled, the republic in which they lived, should not be dominated by these powerful newcomers. In an atmosphere so saturated, policy on both sides was not directed so much to the reasonable adjustment of opposing rights—a task difficult even in a stable and calm situation—as to the assertion of dominance. From the Boer governments came oppressive

treatment, from the mining interests manifestations of
inordinate desire for gain. Gradually the British interests
erected a series of great combinations in which the interests of thousands of shareholders were united, in whose
service men of position and influence in the political and
financial world which ruled London were employed. To
the dramatizing mind of the press and Foreign Office it
seemed that the question of supremacy over all of South
Africa was at stake—Boer, with German leanings, or
Briton. As the dispute sharpened, the British Government
identified itself with the British interests. In war, their
contentions were sustained.

Even in the dominions there arose causes of dispute between British investors and the local governments. The
land tax policy of the New Zealand Government, for example, appeared unjust and iniquitous to British investors
in land companies. "New Zealanders," remarked the editor
of the *Economist* in the issue of June 20, 1891, "while
making laws for themselves, appear to forget that British
capital sunk in the colony is nearly as large as their own."
The power development activities of the Province of Ontario were regarded by those British interests who financed
the Electrical Development Company of Ontario to be an
unjust use of governmental power. Or again, and of more
serious import, British investors in the Grand Trunk Railway of Canada fought long and bitterly the treatment
accorded by the Canadian Government. But disputes such
as these the British Government left, except for amiable
good offices, to the interested parties to settle by themselves through negotiations or the law courts.

In the decade preceding 1914, no outright government
default, save that of Mexico, occurred in which British
interests were heavily involved. Hence the Foreign Secretary was left freer than usual by those who had put their
faith in the credit of foreign governments. But his desk
was never clear of the protests of those on whose investment abroad a shadow was cast by changing political cir-

cumstances or injurious legislation. To them the government gave serious, discriminating attention; often it rendered advice and assistance. But the available records of this range of activity yield little that can be turned into generalization. By a few examples, its variety may be indicated. When the Chinese Government endeavored to reduce the rights of the Chinese Engineering and Mining Company in the Kaiping Basin, the British Government made its opposition effective.[22] When during the second Balkan war, Greece and other Balkan states sequestered revenues collected by the Ottoman Public Debt Administration, the governments of the lending states, Great Britain included, caused them to desist.[23] When the United States was planning to undertake responsibility for the financial reorganization of Liberia, Sir Edward Grey made his consent to the contemplated reorganization loan provisional upon the maintenance of the "preferential rights and privileges of the British bondholders" and "the payment of the outstanding British claims."[24] Such were the instances in which the government looked over the shoulder of its investors.

THE INVESTORS ENDEAVOR TO HELP THEMSELVES

In the late sixties, when the government's attitude was more diffident than it later became, the financial groups interested in foreign securities formed a protective association to enable them to deal more effectively with defaulting states. The Corporation of Foreign Bondholders, after an early period of somewhat doubtful wisdom, established its value to investors in negotiation.[25] Even when the

---

[22] See *Annual Report* of the company, 1909.

[23] *Report of the Council of the Corporation of Foreign Bondholders,* 1912, p. 14.

[24] *Foreign Relations of the United States,* 1910, p. 704.

[25] During the eighties and nineties the Association was repeatedly accused of serving limited interests at the expense of the bondholders. It was later incorporated by Act of Parliament, 1898. Its directing body, known as the Council, consists of 21 members, of whom six are nominated

government's friendly offices or forceful strength were exerted in behalf of the investors, the task of negotiating new agreements remained for private interests to perform. For the scattered bondholders this organization, which appointed on its committees men influential in the large issuing houses and from public life, filled a genuine need. It provided continuity, authority, and disinterestedness in the salvation of disappointed hopes; its memory and stubborn will, when once it had an affair in hand, exceeded the span of individual life. The only defaulting debtors on its list that, during its half-century of existence before 1914, were not brought finally to book in some form or compromise, unsatisfactory as it might be, were the defaulting American states.

Besides its talent for persuasion and for the organization of moral pressure, the Corporation, within the limits of the circumstances of each case, could muster to best advantage the aid of the banking community, the stock exchange, and the government. Defaulting governments found it impossible to secure new financial accommodation while their reckoning remained unsettled. Even before the formation of the Corporation, the stock exchange had used its retaliatory powers against governments which had

by the Central Association of Bankers, six by the London Chamber of Commerce, and the rest by coöption. The Council acted sometimes on its own initiative but usually through the bondholders' committee associated with it. This system of appointment to the Council was devised in 1897, when the Corporation was under criticism for agreements negotiated with Spain, Uruguay, Ecuador, and Cuba, it being declared that its decisions were dominated by the issue houses who wanted to bring out new loans for the defaulting states, and by the speculators who had purchased at depreciated values. *Economist,* September 27, 1884; November 20, 1897; April 4, 1896. For an account of its organization and early activities, see, besides the *Annual Reports* of its Council, Jenks, *op. cit.,* and the articles in the *Economist* cited above. In addition to the Corporation there was founded in 1884 the English Association of American Bond and Shareholders, Ltd. This body took an active part in the reorganization of railroads, the Wabash and Atchison, Topeka & Sante Fe among them; but in addition to its protective activities, it performed various other services for its members. See A. E. Davies, *Investments Abroad* (New York, 1927), pp. 146 *et seq.*

violated the conditions of their loan contracts. New loans
were refused quotation until a settlement had been arranged, and sometimes all the loans of the offending government had been stricken from the list. Spain, Russia,
Austria, and Turkey had been so treated in the past. With
the creation of the Corporation, the stock exchange concerted its action with that of the protective association,
joined to block or reduce the credit in London of the de-
faulter.[26] But as the century drew on the effectiveness of
this stock exchange policy waned, and its inconvenience to
bondholders increased. For the Paris and Berlin markets
grew in capacity, and no arrangement for regular cooperation between the Corporation, the London Stock Exchange and the corresponding institutions in foreign financial centers, endured. The influence of the association
continued to be sufficient to close the London market, but
the trust of the investors in the efficacy of this power
diminished. More need was felt of government assistance.

From the government little help beyond friendly mediation had been expected in the early years of the organization. Indeed, greater help was hardly sought. Thus the
council of the Corporation in its first report (1873) recorded the fact that applications to the government for
aid were made as seldom as circumstances compelled, that

the interests of the bondholders are generally antagonistic to
any measures which can place Her Majesty's Government in
simple antagonism to that of another country, or may cause
hostile interposition which must come home in disturbance of
our own commerce, besides the creation of dangerous complications. The embarrassment which is entailed on bond-

[26] In the first *Report of the Council of Foreign Bondholders,* 1873, p.
50, it is remarked that "the Council have benefited by the friendly offices
of the Stock Exchange on many occasions. The consolidation of the organization of the Bondholders, while it promotes the policy initiated and
pursued by the Committee of the Stock Exchange, tends to relieve it
from many troublesome applications, enabling it to devote its action and
influence with greater effect to the important cases which may come
under their special jurisdiction."

holders by the mere interruption of diplomatic relations is very severely felt, as in the case of Mexico, so that our efforts are rather directed to the restoration of such relations than to any new interference with them.

But this attitude changed somewhat as French, German, and (in Latin-America) American capital became available to countries with which British bondholders were in dispute.

Official advice or assistance was more freely asked and more freely granted. But always the government retained complete liberty of response to any request. The relations between the Corporation and the government remained discontinuous and private. Through the membership of its governing Council, the Corporation could be assured that official circles had full knowledge of its activities and difficulties. The advice of the Bank of England was to be procured in quiet consultation, made easy by the fact that during many years the vice-chairman of the council was on the board of governors of the bank. Applications for aid were asked and considered in friendly intercourse wherein each was conscious of the other's responsibility and position. In this propriety, this understood taciturnity, each reserved for itself the freedom wished. The government avoided unwanted responsibility, the bondholders could concentrate on their interests.

A review of the Corporation's exertions and policies leaves behind impressions of two outstanding qualities, doggedness and moderation. Its annual reports still present the case against the state of Mississippi with the same note of ardor as sounded in 1842; while the Corporation lasts, no old undischarged debt is ever buried. On the other hand, no disposition was shown to prolong disputes to secure the last pound due, or to defend abstract principle. Reasonableness guided the often difficult decisions between the difficulties of the debtor and the rights of the creditor. With steadiness it pursued its intention of ending disputes without creating new ones. Both the banks and the government it relieved of a substantial duty.

CONCLUDING OBSERVATIONS

THE whole nature of the relationships between finance and government in Great Britain displayed those marks which have been considered characteristic of British political life and institutions; a regard for private interest and initiative, a dislike for legislation and regulatory routine, the creation of a code of relationship and action, but withal the easy adaption of action to circumstance, even in violation of the code. The whole made up a skilful and determined combination of self-interest and national interest. This system, for despite all the lack of fixed principles or easily defined arrangements it was a system, worked well. British capital was soundly placed; the essentials of British economic and financial policy were well served; the tasks of empire were well performed. True it is that these judgments evade certain prime questions that might be asked! Would not the masses of the British people have been better off if less capital had gone abroad, if more had been employed by domestic industry, or used by the government for social improvement? Would not various regions of the world have been happier if they still remained unchanged by British enterprise and capital? In such queries as these, one comes close to questioning the whole of modern history, its motives, dominant national ideals, new industrial life and methods. The most intricate economic analysis, the most careful philosophic judgment, would leave behind enough doubt to permit free play to prepossessions. Here the analysis reaches only the near confines of knowledge, the judgments rest on the supposition that there was a large measure of inevitability in the main currents of recent history.

CHAPTER V

FINANCE AND GOVERNMENT IN FRANCE

THE TEXTS

IN France, government supervision of the business of trading in securities goes back to the days of first growth of these operations. This was an inheritance from the period when imperial control extended to all commerce. The security trade and the traders were under imperial regulations in the seventeenth century; in 1720 a group of traders were granted an official monopoly which (with breaches) endures to the present day. The company of stockbrokers, limited to seventy houses in Paris, were named by the President of the Republic and were under the rule and discipline of the Ministers of Finance and Commerce. This government-regulated association (Compagnie des Agents de Change) made up the broad official market. Alongside of them there rose very early a "free market" known as the Coulisse, doing a large and active business in securities not listed on the official market. It encroached besides, under leniently inclined administrations and public opinion, upon the field of the official monopoly, and conducted trade in French *rentes* and railway securities. By virtue of an arrangement of 1891–92, and the decrees and finance law of April 13, 1898, it was permitted to stay in this broader field, under limitations and regulations.[1] Outside these exchanges the banks carried on an independent security trade. The continued tradition

[1] The Coulisse secured the right to deal in French *rentes,* in Egyptian, Spanish, Hungarian, Turkish, and Portuguese government securities, and a great variety of issues not listed on the official Bourse, some of which could not be listed—e.g., because the par value of shares was too small. It was given a legal existence and interior regulations. The struggle broke out again in 1896, and was regulated by an *entente* which provided for a division of commissions. The Coulisse itself divided into different groups.

of government supervision of the stock exchanges made it natural that the government should exercise powers of decision over the trade in foreign securities.

The supervision, it should be observed, extended over the Provincial stock exchanges as well as that of Paris, and the government decrees, in general, applied to them. The most important of the Provincial exchanges was that of Lyon, the prestige and relative activity of which were injured greatly, however, by bank failures in 1881–82. In the trade in foreign government securities the Provincial exchanges played an insignificant rôle. But they, especially that of Lyon, conducted a substantial trade in the securities of foreign industrial enterprises, especially in the securities of foundries, railways, mines, and local public utilities. To a foreign borrower, however, listing on the Provincial exchanges without listing in Paris did not suffice to give a broad market. Besides, these exchanges were governed in their decisions by those reached in Paris. They were, as far as the effective exercise of government influence went, part of the official market.

Under a series of early decrees all dealings in foreign securities had been forbidden to the official brokers. Outside the law, a few private dealers conducted a small, irregular trade. After 1800, the securities of foreign governments, allies or vassals of France, began to appear in Paris. In 1823 such government securities were granted listing on the official Bourse—under the supervision of the Minister of Finance. The 1823 decree explained that it would be wise to give a legal and authentic character to the numerous operations "which already take place in the loans of foreign governments." The government gave warning in granting listing, that this action did not signify any official approbation or intention to help investors who might suffer loss. This decree and a letter of the Minister of Finance of November 12, 1825, to the Paris Stock Exchange remained during the whole of the nineteenth century the text regulating the admission of foreign government securities to listing on the official Bourse. The government right of control was redefined in another letter of August 12, 1873, addressed by the Minister of Finance:

It is necessary that the Minister of Finance and Minister of Foreign Affairs judge, one from the point of view of the Treasury, the other from the point of view of political interest, whether there is any reason for opposing the official listing of foreign government securities, while the Stock Exchange has the duty of forming a judgment as to whether the negotiation is useful and opportune considering the public interest.

From time to time thereafter this government right was reaffirmed.

Foreign securities, other than those issued by foreign governments, were admitted to trading on the official Bourse only by tolerance until 1858–59. By decrees issued in those years they were made legally eligible for official listing. Over their admission (the securities of foreign companies, provinces, and municipalities), official control was also set up. The Decree of 1880 (supplemented by that of 1890, and the laws of 1907 and 1912) defined the basis of the control that was exercised during the pre-war period. These texts gave to the Paris and Provincial stock exchanges the power to grant, refuse, suspend, or forbid the negotiation of securities. The borrower was required to submit enumerated documents in duplicate, one to the proper authorities of the Stock Exchange, one to the Minister of Finance. Article V of the 1880 decree declared that "The Minister of Finance can always forbid the negotiation in France of a foreign security." Usage and circumstance caused both the stock exchanges and the government to interpret with constraint the legal right conveyed by the texts. The officials of stock exchanges construed their power over security negotiations to apply only to the question of official listing, and to dealings between its members.[2] The government did not attempt, as it might have under Article V, to issue any general prohibitions applicable to all and imposing a penalty. It required only that its authorization be secured prior to official listing as in the case of foreign government securities.

Whether the government's supervisory powers over foreign security listings extended, by law, to the outside exchange (Coulisse réglementée) remained in doubt and dispute.[3] But as a matter of fact almost the same degree of control existed. From time to time there was handled through the Coulisse some issue which had met government disapproval, as when, in 1910, a bond issue of the city of Budapest was distributed through its agency without a prior reference to the authorities. But these cases were few. More important limitations to the government's control arose out of the power of the banks to dispose of unlisted securities, and the ease with which banned securities might be bought on foreign stock exchanges, especially that of Brussels. For the French banks had many close connections with Belgian syndicates and often took a share in new emissions made in Belgium.[4] Despite these means of evasion, the powers possessed by the French

[2] See R. Ribière, *De l'Admission de la Cote dans les Bourses Françaises des Valeurs* (Paris, 1913).

[3] For one view, see M. Pluyette, "Devoir ou Droit," *Congrès Internationale des Valeurs Mobilières*, Vol. II. For the opposite, see H. Imbert, *Les Emprunts d'États Étrangers* (Paris, 1905).

[4] F. Baudhuin, *Le Capital de la Belgique* (Louvain, 1924), p. 230, gives the following figures of the per cent of foreign subscriptions to the new capital issues brought out in Belgium, for private companies:

Year	Companies operating in Belgium	Companies operating abroad
1890	12	26
1900	17	59
1910	11	46
1913	22	64

Even if these figures are reliable (they are of the kind which usually baffle computers) the share of French capital in the total is not ascertainable.

Government were sufficient to make its will effective. Listing on the official Bourse or some direct manifestation of
government favor was essential to the success of a large
foreign security emission.

SUPERVISION FOR ECONOMIC ENDS

So much for the substance of the texts upon which the
government supervision rested, the texts which conveyed
authority to changing ministries. An understanding of
their importance is not to be secured by scanning their
wording, but only by a review of actual practice. For no
high court controlled their application; that remained in
the field of official discretion.

The great use made of the foreign securities possessed
by Frenchmen in discharging rapidly the indemnity
claimed by Germany, and so in liberating their country
from German occupation, left a deep mark on French
opinion. For two decades thereafter the purchase of foreign securities was regarded with official and general
favor. This attitude endured despite the shock and losses
into which French investors were led by their eagerness,
especially in the seventies. The losses gave rise to proposals
of a parliamentary investigation of the sort just completed
by Great Britain, and one was actually resolved. But no
official action resulted from the disillusionment. There
resulted a sharper defining of the government right of
supervision but still a sparing use of the right. The market continued to be comparatively free.

But toward the end of the century new forces of interest
and opinion arose, new situations took shape which led to
a frequent exercise of official authority and changed its
purposes. An attitude far less favorable to foreign investment than before prevailed. Supervision was marked
by a resolution to restrain and to turn each loan to concrete advantage. The changed attitude was expressed by
leaders of all shades of political thought. Thus Briand, as
Prime Minister, declared in 1909 that "French gold

trickled over the entire world. If it is permissible to express a single regret or anxiety, it is that it does not remain within the country."[5] Three years later Poincaré, the Prime Minister, assured the Chamber that, above all, his ministry would undertake "to combine with French military and naval power, as converging and connecting forces, the financial power which is so great an aid to France."[6] Caillaux, holding the portfolio of Minister of Finance, on December 15, 1913, declared, glancing back over his terms of office which began in 1899, "I have conducted the public finances for six years; I have admitted to quotation only those foreign loans which assured France political and economic advantages, and I have considered above all else the needs of the Treasury and its resources."[7] The Chamber of Deputies resolved on the same day that "the financial resources of the country should be kept above all for national needs."

As these expressions indicate, the ministries which came into power after 1900 asserted the same general policy. What differences occurred related rather to the merits of a particular case, the claims of a particular borrower. They all maintained a careful supervision and showed a disposition to restrain the outward movement. The French investors and banks submitted to this supervision, though the banks often chafed against the enforced delay and fought with might and main against refusals. Occasionally they circumvented the will of the government, buying and placing securities barred by official action, as episodes recounted at a later point illustrate. But sustained opposition and defiance were cautious and concealed. The ordinary attitude of the banks may be found expressed in the Report of the Board of Directors of the Comptoire National d'Escompte for 1910: "In the selection of securities which we offer to our clientele, we undertake, as

5 *Débats Parl. Chambre de Députés,* November 30, 1909, see speech of M. Henri Michel.
6 *Ibid.,* December 21, 1912.   7 *Ibid.,* December 15, 1913.

a rule, not only to seek security of investment, but also to take into account the views of our government and the economic and political advantages that may be obtained for France by the loans contracted by other countries."[8]

The forces of national interest and opinion which shaped the turn of government policy were deep and numerous. The growth in the volume of foreign borrowing which took place beginning in the nineties raised disturbing doubts. It was natural that the nation should consider afresh whether its best interest was served by so large an outward movement of capital, natural that it should question whether the national economy was strengthened or weakened thereby. It is easier to recognize the immediate loss that results from capital export than to perceive the many indirect benefits. Again it must be remembered that from 1897 interest rates were steadily increasing in France, as in the rest of western Europe, and the terms on which private borrowers and the French Government secured loans were growing harder—moderate as they were compared with post-war rates. Besides, a change occurred in the national psychology. French national pride and ambition recovered from the defeat of 1870 and laid out new claims and hopes. It took to heart the slow development of French industry and commerce as compared with the other great powers, especially as compared with Germany. One of the reasons why French industrial development was slow, a varied body of opinion became convinced, was that financial leadership was evading the duty of undertaking new enterprises, utilizing French talent and resources. It was neglecting this task and opportunity

[8] More than one Ministry had to meet movements in Parliament to subject the foreign loan business to parliamentary control, or to more formal treatment. Thus, on January 21, 1909, the Socialist party (directly seeking to block a loan to Russia) moved that "the Chamber invites the government not to authorize the emission in France of any foreign government securities without having first indicated to Parliament the precautions taken to safeguard national interest." On December 29, 1911, it was proposed that "loans of foreign governments shall be made only after a decree considered in the Council of Ministers."

to cater to the extravagance of foreign states, while the national diligence, creativeness, and daring decayed.

This general judgment suited different conceptions and interests. The Socialist opposition accepted it. It believed foreign investment to be against its interest and partly accountable for the poor condition of industrial life and labor, another proof of the parasitism of the capitalist class. Many industrial employers arrived at the same position by another chain of reasoning. The cost of capital figured in their plans, made easier or harder their struggle with foreign competition. In the final result, it was explained to them, foreign investment increases capital supply and reduces interest rates; but they held the contrary view. Further, they feared lest French capital might serve (instances could be found) to develop competing industries abroad to their loss and difficulty. The owners of local industries and those who hoped to preserve such small-scale enterprises shared this anxiety with more powerful enterprises. It was given voice by employers' associations and found a place in government policy.

The organized employer groups sold their consent to foreign loans for promises that foreign lenders should give French industry special consideration in their expenditure.[9] The government tried to apply this rule as a condition attached to the grant of listing. Loans to directly competing industries were sometimes kept off the French market, as in the case of the refusal in 1909 to grant official listing to the common stock of the United States

[9] The government did not bind itself formally, but did what it could in each instance. *Bulletin de la Fédération des Industriels et des Commerçants Français* of February and March, 1909. In an audience with the Minister of Finance, the Executive Committee of this Federation presented a declaration concerning the advantages to be secured to French industry and agriculture when foreign loans are admitted to official listing. The Minister of Finance replied to the delegates that "whatever his wish might be to secure from foreign states borrowing in France tariff concessions or orders for French producers, it was impossible to proceed on general principle. The condition requested must be a matter of degree, determined by numerous and diverse elements. For example, French prices might be much higher than those of foreign

Steel Corporation. And in general the government endeavored to conform to the resolution passed by the Paris Chamber of Commerce "that whenever a foreign loan is admitted to official listing, admission should be made conditional upon the concession of advantages to French commerce and industry." The heavy metal and construction industries, those which had most to hope from governments engaged in building public works, and adding to armaments, took the lead in the presentation of this policy.

Because of it, there was attached to almost every government loan issued in France in the years just preceding the war, a tale of diplomatic negotiation of which the following are but a few leading instances. In 1909 the government refused listing to a proposed Argentine loan, because that government had decided to purchase cannon in Germany, despite the fact that a technical commission had previously recommended the purchase of French cannon.[10] Later this veto was removed. During loan negotiations with Japan and Russia in 1908 the steel and iron industry petitioned the Ministers of Foreign Affairs, Commerce, and Finance to secure contracts, as a loan condition, and the government so urged the bankers.[11] When Japan gave no order to French shipyards, the Presidents of the Society of Manufacturers and Builders of War Ma-

competitors." The Minister declared, however, that he "would never leave out of sight the terms of the request made to him." It is interesting that no such conditions as those mentioned in the preceding extract were attached to Russian loans though the French Government made friendly representations in favor of French industry. The French industrialists were dissatisfied with the policy pursued by Russia. Again it is interesting to observe that though the merchants of Havre asked the French Government in 1908 to refuse quotation to loans of the state of São Paulo, Brazil, to be used to control coffee production and prices, the government did not grant the request. Compare the American action of 1926 on loans for the same purpose.

[10] *Bulletin des Industriels et Commerçants*, March, 1909.

[11] H. Gans, "Intervention Gouvernementale et l'Accès du Marché Financier," *Revue Politique et Parlementaire*, February, 1909. For this petition and other similar ones, see the files of *Réforme Économique*, 1908–13.

terials, and of the Society of Shipbuilders and Marine Machinery Builders, opposed the loan of 1910. In June of the same year, having heard that Portugal was planning to spend in British shipyards the proceeds of loans which she hoped to contract partly in France, the same executives urged that Portugal be informed that the French market would be closed. Similar protests were made by the Federation of French Manufacturers and Merchants against a contemplated loan by Chile to be used in the purchase in Germany of war materials.[12] In 1912 the city of Prague was asked by the French Government, as a condition of the right to borrow, to give preference to French manufacturers in giving orders for industrial products, and as a result turned to Vienna for the needed loan. Even when the demands of industrial organizations were ineffective, they left some trace on future government policy. M. Pichon, Secretary of Foreign Affairs, informed the Chamber, in 1911:

It is a tradition to which we conform in the Ministry of Foreign Affairs. You can see from the statistics that we have obtained valuable results in this respect, especially for our great metallurgical industries; it is generally thanks to the intervention of our Minister of Foreign Affairs in accord with the Ministers of Finance and Commerce that we have been able to secure important orders.[13]

It was in loans extended to the Balkan states and to Turkey that this policy of securing orders in return for loans was most constantly and effectively applied. The French Government endeavored to insure that these needy and belligerent borrowers placed their orders where they found the favor of a loan. Often in these negotiations, a representative of Creusot, France's greatest maker of steel and war materials, took a direct part, or at all events some bank on whose board Creusot was well represented. Often

[12] *Bulletin des Industriels et Commerçants,* December, 1911.
[13] *Débats Parl. Chambre de Députés,* January 13, 1911.

the armament firms made advances, till the state of the market and disposition of the government should permit the issue of a public loan. This activity of armament firms was international. Sometimes the different national groups of armament makers competed in the supply of funds and pursuit of orders, sometimes they combined. And sometimes the French Government called on these groups to extend loans which had a political object.

Serbia in 1905–6, 1908–9, and 1914 was induced to buy where she borrowed, permitted to borrow to pay for what she had bought. So, too, with Bulgaria, as explained in the Report of the Budget Commission (Ministry of Foreign Affairs) for the year 1906.

In the course of this year, the Department followed with particular care the question of the loan of 100 millions extended to Bulgaria by the French banks, which brought important orders to French industry, especially for war materials. Long and delicate negotiations preceded the signature of this loan contract, and the French Minister of Foreign Affairs and the French representative at Sofia intervened many times most effectively.[14]

Of Turkey the same request was made in 1903, 1905, 1910, and 1914, successful in all but the third instance; that came to nothing since the Turkish Government refused French demands and turned to Berlin and Vienna. The placing of orders was, in 1914, insisted upon with special determination, since Turkey had just used part of the proceeds of a loan contracted in France to buy warships in Germany. From Greece, the fourth of the antagonists of the period, the same condition was, in 1914, exacted that the orders for army, navy, and railroads be reserved for French concerns.[15] From each and all, in that

14 *Rapport du Commission du Budget, Affaires Étrangères,* Exercice, 1906.

15 *Un Livre Noir, Diplomatie d'Avant-guerre d'après les Documents des Archives Russe* (Paris, n.d.), II, 233.

maelstrom of Balkan finance, came orders for the armament firms, easing the way to government consent.

It is worthy of remark that this attempt to bind the borrower to spend the proceeds of his borrowing within France was often justified by industrialists and government officials because such demands were made by the German banks and government. That this was sometimes the case, incidents related in following chapters will indicate. But the German Government and bankers tended, likewise, to justify their course by the necessity of meeting French tactics. They, in fact, often argued that the aid extended to French industry far exceeded that given to the German. Thus Freiherr Von Gamp Massaunen, member of the Reichstag and Prussian House of Delegates, testified in the German Bank Inquiry of 1908:

Yes, indeed; there is often in France an express stipulation that the cannon, firearms and so forth must be ordered in France. The representative of Krupp's will confirm this statement . . . Krupp has lost many orders because the French Government has expressly demanded that these things be made in France . . . But since our banks do not do this . . .[16]

Thus the circle of mutual accusation was formed, gradually catching both governments within its confines and more and more often making suspicion correspond with fact. For the particularly demanding and alert attitude of the French industrial groups there was a special reason. Without government aid, they could not get—merely as a result of the competitive bidding—more than a minor share of the orders for the metallurgical products paid for by loans. Even when French capital retained a directing power over a foreign enterprise it was likely to find that its requirements could be met more cheaply or advanta-

[16] *German Bank Inquiry of 1908, Stenographic Reports* (National Monetary Commission, Washington, 1910), pp. 656–657.

geously elsewhere.[17] A special need for compensation was felt.

Despite the fact that in the discussion of the subject, much was made of the possibility of securing tariff concessions as a compensation for loans, little was actually attempted or achieved in that direction. The refusal to admit to quotation the stock of the United States Steel Corporation may have been prompted in part by resentment at the American tariff; if so, it was a futile action.[18] In 1908 listing was refused to the bonds of the Crédit Foncier of Denmark because of an intended increase of duties on French wines; concessions having been obtained, the veto was later withdrawn.[19] In 1910 Sweden and Norway were asked to reduce the duties on certain French wines before they were permitted to borrow in the official market. Doubtless many other minor concessions were secured in the course of negotiation of commercial treaties. But their trace has not been revealed and their significance must have been small. The general use of "the most-favored-nation clause" in pre-war Europe lessened the importance to France of any concession that might be obtained. The effort seems to have been confined to securing reduction of duties on a few French specialties. An exceptional loan condition seems to have been proposed to Belgium in 1912–13, when that country sought a loan in France—to wit, that she agree to enter into a convention for the exchange of information between the two governments regarding inheritances left by citizens of one country within the other country. The Belgian Government refused and the loan was issued in London.[20]

[17] See the interesting computations of capital investment in and purchases by railways in Argentina, Brazil, and Chile in A. P. Winston, "Does Trade Follow the Dollar?" *American Economic Review*, September, 1927.

[18] *Bulletin des Industriels et Commerçants*, June, 1909.

[19] *Economist*, February 15, 1908.

[20] See lecture of M. Guillain in *Intérêts Économiques et Rapports Internationaux* (Paris, 1915), p. 227.

The same desire which made the French Government endeavor to secure orders from foreigners borrowing in France, prompted it to urge the banks and stock exchange to secure places for Frenchmen on the board of directors or in the management of borrowing enterprises. Critics of the banks made it a mark of shame that in so many parts of the world French capital played but a passive rôle, exerted no control over the direction of the businesses they financed, and did not advance French industry. These assertions, repeated often enough and vigorously enough, gradually shaped government policy. The achievement of the wish was not easy. Neither the head offices of the banks nor their foreign branches were particularly well organized to found enterprises, or control them; and it was difficult to secure place for Frenchmen in enterprises built by foreigners, even though they sought capital in Paris. Local sentiment in foreign lands opposed their introduction; and there were few Frenchmen of marked ability residing in foreign lands who might be placed on such boards. Nevertheless, many Frenchmen were introduced into the direction of enterprises in Russia, Spain, Turkey, the Balkans, and Latin-American states.[21]

According to M. Pichon, Minister of Foreign Affairs, "We ask ordinarily that France be represented in the boards of directors that may be set up as a result of the operation, so that our commerce and industry are enabled to profit as much as possible from the use of the borrowed funds."[22] But the government found, as a matter of fact, that it often was not in a position to make this demand. It tended to pass on to the official stock exchange the duty of presenting it unless some political issue was at stake, as in the case of the Balkan and Bagdad railways. The official stock exchange, through its committee of admis-

[21] *Débats Parl. Chambre de Députés,* January 13, 1911. *La Revue Bleue,* July 23 and August 6, 1910, held a symposium on the subject in which various bank directors described their efforts to secure representation.

[22] *Débats Parl. Chambre de Députés,* January 11, 1912.

sions (Chambre Syndicale), in the years before the war occasionally interposed itself for this purpose into loan negotiations. It had authority for such action in the government decrees of 1880 and 1890.[23] Few specific records of such negotiations either by the Committee of Admissions or the government on this matter are available, even if they exist. In its report for 1909 the Budget Commission (Ministry of Foreign Affairs) noted that "Brazilian public works enterprises whose shares were given listing in the French market during the year, gave a formal undertaking that important place would be given to the French element on the Board of Directors."[24] In its report for 1910 the same body observed again, apropos of South American loans, "as regards the companies whose capital is partly French, the Department has exerted itself, and has to a certain extent succeeded, to procure a greater French representation on the boards of directors." The same report records specific success with the Brazil Railway Company, and various Mexican companies.[25] These instances show the direction of the policy, sustained as opportunity afforded.

A frequent wish was expressed in Parliament and outside that the practice of supervision of foreign borrowing should be extended to prevent the issue of dishonest or too hazardous foreign securities. But no Ministry would possibly accept this responsibility; and as a matter of fact French political policy tended to encourage the extension of loans to countries of doubtful credit. Reliance had to be placed upon the judgment of individual investors and the banks, the sense of responsibility of the stock exchange,

[23] But in passing upon listing applications for the loans of foreign governments the Committee on Admissions reached its decision wholly on technical grounds. R. Ribière, *De l'Admission de la Cote dans les Bourses Françaises des Valeurs* (Paris, 1913).

[24] *Rapport du Commission du Budget, Affaires Étrangères*, Exercice, 1909.

[25] *Ibid.*, Exercice, 1910.

and the protection afforded by the law.[26] But these met the difficulties imperfectly. The banks were sometimes wrong or careless. The financial press was unreliable and venal. Fraudulent securities could be sold though they were quoted on no Bourse. Thus, occasionally, the government seems to have stepped in to guard French savings against what was considered an obvious risk. Brazilian provincial loans were refused listing by the government because their credit was judged to be doubtful and there was no satisfactory recourse in case of default. The distribution of a loan of Paraguay was stopped, because revolution broke out after the loan contract was signed and the loan was disavowed.[27] In 1913, listing was refused to an issue of ten-year 6 per cent Treasury Bonds of the Huerta government in Mexico, since the leaders of the Carranza party notified the French Government that they would not recognize this debt. But only in special circumstances of this kind did the Executive Government use its power to safeguard investors.[28]

THE SEARCH FOR POLITICAL ADVANTAGE

ABOVE and beyond all other considerations which induced French official intervention with the movement of French capital abroad was the wish to make the investment serve the political purposes of the state. The reigning diplomacy of the day was the diplomacy of bargaining, and in that game, played with every resource of power and ingenuity,

---

[26] Rather elaborate safeguards were established by law, prescribing in detail the conditions to be met in the emission, exposition, and sale of securities. The laws were revised in 1907 and 1912—extending the requirements.

[27] *Débats Parl. Chambre de Députés,* December 28, 1911. But the Minister of Finance at the same time said that if official listing was not asked he could not prevent the sale of the loan unless evident fraud was shown.

[28] Still in January, 1909, Caillaux, as Minister of Finance, declared that the government refuses listing "when it appears that French saving may be hurt by this investment." *Débats Parl. Chambre de Députés,* January 2, 1909.

it was but natural that this precious ability to provide resources to needy governments should be fully appraised and used. Borrowing in Paris became as much the work of the foreign ministers as of the ministers of finance of those loan-seeking governments that crowded the official anterooms of the Quai D'Orsay. The saving French people gave this official intervention their approval. Financial nationalism corresponded to the state of mind of France.

The wish to make French lending conform to and aid French political policy led to government intervention of three types. First, the government acted to prevent the arrangement or emission of loans to countries whose political actions were deemed unfriendly, or whose political alliances and interests seemed to clash with those of France. Second, admission to official listing was made conditional upon pledges, assurances, or compensations of a political order. Third, the government used its connections with financial circles, its influence over public opinion and press to facilitate the borrowing of states with which it was allied, or to arrange the sale of loans in return for which political advantages had been secured. In some instances the government itself virtually arranged the borrowing, then selected some banking group to execute it; or, in the case of business which the banks were at the moment reluctant to undertake, it called together the bank executives and secured their coöperation on ground of national welfare.

From 1887 on, the prospective borrower at Paris had to satisfy the nervous judgment of two foreign offices, not one—the French and the Russian. Through the Financial Agent in Paris, through his friends in the French banks, and diplomatic agents in the world's capitals, all whispers of intended transactions reached the Russian Minister for Foreign Affairs as soon as they were uttered. Always alert, possessed of numerous political difficulties at almost all parts of its spreading frontiers, the Russian ally was no more backward in pressing its judgment of proposed loans to other countries than in presenting its own needs. Consent to its wishes in this field was claimed as an essential part of the political alliance. French financial relations with China and Japan, with Persia and Turkey, with the Balkan states and the Central Empires often followed the lines set by Russian political purposes rather than any direct interest of the French people. Russia had favors to bestow upon banks and financial journals so that its desires might be the more easily recognized. The dangers of this policy did not pass entirely unobserved. M. Bompard, Ambassador to Turkey, for example, whose negotiations with Turkey in 1912 were being hindered by Russian exigencies, took the liberty of writing to his superior:

May I add in passing that in my opinion the Russian Government tends to abuse the power of the French market as an instrument of its own political ends; yesterday it was in China, today it is in Turkey; now I hear talk of Austria-Hungary. That course seems to me most dangerous . . . The power of opening or closing the French market to foreign loans is certainly an important weapon for the French Government but it ought to be used to defend French interests only, lest French financial independence be compromised.[29]

But the Russian Government substantially had its way.

The sentiments of regret and bitterness left by 1870, the antagonizing movement of political, military, and commercial affairs in the subsequent era, kept alive in the French mind a hostile regard for Germany. This recorded itself in French financial policy. Loans to the German Government or to German industries violated these sentiments, and were felt even to smack somewhat of treason. Thus, outside of short-time transactions between the money markets, undertaken largely in the natural course of trade, Germany was unable to borrow in France. To

[29] *Documents Diplomatiques Français, 1871–1914,* 3d ser., Vol. I, No. 279.

the German Government and industry, restricted by the frequently strained credit situation within Germany, the power to borrow in the cheap Paris market would have been a valuable advantage. But responsive to the public judgment, the French Government stood ready to refuse official listing to any public issue. No French banking group was willing to risk the certain odium and refusal. At various times, in connection with discussions of Moroccan and Turkish affairs, suggestions of a possible arrangement were put forward by the German Government, but were ignored.

Toward the other members of the Triple Alliance, Austria-Hungary and Italy, official policy was slower to shape itself, and more variable. Until there came into the depths of judgment the almost settled conviction that the alliance would be drawn into war one day or another, Austria-Hungary was a favorite field of investment for the French. The French Government regarded this situation benevolently. But, as public sentiment shifted, official policy shifted also, and pointed and defined the change. The French banks ceased their attempts to sell Austrian Government securities by public issues. The guardianship of the government over the loan market was obviously asserted in the case of a Hungarian government loan that the French bankers proposed to issue in 1909. Official quotation was directly refused. When shortly afterward the French bankers distributed a bond issue of the City of Budapest, for which official listing was not sought, Russian indignation found definite form. "Every loan granted to Austria-Hungary or simply to Hungary would similarly weaken the position of Russia, and consequently of the Dual Alliance," the French Government was informed.[30] During the strained years ahead to 1914 this view prevailed. The French Government detoured all further loan proposals from Austro-Hungarian sources,

[30] *Livre Noir,* I, 90–93.

though the Dual Monarchy held out vague political promises.

The treatment of Italian loans by the French Government ran through the opposite course. When Italy entered into the alliance of the Central Powers, the French grew fearful. Previously the French had invested freely in Italy. Now the drift of public feeling was reflected in official policy. In 1885 the Crédit Mobilier was forced to retire from Italian railroad financing. When two years later the Triple Alliance was renewed and a tariff dispute augmented ill feeling, there spread throughout the French press and banking circles persistent criticism of the Italian financial situation (which was weak), and no less persistent suggestion that Italian securities be sold. Whether the French Government actually initiated the press campaign or not, official sympathy with it was not concealed. For a decade the estrangement lasted, and the Paris market was closed to Italian loans. Then gradually as animosity cooled, as Italian foreign policy displayed an independent tendency and the chances of renewed friendship grew, the market was reopened. With the turn in the political relations, the attitude of the French Government turned, too.

Toward the financial plans of its neighbor, Belgium, the French Government usually showed a welcoming attitude. But reserve was maintained toward the financial solicitations of the Belgian sovereign in behalf of his ambitious plans in the Congo and China. The Congo Free State was permitted to borrow in Paris in 1886, for example, only after a territorial concession, and after France was granted a right of preëmption over the territories of the former International Association in case of liquidation.[31] Not long thereafter the market was again closed to these securities.

Toward the various Balkan states no fixed attitude prevailed. Each of their frequent appearances as borrowers

---

[31] Comte L. De Lichtervelde, *Leopold II* (Paris, 1927), pp. 225 *et seq.*

in Paris was preceded by negotiations with the French Foreign Office. In a single balance, through the years, that authority tried to weigh its desire for peace in the Balkans, its hope of making relations with the small Balkan states intimate and dependable, the need of respecting Russian policy in that area, and the fear of giving aid to some future ally of the Central Powers.

Thus, for example, Bulgaria borrowed freely in France up to 1907. Thereafter the French Ministry and official policy wavered between doubt of Bulgarian intentions and fear lest Germany might acquire new advantages by granting loans to which the Paris market was closed. In 1909 official listing was refused to a Bulgarian loan arranged by the Crédit Mobilier; in 1911 the refusal was repeated. For a short time during the following year Poincaré was prepared to relax his opposition, influenced by the adhesion of Bulgaria to a Balkan understanding of which Russia was the mentor. But a fresh access of mistrust soon led to a reimposition of the ban, which was maintained throughout the Balkan wars in an endeavor to shorten the conflict. The last play of official judgment occurred in the months preceding the Great War. In dire necessity the pro-German cabinet which held office in Bulgaria showed willingness to grant the German banks pledges that appeared to assure German dominance in Bulgarian affairs. The Paris market could offer better financial terms; alternative pledges could be formulated. The French and Russian governments used all the arts of diplomacy to have the French offer accepted. All were of no avail; the contract with the German banks was signed. Similar interventions and byplays marked the borrowing of Roumania.

As the Serbian policy adjusted itself to Russian policy, that country was permitted to borrow freely. Shortly after the termination of the second Balkan war, however, permission to borrow was hesitantly deferred, lest Serbian action lead to a renewal of conflict. But in October, 1913, it was granted in response to the request of the Russian Government. At the time Russia and all of southeastern Europe was seeking to replenish in Paris public treasuries depleted by war or military preparations for further war. The French Government regulated the order of their borrowing. So that Serbia might avoid default, the Russian Government on this occasion gave up its own priority. No less friendliness was shown to Greece by the French Government. The enterprise of the French banks in Greek industrial and railroad development was encouraged as an offset to the German dynastic connection, and fresh concessions were obtained in return for admitting Greek government loans.

As early as 1899, the French Government, moved by Russian aims, had kept strict watch over Turkish borrowing. Regarding the Bagdad railway project as a means of German aggrandizement and as a menace to Russian position in Asia Minor, mistrusting the German offers of complete equality in ownership and management, in 1903 it refused listing to the railroad bonds, which were purchased by the French banks. Until about 1910, however, the French Government permitted the growth of Turkish Government borrowing in Paris in return for the extensive economic concessions upon which they were always conditioned. In 1910 an attempt to exact conditions in return for the right to borrow left Turkey to turn to Berlin. From the Russian Government the suggestion came that before official permission was granted, agreements be obtained which would limit the expansion of the Turkish military forces. This condition the French Government deemed it unwise to impose directly, but in the conditions it did impose Turkey suspected the same motive and decided to borrow elsewhere. In London, too, it found that French and Russian influence prevailed. In Germany, from which the Young Turk Government had at first turned aside, the loan was finally issued. In 1913–14 the drama of negotiations was repeated; its details are related

in another place. This time Turkey accepted the proposed
conditions. Even then, Russia, with prescience, felt uneasy, and expressed fear lest this new financial aid
strengthen the Turkish Government in its dealings with
Greece and itself. But the direct advantages obtained in
return for the loan were too considerable to forego. To
Russia's anxieties only a vague assurance was returned
that the realization of the loan would be made dependent
upon the pacific march of events. Early in 1914 the official
permission was granted and the loan distributed. The en-
suing months demonstrated that Turkish friendship was
not among the benefits obtained.

If the French Government used its powers of guardianship over the loan market to prevent, as habitually as the
preceding illustrations indicate, the use of French savings
for purposes inimicable to French political interests, it
acted no less steadily to stimulate their use for purposes
that served these interests. Often the government was to
be found in the lead in the negotiation of foreign loans
which it wished to see in the possession of Frenchmen. So
it acted in the Bulgarian and Roumanian instances already cited. Often it induced the banks to accept business
of which they were in doubt, coöperated with them in the
public sale of loans by creating a popular understanding
that patriotism demanded their purchase. To bring the
desired financial assistance to its Russian ally, the French
Government exerted itself particularly. Each stage of
Russian borrowing was arranged with the French Government, as well as with the banks. Still, sometimes, the
government stood in the way of Russia's full desires. In
1900, for example, Caillaux refused to extend listing permission to outstanding internal Russian securities in as
unguarded a fashion as was asked. In 1906–7 when
Russian political policy was galling all liberal political
groups, its borrowing was deferred owing to strong parliamentary opposition in France. The loans of 1913–14 were
made conditional upon an increase in Russian military

strength and the construction of certain strategic railways. But these were only temporary difficulties of adjustment between partners. For the most part it was accepted
that the political alliance gave Russia free access to
French savings. This was regarded on both sides as one
of the important rights or privileges by which the alliance
was maintained and supported in its aims.

In China, where so often loans may be said to have borne
a second set of coupons encashable by governments for
political advantage if and when circumstances favored, the
French Government, like the governments of the other
lending states, habitually endeavored to secure business
for the French banks. For example, it offered to guarantee
a loan in France in return for special concessions in the
three Chinese provinces adjoining Indo-China, and supervision rights over Chinese customs—as a means of meeting
Anglo-German competition. In the negotiations for the
never-issued Currency Loan of 1911, and the Reorganization Loan of 1913, by way of further illustration, the
French Government gave steady support to the Four
Power Consortium which was formed, agreeing with its
insistence that sufficient measure of control over the expenditure of the loan proceeds and the administration of
the pledged revenues be assured. Not even the wish of
the Russian Government shook this support. But in response to this wish the French Government aided in get-
ting place for Russia in the Consortium, and pledged
itself to refuse official listing to any loans that were to be
so employed as to weaken Russia's place in Chinese affairs.

Another country in the realm of French political ambition toward which the government exerted its powers to
influence the movement of French capital, was Morocco.
Here the government dictated the whole course of financial
negotiation. The details of that course of policy, which led
finally to the establishment of a French protectorate in
Morocco, must be left for another place. From 1902 on
the French Government encouraged the Sultan to pledge

his domains to the French banks, forced him to accept
their terms, shut off other possible lenders, and added
heavy indemnity claims of its own to the burdens which
that irresponsible and corrupt sovereign accumulated. Financial matters were an important cause of that gradual
disorganization which made it easier for France to assume
control. Here finance and government coöperated in a dis-
guised but stubbornly held purpose in which the wish for
profit and national ambition joined.

These instances of government initiative in loan transactions by no means exhaust the list. The result of them
all was to create a mutual dependence between banks and
governments which could not be limited to situations in
which it arose. France accepted the situation as a means of
carrying out its political objectives.

FAVOR FOR THE COLONIES

SOMEWHAT apart from the ordinary practice of government supervision of foreign lending and differently exercised, was the official policy of facilitating the movement
of French capital into French colonies. Moderation in
colonial borrowing was assured by the financial laws of the
Republic. Under laws passed in 1898 and 1911 all loans of
colonial governments, after being authorized by the local
authorities, had to be approved by a decree of the Conseil
D'État. If the guaranty of the home government was
asked, the proposal had to be submitted to the French
Parliament for legislation. When the government guarantee was accorded to any colonial loan, all subsequent loans
of that colony required parliamentary authorization.[32]
These regulations probably kept down the sum of colonial
borrowing, but, on the other hand, they kept the public
credit of the colonies very high. Besides, colonial borrowers

[32] For the record of this legislation, see any manual of French colonial
legislation, e.g., A. Girault, *Principes de Colonisation et de Législation
Coloniale* (Paris, 1923 ed.), Part 2, Vol. I.

were shown favor in the Paris market in two different ways. Many of their loans were purchased directly, without public issue, by the official institutions which held the small savings or pension funds of millions of people—the Caisse Nationale des Retraites pour la Vieillesse, and the Caisse des Dépôts et Consignations. The Crédit Foncier, in a smaller measure, also took colonial loans in this way. Secondly, the French Government frequently gave its guarantee to colonial loans—as to the Tunisian loan of 1884, the Madagascar conversion loan of 1897, the Indo-Chinese loan of 1896. By virtue of this official safeguarding and assistance, the French Colonial Governments were enabled to borrow very cheaply—usually at not more than 4 per cent—and were always able to find lenders. Thus the French Government strove to make colonial development a preferential use of French savings.

The system of parliamentary authorization was used to assure the expenditure of the loan funds within France. The Chamber of Deputies in granting authorization ordinarily inserted in the law a provision to the effect that any materials for public works to be carried out with the loan funds, which were not found within the borrowing country, should be of French origin and be carried in French ships.[33] The preference was made more certain by the fact that after 1900 most of the railway building in the colonies was carried out by the colonial authorities. Virtually all the other public works and mining resources were reserved for French enterprise. Thereby a sentiment was created in favor of colonial loans.

[33] For discussion of the use of provision, see A. Dardenne, *Les Emprunts Publics* (Paris, 1908), and H. Paulin, *L'Outillage Économique des Colonies Françaises* (Paris, 1911). Typical of these provisions is Article 8 of the 1912 loan for French West Africa, "all materials used for the execution of the work, as well as the stationary material and rolling stock required to operate the projected railroads which is not found within the country, shall be of French origin and be transported on French ships." *Bulletin du Comité de l'Afrique Française,* April, 1912, p. 146.

THE GOVERNMENT'S PART IN SECURING CONCESSIONS

THE positive action of the French Government in turn-ing French savings to purposes agreeable to its judgment did not exhaust itself in the measures which have just been reviewed. Often the resources of its diplomacy were spent to secure for French capital and enterprise, profitable op-portunities of which other governments disposed—to pro-cure concessions. Sometimes economic considerations de-termined its action, sometimes political; sometimes they commingled. All the industrial countries of Europe were exerting themselves for the same objects. Their competi-tion extended over the six continents. But it took its most intensive form in those regions not yet brought under development, not yet commanding capital resources and industrial technique, nor having a capable, managing, stable government.

In later chapters this intricate struggle for concessions is traced out. Here it is possible only to dwell briefly upon a few of its outstanding efforts of the French Government. During the whole course of disturbance and difficulty which finally brought Tunis and Morocco within the French Empire, every concession granted by their rulers was contended for with unrelaxed purpose. To secure the cession to French interests of right to build in these coun-tries roads, railroads, and port works, to exploit mineral deposits, and to found banks, the French representatives used all the arts of pleading. When proof of mutual bene-fit and other forms of inducement failed, and a rival gov-ernment secured rights that might be turned to political claims, financial pressure or forceful menaces were applied to prevent these regions from escaping French hegemony. By these means a monopoly of railroad and port construc-tion was obtained. In Tunis the competitive effort of Italy to procure entry for Italian enterprise was among the influences which brought the French Government to its decision to assume political control. In Morocco, it can be said, concessions were regarded, as between France and Germany, as outright political instruments. For each step in its forward reach French capital depended upon its government's help.

In the Balkans, Turkey, and the Far East, the government pushed forward in behalf of its financial enterprises with more caution, but no less vigor. For railway and banking opportunities in the Balkan states intrusted to French capital, French diplomacy worked in a half dozen capitals—believing that financial enterprise might help to link these countries sympathetically to France, cause them to regard France as a rich and reliable friend. Toward opportunity in Turkey, French capital had early directed itself in large amounts. With the entry of organized German finance, and the growth of German commerce and political influence, a great tension entered into the negotiations for further concessions. The almost perpetual financial troubles of the government and its failing power, the detachment of its European territories, and the steadily grinding political antagonism midst which the country lived, presaged its dissolution. By bargaining, by working in collaboration with Russia, by providing loans to the needy Turkish Government, by the ready interest shown by its banks in Turkish business, the French Government gradually brought into French hands a huge system of concessions throughout the Turkish Empire, but more particularly in Anatolia and Syria.

In China, that other great field of concession rivalry, French aims and claims were well sustained. By treaty, by persistent presentation of its demands, the French Government caused to be set aside for French finance the main railroad and mining opportunities in those provinces of China which bordered on its colony of Indo-China. In several important railroad ventures outside this region the French Government exerted itself to assure adequate consideration for French banking groups with which official relations were maintained. Besides, with the encouragement of the government, French financial participation in the concessions obtained by the Russian Government was arranged. The capacity of French savings and its responsiveness enabled France to acquire a position of parity with the other great powers in the settlement of Chinese affairs; these offset the greater naval and commercial strength of England and Germany, the geographical propinquity of Japan and Russia. While this position was being obtained in China, a somewhat more exclusive one—in regard to railroad and port concessions —was, by treaties with Siam and Great Britain, secured in Siam, the other border state of Indo-China.

These exertions of the government, here only summarily touched upon, drew together closely the government and the powerful financial groups. In the forces of interest and notions of glory which ruled the national state, they were united.

GOVERNMENT PROTECTION OF FOREIGN INVESTMENT

THE government would not, save in a few exceptional circumstances, use its power of supervision over the capital market to safeguard the investors against unsound loans. But less reluctantly it stepped in to aid and protect them in the event of default by a foreign government, or action injurious to an established French financial interest abroad.[34] The course pursued in this matter varied in accord with the ideas and tendency of the ministry in power at any particular time, and adapted itself to the strength, position in international affairs, state of civilization, and character of the action of the defaulting or offending governments.[35]

[34] An effort was made at various times to get the French courts to provide recourse against foreign governments, but this they always refused to do. Imbert, *op. cit.*

[35] For analysis of French policy in the earlier years, see H. Becker, *Les Emprunts d'États Étrangers en France* (Paris, 1880). M. Lewandowski, *De la Protection des Capitaux Empruntés en France* (Paris, 1896). For the later years there is an enormous literature on this

The French Government always insisted on retaining complete liberty of action as regards the aid it might extend to its investors. The wide distribution of security ownership made it relatively easy to stimulate an agitation in favor of intervention in any particular case. Sometimes the government remained entirely unmoved by the appeals of injured creditors, sometimes it resorted merely to a general declaration or use of good offices to satisfy a public wish, sometimes vigorous acts of pressure or intervention were undertaken, alone or collectively. The humiliation, odium, and expense that had been incurred in the disastrous attempt of the Emperor Louis Napoleon and Maximilian to collect debts in Mexico implanted fear of reckless adventures for a considerable period. The decade of the seventies brought heavy losses to the investors in foreign securities. But from all but two of the defaults which occurred, the government stood aside except for the friendly exercise of its influence. Only in Egypt and Turkey was the situation followed up. On the occasion of Egyptian bankruptcy in 1875–76 the French Government used all its power to secure recompense for its bondholders, and ample representation in the international institutions of control which were created. The Crédit Foncier, an official French institution, held 175 million francs of Egyptian securities, risked to maintain French influence in Egyptian affairs. Stubborn refusal to permit adequate debt reduction was among the causes that produced the rebellion which led to British assumption of power. Having refused to share in this final action, France thereafter stubbornly upheld every atom of the legal right of its investors—inspired not only by concern for their interest, but also by the hope that its embarrassment would cause Great Britain to bring its occupation to an end. Not till 1904 was the quarrel settled. Toward Turkey its policy

subject, largely repetitive. A. Wuarin, *Essai sur les Emprunts d'États* (Paris, 1907). A. Guillaume, *L'Épargne Française et les Valeurs Mobilières* (Paris, 1907), are among the best.

ran on parallel lines. International control of revenues
pledged to the bondholders was obtained and vigorously
upheld by the French Government.

In the later years of the nineteenth century and the
early years of the twentieth, French official policy showed
the same variation. Heavy losses were suffered by fresh
suspension of payments of many Latin-American states,
but the French Government resorted only to friendly
mediation for the formulation of new agreements, or the
arrangement of arbitration proceedings. When Great
Britain, Germany, and Italy used force against Venezuela
in 1902-3, the French Government stood passively by. It
is possible, in fact, that the recoil of public opinion in
Europe which followed this intervention, and the attitude
displayed by the American people at the time restrained
France from resorting to forceful pressure at a later time
when the provocation was greater. In 1907, Venezuela
charging that the French Cable Company was aiding a
revolution, and was not fulfilling its contract, closed up
its offices. The French Minister was given his passports.
The Paris market was closed to new Venezuela borrowing
but no more vigorous action was taken. The quarrel was
not settled till 1914. Only toward San Domingo was an
outright show of force made to protect a French interest.
There a French battleship was dispatched in 1892 to support the French-owned national bank against the government; there, too, in 1903-4 a threat was extended that the
customs would be taken over to assure the payment of
French bondholders midst the existing confusion of contending foreign groups.

The Portugal default of 1892 roused particular criticism in France because of the already substantial losses
suffered by French investors in Portuguese securities, and
the widely held opinion that the action was unnecessary,
and unjust. A large party in the French Parliament
pressed the executive to take firm action, and all the peaceful resources of French diplomacy were exerted to secure

improved terms for the investors. The French Government sought, in the course of negotiations, to have the revenues pledged to the loans put under the supervision of the Tobacco Monopoly or the Royal Portuguese Railways, in both of which French influence was substantial. But not only the Portuguese, but the British and German governments opposed any such arrangement. Greater success attended the exertions of the French Government in behalf of investors in the bonds of the Royal Portuguese.Railways, when they were unfairly treated in reorganization proceedings directed by the Portuguese Government; improved terms were secured.[36] Even while French diplomacy was occupied with these matters, it made overtures of further financial assistance to the Portuguese Government. The loans it proffered were to be guaranteed by a mortgage on the revenues of certain colonies, which would have given France a part in settling the disposition of these colonies in the event that default or other circumstances led to their partition. In these attempts it was moved by a knowledge of the Anglo-German agreement dealing with these domains.

Toward Spain, which Cuban and Philippine revolts and the war with the United States left in acute financial distress, the French Government showed itself moderate, though alive to the large interests of its investors in Spanish bonds. When in 1899 the Spanish Government wished, by taxation, to reduce the interest on its external debt, an intimation was conveyed that the French capital market would be closed to its appeals if it did so. But no serious official opposition was manifested when such taxation was applied to the coupons of the mortgage bonds secured on the customs of the Philippines and Cuba, which indebtedness the Spanish Government had to assume when the American Government would not. Some years later, however, the official market was closed to Spanish securities because of the treatment accorded French in-

---

[36] *Report of Council of Foreign Bondholders,* 1893 and 1894.

vestors in the South Spanish Railroad. Bond interest had been suspended and was not resumed though, in the judgment of the French, the road was now able to meet the obligation, and was giving preferment to the Spanish bondholders. Since Spanish law prevented foreclosure by the French investors, and the Spanish Government alone had the power to remedy the wrong, the official ban was applied against its securities.[37]

In the negotiations which led to the establishment of some measure of creditor's control for Serbia in 1895, for Greece in 1898, and for Bulgaria in 1902, the weight of the government was thrown behind the bondholders' proposals. No actual defaults occurred in Serbia and Bulgaria; the supervisory arrangements were introduced as conditions of the conversion loans that enabled the governments to avoid default. The German banks took the initiative in pressing for the Serbian arrangement rather than the French. When in 1898 Greece emerged defeated from a war with Turkey, France followed the German lead in putting the pledged revenues under control.

It was to coerce the governments of two Mohammedan states that the most outright gestures of force, in behalf of French investment abroad, were made. In both instances the French Government sought objects of a wider character than the protection of the threatened investment. When in 1907 Moulay-Hafid overthrew his brother and became Sultan of Morocco, he had no funds to establish order throughout the country, to meet the service of the Moroccan government loans sold in France, or to pay the costs of the French military expedition which were charged up to him. New borrowing was obviously necessary to avoid default. The French banks offered the required loan on conditions which greatly strengthened their control of Moroccan finances. As the Sultan showed signs

[37] A. Leroy-Beaulieu, *L'Économiste Français*, August 13, 1910, and *Report Association Nationale des Porteurs Français de Valeurs Étrangères*, 1908, p. 15.

of preferring default the French Government, with effect, definitely threatened the use of force. It not only sought the extension of French influence; it feared lest the continued postponement of payments due to German interests might provoke German governmental action.

Toward the Turkish Government in 1901 the threat of force passes into its actual display. The episode, commonly known as the Lorando-Tubini affair, had complicated antecedents.[38] Three claims were involved. In 1890 the Turkish Government gave a concession to a French company (Société des quais de Constantinople) for the construction and operation of the quays of Constantinople. After the first quay at Galata was built, opposition against the company appeared; the longshoremen felt the loss of work, local tugboatmen were angered by the company tugs, the local merchants criticized the rates charged though the company had no monopoly. The Sultan refused to continue to carry out the terms of the concession, and hindered its operation. Then he offered to repurchase the concession on terms unacceptable to the company, which wanted an indemnity, and desired to retain the right to exploit the quays. The Turkish Government vacillated in its offers to the company and in its responses to the arguments of the French Government. The French Government wished this particular concession to remain in French hands since the port of Haida-Pasha was being developed by German investors.[39] The matter was taken to involve not only pecuniary interests, but to raise questions "of a wholly different character, touching the position of France on the Bosporus."[40] The other claims were of a purely pecuniary character; they concerned loans

[38] *Documents Diplomatiques, Turquie, 1900–1901;* A. Moncharville, "Le Conflit Franco-Turc," *Revue Générale du Droit International Public,* 1902.

[39] *Die Grosse Politik der Europäischen Kabinette,* Vol. XVII, Nos. 5668, 5669.

[40] *Documents Diplomatiques, Turquie, 1900–1901,* No. 4.

made at 15 per cent interest to the Sultan by Levantine bankers of French citizenship, Lorando and Tubini.

Though the French Government in the past had often ignored such situations as these, in August, 1901, it broke off diplomatic relations with Turkey, recalled its ambassador, and again demanded immediate satisfaction for the claims. Shortly thereafter a satisfactory repurchase agreement for the Constantinople docks was drawn up, and a settlement of the Tubini claims arranged. But the Lorando claim remained open. On October 26, 1901, the French Government again reasserted its demands and now, as compensation for troubles and delays encountered, asked satisfaction of some political matters. The rights of French schools, hospitals, and missions were to be legally recognized and extended; the election by his church of Mgr. Emanuel Thomas, a French *protégé*, as Chaldean Patriarch, was to be sanctioned, and the investiture made. Four days later a naval division was dispatched to Mytilene to seize the customs. M. Delcassé, Minister of Foreign Affairs, declared that "we wish to show that to the long and persistent denials of justice, to the systematic and repeated detractions of our rights and interests, France, after exemplary patience, has something besides protests to put forward."[41] The day after the fleet arrived at Mytilene, the Sultan settled the Lorando claim and satisfied the other French demands.

French calculations in this episode plainly passed beyond the simple intention of assuring just consideration for the three French claims out of which it arose. The French Minister of Foreign Affairs declared to the Chamber of Deputies after the dispatch of the fleet

that he looked with disfavor and apprehension at the disappearance of an enterprise bearing a French name . . . and that the government had felt that it was in the presence of a

[41] *Débats Parl. Chambre de Députés,* November 4, 1901.

system, a prejudice, and that other interests of a more general and elevated character, disputed today, denied tomorrow, violated day after tomorrow . . .[42]

In other words a blow had been struck to leave an impression along the African coast and throughout the Near East that France was determined to maintain its place and program, and powerful enough to do so. The Quays of Constantinople, the claims of Lorando and Tubini were but the "dossiers" on top of the pile.

From among the other instances of later years where the French Government asserted itself to shield French interests abroad (they were not infrequent), special interest attaches to the measures taken in 1912 in behalf of claims against Cuba.[43] These French claims arose out of the 1895 revolt against Spain, and the correspondence they had occasioned grew more faded as it grew more bulky. In 1910 the French Ambassador, joined by the British, who had similar claims to press, served warning that the Paris market would be closed to Cuban security issues in the event of continued refusal. The Banque de L'Union Parisienne, which was negotiating a bond issue for the Crédit Foncier Cubain, ended the discussions rather than face official opposition. On the board of the Crédit Foncier Cubain, Frenchmen, Germans, and Cubans sat side by side. Not long after, the Banque Continentale of Paris, which was the subsidiary of a German bank, prepared to bring out the Crédit Foncier issue, announcing that official listing would be sought. Rejection of this request was asked for in Parliament. The Minister of Foreign Affairs announced that it had already been rejected, explaining, "When a request is addressed to the government, it is examined with an appreciation of the financial interest and French political interests . . . in all requests

[42] *Ibid.*
[43] For an account of this episode, see *ibid.*, February 3, 1912.

the French interest should take precedence over the financial interest . . ."[44]

Though vaguely phrased, this statement indicates the consideration which, more than any other, shaped the policy of the French Government in the matter of extending official protection to French investments abroad—as far as it was not shaped by the accident of personalities and special influence. Governmental intervention in behalf of private investors in a foreign land is a political action, which has political consequences. The French Cabinet was highly sensible to that fact in every instance; and to it other circumstances and conditions were made secondary in the long list of decisions which the government was compelled to make. Eager as it was to protect its investors, influential as these investors were in official circles, it was in a measuring of political advantage or disadvantages that the government found its primary guide.

THE ORGANIZATION OF THE INVESTORS

THE French Government, so that it might keep itself clear of the necessity of intervention, "when foreign governments are concerned, and such intervention would hinder its general policy," encouraged the effective organization of the investors.[45] In 1898 M. Cochery, the Minister of

[44] *Débats Parl. Chambre de Députés,* February 3, 1912. Isvolsky wrote to his government apropos this statement: "That declaration of M. Poincaré differs sensibly from the point of view of Caillaux . . . who . . . as your Excellency knows, regarded analogous operations such as the Hungarian loan or the participation of France in the Chinese Quadruple Syndicate above all from the point of view of the financial advantages obtained. The change in the attitude of the French Government should have a serious and favorable significance for our political interests." *Livre Noir,* I, 188. Isvolsky later modified his judgment of Caillaux somewhat, praising the interest and energy with which the Doumergue-Caillaux Cabinet in 1913–14 arranged for the program of Russian borrowing. *Ibid.,* II, 222.

[45] See Lacombe, "De la Défense des Porteurs de Titres de Fonds d'État Étrangers," *Congrès Internationale des Valeurs Mobilières,* Vol. II, for the origins of the organization. In 1913 its name was changed to L'Office Nationale des Valeurs Mobilières, and its functions broadened somewhat.

Finance, charged the official stock exchange (Chambre
Syndicale des Agents de Change) with the duty of founding an investors' association which could defend French
financial interests abroad, achieve satisfactory settlement
of their difficulties through their own strength and talent.
The association then created (Association Nationale des
Porteurs français de Valeurs Étrangères) sought a wide
membership of individual and corporate investors. The
personnel of its executive bodies and the commissions
through which it negotiated were drawn largely from the
circles of the stock exchange and from government officials or former government officials of high rank. For
aid the Association depended upon both the stock exchange and the government. The stock exchange continued to be its largest financial supporter; it also coördinated its action with that of the Association by barring
from trading the loans of foreign governments with which
the Association was unable to reach agreement. The government's assistance varied from instance to instance. The
diplomatic officials and consuls abroad introduced its
representatives, kept it informed, transmitted its complaints and often fought its battles.

The Association retained, at least nominally, independence of action despite its relations with the public powers.
The Director of the Association explained, "the Minister
himself requires that it be so, as shown by his insistence
that the President retain no connection with the Administration. But the Association receives most precious and
exclusive support from the government."[46] Through its
connections the Association was assured of attentive consideration of its need without any formal arrangements
for the transmission of its wishes, or the reception of those
of the government. A natural coöperation developed in
which the government seemed usually most pleased when
it had to take no share at all in the situations that occupied the Association; that, after all, was the object of

[46] *Association Nationale des Porteurs Français*, 1899–1900, p. 4.

founding it. No doubt the Association now and again
adjusted its policies or demands to the advice of the administration, which it could hardly afford to embarrass.[47]
Their organization enabled the bondholders to act effectively and decisively in defense of their interests. It enabled
the government to free itself, when and as it wished, of an
unpleasant task without exposing itself to the criticism of
leaving an important national interest in neglect. Both the
bondholders and the government found the arrangement
satisfactory.

SOME GENERAL OBSERVATIONS

It is difficult to recall, after surveying the relationship
between finance and government in France, the ruling conception of the economic texts that investment and the business of buying and selling of securities are private activities, decided by the taste and judgment of the savers and
the banks, bringing profit and loss according to the wisdom of private decision. In so many ways did the investment of French capital abroad come within the field of
governmental cognizance and regulation, so regularly
were judgments and favors passed back and forth between governments and banks! Another positive notion
was added to that in the texts; though the action of each
investor and bank remained a private financial operation,
the action of them all over the passing years was a matter
of national consequence and a natural field for government
control. This notion was turned into policy, and the policy
was directed primarily by two sets of conditions and desires. French industry was lagging in its growth behind
that of rival states; French foreign investment must serve

[47] Though only one serious charge of the kind has come to my attention. The Caillaux government was accused of inducing the Association
to accept against its judgment the terms offered by the Spanish Government in 1900; in so acting the government was further accused of having
come under the influence of the large Paris banks. G. Manchez, "La
Rente Extérieure Espagnole et le Projet de Convenio," *Revue Politique
et Parlementaire,* October, 1900.

to aid it. French political destiny was being worked out
from day to day midst a world that included enemies, and
regions that were potential prizes for stronger and more
civilized powers; French foreign investment was one of
the forces by which this destiny might be made safe, perhaps, a triumphant one.

How fully the objects of this policy were realized, what
gains and what disappointments it brought, it is the burden of the preceding survey and of later chapters to ex-
pose. Here is place only for a few incidental observations.
The course of French experience seems to indicate that
international friendships resting upon financial connections are fickle, and international gratitude for financial
aid—in the form of loans—rare. Professions of friendship
may abound when loans are sought; but may last no
longer than the need which occasioned them. The loans
are judged as private profit transactions. Borrowing governments are usually more conscious of the cost of the loan
than of the benefit received. A refusal of a loan because
of government intervention is remembered longer than the
granting of two loans. The official benevolence shown to
Russia undoubtedly strengthened the Russian alliance but
strong common political objects bound the two governments together. It successfully promoted French policy
in Serbia and Japan. But where political currents were
unfavorable, as with Turkey and Bulgaria, the connections built through financial aid fell apart.

Foreign borrowers, especially foreign governments, had
not only to satisfy the bankers of the soundness of their
credit and their plans; they had to satisfy the French
Government, popular opinion and the press which led it, of
their purposes. This necessity contributed to the formation
of an unhealthy relationship between the governments, the
banks, and press. When opposition was expected, all possible channels of influence were used. The press was bribed
—sometimes with the knowledge and advice of the French
Ministers who also had to reckon with outside opinion;

the way was opened for blackmail by the press.[48] The borrowing governments did not even hesitate to appeal to personal advantage. Thus the Russian Foreign Office, when instructing its Ambassador at Paris to seek permission for a contemplated loan suggested that it was advisable "to permit participation not only of a group of great banks headed by the Crédit Lyonnais and the Banque de Paris, but also of a new group of second rate provincial banks led by the influential Cochery. By satisfying him, we shall no doubt please the French Government and diminish opposition in the Parliament and press."[49] With or without basis in truth, a large part of public opinion believed that their public officials were corrupted in this process of passing upon foreign loans—whether for personal or party benefit.[50]

Between the banks and the government exceptional intimacy with mutual temptations arose. Subject to official supervision in their foreign loan arrangements the banks were under the necessity of not giving offense, could not easily resist claims for special favor. For instance, they

[48] See the correspondence of A. Raffalovitch, financial agent of the Russian Government, published in *L'Humanité*, December, 1923–March, 1924. Raffalovitch mentions the Serbian, Argentine, and Brazilian governments as making payments to the press. J. Caillaux, *Mes Prisons* (Paris, 1921), p. 186, in denying that he demanded a contribution to party funds in return for permission to list Turkish securities, asserts that the Turkish Government had spent three million francs for newspaper publicity with the knowledge of the Foreign Minister. Bribery of the press took many forms—money, options, decorations, jobs. The practice was not limited to foreign governments; an official investigation revealed that the newspapers were paid seven million francs for assistance in issuing the Panama Canal Loan of 1888. R. Poincaré, *Au Service de la France* (Paris, 1926), III, 97, states that Russia made large payments to the French press in 1904–6 with the cabinet's knowledge; the Italian and Austrian governments did the same. In this chapter he asserts that Isvolsky falsely gave the St. Petersburg Government to understand that he, Poincaré, as President of the Republic, urged that the Russian Government bribe the press, so that funds would be supplied.

[49] *Livre Noir*, II, 455.

[50] E.g., G. Manchez, *Sociétés de Dépôt, Banques d'Affaires* (Paris, 1918), pp. 97–98.

were expected to reserve place upon their directorates for discharged ambassadors and retired officers of the Ministry of Finance.[51] Such places were prizes dangled before officials provided the banks found their services valuable. While on the other hand, the government, in its efforts to influence French investment for political ends, had to rely steadily upon the banks. Even though it be assumed that both groups were governed by most rigorous standards of honesty and public welfare, doubts must remain as to the wisdom of creating so close an association between any single set of private interests and the state. For France, it cannot be said to have promoted faith in the government.

[51] Poincaré, *op. cit.*, I, 268, made reservations for Philip Crozier, Ambassador to Vienna, and for George Louis, Ambassador to St. Petersburg. E. Judet, *George Louis* (Paris, 1925), p. 248. The Banque de L'Indo-Chine, in particular, was expected to make place for such officials and some were always on its board of directors.

CHAPTER VI

FINANCE AND GOVERNMENT IN GERMANY

THE GROWTH OF A DOCTRINE

THERE never was in Germany a large amount of easily spared capital. Thus there always existed in industrial and official circles, not far out of sight, an anxiety lest too open a reception to foreign loans might make difficult the satisfaction of their own wants. German industry, while seeking and planning foreign expansion, was not, therefore, entirely unsympathetic to some measure of guardianship of the loan market; it was not willing to trust solely to the movement of relative interest rates, to the long-time results of foreign investment. In addition, two strong bodies of opinion within the country were antipathetic to the movement of capital abroad—the agriculturists and the Socialists. By the agriculturists such investment was deemed a cause of higher interest rates for agricultural credit; besides, they feared lest the growth of German financial and industrial interests abroad would cause the agricultural interests to be sacrificed in tariff bargaining. By the Socialists it was regarded as bringing oppression of weaker races in its train and as certain to involve the country in international conflict. These influences combined to foster the notion that foreign investment should be submitted to regulation, to create a current of feeling that its total amount should be kept down. Intermittently this demand attained articulate and forceful expression. The banks and public powers were not altogether heedless of it.

From the time of Bismarck's passing—even in the last years of his chancellorship—it is true that German industry and the German Government worked might and main to develop their foreign influence, to expand foreign sales, to build up foreign banking connections, to win place for German capital and enterprise, to acquire spheres of influence and colonies. It was recognized that the investment of capital abroad was essential to all these ends. Thus the dominant mood and calculation of the government, the big banks, and the powerful German industries, were to look with favor and hope upon that investment—though, as has been indicated, not entirely with ease of mind.[1] Out of the conflict of influences and computations there grew, especially after the turn of the century, an attitude of "management," of "amanagement" such as a housewife practices with not too great a weekly budget. The attitude of management fitted in naturally with various strains in German foreign policy, with the mixed note of striving ambition and harassment which marked that policy, the psychological compulsion to go forward, the sense that the only way forward lay in combat with unfriendly nations possessed of earlier advantages. In the grip of these feelings, the government tended increasingly to look for evident return, in the way of economic advantage or political favor, from its foreign investment.

In this matter of foreign investment there is a great gap between conceptions which may be formulated as guides and the actual events. Investors, no matter how patriotic, have judgments and tastes of their own; banks, no matter how desirous of serving the nation, have obligations, in-

[1] The different attitudes were well summarized by Herr Mueller, Director of the Dresdner Bank. "The participation of the German Banking community in foreign government and municipal loans is often regarded in circles not connected with business as undesirable and sometimes dangerous to the public welfare. Even German Ministers of Finance have been inclined to view the questions from this standpoint. The Imperial Chancellor and the Minister of Foreign Affairs have always held a different opinion and have recognized that it is imperatively necessary for the international position of Germany, for German export trade and consequently for the development of the German Merchant Marine Navy, to compete with England and France in lending money to foreign and transatlantic countries." *Miscellaneous Articles on German Banking* (National Monetary Commission, Washington, 1910), p. 152.

terests, connections which they steadily preserve. Thus only from the actual events can the actual course of policy be discerned. But out of the controversies within Germany before the war, there did arise a substantial measure of agreement upon a conception of policy. This the government and predominant opinion tended to accept as a theoretical basis for action. In a book which had great influence, the elements of the conception were given precise formulation.[2]

1. The issue of foreign securities in the domestic market, like the establishment of branches of domestic enterprises and participations abroad, is permissible only after the domestic demand for capital has been fully satisfied, since the first duty of the banks is to use the available funds of the nation for increasing the national productive and purchasing power and for strengthening the home market.

2. International commercial dealings as well as international flotations ought to be but the means for attaining national ends and must be placed in the service of national labor.

3. Even when the two foregoing conditions have been fulfilled the greatest care will have to be used in selecting the securities to be floated.

These general propositions are vague. They were extremely difficult to translate amidst the circumstances of the particular cases which always present the question of "more or less." They may set out objects for government intervention which are more likely to be achieved by the unhindered operation of private judgment. Yet in substance they represented the general attitude which tended to prevail in Germany before the war and the general objects which the government tried by its supervision to achieve.

[2] J. Riesser, *The German Great Banks and Their Concentration*, p. 384.

MEANS AND METHODS

FOR the advancement of these purposes the government trusted to a large degree to the instinct of the private investor and the judgment and initiative of the Great Banks. It did not wish to introduce itself formally and regularly into the affairs of the money market or of the banks. All suggestions for the establishment of a *régime* under which the opinion of the government was to be formally asked before each emission were regarded with disfavor. The undesirability of having responsibility imputed to it for judgment of loan issues and the risk of giving offense to other governments were recognized. But occasionally, to check some loan, the formal exercise of legal power was used. For under the laws of the empire, the government was able to exercise legal control over loan operations through several official institutions.[3]

Indirectly the admission of securities to listing and trading on the German Stock Exchange could be influenced under the arrangements established by the Stock Exchange Act of 1896.[4] Regulation of admissions was inaugurated in the eighties, provoked by the heavy losses of investors. Renewed defaults of foreign governments and strong opposition to the large amount of current foreign investment were among the causes which led to the holding of a stock exchange inquiry in 1892 from which issued the regulating act of 1896. This act and subsequent amending acts created boards of admission on the German stock exchanges upon which interests not professionally engaged in the security business were given substantial representation.[5] It was hoped to safeguard the agricul-

[3] A detailed study of the legal basis of control has been made by W. H. Laves, *German Governmental Influence on Foreign Investments, 1871–1914* (Thesis, University of Chicago, 1927); I have drawn upon it for this chapter.

[4] W. Lexis, "The New German Exchange Act," *Economic Journal*, September, 1897.

[5] The provision as revised by the 1908 Law and the Berlin Stock Exchange ordinance, Art. 24, reads "at least half not active in stock

tural and industrial interests of the country against the possibility that the banks, with their great powers of security distribution, might err, or sacrifice internal development for easy profit. The act defined the procedure and conditions of admission to be observed by the boards of admission. For the Berlin Exchange these conditions were also regulated by a law passed by the Prussian Bundesrat. Despite their composition, these boards of admission interfered but little on their own initiative with the course of security issue in Germany except on technical grounds, or to improve prospectuses, or to prevent evident error or fraud.[6] Such seems to have been the fact though a wide field of discretion was opened by the law in authorizing the boards to exclude securities which endanger "a public interest" ("ein erhebliches allgemeines Interesse"). In the interpretation of this provision, however, the boards dared not venture far outside of the grounds of technical correctness. Since most objects of national policy were matters of public debate, of party or sectional difference, they could hardly attempt to shape them by their decisions. Still these boards were agencies through which the views of the business community and government might be conveyed to the banks with a certain measure of authority. Objections to foreign loans, in gen-

exchange business." In 1913 out of a board of 28 members and 8 alternates, 20 were active or retired bankers, 7 industrial representatives, 3 representatives of produce exchanges and metal markets.

[6] For analysis and record of their activity, see P. Jacobs, *Die Zulassung von Wertpapieren zum Börsenhandel* (Berlin, 1914), and H. Zichert, *Die Kapitalsanlage in Ausländischen Wertpapieren* (Berlin, 1911). Jacobs cites various refusals on special grounds, e.g., of the Luxembourg Union Bank because of its corporate form, of the Deutsche Erdöl Gesellschaft in 1912 because of the possible interference with the plans for a German government monopoly and deleterious effect of such a monopoly upon the shares (all this under par. 3, sec. 36—the "public interest" clause), also instances in which further information or improved prospectus was required, e.g., a Turkish Loan of 1905, a Canadian Pacific bond issue of 1913. As early as 1896 the Committee at Berlin refused admission to a Mexican loan because the legality of the pledges assigned was considered doubtful. Zichert asserts, however, that the Boards of Admission were dominated by the banks.

eral or particular, could be and were brought forward for discussion; and to some extent the banks were guided thereby.[7]

The various state governments within whose territories the several stock exchanges were could intervene in the decisions of these boards of admission. To each was appointed a state Commissar whose duty it was to see that the laws regulating the exchange were observed. Of these appointments the most significant was that of the Commissar of the Berlin Stock Exchange which was made by the Prussian Minister President who was at the same time Chancellor of the Empire. Here was a direct line for the exercise of the will of the Imperial Government. But the Commissars, including the one at Berlin, in general played a passive rôle. Their powers were poorly defined and the government showed little disposition to extend them by a broad interpretation of the legal provision regarding the public interest.[8] The known instances of intervention by the government through this channel are few; but the government steadily upheld the right to use it. Thus, for example (February 20, 1913), the Prussian Minister of Commerce declared before the Prussian Landtag, apropos of the barring of the bonds of the Chicago, Milwaukee & St. Paul Railway from the Berlin Exchange, "My right to interfere at the place of admission has never been denied in the Prussian Legislature . . . and objection has not been raised to the right of the state to determine whether a general public interest has been endangered." To make it more effective, the law of 1896 provided that when a security had been refused admission by one stock exchange in Germany, no other exchange could admit it unless the reasons for exclusion were of a local character. This created a unity of control within the power of the

[7] Testimony of Dr. Paul Wachler, *German Bank Inquiry of 1908* (National Monetary Commission, Washington, 1910), pp. 665–668.

[8] Testimony of Count Von Kanitz, *ibid.*, pp. 580–581, and B. Dernburg, *Kapital und Staatsaufsicht* (Berlin, 1911).

Imperial Government when it chose to exert it. But the government emphasized how sparingly this power had been and must be used.

Through its powers of dictation over the Reichsbank, the government possessed another formal means of influencing the course of German investment. The directing board of the Reichsbank was made up of the Chancellor and four other members, one of whom was appointed by the Emperor, and the other three by the Bundesrat. The Reichsbank's right to regulate rediscount rates enabled it to influence capital movements, to regulate them in the interest of the German money market. But this was a delicate instrument which might react upon business; moreover, in its effects, no discrimination could be made between foreign loans that were favored and those that were not. Of greater use for the purpose was the dependence of the large banks upon the aid of the central bank, which fact assured effectiveness for its suggestions. Moreover, the Reichsbank, as a source of credit for these banks, could make its own rules on collateral security. Its acceptance or rejection of the securities of a foreign country as collateral was certain to affect their place in the German market; banks would not long hold securities declared ineligible. These combinations of powers sufficed to prevent the introduction of securities into Germany against an evident official opinion.[9] But the government was reluctant to use them and give offense thereby.

It was by private, direct, unofficial but steady communication with the directing heads of the important banks that the Kaiser and the Foreign Office assured themselves of the adjustment of capital movements to their judgments and policies. Such communication permitted secrecy, flexibility of judgment, and formulation of terms of common advantage. Before the great industrial de-

[9] Testimony of Herr Roland-Lucke, formerly Director of the Deutsche Bank, in *German Bank Inquiry of 1908, op. cit.,* pp. 350–351; Zichert, *op. cit.*

velopment of Germany, before the birth of the ambition to become a world empire, there was little social intercourse, little coördination of activity between financial and official circles, though the Emperor and the Chancellor might have entertained a personal intimacy with a Bleichröder or a Rothschild. But with the drawing together within the same circles of ambition of the monarchy, the naval and military advocates, and the commercial and financial interests, both business and social communications became common and accepted, with the Kaiser in the center of the circle. The leading figures in the Deutsche Bank, the Diskonto-Gesellschaft and in Bleichröder (Berlin connection of the Rothschilds) were most frequently found within it. All of the successors of Bismarck were convinced that their place as a world power depended upon the expansion of German enterprise and capital abroad. Kaiser Wilhelm II watched carefully every move in that process of expansion and labored for it; the reins were in his hands.[10] The banks often drew back from the impetuosity of official purposes and strove to moderate the frictions which they generated.

It became customary on the part of the banks to consult the Foreign Office in regard to foreign loans to which a political interest might attach, or to which serious objection might be entertained, though no formal require-

[10] See the life of *Georg Von Siemens* (Berlin, 1923), by K. Helfferich for a picture of this activity. Other examples are given in B. Hulderman, *Albert Ballin* (Oldenburg, 1922); Ballin relates that when he was negotiating with the Morgan group in 1902 in regard to the formation of the International Mercantile Marine and community of interest plan, the Kaiser followed every step, of the negotiations and caused the arrangements to be modified; so, too, when Ballin set off to create a Japanese-German Bank, he was called to Kiel to confer with the Kaiser and Chancellor on the subject.

The relationships between the Foreign Office and Bleichröder are recorded in considerable detail in the book and papers of Paul H. Von Schwabach, of which an account is given in *Europaische Gespräche,* June, 1929. Often Schwabach was intrusted with errands intended to further international understanding. His communications with the Rothschilds show a steady concern for peace.

ment of the kind was ever made by the government.[11] As
the interests of the banks increased in regions where their
safety was largely dependent upon their government, as
prospects of future opportunities became plainer, they
took pains to make their actions fit and respond to official
indications. Sometimes these indications came directly,
sometimes they were conveyed deviously through the admission committee of the Berlin Stock Exchange, the
Reichsbank, or the semiofficial press.

It was upon these quiet, informal procedures that the
German Government relied to turn the process of foreign
investment to what it conceived to be the greatest national
advantage and to regulate its movement. A director of
the Krupp's bore witness to the effectiveness of these
means. "I believe," he told the German Bank Inquiry of
1908, "that the existing state of things suffices to enable
the government to hold up undesirable loans or prevent
their being placed at an inopportune moment."[12] The
close connection between the banks and industries gave
sufficient assurance that the banks would work directly
for German industry. The representation of the Great
Banks on the boards of directors of the main industrial
companies of Germany, their continuing investment in the
securities of these companies and general financial inter-
dependence was a guarantee that the banks would exert
themselves to secure favor for German industry according
to their judgment of the possible. This was one of the most
urgent of official desires. For in Germany, as in France,
only wavering credence was given to the theory that even
in the absence of special provisions or arrangements, foreign lending must benefit foreign commerce; and besides,

[11] This was brought out clearly in the German Bank Inquiry of 1908,
and has been affirmed and illustrated by many German authors. For good
examples, see H. Dove, "Der Einfluss der Boersengesetzlichen Vorschrif-
ten," *Bank-Archiv*, April, 1911, p. 223; M. Brabdt, "Die Einführung
Ausländischer Anleihen," *Bank-Archiv*, April, 1911, p. 221.

[12] *German Bank Inquiry of 1908–1909* (National Monetary Commission, Washington, 1910), I, 420–421.

German opinion was always concerned with the balance of trade, lest gold be lost and credit be restricted.

Another reason why formal regulation was dispensed with lay in the fact that the other important aims of the government could be attained only by informal, personal action. For they required a positive response. The government, despite its recognition of the many demands for available German capital often sought to induce the banks and investors to finance projects deemed essential to the advancement of imperial aims, to sway judgment and action in favor of lands where a prospect of increased German trade and power was seen. The German Government found tasks for German capital to perform; that was the most important way in which it influenced the course of German investment.

THE ACTUAL EXERCISE OF GOVERNMENT INFLUENCE

THERE was in Germany, it has already been observed, an undercurrent of protest against the movement abroad of capital in what was considered too great volume. This rose from popular and party sentiment, not from the directing center of government. As a manifestation of a popular feeling of some strength, it bore down upon the banks and government. It is impossible to measure to what extent it may have been reckoned with, acted upon, by those who directed official policy, to know to what extent the general movement of capital may have been constrained by official influence in deference to that sentiment. All that is certain is that there was present in the minds of the banks, the Reichsbank, the government, the necessity of "managing" the employment of German capital, so that it might perform its most urgent tasks. Often—both the current comment on the matter and the testimony of the banks indicate—this created a general constraint, a caution, in the flotation of foreign loans. Such constraint was to some extent the reason, it is likely, for the small volume of foreign lending in the years 1905–9 and 1911–14. But it was certainly not as strong an influence as the basic condition of the capital market.

From time to time the government gave direct or indirect indication that the time was not favorable to foreign loans. Thus the Minister of the Interior, Delbrück, avowed before the Reichstag (February 11, 1911) a policy of maintaining such a proportion between domestic and foreign securities as would maintain the price of government securities. When, to use his words, "the cup is too full," the government would intervene, as it did to prevent the listing of American railway bonds in 1911. So too, in 1913–14, the government conveyed through its semi-official press the opinion that foreign loans which were not especially advantageous for economic and political reasons should be restricted to the utmost. The German Government itself was then under the necessity of borrowing heavily.[13] The discount rate had risen to almost 6 per cent, the rate for short-time advances on securities to almost 7 per cent. Both German industry and the German Government believed that they could ill afford any foreign drafts upon the savings of the country. Thus the Prussian Minister of Commerce intervened to bar from the Berlin exchange a bond issue of the Mexican Government and short-time notes of the Mexican National Railways. In addition to the fact that the Imperial Government was about to issue a loan, the Minister was moved in this action by his judgment that the Huerta Administration, unrecognized by the United States, offered a dangerous risk.

But even while it was attempting to control the volume of foreign investment, the government realized that it could only hope for partial success. It recognized that the economic forces, the private calculations, which determined whether capital should stay at home or move abroad,

[13] For an account of this exercise of official influence, see A. Lansburgh, "Die Staat und Ausländsleihen," *Die Bank,* July, 1913; S. Schilder, *Die Auswärtigen Kapitalsanlage vor und nach dem Weltkreig* (Berlin, 1918), pp. 28 *et seq.*

had a will of their own. The business of loan issue was a delicate one, not to be interrupted at will. Or, as the head of a large private bank explained to the members of the Bank Inquiry of 1908:

Desirable as it is to choose the moment wisely, still we are not always in a position to seek such financial operations according to our pleasure. If, for example, a country has for ten years made no loans, and if at a certain time it has need of money, then it is not at all likely that we could say, "Would it not be better if you were to wait a year?" By such conduct as this we should often wantonly and foolishly lose valuable connections.[14]

And lastly, the government itself was usually divided in its wishes. Even when it might have appeared desirable to restrict foreign lending in order to ease the domestic capital situation, various phases of its program of economic and political expansion required foreign lending. Herr Dernburg, ex-Minister of Colonies, in criticizing the restraint upon foreign investment imposed in 1911, asked how these cross-purposes were to be reconciled.

What is to become of the negotiations of the great Chinese Hu-Kwang loan, carried on for several years, which German diplomacy advocates so eagerly? . . . What will happen also to the Santa-Catherina and Manchurian loans, which the Foreign Office supports? On the one side we have the Minister of Foreign Affairs urging forward, on the other side the Minister of Commerce putting on the brakes.[15]

The chief reasons for government intervention to check specific proposed loans, or the loans of a specific country, were political. These interventions concerned the borrowings of Serbia, Russia, and Bulgaria. Twice, in 1893 and

14 Herr Fischel of Mendelssohn & Co., *German Bank Inquiry of 1908–1909,* I, 479–480.

15 Dernburg, *op. cit.,* p. 22. This short volume is the most effective argument against the exercise of government control written in Germany before the war.

1906, Serbian borrowing in Germany seems to have been arranged with the banks, but not carried through. The circumstances which led to the withdrawal of the banks in these instances remain somewhat obscure. But contemporary observers attributed the action to the decision of the government. In the 1906 episode, the distribution of armament orders, which the French banks and government were also demanding as a condition of a loan, was at the center of the controversy.

Toward Russia the action taken was dramatic and repeated. German capital had contributed largely to the needs of the Russian Government and to the construction of Russian railways in the seventies and early eighties. But during 1886–87 the state of feeling between the two countries greatly changed. Fear and antagonism succeeded friendliness. Bismarck ordered the Reichsbank to refuse to accept Russian bonds as collateral security; sympathy, if not stimulant, was extended to a press campaign directed against Russian securities. They were sold outside of Germany. The decree was kept in effect until 1894. Thereafter, until 1906, Russia was intermittently permitted to borrow in Berlin. In 1906 the German Government again caused the banks to renounce Russian government loans. The force of Russian diplomacy had been turned against Germany in the preceding years. No further Russian government borrowing occurred in Berlin. But the market was left open to Russian industrial securities; for the entry of German private enterprise into Russia was deemed an economic gain.

When Bulgaria in 1909 met refusal in Paris, it turned to Vienna and Berlin. The German Government blocked the listing of the loan on the Berlin and Hamburg exchanges. By 1911 a satisfactory commercial treaty was signed. Then the Hamburg Exchange was open to the loan. Two years later, when France and Russia were extending loan offers to the Bulgarian monarch on condition that the pro-German Ministry should be turned out of power, when the German banks were asking loan security that was unpopular among the peasants, the German Government urged its banks to grant the required loan and exerted itself to have the requirements of the German banks modified, so that the French-Russian offers might be refused.

These actions are simply understood in the light of the continental political situation. The refusal of listing by the Prussian Government to the bonds of the Chicago, Milwaukee & St. Paul Railway in 1911 was of a more unusual nature. Its explanation still lies in a field of conjecture composed of the dozen possible reasons. The condition of the German capital market was the chief explanation offered. The demands on the capital market were numerous at the time; the government borrowing plans had been deferred. But there were special influences and interests which caused the government action to be taken just then, and against the American bond issue rather than the other foreign issues which were admitted during the same year. The issue was unpopular in industrial circles as possibly aiding American industry; agricultural opposition to foreign lending was vocal and active; the occasion was a good one to make a gesture pleasing to these circles of opinion. Besides the German Government and the American had been exchanging forthright notes concerning the German Potash Law of 1910, which was judged by the United States to affect adversely contracts previously made by Americans with independent German producers. The high American tariff was creating antipathy.[16] The closing of the Berlin Exchange might have been caused by the antagonism that was roused, might have been intended as a notice to the American Government that German financial aid would be unavailable till the spirit of concession was shown. Certainly the debate occasioned by the action took on a distinctly anti-American character in the speeches of the Conservative, Clerical,

[16] *Foreign Relations of the United States,* 1911.

and anti-Semite factions. But this explanation is only conjecture, though a likely one.

Only in these few instances, as far as is known, did the
government intervene formally to check the loan arrangements of the banks. For the rest it trusted their judgment
and their ability to understand veiled suggestions. The
investments made in banks and industries in Russia,
France, Great Britain, and Serbia—four potentially
hostile countries—were not opposed. They were accepted
as remaining under German control and strengthening
German industry and commerce. Economic influences were
permitted to prevail, to form their own connections.

The government, as has been already emphasized, addressed the banks not so much to restrain them as to induce them to accept new responsibilities, to undertake
loans and enterprises deemed of service to the German
state and German economy. The range of its activity was
indicated by the Director of the Dresdner Bank.

The Foreign Office has frequently stimulated the German
banks to enter into competition for Italian, Austro-Hungarian, Turkish, Roumanian, Serbian, Chinese, Japanese,
and South American loans. Even when the banks are approached from other quarters, the first move made is to ask
the consent of the Foreign Office for carrying on the negotiations. If the consent is given, then ministers, ambassadors, and consuls frequently support the representatives of
the German banks by word and deed.[17]

On three striking occasions, to illustrate the course of
activity, the government stepped forward to induce the

[17] W. Mueller, *Miscellaneous Articles on German Banking* (National
Monetary Commission, Washington, 1910), pp. 152–153. Herr Schinkel,
partner and director of the Diskonto-Gesellschaft, presented the matter
to the German Bank Inquiry this way: "Often it is our own government that imposes the duty upon us under all circumstances to cultivate
good relations with Brazil, East Asia, Chile, or Argentina, inasmuch as
these countries still constitute a neutral ground which, unless we look
out, will be wrested from us without ceremony by the English and
Americans." *German Bank Inquiry of 1908–1909*, II, 249.

banks to extend financial aid to friendly powers, after they had encountered refusals in Paris. Italy, which had hitherto borrowed chiefly in France, in 1882, formed alliance with the Central Powers. Within the next five years, the German banks, under instruction of their government, undertook the task (and opportunity) of financing the Italian state and railways. In 1887 the French Government closed the Paris market, and instigated the resale of Italian securities held by its citizens. Bismarck and the Italian Prime Minister brought the German banks together in a syndicate to support the Italian Government through the succeeding years, when the fear of bankruptcy was acute. The coöperation was carried into the field of private banking and industry. Germany thought to cement to itself a valuable ally, and while the Italian need was great, it did. But with the gradual cooling of Italian relations with the Central Powers, and the readmission of Italian securities to the more capacious French market, the financial connection dwindled.

In 1910 the German Government in similar fashion pressed the banks to undertake financial operations for Turkey and Hungary. The banks feared that the Turkish credit was not good enough to enable them to sell a large Turkish loan in a strained market—a loan which the French and British governments had kept off their markets. Only the earnest insistence of the Kaiser and Chancellor prevailed upon them to accept the risk. The Kaiser seized the opportunity of putting Germany in favor by helping where others refused. Shortly before, Hungary, too, had come to Berlin after meeting the veto of the French Government, and found through official intervention the loan it sought. Under no less dramatic conditions the German banks were led forward in loan negotiations with Roumania in 1913 and with Bulgaria in 1914.

Outside of the continent, and especially in China and South America, the banks were urged forward by sympathetic coöperation and support rather than by direct suggestion and request, though such were made from time to time. In China, the government showed itself, as did the other Great Powers, eager for full German participation in Chinese government and railway finance and exerted itself that its banks might possess a leading share.

GOVERNMENT AID IN SECURING CONCESSIONS

DURING the last quarter of the nineteenth century the world of purposes and fantasies within which German popular sentiment, German industrial and financial interests moved, underwent a transformation. A mystic sense of great destiny—such as possesses all nations from time to time—of larger goal, began to shape national feeling and national ideals. Such vague movements of national consciousness usually seek expression in very ordinary and concrete efforts and aims. These were supplied in Germany by the commercial, industrial, and financial groups which were attaining strength and by the ambitions of the rulers. German commerce had acquired system and foresight; German industry had shown a capacity to apply technical discovery and to organize its operations in large and effective units; German finance was attaining concentrated control over growing capital sums, and was ready for adventure. All felt that their future growth depended upon the acquisition, under their direction and influence, of markets, of raw material supplies, of lucrative opportunities, in foreign regions. With this sense of need and ambition, the Kaiser and most of those who surrounded him sympathized. In thought and plan these desires for commercial and financial expansion became fused with dreams of an extension of German political dominion. The talent and power of Germany proven on battlefields and now in the workshops, the judgment took firm hold, gave it the right to share more fully in settling the political fate of the world, in exercising political dominion over primitive regions or countries submerged by the advance of European civilization. Germany, thus moved and thus led, entered the competition with Great Britain and France for foreign commerce, concessions, financial advantages, colonies, control.

Circumstances combined with the seriousness of mind and purpose, which is part of the German character, to impart to the German effort tense and unsparing quality. For already other countries, and especially Great Britain, possessed vast colonial areas, had established claims and privileges through precedent and treaty, built up worldwide banking systems, come into the ownership of so much of the best opportunity, were already engaged in the exploitation of most of the favored regions. A consciousness of handicap came to characterize the German effort. Of the limited chances which remained, none must be overlooked, all must be pursued.

The manner and extent of the government exertions in behalf of concession opportunity differed, as did those of the British and French governments, according to the character and strength of the government and people within whose domain the concession was sought. On the continent of Europe, diplomacy was restricted to the cultivation of friendship, to friendly pleadings or interposition, to the suggestion of compensating advantages; though in the small Balkan states it took occasionally a sharper turn. Along such amiable though serious lines the negotiations undertaken with Latin-American states also ran. It was in the Near East, in China, Morocco, and Africa that the German Government assumed an active, leading rôle.

German enterprise and capital investment in Turkey centered in the Anatolian and Bagdad railways. The concession for the Anatolian railway was obtained by an international syndicate in which the German interest dominated. Bismarck viewed the plans of the syndicate with misgiving, foreseeing the international hostility that would arise. But once the decision of the group was made, he pushed its claims against foreign opposition. There-

after, through years of careful planning and diplomatic
support and arrangement, the German Government labored to bring the German railway projects to completion.
An impoverished, decaying, confused Turkish Government had to be kept together and supported in crises; the
confidence of a suspicious Sultan had to be retained. Then
later the trust of a rebellious Young Turk Ministry had
to be won. The effective powers of opposition of Russia,
Great Britain, and France had to be overcome by bargaining and arrangement. Not least important, the German banks had to be induced to engage more and more of
their resources in a venture of great and uncertain cost,
and hardly more certain return. In 1914 the final achievement of all this seemed assured.

It was with the Bagdad railway in mind, not because
of any interest in the possibilities of Persia, that the
German Government negotiated for concessions in Persia.
Thus always, these efforts and the movements of German enterprise were guarded and constrained lest .
sia and Great Britain be provoked to make a direct
issue of them. They were renounced in that zone of influence which Russia claimed, when Russia in return consented to ease the way of the Bagdad railway. In another
far-distant country, a similar renunciation was made, for
the benefit of German policy elsewhere. German capital
had assisted in financing the construction of railways in
the Boer Republics of South Africa and was seeking other
opportunity in these lands. In a succession of official declarations and gestures, of which the Kaiser's telegram to
President Kruger upon the repulse of the Jameson Raid
was the most spectacular, the German Government was
creating an impression of friendship and support. But its
real plans and aims were elsewhere, in the hopes of a division of the Portuguese colonies. When once they were met,
as far as they could be under the circumstances, by an
agreement with Great Britain, no further effort was made
to gain concessions in the Boer Republics. Rather, German

capital was encouraged to seek opportunities in those portions of the Portuguese colonies assigned to German control in the event of the bankruptcy of Portugal.

In China the German Government secured exclusive
opportunity for German capital in the province of Shantung, bestowing the mining and railway rights upon companies created under imperial control and subject to
imperial direction. That German capital might share more
effectively in Chinese government loans and be brought
more readily to finance such concessions as these, all the
powerful German banks had, at the suggestion of the
government, grouped together to establish the Deutsche
Asiatische Bank. In the ownership of this institution the
Seehandlung, State Bank of Prussia, joined with the private banks. Behind the Deutsche Asiatische Bank, both in
its individual efforts and as a member of the International
Consortium, the German Government stood, coming to the
fore when needed, and encouraging its determined and
successful efforts to share substantially in all Chinese financing. Prestige, commercial and financial benefit, the
right to share in the settlement of Far Eastern affairs—
these were the aims of policy as far as they had shaped
themselves.

These, too, inspired the stubborn striving of the German Government to make place for German capital and
enterprise in Morocco. The course of German action, with
all its variations and complexities, cannot be interpreted
with certainty despite the immense amount of information
that has come from official archives. In that range of argument by which the German Government explained and
defended its actions, a dozen conceptions and states of feeling appear—injured political pride, fear that Morocco
would be closed by France to German commerce and enterprise (a fear accentuated by the fact that so much of
Africa was already in French or British hands and com-
pounded with envy), a belief that as England and Spain
had been compensated for withdrawing from Morocco,

Germany, too, deserved compensation—these do not exhaust the list. For over ten dramatic years, while disorder grew and disaster became imminent, the German Government encouraged the entry of German financial enterprise and exerted the full strength of its diplomacy to gain a share in the development of Morocco, second to that of no other country. Twice the determination was shown to resort to armed force rather than consent to the establishment of French control. Of all the strivings of the German Government to secure opportunity for German capital, this was the most resolute and most reckless. In the second Moroccan crisis the battle-lines of the coming World War were drawn.

At the end of a quarter century of effort German enterprise held place in most of the contested areas of the world. Through the concentration of banking forces and the zeal of the government enough capital for the purpose had been found. To make these foreign enterprises more independent, to build up German commerce, to satisfy national pride, a self-sufficient merchant marine, a group of German banks in foreign countries, and a German-owned cable system, were found necessary. In all these fields British private enterprises had gained predominance by slow acquisition and growth throughout the century. For a similar slow growth neither German commerce nor the German Government could wait with patient trust. A special effort was exacted of that close combination of financial forces of which the Great Banks were the head.[18]

18 Of the banks Riesser, *op. cit.*, p. 529, wrote that the Great Banks "also coöperated with the government policies regarding the colonies, navigation, canals, the navy, and cable connections, all of which bore the closest relations to the above business policies." In all regions, however, it was difficult (not only for Germany, but for France and England as well) to make banks located abroad serve political purposes. For, in order to support themselves, they had to fit into the local situation and seek an international clientele. When the wish of the Government did not serve their private interest, they were loath to risk their money. For example, the Deutsche-Orient bank refused to go ahead with the concession obtained for it in Persia, despite the urgency of the Foreign Office.

For the cable companies which were formed the government gave subventions and the support of government departments. Its skill and power were exercised to secure the required consent and coöperation of other governments. For the establishment of banks abroad the way of the Great Banks was eased by diplomatic intercession; and at times it was the government which asked that their creation be undertaken and that the necessary capital be found. By similar initiative, by an unflagging display of interest and of favor, by stimulating banking support, the merchant marine was built. The German people and their government were trying to overcome the tardiness of their attainment of great national strength by systematic, united use of it. In this unity of interest all foreign enterprise took on a faint official tinge. The rest of the world recognized the fact, exaggerated it, and though striving for the same purposes, resented it.

GERMAN CAPITAL AND THE COLONIES

THE historians of the German colonies have tended to distinguish three different, successive, positions taken by the German Government toward those activities of private enterprise which contributed to the acquisition of German colonies. In the first, taken by Bismarck up to 1880–84, the government gave protection to the rights of private ventures when the necessity was clear, while avoiding the assumption of any political responsibility and any conflict of claims with foreign powers. In the second, the government forsook its Kontinental Politik, began to extend protection and aid against the rivals to German enterprise in areas that might be turned into colonies, and accepted responsibility for the government of areas brought under German control. In the third, the acquisition of colonies became an active aspiration and the government engaged all its diplomatic skill and power to secure for its subjects concession opportunities, which might lead to the extension of German political dominion. In all stages the capital

for pioneering in colonial areas and for the development
of acquired colonies was furnished primarily through the
agency of the Great Banks and a few private banks which
formed subsidiary companies to operate there.[19] On the
one hand these banks were usually ready to respond to
official suggestion and undertake initiative when asked as
a patriotic duty.[20] On the other hand the government usually conveyed to these banks the privileges and opportunities available in the acquired colonies. Government stimu-
lation of colonial ventures and investments did not grow
less necessary as the colonial domains expanded, because
of the unsatisfactory financial returns of many of the ventures. In the nineties, for example, despite the appeal of
the Chancellor and the colonial societies, sufficient capital
could not be found to finance the development of German
Southwest Africa and the government was forced to consent to the admission of English capital to a large share
of the undertaking. That the field was not left to a still
greater extent to the British enterprise was due to the
pressure of the Chancellor. In German East Africa, both
the Seehandlung and the Kaiser himself gave financial
aid to the chartered company which was created. Over
most of the larger concessionary companies and the colonial banks and chartered companies which were established, the Imperial Government maintained a guiding
control. The imperial guarantee was given for a substantial part of the borrowing undertaken for the construction
of railways; the colonial banks which were created were
kept under the direct supervision of the Imperial Chancellor.[21]

[19] J. Scharlach, "Unsere Banken und die Kolonien," *Bank Archiv,*
June, 1906. The argument for investment in the colonies was well presented by Dernburg, *Zeilpunkte des Deutschen Kolonialwesens* (Berlin,
1907).

[20] Especially Herr Hanseman of the Diskonto-Gesellschaft in the first
ventures.

[21] P. Schutte, *Die Frage einer Regelung der Wertpapier Einfuhr*
(Iserlohn, 1914).

The close association between government and financial enterprise in colonial expansion and development is not to be explained so much by the preference of the government or the form of the banking system as by what may be called (accepting the doctrine of colonial expansion for purposes of explanation) the conditions and necessities of the case. None of the German colonial empire was especially suitable for white settlement, nor possessed responsible government, nor, taken as a whole, richly endowed with easily developed resources. German capital, for example, was drawn far more quickly to the gold fields of South Africa than to the mines of German Southwest Africa. There did not exist in Germany as in Great Britain half a thousand groups whose experience and financial venturesomeness no strangeness or difficulty could appall, who knew how to work mines at any height or climate, and hew plantations out of jungles, who for a century had been opening up hidden resources of distant interiors. Upon the government fell the burden, since colonies were desired, of counterbalancing these deficiencies by will and organization. Despite their exercise, the amount of capital that went to the colonies was small.

THE PROTECTION OF THE FOREIGN INVESTMENT

In the decades of the seventies and eighties the German owners of foreign securities suffered many invasions of their rights and heavy losses. Financial circles were shocked, irritated, and depressed. The government was led to a more serious consideration of the demands for the use of its influence and retaliatory powers than before. Its policy and action, like those of Great Britain and France, were guided by judgment of how national interest was in each instance best served rather than by any outright acceptance of a duty toward the bondholders or any abstract law or right. The measures taken were, except toward Egypt and Turkey, limited to friendly and moderate diplomatic intercession. The investors' organizations and the stock exchange were left to guide the settlements. Bismarck shared the widespread feeling that the previous investment had been excessive, and a lack of enthusiasm in encouraging it in the future by saving the bondholders from their misfortunes. Again, in most of the defaults the German financial interest was smaller than that of the French and English; the bondholders and the government were compelled by this circumstance to conform their action to that taken by the greater interest. In the Turkish and Egyptian defaults, Germany followed along the French and British course, accepting a secondary place.

The defaults of the nineties have already been recounted. The misfortunes encountered in the Latin-American countries the government left to the banks to master, with its friendly aid. Toward Portugal more vigorous action would have been taken, there is no doubt, if it had not been for the opposition which would have come from Great Britain and France. For the German bondholders had suffered from previous Portuguese actions, and Portuguese securities had been admitted again to quotation only in 1886. The remonstrances of the German Government were sufficiently strong to cause Portugal to revive the Junta de Credito Publico and intrust to it revenues assigned as securities for the foreign loans. In the succeeding years of reproachful negotiations between the bondholders and the Portuguese Government for a new settlement, the efforts of the German Government were bent first toward the establishment of international financial control, later toward agreement with Great Britain concerning future Portuguese loans, to be secured on the revenues of the Portuguese colonies.

To the appeals of the holders of Greek bonds, when default first occurred in 1893, Chancellor Caprivi merely responded with the advice that they should concert themselves with the British bondholders and arrange the matter with the Greek Government. But in the following year the suggestion that joint intervention be undertaken was conveyed to the French and British governments. By 1898 when Greece issued defeated from war with Turkey, whose favor Germany was then seeking, official determination was crystallized. The German representative at the conference which settled the terms of peace took the initiative in bringing sufficient Greek revenues under international control to assure the service of the foreign debt. Here probably a political aim was being served as well as a private financial interest. To establish a plan for bondholders supervision in Serbia in 1895 proved an easier task. It was achieved by those German and French banking institutions which undertook the required conversion loan without the open display of the government's will. The unfortunate holders of American railway bonds were left to get what they could out of the American railway reorganizations in which they were represented by their banks.

Before the later defaults of the Latin-American countries the government remained vexed but passive—with one striking exception. True, in 1901 Germany joined in a protest to Honduras threatening the use of force if American claims were settled and German claims were neglected; but that was a minor incident. The use of armed force against Venezuela stirred world-wide feeling. German injuries, like the British, were of a varied character. The bond issue sold in Germany to build a railroad was in default; German citizens had been unpaid for construction work done for the government, and had suffered losses through war damages, forced loans, and requisitions. By the violence of the action undertaken, Latin-American feeling was aroused, and an undercurrent of hostility made itself felt in the United States, though nowhere was any approval of the attitude of the Venezuelan Government to be found. In the published official documents there appear, to account for the vigor of German action, a sense of baffled justice, of fear that if one of the Latin-American countries were permitted to mistreat European enterprise with impunity, all of it would be liable to similar treatment, perhaps a hope of special privilege to be obtained. The German action was never repeated; it may have been regretted.

All these exertions of the German Government were concerned with losses suffered by investors in foreign government bonds. When once German enterprise was settled in a foreign land, the German Government tended to stand aside and leave it to manage its relations with the foreign government and people except in such regions as Morocco, Africa, and China. But now and again the government took formal action, often enough to give a sense of guardianship. The English Government was urged in a series of serious diplomatic conversations, in some of which the Kaiser took the lead, to compensate the German investors in the Netherlands-South African Railway (in the Transvaal), taken over by the British Government after the Boer War. The Balkan states were called upon to respect the private ownership of the properties of the Oriental Railway Company within the territories acquired from Turkey. In 1908, for example, Germany refused to recognize the independence of Bulgaria until it agreed to indemnify the company for losses incurred through the Bulgarian seizure of part of the line; and later Germany opposed the inclusion of those parts of the line which remained in Turkish territory in a scheme for internationalization under study by France, Austria, and the Balkan states. Here again a desire to manifest friendship for Turkey made up part of the play. German concessions in Madeira were in 1905 defended with a determination not untouched by thoughts of possible future territorial acquisition. Most stubbornly of all were the rights and claims of German concessions in Morocco defended and pressed against the bankrupt Sultan and the opposed French. In China and Africa, German policy followed the same line of purposeful determination as was pursued by the other powers, perhaps more clumsily than France, more aggressively than England.

CONCLUDING OBSERVATIONS

To a student of German economic and financial affairs before the war, the nature and distribution of German foreign investment must have seemed satisfactory. With capital hardly more than sufficient to finance the advance of domestic enterprise, without many long-standing financial relationships with foreign countries, the German foreign investment seemed well placed where it could give most support to German economic life and policy. Of the foreign government bonds possessed, the largest part were bonds of the countries with which Germany wished to maintain close and friendly political relations and with which German commerce and industrial connections were growing stronger. The investment in industrial enterprises abroad, "undertaking capital" as it was called in Germany, had gone mainly where it seemed likely to establish the leadership of German commerce and industry—in Central and Eastern Europe, North and South America. The German Government had, in general, permitted trade connections, natural diversity of resources and abilities, geographical propinquity, to have their effect. When this fact and the comparative absence of any formal government control of that investment are considered, some perplexing questions present themselves. Why did this investment create so much uneasy criticism and distrust in other countries? Why in the final outcome did the private German investor lose almost all his holdings? Part of the answer to the first question is to be found merely in the fact that this investment represented a vigorous and effective new current of financial and commercial competition. Other countries, especially Great Britain and France, feared and fought displacement. Further, despite the absence of formal supervision, the close partnership of effort between the government and the banks was discerned; the government was felt to be the driving power in much of German foreign investment. Hence the idea grew that this investment was not merely a private venture but part of an official scheme, aiming at commercial, perhaps political, hegemony. As such, even countries largely dependent upon German finance, like Turkey and Roumania, from time to time, showed fear of that dependence. To the fears thus engendered, the steady rise of German strength, particularly of military strength, and the blunt assertion of that strength, gave added force. Since directly or indirectly it served German policy, German foreign enterprise was inevitably disliked by the members of the Triple Entente.

The German investors found themselves in possession of a comparatively small amount of securities which remained safe during the war. This has been adduced as proof that German financial and industrial circles did not desire war. It can be accepted as such though it could hardly have been foreseen that war would draw into the circle of enemies such distant regions as China, the United States, and part of South America. What it reveals is a certain blindness as to the amount of antagonism roused by that coordinated nationality-conscious, vigorous attempt to gain for German commerce, industry, and state, a large share of power and advantage in regions where national ambitions clashed. German foreign investment, so integral a part of the German outward thrust, was lost with the failure of that thrust.

PART III

STUDIES IN LENDING AND BORROWING

CHAPTER VII

INTRODUCTION

BY the fact that the people of some countries of Western Europe accumulated more capital than they chose to employ at home, or could employ to their greatest advantage, by the fact that the people and governments of other regions offered return for the use of that capital, a creditor-debtor world came into existence. In this sphere of experience there was no end of variety. At some times and places it was a friendly and satisfied world in which lenders sought only fair terms, proceeds were fruitfully employed and debtors met their obligations fully; mutual respect between debtor and creditor and common gain prevailed. At other times and places it was a world of suspicion, duplicity, and disappointment, in which creditors sought to take advantage of need or weakness, in which lending took a sinister turn, and borrowers misused the intrusted resources, or defaulted in their obligations; then the rancor, the scheming propensities, the ill-will of mankind were aroused. The contrast, the variety, were most natural. For in this world of borrowing and lending the participants were of very different condition, power, and ability to conduct themselves well under the exigencies of modern industry and finance. The most debauched and lavish Oriental monarch might come into the loan market on the same day as the most serious, disciplined and trained American railway executive; behind one might stand nobody but a handful of court officials eager to get their hands in his pockets, behind the other, the whole force of an organized nation.

To understand behavior in this lending and borrowing world, and to reveal what a wise nation should cultivate or avoid, it is necessary to follow the dealings between a great number of separate borrowing countries or regions and those which made loans or investments to them—in short, to make a series of studies in borrowing and lending. But in this matter, as in others, the annals of the happy are brief. The dealings are suitably confined to the quiet process of investment, effort, and payment. The results lay in the sphere of economic and commercial development where they have been already marked. The record of foreign investment in the United States, Canada, Switzerland, Denmark, during the half-century before the war, is, for example, quickly written and the consequences are easily understood. It has been when the process of borrowing and lending was affected by political influences, when it has created situations which led to political action, or been used to create such situations, that the record has grown long and involved. It has been when irregular and troublesome events have followed the act of borrowing, and the destiny of peoples was brought into the question, that the record presents difficulties to the judgment.

So the studies in lending and borrowing which follow, are mainly studies in difficulty and conflict. But here again it must be remembered that difficulty and conflict are the inevitable accompaniments of change. Capital, allied with modern technology, is a force which compels change. And then, too, political relations were undergoing rapid transformation in the period under review. The struggle for power among the nations left no economic action free. Some of the good results of these changes will far outlive the difficulties and conflicts which fill the studies. Human weakness, abuse, and oppression appear in plenty in the record, but they should be held in the perspective of the great transformation to which they were often but incident, but which they, indeed, tended to deteriorate and warp.[1]

[1] The reader may miss from among the following series, studies of foreign investment in the Central American and South American countries, in which regions about one-sixth of the total European foreign investment was made. But the task was beyond this opportunity. It would have required a volume in itself to present in detail the course of relationship between European capital and the score of independent Latin-

American governments south of the Rio Grande, another volume to trace the investment and its outcome in the territories forming these national states. That study of enormous scope and detail could not be fitted into the outlines of this work. Various other considerations make the omission natural as well as necessary. In the other regions which are studied the period 1870–1914 formed a fairly definite epoch, with a clear and dramatic close; the events related were part of the scheme of things which brought the period to its end. But in Latin-America the course of activity of outside capital was only interrupted and deflected by the war. A whole new map has not been drawn, political and social systems have not been revolutionized. The forces at work remain essentially the same. In one respect, it is true, the outside conditions under which the Latin-American states draw their capital for their development have changed—the United States has gained so greatly in political power, and its capital has moved with overwhelming energy into the Latin-American lands. But that fact, in itself, is stimulating the studies which must be omitted here; an important literature dealing with American financial expansion is being born, to which the reader may turn. The following paragraphs are but a few general observations offered as a footnote to that literature.

European capital and enterprise, above all British capital, entered with hope and vigor all the republics of Central and South America. It supported land and exploration companies, railroads, ports, municipal public utilities and construction enterprises, operated mines and industries, exploited timber and pasture lands—and financed governments in their political aims and economic undertakings. With the help of this capital the peoples of these republics were able to become important suppliers of foodstuffs and raw materials needed by the older industrial countries, and purchasers of large amounts of manufactured goods. Despite the heavy losses and difficulties suffered from time to time, especially in the eighties and nineties, by the foreign investors in these lands, the volume of investment expanded from decade to decade. Precise measurement of the total European investment in Latin-American countries appears to be unachievable. From the estimations made in the creditor countries, as of 1914, a total of something over 6 billion dollars appears, of which about 4 billions were British and something over 600 millions German. The estimates of French investment are most uncertain of all; a billion is perhaps not too far from the actual mark. Of the 6 billion dollars, over a third (almost entirely British) was in the Argentine Republic, about a sixth in Brazil, not far short of that in Mexico. More than half of the total was probably devoted to railway construction, either directly by foreign companies or through the foreign borrowing of the governments.

In the earlier period of borrowing lenders and borrowers often dealt with each other irresponsibly and dishonestly. The terms of lending were really terms of gambling; and the acquisition of concessions was often marked by corruption, double dealing, and political manipulation on the part of either of the negotiators, or both. The weaker, less responsible governments tended to develop a rather definite technique for cheating their creditors—honest and dishonest alike. Loans were contracted bear-

ing high interest and commission charges; irresponsible government administration or political upheaval led to default and neglect of creditors'
claims; when the government felt itself in need again, or some hungry
government official wanted to line his purse, the outstanding debt was
converted into one of smaller principal or lower interest—the debt
having changed owners in the meantime at a depreciated price; new
loans were then issued in amounts greater than required to discharge
the former debt in order that a floating debt might be paid off or public
works undertaken; thus the way was paved for a repetition of the same
cycle of events. That this process could continue without leading to the
extension of control on the part of the governments of the European
lending countries was due partly to the fact that these countries were
outside the main arena of European rivalries, partly to the hostility that
would have stirred throughout Latin-America by such a move, and above
all by the protection afforded by the Monroe Doctrine. It was the existence of this doctrine and the assurance that the United States would
support it, which prevented intervention on more than one occasion, and
ended it on several; which on the other hand sometimes gave the government of the borrowing state an illusion of safety that fostered irresponsibility as regards just claims of lenders or investors.

After 1900 the larger and more firmly established states, Brazil,
Argentina, Chile, and Peru gained steadily in stability, economic effectiveness, and their standing in the world's money markets. Through
all internal and financial difficulties, the economic development of these
countries, and of the other Latin-American states, moved on. Their
public credit distinctly improved in comparison with that of most states
on the European continent. How the market value of their bonds rose
in London is illustrated by the following table, which covers a period
of rising interest rates.

	1898		1903		1908	
	High	Low	High	Low	High	Low
Argentine loan, 1886–87	94	84	102	97	105	100
Brazil loan, 1883	63	44	85	79	92	83
Chile loan, 1885	84	63	87	80	97	84
Uruguay 3½ per cent loan, 1891	46	46	63	54	73	66

Securities of countries with weak credit, bearing reduced interest

Colombia external, 1896	19	16	32	16	46	42
Nicaragua railways	53	40	65	59	66	58
Paraguay, 1886 loan	17	14	33	28	52	45
Venezuela, 1896 loan	39	30	38	26	49	43

At the beginning of 1914 Mexico and Honduras were the only two Latin-
American states on the Council of Foreign Bondholders' lists of de-
faulters; and Mexico's default had come after thirty years of exemplary
financial behavior, and the moderate and useful application of foreign
resources. The gradual strengthening of the credit of the Latin-American
states was due in substantial measure to the economic development
which took place under the leadership of foreign-owned and managed
corporations. The excellent financial record of most Latin-American

governments during the strain of the war, their sincere effort to meet their obligations were a striking indication of the increasing financial and political stability they had attained.

The French and German governments from time to time exercised control over banking negotiations with the Latin-American states. They asked in return for loans that the proceeds be spent in purchases from their industries, or that their citizens be given place in the management of some enterprise. But in general they, as well as the British Government, favored the course of investment in Latin-America as a means of planting their enterprise in these countries and of assuring markets for their industries. They besides were rather eager to enable their banks to share more largely in the profits of Latin-American finance, which had been dominated by British institutions. After 1900 the German and French competition for government issues and for concessions became much more effectively active—especially in Argentina, Brazil, and Mexico. European investment in Latin-American countries was being augmented as rapidly as that in any part of the outside world—perhaps excepting Canada and Australia.

The future growth of American activity was already clearly foreshadowed. In many of the railroad enterprises, early and late, American adventurers, reputable and disreputable, had drawn the first plans and gathered together the necessary resources. In the mining and petroleum industries substantial investment was being made by well-established American groups, who possessed the resources to expand abroad as rapidly as they had at home. The Spanish-American War had left us with Caribbean possessions; the completion of the Panama Canal had signified the broadening of our circuit of commercial influence; we had intervened to take charge of the financial affairs of several small Caribbean states. Even in 1914 the record of foreign financial activity in Latin-America could not be written solely as a chapter of the outward spread of European savings.

CHAPTER VIII

NONINTERCOURSE BETWEEN FRANCE AND THE CENTRAL POWERS

THE BAN AGAINST GERMAN SECURITIES

EVEN between rival and inimical powers capital seeks to move, to pass frontiers ringed with bayonets, responding to some clearly perceived banking opportunity, some personal tie, or some need of home industry. But such movements are hesitant, and at the mercy of criticism. A few bankers and statesmen may believe that financial coöperation will create the means of compromising clashing interests and initiate political understanding. But if the antagonism and mutual fear be strong this is dismissed by others as a self-interested delusion. Thus when at the bottom of men's hearts and minds rests a sense that differences between their nation and another nation cannot be healed, financial coöperation loses force. It is restrained by governments which, expecting war, fear that their enemy will be strengthened; the restraint in itself becomes a source of antagonism as well as a standing notice of it. Such was the situation between France and the Central Powers.

French and German banking syndicates participated jointly in many loans that were issued in both markets, but this is merely a fugitive and not binding form of coöperation. There were a few personal and financial connections between the investment banks of the two countries. The German banks had participated in a few Paris houses. The National Bank für Deutschland was a shareholder in the Crédit Mobilier, the Deutsche Bank in Alfred Gans and Company, the Dresdner Bank controlled the Banque Allard. On the directorates of the largest French institutions were men of Austrian and German origin, who had retained banking connections with their former countries. French and German banks participated in the ownership of institutions in Holland and Belgium. Now and again, when the banks of both countries were drawn into the same situation they ventured upon a joint undertaking. The Deutsche Bank and the Banque Impériale Ottomane shared the launching of the Bagdad railway; German and French banks worked together in the Banca Commerciale Italiana, in a Consortium for Enterprises in Constantinople, and in the State Bank of Morocco. Besides, they participated jointly (along, often, with Belgian, Austrian, and English capital) in public utility enterprises and concessionary companies in Spain, Russia, South America, and Africa. But these were private participations by the investment banks which often did not appear in their balance sheets. No attempt was made to secure official listing for the securities of these enterprises; ordinarily, in fact, they were held closely by the banks and not offered for public sale. Even so, this coöperation was under criticism in France by a large section of opinion— and in the years directly before 1914 appears to have come to a standstill. The leaning toward coöperation grew weaker within the banking organizations themselves.[1]

The most important financial dealings between the two countries were through the free short-time loan market. The course of trade and the difference of interest rates between the two centers induced the French banks to make short-time loans to the German bankers secured on collateral or commercial paper, and to discount bills of exchange due in Germany. This was an aid to the commerce of both countries and continued despite a certain amount of popular dissatisfaction in France. After the Algeciras scare which occasioned a withdrawal of French funds, the amount of such short-time lending was reduced.

[1] For a detailed but somewhat unbalanced review of such Franco-German connections and coöperation by critics of them, see J. E. Favre, *Le Capital Français au Service de L'Étranger* (Paris, 1917), and Lysis, *Les Capitalistes Français contre la France* (Paris, 1909).

The course of industrial development in the two countries, especially the poverty of France in coal, and of Germany in iron ore, led to a certain amount of direct investment by the industrialists of each within the territories of the other. The French iron industry acquired ownership of coal properties and some factories in Germany. French commerce established branch offices. Frenchmen retained much property in Alsace-Lorraine.[2]

The German dye, chemical, and electrical industries set up branch factories or distributing plants in France. The German metallurgists and colliery owners acquired ore properties in the Meurthe and Moselle Basin, and in Normandy. Germany furnished half of the coke used by blast furnaces of Longwy-Briey and Nancy in France, while France shipped iron ore to the Westphalian iron and steel plants.[3] Therefore, an *entente* was arranged between French and German steel plants by which the French took financial participation in the German enterprise (Roechling) and obtained representation in the management. In return the German plants were given a share in French iron properties (the Aciéries de Longwy, at Valleroy) and financial participation in the company exploiting them. Thyssen owned two unexploited fields in the same basin and small properties elsewhere. But when he sought to extend this ownership in Normandy, to build a coking plant and foundry and run a railroad between mine and plant, opposition within France compelled him to accept a minority position in the venture; in return he was granted an option upon 40 per cent of the mineral product. All this German investment was, in the jingo press, denounced as a destructive and spy organization. It was attacked with excitement in every crisis in French-German relations.

2 F. Eccard, *Biens et Intérêts Français en Allemagne* (Paris, 1917).
3 M. Vigne, "Le Bassin de Briey," *Revue d'Économie Politique*, January–February, 1913; "Les Participations Français dans les Mines en Allemagne," *L'Information*, January 8, 1913.

In Algeria and Morocco, too, the German steel industry sought ore supplies by capital investment. The course of events in Morocco is related elsewhere. In Algeria the ore sought was located in the interior at L'Ouenza. Its utilization required the construction of a railroad of 240 kilometers to the port of Bône. The Algerian administration entered into agreements for the construction of this road with the International Consortium (French, German, and English) which had a concession for mining the ore, the Société des Mines de L'Ouenza. In this consortium the armament makers of all three countries were combined. The project was defeated, April, 1910, in the Chamber of Deputies, in a debate in which the German participation in the consortium was much emphasized. The Socialist party, disliking the combination of armament interests, also shared in the vote against the project. Out of the eighteen directors of the road, eleven were to have been French, as well as all the higher personnel.[4]

There can be little doubt that French public investment in German securities would have grown if they had been admitted to trading on the Paris Bourse. But the official though tacit ban applied after 1870 was never lifted. During that period when the Fashoda incident brought France near to Germany, a few German industrial securities were admitted to the Bourse, as, for example, the shares of the Goerz Company; but that period was brief.

Several times this official ban was brought into question when plans of French-German financial coöperation were considered as a way of easing political differences between the two countries. But these plans faded out and the ban remained. Certain French statesmen, notably Rouvier, up to September, 1905, and later Caillaux, favored such coöperation in the hope of bringing about a French-German

[4] *Le Marché Financier,* 1909–10, p. 857; P. Albin, *Le Coup D'Agadir* (Paris, 1912), pp. 129 *et seq.; Revue Politique et Parlementaire,* September, 1908, p. 624.

rapprochement, but this "financial pacifism," as it was called, was blocked by contrary opinion and events. The idea of collaboration between the financial enterprise of the two countries was put forward most seriously in the course of controversy over Morocco, and was arranged for in the accord of 1909. The German Government was ready to believe that this accord would broaden in significance and prepare the way for the introduction of German securities on the Paris Exchange. A few French banking houses were ready to give their friendly support, especially the Banque Impériale Ottomane and the Banque de Paris et Pays Bas, which wished to share in the German development in Turkey. But the main industrial and commercial groups fought the notion of collaboration and the admission of German securities with all their influence.[5] The accord collapsed, leaving only hard feeling behind it, and with it collapsed the possibility that German securities would be admitted to the Paris Bourse. When in 1911 the head of the Deutsche Bank, Von Gwinner, and the German Secretary of Foreign Affairs, proposed to the French Government that the privilege of official listing be granted in return for a free hand in Morocco, the proposal was not even discussed.[6] The lines of opposition were drawn too fast to hope for any useful consequence. In the state of feeling that existed financial intercourse, like all other intercourse between the two countries, would have ended only in resentment. The French policy must be regarded as merely one phase of the armed truce that prevailed. The

5 *Bulletin de la Fédération des Industriels et Commerçants Français,* June, 1909, and October, 1911.

6 J. Caillaux, *Agadir* (Paris, 1919); *ibid., Mes Prisons* (Paris, 1921), p. 12. The author declares that the Dresdner Bank bought an interest in the *Figaro,* which urged editorially (September, 1911) that German securities be admitted to the Bourse. An indication of how complete the French tried to make the embargo is given by the fact that during 1913, when the Sextuple Group loan to China was being negotiated, France opposed the issue of bonds that could be sold freely on all markets lest Germany sell its portion in Paris later. *Foreign Relations of the United States,* 1913, pp. 149–150.

ban itself emphasized the existing antagonism and made it more evident; but France chose not to risk having the force of loaned capital turned upon herself.

AUSTRIA-HUNGARY: THE ENDING OF A FINANCIAL FRIENDSHIP

FINANCIAL relations between France and Austria-Hungary changed significantly as Europe formed into two antagonistic groups. French capital, before and after 1870, financed the construction of two of the most important railroads in the Dual Monarchy, the Southern Railroad (Lombard), and the State Railroad. The securities of these roads were listed on the Paris Bourse. A Council of Administration representing the French interest met in Paris, and French investment therein remained substantial despite unsatisfactory treatment by the Austro-Hungarian Government. It was chiefly in the Dual Monarchy that the ill-fated Banque de Lyon et Loire and L'Union Générale carried out their work of phenomenal expansion, financing governments, banks, railways, port construction, till they failed in 1882. Up to 1890 Paris was a large purchaser of Austrian government securities, and the largest purchaser of Hungarian government securities. George Raphael Levy estimated that in the nineties the French investment stood at two billion francs.[7] That the gradual intensification of antipathy did not lead Frenchmen to dispose entirely of their holdings was shown in the post-war discussions of Austrian and Hungarian debt. Of the securities admitted under the Innsbruck Convention (Austrian and Hungarian government bonds and those of the State Railway Company), French investors were found to possess 35 millions of pounds sterling, German 27.6 millions of pounds, and

[7] G. R. Levy, "Les Capitaux Français à L'Étranger," *Revue des Deux Mondes*, March 15, 1897.

British 6.8 millions of pounds.[8] French-Austrian banking connections remained friendly. The Rothschild house in Paris worked intimately with the Austrian Rothschild. The French retained an interest in the important Austrian Länderbank, and with it and through its subsidiaries coöperated in the financing of Balkan governments and railways. They retained an interest in the Austrian and Hungarian Mortgage Banks. The Société Générale et Comptoir Nationale D'Escompte drew some of their higher officials from Austrian banking circles.[9]

But as continental alliances became fixed and French opinions came to regard Austrian policy as subordinated to German, as the tension between Austria and Russia grew acute, this financial coöperation fell under suspicion in France. Austrian securities were tacitly refused admission to the Paris Bourse. The ban was applied with a few exceptions to both industrial and government securities despite the pressure of interested banks.[10] At various times the government of the Dual Monarchy, like the German Government, sought to regain access. The matter was broached in connection with many of the diplomatic situations in which the interests of the two countries touched. As early as 1905–6 a disposition was indicated to make concessions for the privilege of borrowing in France. During the Moroccan crisis of that period, Von Aehrenthal, the Austro-Hungarian Foreign Minister, for this reason, shifted back and forth endeavoring to convince France of the Austro-Hungarian independence of Germany, and yet keep Germany reassured of his support.

[8] *Report of Council of Foreign Bondholders,* 1925, p. 80. The total French investment in Austria-Hungary was greatly in excess of this. One estimate of the Association Nationale des Porteurs Français puts it as high as 6.5 billion francs.

[9] For a detailed account of French-Austrian financial connections, see the "Mémoire" by N. L. Raffalovitch, the secret agent of the Russian Finance Ministry at Paris, *Livre Noir,* II, 262 *et seq.*

[10] In 1912 Poincaré, having refused listing to Hungarian government bonds, gave his sanction to small issues of the Crédit Foncier Autrichien.

The French market was held open to Hungarian securities after it had been closed to Austrian issues. French opinion was traditionally favorable to Magyar aims. For a long period it appears to have thought possible a dissolution of the Dual Monarchy. But after the Bosnian crisis of 1908–9, Hungarian government securities came under the ban. Even toward industrial and public utility securities it tended to apply. Russian opposition to their admission became firm and permanent. The French position became clear when Hungary, negotiating through Rothschilds, tried to use its former privilege of borrowing in Paris, in 1909, not long after the annexation of Bosnia and Herzegovina. Though Hungary asserted that the loan was to be used for other purposes, French and Russian opinion held that it would serve to pay off treasury bonds to defray expenses in the newly annexed provinces, and to strengthen military forces and fortifications. The opinion was correct.[11] Russia and the smaller Slav states immediately manifested opposition. Furthermore, French financial circles were incensed at the treatment received and losses sustained by the French bondholders of the South Austrian Railway.[12] The French Government appears to have asked as a condition of listing various minor economic concessions and guarantees that the loan funds would be used only for pacific purposes.[13] Intrigue, the ways of which have not been too clearly revealed, attended the discussions. According to M. Crozier, then French Ambas-

[11] The 1910 budget contained items of 339 thousand pounds for expenditures in the provinces, and 13.5 million pounds for army expenditure—an increase of 875 thousand pounds as compared with the preceding year, also 2.6 million pounds for naval expenditure. See analysis, "The Finances of Austria-Hungary," Great Britain. *Diplomatic and Consular Report No. 4367* (Cd. 4446–191, 1908–9).

[12] P. Leroy-Beaulieu, *Économiste Française,* August 13, 1910, pp. 234–235; *Le Marché Financier,* 1909–10, p. 83. French capital had participated largely in the financing of these railways by bond purchases. The French bondholders attributed their difficulties to the establishment of a competing line by the Austrian Government.

[13] Leroy-Beaulieu, *ibid.,* and France, *Commission du Budget, Affaires Étrangères,* Exercice, 1910, pp. 33–34.

sador to Vienna, the consent of the French Government was at one moment obtained; but in the final outcome the conditions proposed by the French Government were refused.[14] Terms, albeit poorer in their financial aspects than those obtainable in France, were arranged with a German and Austrian syndicate. The incident emphasized the antagonism between the continental alliances. Herr Kinderlen-Waechter, German Secretary of State for Foreign Affairs, publicly declared at the time: "The lesson shall not be lost. The conclusion of the loan will strengthen further the bonds which unite Germany and Austria-Hungary and mark the success of the countries that the French financial market wished to injure."[15]

In 1911 the French bankers headed by the Crédit Lyonnais distributed in Paris a bond issue of the City of Budapest, asking no official listing. The Russian Government was roused, though admitting that its French ally had no legal power to prevent the transaction. The Russian Minister at Paris, Isvolsky, stated fully the views of his government.

I have had recently to call the attention of the French Government repeatedly to the serious injury that certain financial enterprises undertaken by the French banks might cause to the essential Russian interest. Because of its enormous extension and its geographic peculiarities Russia is vulnerable on all parts of its periphery and cannot be equally strong on all fronts. . . .

The Ambassador continued:

It seems to me that the question of loans and of financial undertakings is precisely one wherein the unity of the major political interest of Russia and France should show itself most clearly. We must follow with an extremely vigilant eye French financial projects, and when these menace our in-

[14] P. Crozier, "L'Autriche et L'Avant-Guerre," *Revue de France,* June 1, 1921, p. 607.

[15] R. Recouly, *Revue Politique et Parlementaire,* October, 1910.

terest, exercise strong enough pressure on the French Government to check them.[16]

Despite all official assurance Russia remained anxious, fearful of the influence of financial circles upon the decisions of the French Government. But French official opinion was in accord with that of M. Isvolsky as shown in episodes arising thereafter. So were industrial circles with the possible exception of a few large groups having international connections.[17]

In November 1911, Count Von Aehrenthal, Foreign Secretary for Austria-Hungary, while discussing the question of adhesion to the Franco-German accord regarding Morocco, stated that this friendly action, taken without material compensation, ought to be reciprocated.[18] Shortly thereafter he made it clear that the form of reciprocation most desired was permission to borrow in Paris. The political relations between the two countries being excellent, he argued, economic coöperation should be encouraged also. He mentioned Morocco and the Orient as fields in which Austro-Hungarian political assistance might be extended. A vista of even further concession was vaguely painted. "We expect," the imperial official wrote, "to ask for the good-will of the French Government in the interest of Austrian and Hungarian finances. We shall choose for this demand a moment when the international political situation is favorable to transactions of the kind."[19] Von Aehrenthal consulted with the Hungarian Minister of Finance as to the form and substance of the favor to be asked. It was decided that the French Government be asked merely for a secret declaration that if the Imperial Government should seek to borrow in Paris dur-

---

[16] *Livre Noir*, I, 90–93.

[17] See, e.g., article in the *Bulletin des Industriels et Commerçants*, June, 1909, for the point of view of industrial circles.

[18] Crozier, *op. cit.*, p. 616; *Documents Diplomatiques Français, 1871–1914*, 3d ser., Vol. I, No. 10.

[19] *Documents Diplomatiques Français, 1871–1914*, 3d ser., Vol. I, Nos. 152, 168.

206   *Europe: The World's Banker: 1870–1914*

ing the next three years up to a billion crowns—half for
Austria and half for Hungary—that the French Government would place no obstacle in the way of the transaction.[20]

M. Crozier, French Ambassador in Vienna, urged that
the occasion be seized to weaken the Austro-Hungarian
Alliance with Germany. In the sketch of his hopes, Austria-Hungary was to give a promise that she would not
support Germany in aggressive war, and France was to
act to bring Austria-Hungary and Russia closer together.
At the time it was widely believed that Caillaux was sympathetic to the arrangement for admitting Austrian loans
with some such general purpose.[21] But the official documents indicate the contrary; Caillaux rebuffed the advance.[22] Fires of criticism had previously been lit in press
and Parliament by the flying sparks of rumor.[23] When
Poincaré succeeded Caillaux into power, he repeated the
refusal and gave the Russian Government assurance that
it would be maintained.[24] Upon Crozier's interest, upon
his expression of hope of a reconciliation between Austria-
Hungary and the French-Russian allies, Poincaré casts a
peculiar light. "The exceptional interest that our Ambassador showed in the financial relations of France and the
Monarchy decided the government to replace him by a
less fantastic diplomat and to ask M. Klotz to have a director's post reserved for him in a bank."[25]

[20] *Österreich-Ungarns Aussenpolitik,* Vol. III, Nos. 2877, 2885, 2902,
2937, 2942.

[21] Crozier, *op. cit.,* p. 616; R. Poincaré, *Au Service de la France,* I,
244.

[22] The Foreign Minister, De Selves, seems to have managed to give
the impression to the Austro-Hungarian Government that he personally
was favorable to the plan, while indicating to the Serbian Government
that he opposed it. Compare *Österreich-Ungarns Aussenpolitik,* Vol. III,
Nos. 3050, 3080, and M. Boghitschevitsch, *Die Auswärtige Politik
Serbiens, 1903–1914,* No. 1621.

[23] *Débats Parl. Chambre de Députés,* December 19, 1911.

[24] *Documents Diplomatiques Français, 1871–1914,* 3d ser., Vol. I, Nos.
329, 371, 382, 425.

[25] Poincaré, *op. cit.,* p. 268. Crozier became a director of the Société
Générale and of the Austrian Agrarian Bank.

The French refusal caused embarrassment in Vienna. Austria-Hungary was forced to issue treasury bonds for military expenses and resort even to the costly New York market to dispose of some.[26] Though the Imperial Government resented the refusal, the stimulus of further need made steadily more acute by the growth of military expenditure, led it again to risk refusal in 1913–14.[27] The outlay for military preparation had increased over 40 per cent in five years. A favorable opportunity seemed to present itself in connection with a plan of internationalizing the Balkan railways as a means of ending the strife of which they were the subject. The Dual Monarchy showed itself willing to admit French capital to almost controlling ownership in the international system which was to comprehend lines in Serbia, Greece, and those of the Oriental railways, the shares of which were then in the hands of the Austrian banks. It accepted the idea that the president of the managing company should be French. M. Pichon, the Secretary of Foreign Affairs, appears to have been well disposed to the plan of internationalization, to have at least lent ear to the arguments of the French financiers that the arrangement should be a prelude to a *détente* in the Balkans.[28] The financial groups in charge of the negotiations were led by Count Vitali and Herr Sieghart, Governor-General of the Austrian Boden-Kreditanstalt, in which the Banque de Paris et Pays Bas had an interest; included in it also were M. Doumer, former French Minister of Finance. Through these the Austro-Hungarian Government hoped to regain access to the Paris market.[29]

[26] *Le Marché Financier,* 1912–13, pp. 604–605; *Österreich-Ungarns Aussenpolitik,* Vol. V, No. 4763.

[27] The army estimates had by 1913 mounted to 18.9 million pounds, the naval estimates to 5.9 million pounds. "The Finances of Austria-Hungary, 1913," Great Britain. *Diplomatic and Consular Report No. 5321* (Cd. 7048–47, 1913).

[28] *Die Grosse Politik,* Vol. XXXVII, No. 15126, footnote 15130, footnote 15131.

[29] *Ibid.,* No. 15140. It tried to connect the discussions at one point

So strong was the wish to obtain its aim that the Austro-Hungarian Government made concessions that would
have weakened its former Balkan policy. So strong it was
that the government withstood, throughout a tense argument, the demand of the German Government that German interests in the Turkish railways be safeguarded by
excluding from the scheme the eastern lines of the Oriental
railways—those connecting with the Anatolian railway
and remaining in Turkish territory.[30] The German banks,
supported by their government, wished to repurchase the
shares that would give control of these lines; or, failing
that, they asked that the lines be kept in Austro-Hungarian ownership and that they be given representation on
the directing board. From the shifting arguments put
forward by the Austro-Hungarian Foreign Office, it does
not appear clearly whether the French group and government had been promised a share in the eastern lines.
The Austro-Hungarian Government denied it in February, 1914, yet showed itself resistant to German
requests, and fearful of losing French favor. A compromise was being arranged when the general plan of internationalization began to sag toward failure.

As related elsewhere, the causes of the failure were
complex and numerous. It remains doubtful whether the
French Government would have reversed its policy toward
Austrian and Hungarian loans, even though the plan had
been matured. On that point the whole affair was probably
little more than a trial of wits, in which Austria-Hungary
tried to find a way out of its controversy with Serbia and
to borrow in France without any basic shift in policy. The
French and Russian Government demands, in the last instance, would probably have cut deeper into the Austro-

with the question of admission to listing of the bonds of the Metropoli-
tan Street Railway of Vienna, but the French Government ignored the
approach. *Livre Noir*, II, 215.

[30] *Die Grosse Politik*, Vol. XXXVII, Nos. 15132, 15133, 15135, 15137,
15140 contain the gist of the discussions.

Hungarian position than these preliminary negotiations reveal. The French market remained closed, a standing mark of the opposition soon to be stirred to war. Austro-Hungarian financial necessities remained embarrassing.

CHAPTER IX

THE FINANCING OF IMPERIAL RUSSIA

THE LARGEST BORROWER IN EUROPE

RUSSIA was the largest borrowing country of pre-war Europe, and the greatest undeveloped region. Its own people, gifted in so many directions, showed only small capacity for modern industrial activity, and the energies of its absolute government were all too much absorbed in court intrigue and military ambition. The system of taxation was ineffective. The available domestic capital was insufficient for the introduction of modern industry, for public works, or for the needs of a government budget that bore the cost of large military forces and a program of railroad construction over immense areas. Russia turned to foreign capital.

The investment of foreign capital in Russia rose steadily from 1870 to 1914. From 1893 to 1912, taking the ordinary and extraordinary budgets together, the Russian Treasury had an almost uninterrupted deficit. The directly incurred debt of the Russian Government mounted as follows:[1]

Year	Amount (millions of rubles)	Per cent held by foreigners
1895	5,775	30
1899	6,122	37
1904	6,681	46
1909	8,850	46
1914	8,811	48

In 1914, in addition, foreign investors held 870 millions of rubles of other securities bearing the government guaranty, 422 millions of rubles of Russian municipal loans.

[1] L. Pasvolsky and H. G. Moulton, *Russian Debts and Reconstruction* (New York, 1924), pp. 17–21. This is somewhat lower than most estimates—compare L. Martin, *Revue Politique et Parlementaire*, February, 1921.

Still it is to be observed that between 1909 and 1914 Russian public credit improved along with Russian production and trade. The direct government obligations were selling in 1914 to yield little in excess of that of German government securities. The service of these direct obligations in 1913–14 made up about 13.7 per cent of the ordinary public expenditure; the total government debt, foreign and domestic, required about 21 per cent.[2] But these figures minimize the burden. For the revenue-collecting power of the government remained small and handicapped. Direct taxes yielded little. More than half the total revenue was derived from the sale of alcohol and the revenues of the railways (which, however, required a larger current expenditure than the revenues they brought). From the other economic activities of the country, not much was secured for the government purse. Of the total government borrowing more than a third was incurred for railroad construction. But according to Count Witte, about 37 per cent of the railways constructed had been built primarily for political and military reasons, not economic. Of the direct government debt owned abroad in 1914, 80 per cent was held in France, 14 per cent in Great Britain.

The sum of foreign capital invested in private enterprise exceeded two billions of rubles—par value. The French were the largest investors in private enterprise, as well as the freest lenders to the government. They owned about one-third of the investment, the British slightly less than one-quarter, the Germans about one-fifth.[3] Such were the sums of foreign capital which came to finance the Russian Government and to build Russian industry. This

[2] See P. N. Apostol's study entitled "Credit Operations" in volume entitled *Russian Public Finance During the War* (New Haven, 1928).

[3] L. J. Lewery, *Foreign Capital Investments in Russian Industries and Commerce* (United States Bureau of Foreign and Domestic Commerce, Miscellaneous Series, No. 124, Washington, 1923), p. 5. These figures are only rough approximations because of the complex difficulties of evaluation. They are derived from original data collected by the Russian Commissariat of Finance, Institute of Economic Research. The totals given do not include investment in railways.

movement of capital was influenced and guided not only
by pecuniary calculation, by economic plans, but by the
stir of political arrangements. No capital movement was
more important in shaping the destinies of the continent.

FRENCH CAPITAL SERVES THE ALLIANCE

NEIGHBORING Germany up to 1886–87 was a large sub-
scriber to Russian loans. German capital had been drawn
into Russia by the friendliness of the monarchs, and the
attraction to German technical and financial competence
of Russia's resources and markets. Its free movement was
interrupted by an action of Chancellor Bismarck in 1887.
Up to almost the year it was taken, the Chancellor had
regarded with satisfaction the Russian drafts upon Germany's increasing capital strength. In 1884 he even permitted the Seehandlung, the Prussian state bank, to receive subscriptions for a large Russian loan, so that its
success might be assured by this sign of official favor.

Shortly after, however, Germany began to draw back
from further commitments. Within German financial
circles doubts were entertained as to Russia's solvency.
Early in 1886 Russia's negotiations with the Diskonto-
Gesellschaft, Rothschild, and other German bankers for
the conversion of large amounts of government and railway debt failed. The failure was repeated later in the
year when a new loan was sought. In January, 1887,
Chancellor Bismarck emphasized the fact that Germany
had already absorbed 1,200 million rubles of Russian
securities while British investors were selling them. The
manner of statement was taken to be a warning against
further German investment. Various economic and political matters at issue between the two countries created
an atmosphere of nervous sharpness and suspicion. Russia had passed a decree prohibiting alien ownership of
landed property near its western frontier, and the employment of aliens as estate managers in these regions; this
affected German interests adversely. The two governments

were in dispute over tariff matters. Discussions regarding the renewal of the Dreikaiserbund did not progress and the renewal of the Triple Alliance made Russia suspicious.[4] The Russian press was showing hostility to Austria and Bulgaria. Out of this swirl of ill-feeling a press campaign arose in Germany urging the sale of Russian securities. If Bismarck did nothing to stimulate this campaign, which is doubtful, he certainly did nothing to check it.[5] The campaign took effect and Russian securities fell seriously in value, but Russia did not yield to the pressure.

In November, 1887, Bismarck made the final irritated move, and instructed the Reichsbank to refuse to accept Russian bonds as collateral security for loans, and to inform its customers that Russian credit was not sound.[6] Simultaneously, the press campaign increased its intensity. Whether mistrust, wrath, or overconfidence, or all three, dictated this overt action, it is impossible to be sure.[7] That Bismarck did not want to alienate Russia permanently is shown by the pains he had taken during the year to satisfy Russian complaints against Austria, and the concessions he made in the drafting of the Reinsurance Treaty signed with Russia in June, 1887. Probably the action would never have been taken if Bismarck had not mistakenly believed that Russia's financial dependence on Germany would cause her to show herself more compliant

[4] Among the incidents contributing to the suspicion was the publication of a forged letter of Bismarck promising support against Russia to Ferdinand if he accepted the throne of Bulgaria.

[5] *Geschichte der Frankfurter Zeitung* (Frankfurt, 1911), pp. 584 *et seq.*

[6] *Die Grosse Politik*, Vol. V, No. 1142. As J. Viner, "International Finance and Balance of Power Diplomacy, 1890–1914," *Southwestern Political and Social Science Quarterly*, March, 1929, p. 3, points out, the direct financial effects of this action were small. The importance was in the emphatic indication of an official veto on Russian loans. It was accompanied by decisions of the German courts declaring Russian securities ineligible for trust funds in Germany; *Economist*, July 16, 1887, p. 911.

[7] *Die Grosse Politik*, Vol. V, No. 1140. None of the published documents furnish an adequate account of Bismarck's reasoning.

to German wishes. It was a maneuver intended to weaken
Russian credit, to remind her of German strength. That
it should have been used by a diplomat of Bismarck's
astuteness remains a puzzling matter despite the opening
of the archives. For it failed completely of effect, and the
danger of which Bismarck was acutely aware—that Russia transfer its allegiance to France—soon became reality.
Russia found the means of meeting its emergency needs
in France. During 1888 Bismarck struck out at Russia
and began to talk of the necessity of defense on two sides.[8]
Bismarck's emphatic gesture became a milestone for great
events. In 1893 the German Ambassador at St. Petersburg
reported that De Giers, the Russian Foreign Minister,
said to him: "Bismarck drove us into the arms of France,
especially through his financial measures. How was it possible to exclude Russian securities from the Reichsbank
just a few days before the arrival of the Czar?"[9] Though
this statement may be regarded as deliberate overem-
phasis, it is undoubtedly true that the shift of Russian
financial connections became a vital element in the making
of new alliances that was to follow. A page had been flung
back in mistrust or anger. Bismarck and his successors
could never again find the same place in the story.

In France, Russian borrowing found scope and encouragement. Discussions about new loans alternated with,
became an essential part of, discussions regarding political
alliance. It was no easy task for these two countries to
find and define a jointly acceptable basis for alliance; in
particular it was no easy task to overcome the Czar's dislike for the democratic, anticlerical French state, and
his discomfort over separation from the imperial dynasties
of Germany and Austria. But stage by stage Russian
policy was influenced in that direction. Probably among
the attractions offered to the Czar by this new policy was
the opportunity to complete the Trans-Siberian Railway,

[8] P. Albin, *La Paix Armée* (Paris, 1913), pp. 255 *et seq.*
[9] *Die Grosse Politik,* Vol. VII, No. 1655.

and the satisfaction of showing Russia to be capable of standing up to Germany.

It is clear that negotiations for borrowing in France were already under way before Bismarck's declaration. The financial agent of the Russian Government in Paris at the time, De Cyon, relates that even prior to it he was cultivating connections and formulating plans to make Paris the main market for Russian securities, and that French banks, including Rothschild, had indicated their willingness to coöperate.[10] A minor conversion loan had been carried through successfully and official listing had been granted to the Russian loans of 1867 and 1869. After Bismarck's declaration a syndicate was organized in Paris to support Russian securities and to undertake the flotation of Russian loans. It had the favoring support of the French Government. Speedily thereafter Russian borrowing assumed large dimensions. Within ten years the French came to possess Russian government and industrial securities in excess of three billions of rubles.

These were the years in which the Alliance was elaborated. As early as 1887 the French Government had begun to indicate its desire for an alliance and to make clear that assurance of continued political friendship was desirable if Russia was to benefit greatly from French financial aid.[11] The idea of an alliance received clear utterance in August, 1890, in which year Germany had refused to renew its "re-insurance" treaty with Russia, since it did not wish to support Russian aims in the Near East, and regarded the treaty as incompatible with its obligations to its other allies. In August, 1891, a general and rather

10 E. De Cyon, *Histoire de l'Entente Franco-Russe* (3d ed., Paris, 1895), p. 237. This narrative account by the Russian agent contains many details that cannot be corroborated. It is disorderly, packed by hatreds, and makes inordinate claims for the author. De Cyon, p. 238, claims to have been the moving spirit in these arrangements. Other authors ascribe the initiative to the banking firm of Hoskier, e.g., G. Michon, *L'Alliance Franco-Russe* (Paris, 1927), p. 3. But this De Cyon, with deprecatory comments, denies.

11 Michon, *loc. cit.*

vague understanding was negotiated between the two governments. But earlier in that year, while the Czar was still holding back his final approval of this step, Russian plans for borrowing in Paris were badly upset.

A large Russian loan had been arranged with a syndicate headed by the Rothschilds, who had handled much of the previous borrowing. This firm, on short notice, withdrew from the arrangements, explaining its action by the persecution of the Jews within Russia. The loan could not be carried through. By various authorities this action has been construed to be an "ill-concealed" pretext to force the Russian Government to sign the desired understanding.[12] So it was construed at the time by the Russian and German governments.[13] Certainly, too, the Russian Treasury was seriously embarrassed and made excited efforts to meet their needs by other arrangements. But there is no evidence to prove that the Rothschilds acted on the instructions of the French Government, rather than on their own initiative; the evidence tends to run the other way.[14]

The Crédit Lyonnais, with the consent of the French Government, undertook the loan later in the year. Thereafter that establishment became the chief financial counselor and distributing agent of Russian loans in France.[15] Unsure of the success of this new syndicate, the Russian Government asked the French Minister to permit the Crédit Foncier, an institution under official direction, to participate. With reluctance the necessary authority was granted.[16] The loan was issued in October, 1891. The German Government had discouraged German participation. Despite an initial oversubscription, its value began to de-

[12] E.g., W. L. Langer, "The Franco-Russian Alliance," *Slavonic Review*, III, 566–570.

[13] *Ibid.*, IV, 86.   [14] Viner, *op. cit.*, p. 5.

[15] Michon, *op. cit.*, p. 25.

[16] E. Daudet, *Histoire Diplomatique de l'Alliance Franco-Russe, 1873–1893* (3d ed., Paris, 1894), pp. 262 *et seq.*

cline. The Russian Treasury had to organize a syndicate to support it by repurchase of the undigested supply.[17]

A keen awareness of financial need and financial dependence, strikingly displayed in this episode, must have been among the influences which led the Czar to accept the understanding in August, 1891.[18] But strong circumstances of a political nature were also drawing the two countries together. They had reason to suppose that Great Britain had joined the Triple Alliance and that Germany had become a party to British arrangements for maintaining the *status quo* throughout the Mediterranean area.[19] France and Russia both felt isolated by these arrangements, and each entertained wishes to disturb the distribution of power along the Mediterranean. This first vague Franco-Russian understanding was given precision by the signature of a military convention in 1892 which was finally ratified by Russia in 1893. French skill in allaying the mistrust of the Czar and manipulation of the inducements proved effective.

Throughout the period of the alliance the sale of Russian securities was aided by government favor which found a response in the concerted and widespread efforts of the banks. At the outbreak of the war, French investors held between eleven and twelve billion francs of Russian securities of which over nine billion were direct or indirect obligations of the Russian Government; 52 loans of this character were admitted to official quotation. No securities,

---

[17] *Die Grosse Politik,* Vol. VII, No. 1516; Report of M. Margaine, *Rapport sur le Livre Jaune Relatif à l'Alliance Franco-Russe* (Chambre de Députés, Document No. 6036, 1919), p. 17.

[18] Langer, *op. cit.,* p. 170, states that the French Government "had made it obvious that a loan could only be had in return for an alliance." After the signature of the military convention in 1893 the German Ambassador in Paris expressed the judgment that financial reasons were a factor of some importance in Russian action but not the leading one. *Die Grosse Politik,* Vol. VII, No. 1533.

[19] Langer, *op. cit.,* p. 169, and his later, more complete study, *The Franco-Russian Alliance, 1890–1894* (Cambridge, 1929); See also *Documents Diplomatiques. L'Alliance Franco-Russe* (1918), p. 4, and the report of Margaine, *op. cit.*

except the French *rentes*, were more widely owned by
people of small savings—clerks, shopkeepers, industrial
workers, peasants. The Property Office (L'Office des biens
et intérêts privés) established by the French Government
after the war received 1,600,000 individual declarations
from owners of Russian securities. The forces of patriotic
feeling, of government persuasion, and of banking effort,
did their work thoroughly. Step by step the French Government was led by the turns and developments of its
political situation and of the alliance. The banks, called
in repeatedly to aid, undertook the assignment not unwill-
ingly. Many of these Russian loans brought unusually
large commissions, and the placement was easy and soon
accomplished. Besides, they and their clients gradually
acquired ownership of Russian resources and enterprises
which needed government orders to prosper. Toward the
end the large volume of Russian securities already possessed by their depositors would have compelled them to
support Russian credit, even though they might have
wished to curtail new loans. The Russian Government
fought doubts and criticism by argument, by publicity, by
decorations, and by bribery of virtually all the Paris
press.[20] In over a hundred banks, the Russian Government
and its Imperial Bank kept large sums on deposit (over
700 million rubles, June 11, 1913), whenever its resources
permitted—sums which drew but 2 to 3 per cent interest;
more than half of these were left in the French banks.

The loans of the early period were issued at an average
effective interest rate of little over 4 per cent; for the
loans of the later years, especially after 1904, the effective
interest well exceeded 5 per cent but in the interval the
yield of most bonds underwent a corresponding change.

Each Russian entry into the Paris market was preceded
by discussions between the two governments which touched
upon the uses of their funds and many aspects of their

[20] See documents published in *L'Humanité,* December, 1923–March,
1924.

joint policy.[21] The Russian Government maintained in Paris a representative to guard and manage its credit there, negotiate with government officials, bankers, and journalists. But important loan transactions were handled directly by the Ministers of Finance and Foreign Affairs (or even the Czar occasionally). The French Cabinet, through agents in Russia, kept vigilantly informed of the state of Russian finances and expressed their anxieties in interministerial notes. For the course of borrowing did not always run smoothly. Deferring to the popular opposition which manifested itself from time to time, or worried over some phase of Russian policy, the French Government often evaded, postponed or made conditional the financial requests of the Russian Government, and tried to turn them to political or economic advantage. In the earlier years the chief grounds for objection were financial, in the later years, political. In 1897, the French Ministry of Finance voiced protest against the introduction of various issues of Russian securities into France by the Crédit Lyonnais, which disposed of them by private sale and did not ask official listing. In 1899 other protests were made against the introduction of a Russian internal loan.[22] In 1900, Caillaux, holding the portfolio of finance for the time being refused official listing to all new Russian borrowing.[23] The opposition was overcome in 1901 when Russia promised to devote the proceeds of the borrowing primarily to strategic railways agreed upon by the French and Russian General staffs.[24]

During the war with Japan, Russia relied mainly on the French market for war loans, and the French Government and banks exerted themselves in Russia's behalf.

21 See report of Margaine, *op. cit.*
22 Michon, *op. cit.*, pp. 128 *et seq.*
23 *Ibid.*, p. 227.
24 *Documents Diplomatiques Français* (1871–1914), 2d ser., Nos. 159, 239, 251, 263, 329. On the one end the Emperor overruled Witte, on the other Delcassé convinced Caillaux. The lines were to hasten Russian concentration at the Prussian front 4 days.

But by the end of 1905 Russian credit even in France was exhausted. Count Witte proceeded to the peace negotiations at Portsmouth, knowing that he could borrow no more till peace was arranged.[25] After the conclusion of peace new difficulties presented themselves. The continuous financial aid of a tyrannous government was subjected to bitter criticism by the French radical and socialist groups. They resisted the issue of new loans which would enable the Russian Government to cement its absolutism, and suppress by violence the constitutional movement.[26] Count Witte had opened loan negotiations in Paris almost immediately after the peace treaty was signed. He made known how imperative it was that the loan be procured before the Duma met in the following May for that body would ask that the ministers be responsible to it. Some doubt existed as to the legality under the new constitution of a loan issued without the approval of the Duma.[27] Rothschild refused to participate, and the other banks held back in the face of the criticism.[28] But the banks yielded to the appeal of the Premier, who had probably secured in return a promise of support in the conference at Algeciras.[29] The issue of the loan was deferred while that conference dragged on, but finally in April, 1906, it was sold. This was the loan which was characterized as "the loan that saved Russia" by enabling it to suppress revolution and to maintain the gold standard. Of it, Gorki remarked, "Every French citizen who buys the loan is an accomplice in the organized murder of a people." While Clémenceau wrote in the *Aurore*, "After having furnished the Czar with the financial resources which were destined to lead to his defeat abroad, it now remains for us to sup-

---

[25] T. Dennet, *Roosevelt and the Russo-Japanese War* (New York, 1925), p. 310. See also M. A. DeW. Howe, *G. Von Lengerke Meyer* (New York, 1920), pp. 202, 231.

[26] *Débats Parl. Chambre de Députés,* February 8, 1907.

[27] Viner, *op. cit.,* p. 10.

[28] *L'Européen,* January 20, 1906.

[29] *Ibid.,* and Michon, *op. cit.,* p. 133.

ply him with the financial resources destined to assure his victory over his own subjects."[30] The loan was to have been issued in New York, Berlin, and London, as well as Paris. But the American bankers retired, and the German bankers were instructed by their government to do likewise. The British participation prepared the way for the Russo-British understanding. Renewed criticism greeted the issue of the loan. M. Pichon promised the Chamber of Deputies, early in 1907, that there would be no further immediate Russian borrowing.[31] But M. Isvolsky rushed to Paris to meet the crisis by securing credit in the form of orders executed in France and payable in the future. Thus the promise was evaded. Ministerial declarations ran one way, action the other way.[32] Strengthened by the funds it now possessed the Imperial Government soon dissolved the Duma. That body, meeting after dissolution, resolved that they would not recognize the loan of 1906.

Because of the undercurrent of hostility kept alive in radical circles, the Russian Government followed the rise and fall of French cabinets with intense care, working out fresh plans and combinations of influences to assure its position in the capital market under quickly changing ministries. In 1912 the Russian Minister in Paris informed his Foreign Office:

I've just received a visit from M. Poincaré, the new Prime Minister and Minister of Foreign Affairs . . . I did not dissimulate that in certain questions, for example, in the affair of the Quadruple Syndicate, his predecessor, M. Caillaux, had not considered our interests sufficiently, and I expressed the hope that under him, these matters would take a more favorable turn.[33]

[30] Quoted in B. Russell, *The Policy of the Entente, 1909–1914,* pp. 43–44.

[31] *Débats Parl. Chambre de Députés,* February 8, 1907; *British Documents,* IV, 274.

[32] R. Millet, *Revue Politique et Parlementaire,* March, 1907.

[33] *Livre Noir,* I, 180.

In 1913 when avid borrowers, especially the Balkan states, were waiting their turn to approach the French investors, and the French Government itself contemplated a loan, the Russian Government sought permission to arrange for the flotation of railway securities at the rate of a half billion francs annually for a number of years. The French Government gave its assent only after it secured a promise that the effective military strength of the Russian army should be increased, and that Russia would commence immediately the construction of designated strategic railroad lines, agreed upon in advance with the French General Staff, a condition for which a more elastic formula was substituted in later negotiations.[34] One of the appreciated advantages to Russia of this agreement was that for a period of years it safeguarded the Russian Treasury against changes of ministry in France and the advent into power of leaders not as friendly as Poincaré.[35] In such arrangements as these the two governments adjusted their interests and purposes.

Besides the direct obligations of the Imperial Government, and the railway and bank securities to which it gave its guarantee, numerous loan issues of Russian cities found a market in France. In large volume, too, French capital undertook the development of industrial enterprises in Russia, investing over a billion and a half francs. This went partly into banks, insurance companies, public utilities, naval constructions, but above all into mines, textile and metallurgical works. The metallurgical works were dependent upon the Russian Government for armament and railroad equipment orders, and were in intimate relations with both governments.[36] The L'Union Parisienne, the Paris bank which took the lead in financing this industrial development, had close connection with Schneider & Company (French armament interests) and with them "began in 1912 to work out a general plan to participate

---

[34] *Livre Noir*, II, 439 *et seq.*   [35] *Ibid.*, p. 409.
[36] E. Baldy, *Les Banques des Affaires* (Paris, 1922), p. 162.

in the munitions and materials orders for the Russian army and navy."[37] The French Government encouraged this process of investment and occasionally took measures to advance it.[38]

The heavy accumulated investment of the French in Russian securities (they formed 25 per cent of all French foreign investments) was a direct consequence of the alliance. The continued dependence of Russia upon French finance enabled the French Government to exercise a measure of control or influence over Russian policy—to restrain its actions in the Near East and sustain its opposition to Germany. On the other hand, once the sums loaned had grown great they strengthened the necessity of making French foreign policy conform to Russian aims, a further cause of unwillingness to risk the rupture of the alliance. Debtor and creditor were firmly bound to each other, but debtor, in this case, was the more exigent and the more aggressive in political plans. A succinct judgment of Mr. Hawtrey upon some results of the relationship deserves quotation.

For a class of people whose motive was to lay by for the future, the lending of money to a reactionary and corrupt autocracy whose history was visibly written in terms of war

[37] Report of the L'Union Parisienne, 1913.

[38] *Rapport du Commission du Budget, Affaires Étrangères,* Exercice, 1914. For example, in March, 1914, the Russian metallurgical factories, Poutiloff, wanted to increase their capital, and gave an option to a Russian private bank, in which Krupp possessed an interest. The French Government caused this arrangement to be set aside and induced Creusot to enter negotiations to supply the capital. See *Livre Noir,* II, 254–255. For another interpretation of the incident, which it is difficult to check up, see F. Delaisi, *La Paix par le Droit,* February and May, 1914. According to this author this plant made artillery of both French and German models and employed French and German personnel and was controlled by French armament firms. A rival French-English group, formed by Vickers, Maxim, and la Société Homecourt, supported by the Société Générale, entered the field and stirred up the first group which was having difficulty in securing further financial aid in France The outcry against the growth of German influence was, according t(Delaisi, cover for an attempt to force the French banks to furnish mor' capital.

and revolution seems to be a curious choice. But if we regard mercantilism, like diplomacy, as virtual war, the system grows more intelligible. Instead of leaving the investor to choose sound international securities, which could be realized in time of war, he was induced to hand over his money directly to pay for the construction of railways and munitions for an allied country by way of preparation. The investor lost his money, because when the war came, the ally could not stand the strain. The strategic railways were not finished, the munitions were inadequate, the government was inefficient and corrupt. Still the investment was not wholly fruitless. Russia, at any rate, kept seventy divisions occupied for three years. And the investor might have chosen apparently much sounder investments . . . with no better pecuniary result.[39]

THE GERMAN GOVERNMENT INTERVENES

THE decree issued by Bismarck in 1887 remained in force until 1894. It was repealed in that year after the two countries had negotiated a new commercial treaty which settled tariff matters between them for a few years. While the decree was in force no new Russian public borrowing took place in Berlin, though some conversions, especially of railroad securities, occurred, and the German banks and investors may have bought Russian short-time treasury bonds. Bismarck had been willing to modify its force in the summer of 1889 when Russia sought admission to listing on the Berlin Stock Exchange of railway bonds issued as part of its conversion plans. But the Kaiser and his advisers opposed the request, arguing that German capital must not be used to strengthen Russia and criticizing Bismarck for his conciliatory inclinations.[40] The re-

---

[39] R. G. Hawtrey, *The Economic Problem* (London, 1925), p. 282.

[40] W. L. Langer, *The Franco-Russian Alliance, 1890–1894*, pp. 34–35. The Berlin market took a small share of the Russian 4 per cent Conversion Loan in December, 1888, but the Reichsbank raised its rate at the time of the issue. *Economist*, December 15, 1888. See also W. H. C. Laves, *German Governmental Influence on Foreign Investments, 1871–1914*.

fusal further strengthened the suspicions of the Czar. The difference of opinion between Bismarck and the Kaiser forecast the more violent differences on the same subject which ended in the dismissal of Bismarck, and the refusal to renew the treaty with Russia.

In 1891, Russia, pushing forward with railroad construction and eager to improve its military equipment, contemplated a large program of borrowing. There was doubt whether the Paris market could meet the need, even with the assistance of Amsterdam and Brussels, because of contemporaneous financial troubles and resentment by Jewish bankers of the persecutions of the Jews in Russia. As already related, borrowing arrangements made in Paris were disrupted by the withdrawal of the Rothschild firm. When a new syndicate was formed, German participation was invited by De Giers, the Russian Foreign Minister. Two important German banks were prepared to share in the issue. The German Government, when consulted, gave a noncommittal reply. But it indicated through a semiofficial organ that the Lombard Verbot still stood. The banks withdrew. Though the German Government assured the Russian that it had maintained a passive attitude and that the bankers had been driven by public opinion, it is probable that definite instructions to abstain were conveyed to the bankers.[41] Chancellor Caprivi was probably fearful lest he further aggravate ill-feeling in Russia, but doubtful as to the wisdom of permitting this loan which would be used to strengthen Russia's railways. Too, much of German opinion was hostile. Commercial relations were still strained; Jewish banking circles were antagonistic; agricultural interests were opposed to foreign lending in general; current losses in foreign investment were great. The Kaiser appears to have held to the belief that a Franco-Russian alliance was out of the question.[42] Throughout 1892 the German market continued

[41] *Die Grosse Politik,* Vol. VII, No. 1515; Langer, *Slavonic Review,* IV, 86.

[42] *Die Grosse Politik,* Vol. VII, No. 1522.

to turn aside Russian advances, and the German Government continued to assert that it was neutral in the matter. However, by the end of that year it had awakened to the probability of a Russian-French alliance, and was construing the renewed French financial assistance as a sign of agreement.[43] After the repeal of the Lombard Verbot in 1894, German banks participated in a large Russian conversion loan. They had in the main resented the enforced sacrifice and loss of business.

Shortly after the beginning of the new century the Russian Government was again admitted to the official German market. The German bankers were apparently approached in 1900. The German representative in London relates that in June, 1900, he was recalled to Berlin for a conference in the Foreign Office convoked to consider whether Russian loans should be permitted.[44] Shortly thereafter, under instruction from the Foreign Office and with the aid of the London house of Rothschild, this diplomat organized a campaign against Russian finance in the English press, employing false telegrams.[45] But a Russian loan was announced while the German Emperor was entertaining the Czar, and issued in 1902. Both Chancellor Von Bülow and the Kaiser would have liked to restrain the lending banks, unless Russia gave pledges in regard to future tariff policy, but acted cautiously lest they again embitter the situation.[46] A refusal would have emphasized too strongly, it was judged, France's value as an ally.[47] After the loan was made it was revealed that Witte had resorted to the German market in order to prove to the French Government that other resources were

43 *Die Grosse Politik,* Vol. VII, No. 1522.

44 Von Eckardstein, *op. cit.,* II, 182.

45 *Ibid.,* pp. 240 *et seq.*

46 *Die Grosse Politik,* Vol. XVIII, Nos. 5404, 5405, 5407. The Chancellor expressed the opinion that Mendelssohn must not put his interest above state interest, and that "His Majesty is ready to use moral and other pressure on Mendelssohn to attain the desired end, and he will not be trifled with." No. 5405.

47 *Ibid.,* Nos. 5406, 5407.

available.[48] The German financial press at the time expressed the opinion that most of the loan was resold in France. Immediately after, the German market was shut again. In March, 1903, the Kaiser made clear that no Russian loans would be admitted.[49] On May 13, 1903, the Chancellor Von Bülow wrote to his Ambassador at Paris:

As is known to your excellency the Imperial Government exercises upon the money market a certain influence to assure the maintenance of reserve toward Russian demands until the commercial treaty matters are settled. Thus, quite recently the Prussian Secretary of Commerce has indicated his intention of preventing the 72 million rubles issue of the Reich-Adels-Agrar Bank from being placed wholly or partly in Germany.[50]

But the Chancellor was also aware that Russia, aided by the French financiers, was negotiating in London, and added, "But if a Russian-British agreement is imminent, we must consider whether it is advisable to stretch the string so taut, as to whether conciliation may not be the wiser policy."[51] The negotiations in London failed, however, and the German Government did not modify its policy until the next year.

During the next three years Russia borrowed much in Germany. A satisfactory commercial treaty was negotiated in 1904. Count Witte secured access to the German market as part of the negotiations.[52] During 1904–5, years of war with Japan, the Germans bought large amounts of short-time Russian treasury bonds, and subscribed to long-time loans. Some previous loans, theretofore not listed in Germany, were admitted to official quo-

---

[48] *Ibid.*, No. 5408.

[49] *Die Grosse Politik*, Vol. XVIII, No. 5909.

[50] *Ibid.*, Vol. XVII, No. 5370.

[51] *Ibid.*, Nos. 5370, 5372. German anxiety lest Russia succeed in borrowing in London before the commercial treaty negotiations with Russia were satisfactorily settled, was evident. *Ibid.*, Nos. 5369–5376.

[52] *Memoirs of Count Witte* (New York, 1921), p. 292.

tation. But by the end of 1905 German sympathy declined. In the Russian Government's plans for borrowing before the Duma met, Berlin was included. But government intervention kept the German market closed. Chancellor Von Bülow explained his action by the financial stringency in Germany.[53] But the published correspondence and attendant circumstance supply adequate grounds for believing that the reason was political. Count Witte in February, 1906, apparently tried to persuade the German Government to consent to Russian borrowing by arguing that if Russia had to depend on France, the government of that country would insist on receiving Russian support at the Algeciras Conference, and he pleaded with Germany to show generosity in the negotiations.[54] The German Chancellor replied that if Russia needed money very badly and if she could not obtain it before the Conference was over, she should bring pressure on France.[55] Witte might have wished to pursue this course; he professed to be recommending conciliation to the French.[56] But Russian support was in the upshot extended to France, possibly as a condition of borrowing.[57] This action was harshly resented in Germany, along with the failure of the Russian Government to ratify the agreement made between the Kaiser and the Czar at Bjoerkoe. Again the German Government was probably aware of the approaches which Count Witte was making at the same time to the British Government. The actual state of German official feeling is indicated by a marginal note of the

[53] *Die Grosse Politik*, Vol. XXI, Nos. 7153, 7154.

[54] *Ibid.*, No. 7027. The Kaiser, a month previously, when informed that the French Government had told the Russian Government that no borrowing would be possible until the Moroccan trouble was settled, defended himself to the Czar by arguing that this was merely a pretext. *Ibid.*, No. 6969. Sir Edward Grey's slant on the situation was different. He wrote on January 15, 1906, that "Russia demanded a loan on improper terms as the price of her support." *British Documents*, III, 178.

[55] *Die Grosse Politik*, Vol. XXI, No. 7028.

[56] *Ibid.*, No. 7029.

[57] *Ibid.*, Nos. 7052, 7068.

Kaiser's written on a report sent March 31, 1906, by the Ambassador to London, setting forth the opposition Russian borrowing was encountering there. "I'm very glad to hear it," ran the note, "not a penny will they get from us."[58] This was the loan so bitterly criticized by liberal groups in France and England as enabling the Czar to cement his absolutism. By the monarch of Germany it was rejected. A major policy must have been at stake. The German bankers, it may be added as parenthesis, subscribed for part of the loan through purchases abroad.[59]

In the subsequent years no new Russian government loans were issued in Germany, though no open expression of opposition came from the government. Some conversions occurred. The small portion of Russian government debt held in Germany in 1914 implies that the sales exceeded the new purchases. But Russian industrial, petroleum, bank, and railroad securities were admitted to quotation on the Berlin Exchange. These presumably found justification in the orders and opportunities which they brought to German industry. As late as June, 1914, admission was granted to the securities of the Azow-Don Commerz Bank and the Russian Bank for Foreign Trade of St. Petersburg. As a neighbor of Russia, as a nation of great industrial enterprise, it was natural that Germany should finance Russian economic development. Only the doubtfulness of Russian credit, the fact that so much of this development was government-controlled, and the undercurrent of political suspicion and antagonism between the two countries prevented the German investment from growing much greater than its actual amount.

UPON ACCORD, BRITISH INVESTMENT FOLLOWS

THE British share in financing the Russian Government was also comparatively small though that government began to borrow in London as early as 1822. But during the

---

[58] *Ibid.*, Vol. XXV, No. 8503.
[59] Witte, *op. cit.*, p. 306.

eighties and nineties when Russia was making new loans
for railroad and governmental purposes, the British investors took virtually no share of them. Whether this prolonged financial alienation rested solely on the inclination
of the British bankers and investing public, or whether
the British Government used its influence to sustain it,
is uncertain.[60] Industrial and railroad securities were
bought but not in great volume; some conversions took
place. British and Russian relations retained the note of
antagonism that had expressed itself in the Crimean War.
Over Turkey, Persia, Thibet, and Afghanistan, and in
the Far East the two countries met in dispute and rivalry.

The Russian approach to British investors took a con-
sequential turn during the first half of 1903. Count
Witte's demands in Paris were causing anxiety to the
French investors and Foreign Office.[61] The French banks,
seeking a partner in their heavy undertakings, apparently
acted as mediators with the British banks. The German
Foreign Office, worried lest Russia secure a loan in London before commercial treaty matters were satisfactorily
settled, was of the opinion that the French Government
was trying to smooth Russia's way on Downing and Lombard Streets.[62] Rumors to the effect that a loan agreement
had been reached and that Rothschild had ceased to be
unfriendly to Russian loans were sufficient to make the
German Government believe that a rapprochement had
been reached.[63] But the London market finally refused to

[60] I have found no convincing evidence of government action. Viner,
op. cit., p. 2, cites O. Becker, *Das Französisch-Russische Bündnis* (Berlin, 1925), p. 288, to the effect that Prince William of Prussia, later
Kaiser Wilhelm II, in a letter to the Czar alleged that the Prince of
Wales, later King Edward VII, had asked Bleichröder to aid British
bankers to lower Russian funds. The amounts of Russian bonds assessed
for income tax (this is not a comprehensive figure) were £2,360,872 in
1877, £941,623 in 1881, £744,057 in 1884. They had mainly been sold on
the German market.
[61] *Die Grosse Politik,* Vol. XVIII, No. 5909.
[62] *Ibid.,* Vol. XVII, Nos. 5369, 5371, 5372, 5375.
[63] *Ibid.,* No. 5374.

go forward with the loan plans; new persecution of the
Jews rearoused Rothschild hostility. The required funds
were secured in France, and in 1904 the German market
was opened again. During the Russo-Japanese War, Russia found the capacious and reasonable London market
available only to its enemy.

That war reduced Russia's capacity for aggression in
China and Persia, and increased its financial dependence.
The revolutionary agitation forced the Czar to grant a
constitution, to permit the establishment of a legislative
body, the Duma, which was certain, it was thought, to curb
the will and policies of the Czar and cabinet. To secure
the means of avoiding financial chaos and of dominating
the Duma, the Russian Government eagerly sought new
political connections which could furnish financial means.
Great Britain had the means. By moderate sacrifices a
crippled Russia could secure access to them. There is little
doubt that Russia's financial needs impelled her to take
the initiative which brought forth the Anglo-Russian
Treaty of 1907 and enabled her to borrow in London. In
January, 1906, Count Witte in expounding his purposes
to a well-known British journalist declared: "that Germany could give a finger's length of help and England an
arm's length. France was so deeply implicated in Russia's
financial situation that her opinion was discounted."[64]

The Russian Government was negotiating with British
bankers in October, 1905, shortly after the text of the
Anglo-Japanese Treaty was made public.[65] The British
Ambassador at St. Petersburg, into whose circle of discussion the proposal of an Anglo-Russian understanding
had entered often in recent months, feared that Russian
resentment might induce her to turn to Germany. He suggested to Lord Lansdowne, Secretary of Foreign Affairs,
that His Majesty's government make some friendly advance to Russia, combining such action with the financial

[64] *British Documents*, IV, 219.   [65] *Ibid.*, p. 210.

negotiations then going on in London.[66] Lord Lansdowne
advised that the financial negotiations be allowed to take
their course independently of negotiations having reference to political affairs.[67] Still within the same month, the
British Ambassador was impressing the Czar with the fact
that Lord Revelstoke (of Baring Brothers) was in St.
Petersburg with the countenance of His Majesty's government, endeavoring to negotiate a loan.[68] Suggestions
for an understanding were circulated freely through the
embassies, but they and the conclusion of financial arrangements lagged until Sir Edward Grey came into office in December, 1905.

By January, 1906, Russian financial anxieties deepened. Criticism of all loans to Russia became more vocal
and determined in French and English liberal circles.
Witte's fears lest he should have to submit his financial
plans to the Duma grew intense; it was plain that in the
Duma these plans would meet bitter and talented opposition. A loan contract with Lord Revelstoke and an international banking syndicate had already been signed, but
the bankers still hesitated awaiting an opportune time.
The French Government still wavered. Witte made no
secret of his wish for an agreement with Great Britain.[69]
The British Government was probably of the opinion held
by Spring-Rice, Councilor of the Embassy at St.
Petersburg, that Russia was not yet prepared to make
permanent or serious concessions. By April, 1906, however, this same informant was saying that perhaps some
concessions would be given in return for a loan. That
month the loan was issued in London. That the British
bankers had assured themselves of British official consent
is virtually certain; that the British Government actually

[66] *British Documents,* IV, 210.
[67] *Ibid.*   [68] *Ibid.,* p. 215.
[69] *Ibid.,* pp. 221, 280. He wished to persuade King Edward to come
to Russia and negotiate personally with the Czar. On the strength of
the news he believed a loan could be arranged. *The Letters and Friendships of Sir Cecil Spring-Rice* (New York, 1929), II, 25.

urged the bankers to go forward with the loan has been
asserted.[70] How far the discussion concerned with an understanding between the two governments had advanced
at the time the loan was issued, it is difficult to ascertain.
The interruptions of the later negotiations indicate that
they had gone but little beyond an expression of intention.[71] However, the German Government took the emission of the loan to be an almost conclusive sign that an
agreement was in the making.[72] The judgment was correct. What part the British bankers may have played in
leading the two countries together, how far Russia was
swayed by financial argument toward compromising her
aims—these subtle matters no intimate witness has yet
revealed in detail.

Thus the Russian government loan of 1906 was issued,
in part, in London, the first large new direct Russian
government loan in that market in three decades. It
marked the encouraging advancement of a project of understanding which was embodied in the Anglo-Russian
Agreement of 1907. It signified the evolution into intimacy
of the Triple Entente. In 1909 another Russian government loan was issued in London. Earlier government issues were admitted to the stock exchange price list. British
promoters and capitalists took a new interest in Russian
private enterprise, and put their capital in banks, industries, oil fields, and mines. The oil enterprises in which
British capital had a share controlled three-fourths of the
Russian oil trade and half the total Russian production.

[70] In the report of the Ambassador of Belgium in London, B. H.
Schwertfeger, *Zur Europaischen Politik, 1897–1914* (Berlin, 1919), II,
112.

[71] It is possible that Sir Edward Grey was of the opinion that the
degree of agreement reached was greater than it actually was. When
pressed by the Persian Minister in London, March 6, 1906, he replied
no more conclusively than to state that "we had not got any definite
agreement with Russia about details, as we had with France." *British
Documents,* IV, 380.

[72] *Die Grosse Politik,* Vol. XXV, No. 8505; *British Documents,* IV,
230.

For that part of the Baku petroleum industry in which
it had little direct ownership, British-Dutch enterprise
marketed the product. "The entire Baku petroleum industry was concentrated, through the cementing medium of
British capital, in the hands of two cardinal groups
. . ."[73] In the copper, gold, and lead mines British investment was also large and growing. With their country's
policy, the ventures of British savers changed. While there
is no evidence to show that the British Government intervened in the process officially its favor was, however, assured.[74] The adjustment of political relationships permitted economic incentives to operate.

[73] Lewery, *op. cit.,* p. 17.
[74] An interesting episode in connection with Russian financing that
would seem to indicate King Edward's familiarity with the situation
occurred in 1907. Sir Ernest Cassel, private financial adviser to the
King, asked him to intercede with the Czar in regard to a proposed
loan Cassel was trying to negotiate. The King consented to ask the
Czar to receive the financier. Sir S. Lee, *King Edward VII* (New York,
1927), II, 595. See, in connection with Cassel's negotiations, J. H. Schiff,
Life and Letters (New York, 1928), II, 141.

CHAPTER X

THE FINANCING OF ITALY BY
RIVAL ALLIANCES

THE course of investment in Italian securities, and the response of the continental money markets to the needs of the Italian Government were deflected several times by the state of the continental alliances. From the birth of the Italian kingdom to the formation of the Triple Alliance, French investors furnished the chief external financial support. Of the consolidated debt held abroad in 1884 the French owned over 80 per cent, the English almost all the rest, the Germans little more than 3 per cent. Total French investment in Italian government securities was estimated to be in the neighborhood of two billion francs. The Paris house of Rothschild held established place as government banker to the Italian Government.[1] The occupation of Tunis by France after an acute contest over economic concessions, roused the latent rivalry and ill-feeling between the two countries. In May, 1882, the Treaty of Triple Alliance was signed between Germany, Austria, and Italy. In the following month Von Siemens of the Deutsche Bank first entered into financial relations with the Italian Ministry of Finance; a government loan was arranged "to be kept secret so that hostile French bankers should not create obstacles to that operation."[2] In the following year the Deutsche Bank undertook a large bond issue for the City of Rome despite unfavorable conditions in all the money markets. The loan gave assurance to Italy that it would not suffer as a result of its allegiance to the Central Powers.[3] In May, 1884, the Reichsbank Committee resolved to include the Italian

[1] I. Sachs, *L'Italie—ses Finances et son Développement Économique* (London, 1885), p. 487.
[2] G. Giolitti, *Memoirs of My Life* (London, 1923), p. 63.
[3] K. Helfferich, *Georg Von Siemens*, II, 207–211.

rente in the list of securities acceptable as collateral. Not long thereafter the German banks agreed upon a plan to finance the reorganization and improvement of the Italian railroads, and in 1885 a syndicate led by the Diskonto-Gesellschaft took over the first of the contemplated railroad loans. These plans were extended in 1887. It was expected that the Crédit Mobilier would participate in this railroad financing. But the French Government intervened to force it to abstain. Word spread of an official ban upon all new issues of Italian securities.

This French action had been brewing for five years, as a potion brews; for Italian resentment of the French victory of Tunis remained vigorously alive and created reciprocal resentment. The French Government had continued to permit French capital to share in the financing of Italy probably hoping that the Triple Alliance agreement, the first term of which expired in 1887, would not be renewed. But in March Italy decided to renew its membership despite German refusal to accede fully to its wishes, and signed a secret treaty with Germany which provided, among other measures, for the coöperation of the two countries in resistance to further French expansion in North Africa. Tariff negotiations between France and Italy ended in a rupture of trade relations; each began to block the other's commerce by high and combative rates of duty.[4] The two countries were also at odds over navigation matters, the old treaty of 1862 having expired, and the draft of a new one having been rejected by the French Chamber of Deputies.

Italy suffered throughout 1887–88 from agricultural, commercial, and financial depression, caused in part by the tariff war. The foreign exchanges were unfavorable. Much having been spent in public improvements, the budget was in deficit. This public expenditure had stimulated a real estate and building boom which was verging on collapse.[5]

[4] *The Memoirs of Francesco Crispi* (London, 1914), II, 169.
[5] A. Billot, *La France et L'Italie* (Paris, 1905), I, 142 *et seq.*

It was under these circumstances that the French press undertook a strident campaign of criticism against Italian credit, advocating the sale of French-owned securities. The French banks ceased to honor Italian commercial bills and withdrew their real estate credits. True, the circumstances gave cause for fear of private and public solvency. But the Italians believed that the French Government had encouraged the press campaign despite the official French denials.[6] In view of the intimate relations between the French press and foreign office, it is certain that the French Government favored the campaign even if it had not arranged it. The cessation of new financing on the French market is further indication of the same probability, for left to themselves, there can be no doubt that the French banks would have found a way to help in the emergency. The Crédit Mobilier, as has been stated, had already withdrawn from its customary participation in Italian railway financing.[7] Unsustained by the usual French financial support, the already overstrained economic situation turned into a general crash. Numerous banks and industrial firms failed. The budget continued in deficit, the currency in chaos. The commercial and agricultural depression became intensified. With the criticism on one side, the suffering on the other, tension grew almost to war pitch in 1889–90. French investors continued to sell their Italian bonds.

But the German banks and German Government strained themselves to give the required support refused by France. In 1888 Bismarck, responding to the appeals of the Italian prime minister, encouraged the German banks to form a strong syndicate to support Italian credit by buying Italian securities and honoring Italian commercial bills. With the German banks Hambros and

[6] Crispi, *op. cit.*, II, 420 *et seq.*

[7] For the main events, *ibid.*, III, 209–223; Giolitti, *op. cit.*, pp. 62 *et seq.*; G. H. Fiamingo, "Les Raisons Économiques de la Politique Étrangère de l'Italie," *Revue Politique et Parlementaire*, July, 1907; Helfferich, *op. cit.*, II, 207 *et seq.*

Baring Bros. of London associated themselves. "In consideration, however," the German Government informed the Italian, "of the fact that such operations not only do not offer any probability of profit, but may even mean a certain amount of risk, the group above named desires that in compensation, the Italian Government in its future financial operations in foreign countries, should apply to its members before concluding elsewhere." The Italian Government gave the desired promise. In July, 1889, when the French polemic against Italian securities reached its highest pitch, Bismarck arranged for favorable comment in the German press. Since this in itself did not prove sufficient, the German bankers were again prevailed upon to support the market, being given renewed assurance of preference in future Italian railroad financing.

The difficulties continued, however. So in August, 1890, Crispi and the German Chancellor arranged for the foundation of a bank through which special support could be given to public credit—the Instituto di Credito Fondiario. The funds were supplied by a German syndicate headed by Bleichröder and the Deutsche Bank. This syndicate enabled Italy to avert public bankruptcy by granting Italy loans in 1890–91 and gave its support in the market for Italian securities for several years thereafter. In this effort the German Government endeavored to induce the British, associated with Italy in Mediterranean policy, to assist; and from time to time British banks worked with the German syndicate.[8] A clear realization was shared by the German banks and German Government that Italy's allegiance to the Central Powers could be assured only if Italy were enabled to dispense with French financial aid. In addition it was judged important that the financial plans of the Crispi Ministry be not allowed to fail, for that ministry represented the elements most favorable to Germany.[9] As the financial strain continued in Italy, the Ger-

[8] *Die Grosse Politik,* Vol. IX, No. 2161.
[9] Helfferich, *op. cit.,* II, 217–218.

man Government realized that it must act with caution
and moderation in trying to influence the Italian to maintain its government expenditure in behalf of the Alliance,
lest financial ruin result and the loss fall on German investors.[10]

German financial assistance in the field of private
enterprise was also arranged and strongly developed. In
1887–88 the German banks bought an interest in Italian
banking institutions, which made mortgage and industrial
development loans. In 1893 the whole of the private credit
structure of Italy was shaken by the failure of three large
banks. Outside aid was needed to build up banking activity
again. The Italian Government wished the German banks
to take over the two bankrupt institutions, but this they
refused to do. In 1894, however, the German syndicate
with Austrian, Swiss, and Italian aid, founded the Banca
Commerciale Italiano, under the urging of the German
Government, with the idea of grouping under this bank
their existing and contemplated industrial and banking
ventures in Italy. This bank helped greatly in the financial
liquidation through which Italy was passing. Later it
founded numerous industrial enterprises especially in the
chemical, textile, and electrical equipment, hydroelectric
and marine industries, in the ownership or management of
many of which the German interests shared.[11]

During these troubled years attempts had been made to
regain entry into the French market, but these failed. In
January, 1891, the Crispi Ministry fell, and was succeeded by one headed by Rudini, which indicated its desire
for a settlement of the difficulties with France; it indicated

[10] *Die Grosse Politik,* Vol. VII, No. 1437.

[11] The activities of this bank were denounced during the war years
by various French and Italian authorities as conspiratorial and designed
to subject all of Italian economic life to German dictation. E.g., G.
Preziosi, *L'Allemagne à la Conquête de l'Italie* (Paris, 1916). The evidence available, however, reveals nothing more than the great and varied
activity carried on along German banking lines, and close working connections between some of the industrial enterprises founded by the bank
and German industry.

furthermore that unless France extended help, a ministry less friendly to France would again return to power. Shortly thereafter, Rudini, seeking funds to pay the next coupons on the government bonds and wishing to float a new railway loan, entered into negotiations with the French Government and bankers. Billot, the French Ambassador, informed the King of Italy that France would remain suspicious as long as the treaty with Germany remained unpublished, and that the French would not invest in a country which might prove to be an enemy.[12] Billot, in his own account of the episode, attributes his stand to the hesitation of the bankers. The French Government urged them to participate in the loans sought by Rudini, he asserts. But the bankers, he explained, believed that the French investors had been so educated in distrust during the previous four years, in a distrust which would last while the Triple Alliance lasted, that they would not make loans until Italy showed a new disposition by overt action.[13] This view may be regarded as manufactured for purposes of diplomacy; the French Government could not be expected to favor loans to a government still bound by hostile treaties unless definite promises were given in exchange. At all events in the following months the Paris house of Rothschild, with the probable consent of the French Foreign Office, in offering Italy a loan, no longer asked publication of the treaty with Germany, but merely a secret declaration by the Italian Government to the French of the situations and conditions under which it would participate in a war against France.[14]

These French attempts to wean Italy away from the Triple Alliance by promise of financial aid, failed. They appear rather to have fed Italian resentment. Billot was of the opinion, in fact, that they disposed Italy still more firmly to a renewal of the Alliance. The Italian Prime

---

12 *Die Grosse Politik*, Vol. VII, No. 1418.
13 Billot, *op. cit.*, pp. 289–294.
14 *Die Grosse Politik*, Vol. VII, No. 1418.

Minister responded to the French proposals in June, 1891, "France offers me its financial help like a piece of sugar at the end of a string; that is a humiliating game in which I shall not play."[15] The Triple Alliance was again renewed a year before the date of its expiration.[16] During 1892 Rudini was succeeded by Giolitti who endeavored to convince the French public of the friendly intentions of Italy, but without success. French finance still abstained from all ventures in Italy.

But by 1895–96 Italian government securities were regaining stability, and were being quietly repurchased on the French Bourse.[17] Italy's acute need for outside help was at an end; and the Italian Government began to draw back from too intimate association with the Central Powers. It began to develop independent political aims which diverged in part from those of Germany. A friendly convention with France dealing with Tunis was passed in 1896. The tariff war was terminated by a new commercial treaty in 1897. Despite the efforts of Von Siemens, the desire to draw German capital into Italian industry by giving it special place began to wane; the German capital market could not offer as easy terms as the French.[18] When the capital of the Banca Commerciale Italiano was enlarged, French participation was arranged and this in time outgrew the German. Up to 1914, however, the Ger-

15 Billot, *op. cit.*, p. 294; G. Giacometti, "Cinq Mois de Politique Italienne," *Revue des Deux Mondes,* September 15, 1891, pp. 389–390.

16 J. Viner, "International Finance and Balance of Power Diplomacy, 1890–1914." *Southwestern Political and Social Science Quarterly,* March, 1929, p. 16, suggests that Rudini's indignation may have been cover for his firm intention to renew Italy's membership in the Triple Alliance and a means of justifying that action. He points out that Rudini had informed the German Ambassador to Rome that the treaty would be renewed before his conversation with Rothschild. But Billot's conversation with the King took place before that of Rudini with Rothschild, and may have been preceded by earlier conversations. *Die Grosse Politik,* Vol. VII, No. 1418. See the analysis of the situation in W. L. Langer, *The Franco-Russian Alliance, 1890–1894,* p. 156.

17 R. Viviani, *Revue Politique et Parlementaire,* April, 1914.

18 Helfferich, *op. cit.,* II, 219 *et seq.*

man representation on the Board of Directors remained a powerful minority, and among the executive personnel, a directing force. By 1906 Paris had become again the chief market for new Italian loans; French finance took a leading part in the large conversion operation of that year. The Italian Government informed the German that in order to get that assistance, it was forced to accept friendly manifestations from the French, which were likely to give a false idea of its relations with Germany.[19] But they were in fact drifting apart. Italy was no longer a sure ally in case of war. During 1912, of 42.9 million lira paid abroad for public debt service, 28.5 were made through French banks, 4.9 through English, and only 3.0 through German.

But the Italy of the twentieth century never became as dependent upon foreign money markets, as in the eighties and nineties of the previous century. Italian public finances recorded a steady improvement, and an increasing proportion of the external debt was repurchased by the Italians. The experience of the nineties undoubtedly sharpened the wish for financial independence. German financial aid proved an insufficient force to cement permanently the Triple Alliance in the face of a competing money market and a growing national ambition.

[19] *Die Grosse Politik*, Vol. XXI, No. 7151.

CHAPTER XI

THE FINANCING OF PORTUGAL—A DEBTOR WITH A NOBLE PAST

DEFAULT FOLLOWS UPON DEFAULT

THE decaying monarchy of Portugal was a steady borrower in the world's money markets during the second half of the nineteenth century. Its defaults severely taxed the patience of the investors who enabled it to conduct a government with almost continuous deficits for forty years. These would have sought to control Portuguese finances to recoup their losses, but the long record of Portuguese magnificence and independence and the presence of powerful protectors stayed their hands. What political ambitions the governments of the lending states had, were turned toward the Portuguese colonies not the state itself.

From 1851 on, Portuguese finances were in perpetual deficit and the government borrowed at home and abroad, often at heavy discount. The new loans were used to pay the interest of older ones, while the government built railways and strove to maintain an army and navy adequate to its memories of historic greatness. The colonies, inherited from the period of greatness, drew on the exchequer of the mother country. British and French investors were the chief buyers of the loans, though in the eighties German investment rapidly increased. The Portuguese government debt totaled 27.8 millions of pounds in 1860, 66.2 millions of pounds in 1870, 97.0 millions of pounds in 1880, 140 millions of pounds in 1890. In 1891–92 a crisis in Brazilian finance provoked a similar crisis in Portugal. The government, in serious need, found its credit exhausted. In January, 1892, it was unable to meet the interest it had guaranteed on railroad bonds. Six foreign representatives were admitted to membership on the Board of Directors of the railways. Shortly thereafter, though it failed to secure the consent of the foreign bondholders, it reduced interest on all government loans, except one, to 33 per cent in gold. To meet criticism the pledged revenues were put under the control of a semi-autonomous Portuguese official body, the Junta de Credito Publico.[1] The government declared itself ready to negotiate with the bondholders in regard to permanent terms of settlement.

This default incensed financial circles. Portugal had put through a costly series of forced conversions in the middle of the century. Now the French Bourse refused to recognize dealings in the new securities. In the French Parliament a strong party pressed the ministry to take action—facing the government with the question, "Can the French Government intervene in Portugal to protect effectively the interests of its nationals, ought it, does it wish to?"[2] The French Minister of Finance would only promise vaguely "to do all in his power to secure fair treatment from Portugal." The German Government's mood of irritation found more active expression. The German investment was of but a few years' standing (listing had only been given in 1886), and the Portuguese default followed closely upon other disillusionments of the same kind. It was German pressure that caused the Junta de Credito Publico to be revived and put in charge of the assigned revenues.[3] In June, 1893, the German Ambassador declared to the Portuguese Government, "In presence of this arbitrary procedure I am charged, and hereby carry out the charge to notify the Portuguese Government of the formal protest of the Imperial Government against

[1] The Junta was composed of five members, all Portuguese; one was elected by the Chamber of Peers, one by the Chamber of Deputies, one by the Cabinet, and two by the holders of the Consolidated Bonds.

[2] H. Imbert, *Les Emprunts D'États*, pp. 77–78.

[3] "Note sur la Dette Extérieure de Portugal," *Association Nationale des Porteurs Français*, 1902–3, pp. 39 *et seq.*

the present decree which injures the rights guaranteed by treaty to the German creditors." The British Stock Exchange banned all dealings in the new securities.

But in face of all this agitation the Portuguese Government declared itself helpless—which was pretty much the case in the absence of government reform—but willing to enter further negotiations. These negotiations dragged without issue for almost ten years. The lending powers would not use strong coercive measures against a state of similar civilization in order to collect debts owed to their private citizens.

In 1893 the French Government did intervene with firmness to protect the interests of the French investors in the Royal Portuguese railways. The Portuguese Government rather arbitrarily declared the company in bankruptcy on the score of an unpaid debt to it. On the official committee of liquidation, the foreign investors who had by far the largest capital at stake in the railway, were given small minority representation; the scheme of reorganization was put through by official edict though wholly unacceptable to the foreign bondholders.[4] The French Senate undertook an investigation of the episode and passed a resolution criticizing the Portuguese Government and stating that they "were trusting in the will of the (French) Government to protect the interest of its nationals."[5] The French Prime Minister remonstrated vigorously, and put at the service of the bondholders for the conduct of the negotiations, a French Inspector of Finances with official backing. The Portuguese Government yielded and revised the terms accorded.[6]

During the negotiation of terms for the settlement of the general government debt, the bondholders endeavored to secure some measure of supervision over the pledged revenues, and other arrangements calculated to improve

4 *Report of Council of Foreign Bondholders,* 1893, pp. 280–281.
5 *Débats Parl. Sénat,* March 10, 1894.
6 *Report of Council of Foreign Bondholders,* 1894, pp. 295 *et seq.*

their security. In 1899 the Portuguese Ministry in power appears to have offered place on the Junta to foreign representatives.[7] But Portuguese public opinion resented this concession and the cabinet was overthrown. The new ministry disavowed the proposals of its predecessor, even refusing to confirm the assignment of the pledged revenues by formal agreement. In 1901 the French Government resorted to an open threat. M. Delcassé, Minister of Foreign Affairs, said in the Senate:

> I would hope, gentlemen, that the Portuguese Government will recognize that it is in the interest of Portugal to give to the foreign bondholders that satisfaction which they have so long awaited. The government is aware that we do not lack the means of supporting the just claims of our countrymen, and it cannot doubt that in case of need we are fully resolved to employ them.[8]

In 1902 an agreement was reached with the French bondholders which the French Government judged acceptable.[9] It provided for reduction of interest to 3 per cent and a reduction of capital to 50–75 per cent of the various original issue prices. The German bondholders insisted upon minute regulation in the conversion law of the plan of payment of the pledged customs revenues, as a condition of acceptance. The British bondholders accepted despite dissatisfaction. The Report of the Council of Foreign Bondholders for 1901–2 explains the acceptance by the fact of previous acceptance of the French and German groups, then adds, "There were other considerations of a confidential character which weighed with the Committee in arriving at a conclusion."[10] The nature of these considerations remains unrevealed. Not long before the French Government was seeking to have the pledged revenues put under the control of the Tobacco Monopoly

---

[7] *Report of Council of Foreign Bondholders,* 1901–2, p. 303.

[8] *Débats Parl. Sénat,* February 25, 1901.

[9] *Association Nationale des Porteurs Français,* 1902–3.

[10] *Report of Council of Foreign Bondholders,* 1901–2, p. 309.

or Royal Portuguese Railway Company in both of which French influence was strong.[11] But the more likely explanation is that the British Government was anxious lest further delay in settlement would lead to decisive action on the part of Germany as regards the Portuguese colonies. The proposal had been steadily in the area of discussion and Germany and Great Britain had signed a convention looking in that direction. The final agreement provided for daily payment of the pledged customs revenues to the Junta de Credito Publico, to be set aside for the debt service, but introduced no foreign representatives upon that body.

From 1902 on Portugal met the reduced debt service. From that date on the government issued only one external loan, and that through the Tobacco Monopoly. Its struggling public finances were supported, when need there was, by issues of paper money and short-time advances of the bankers of Lisbon and elsewhere. Governing it was the fear that new loans would mean either foreign supervision of its finances or detachment of colonial possessions. These risks, inherent in the financial situation, were among the unstabilizing forces which brought on the Revolution, 1911–12.

ATTENTION TURNS TO THE PORTUGUESE COLONIES

FROM the earlier explorations of Portuguese adventurers there were left to Portuguese sovereignty two important colonies on the African mainland, Mozambique on the east coast and Angola on the west coast. In addition, Portugal up to 1890 claimed the vast stretch of interior between them, but this claim was ignored in the parceling out of African territory. The revenues of these colonies never were sufficient to meet the cost of their administration. The

---

11 La Société des Tabacs du Portugal was established in 1891; its ownership was divided between French and Portuguese banks. It paid the government 60 per cent of its net profits above a fixed minimum, and a fixed annuity.

administration itself was notoriously inefficient and brutal, neither developing the resources of the country nor concerning itself with the welfare of the inhabitants. Part of the public borrowings of the Portuguese Government were used to sustain the colonies and to provide a defense organization which would never have been of the slightest use against the potential adversaries. The disposable resources of the Portuguese Government fell far below the actual need, and private capital from other lands came forward. These private ventures became the objects and instruments of political ambitions, and their plans and actions immediately acquired political significance.

During the last two decades of the nineteenth century, while the territorial division of Africa was proceeding rapidly, Great Britain and Germany suspected each other of designs upon these colonies, and Portugal entertained fear and suspicion of both. In 1889 a dispute arose between Portugal and Great Britain because of the cancellation of a contract held by a British company for the construction of a railway from Lorenzo Marques (on Delagoa Bay, the finest port on the lower part of the East African coast) to the Transvaal. The concession was originally granted to an American. Portugal defended its action on technical grounds in the contract but its real motive was unquestionably fear of British dictation. The British Government sustained the company's demand for an indemnity. Many observers imputed to this action the calculation that the indemnity would be beyond Portugal's capacity to pay and that territory would be ceded in recompense; for Portugal's borrowing power was exhausted at the time. There are implications in the British official documents which support this idea.[12] The arbitral body rendered damages which, though substantial, were little more than half of the original British claims; the claims of the American Government in behalf of the widow of the American con-

12 Memorandum by J. A. C. Tilley respecting the "Relations between Germany and Great Britain, 1892–1904," *British Documents,* I, 322.

cessionaire received no recognition. Portugal managed to borrow the necessary funds from its Tobacco Monopoly, which was financed by French capital. The railroad was completed by the government to the borders of the Portuguese colony, then by arrangement with the Boer Government of the Transvaal was carried to Pretoria and Johannesburg. English effort to acquire the road continued. Cecil Rhodes and Rothschild in turn endeavored to induce the Portuguese Government to part with the railway and with the Mozambique colony.[13] On the other hand German capital participated in the extension of the road and supported offers for the lease or sale of the road to the Transvaal Government. But the British Government protested against any such transaction on treaty and other legal grounds, and Portugal itself was not favorably inclined. Germany maintained interest in the prospect, and encouraged German traders to acquire land in the neighborhood of Delagoa Bay.[14] It was determined at all events that the road should not fall into British hands.[15]

Because of the uncertainty of Portuguese finances the colonies remained in the field of possible bargaining, and provoked the moves and countermoves of rival empires. When in 1894 a native insurrection broke out at Lorenzo Marques (an insurrection ascribed at Berlin and Lisbon to the intrigues of Cecil Rhodes who had been disappointed in his attempt to buy the railway), His Majesty's consul landed bluejackets without consulting the Portuguese Government. Upon the protest of the Portuguese Government they were withdrawn; but the British Government would not give its consent to the recruitment of volunteers to suppress the rebellion. Germany, not to be

13 W. B. Worsfold, *The Reconstruction of the new Colonies under Lord Milner* (London, 1913), pp. 117 *et seq.* Mr. Worsfold had access to the Milner papers.

14 Memorandum by E. Crowe on "The Present State of British Relations with France and Germany," January 1, 1907, *British Documents*, Vol. III, Appendix A.

15 *Die Grosse Politik,* Vol. XI, No. 2578.

behindhand, sent two men-of-war to Delagoa Bay to safeguard "the large German interests involved, both on the
coast and in the Transvaal." For Germany was courting
the Transvaal Government. When the Delagoa Bay Railway was opened, a deputation of German naval officers
visited Pretoria, and the Kaiser, in congratulating President Kruger, pronounced the railroad "a means of drawing closer the bonds which connect the two countries."

Negotiations between Portugal and its foreign creditors
over the revision of the terms of the arbitrarily imposed
debt settlement were dragging, while the irritations of
governments were growing and the financial needs of
Portugal were still acute. In 1897–98 Great Britain proposed various plans of financial assistance which were
designated also to safeguard against the possible alienation of Mozambique to the Transvaal or any other foreign
power. The first proposal made was that Great Britain
should guarantee Portugal's African possessions in return
for British official participation in the control of the Delagoa Bay Railway, and a veto power over concessions in
the region of that bay. Mr. Chamberlain suggested in
addition that Portugal raise a loan on the mortgage of
the African possession, and the revenues of the railway
and colony. The Portuguese Government refused. The
German Government, alarmed at the course of the discussions, recalled its Minister to Portugal for not supporting
German interests with sufficient firmness. Various alternatives were put forward from London, all of them designed
to secure in return for financial assistance control over the
economic life of the Delagoa Bay region and protection
against the possible extension of privileges to the nationals
of Germany or France.[16] English persistence in these loan
proposals, English willingness to take the exceptional
course of making a direct governmental loan to Portugal,
arose from fear that if Portugal borrowed elsewhere it
might mortgage the customs revenues of its colonies.

[16] Memorandum by Mr. Bertie, *British Documents*, I, 45–47.

The scheme of an Anglo-German agreement upon the Portuguese colonies grew out of this situation. On June 22, 1898, the German Government, aroused by the direction which British proposals were apparently taking at the time, peremptorily warned the Portuguese Government that Germany would not remain on friendly terms if Germany's interests were disregarded.[17] The French Government made a similar declaration. Mr. Chamberlain suggested to the Portuguese Minister that Germany might share in the loan under discussion, taking her security on some of the Western possessions.[18] On June 23, 1898, Germany advanced proposals looking toward the eventual division of the African colonies.[19] In the discussions which ensued between Great Britain and Germany the proposals for an immediate loan dropped out of sight, but an agreement for the colonies was brought to a successful conclusion. For advantages obtained Germany abandoned all ideas of support of the Boers, while Great Britain abandoned, for the time being at least, her traditional ally. The unfitness of Portugal for colonial rule seemed to justify the action taken.[20]

England and Germany signed (August 30, 1898) two conventions dealing with the Portuguese colonies. In that made publicly known, they agreed to ask each other to share in any loans that might be asked by Portugal on the security of the customs or other revenues of the African colonies. In the event of such a loan the British share was to be secured by the customs of the Mozambique Province south of the Zambesi River, and of a designated part of Angola; the German share was to be secured by the customs of the remainder of these colonies. Each was to limit its efforts to obtain new concessions to those sections, the customs revenues of which were assigned to their respective loans. Any control of customs undertaken in event of de-

---

[17] *British Documents*, Vol. I, No. 68.
[18] *Ibid.*, Tilley Memorandum.   [19] *Ibid.*, No. 70.
[20] For the German correspondence on the subject, see *Die Grosse Politik*, Vol. XIV, Part I, pp. 257 *et seq.*

fault should be likewise so partitioned. In the accompany-
ing secret convention the two powers agreed to oppose the
entry ("intervention" is the word used) of any third
power either by way of loans on security of colonial revenues, by way of lease, cession, or purchase of territory. It
contained provisions safeguarding the private rights of
the nationals of the contracting powers "in case Portugal
renounces her sovereign rights . . . or loses these territories in any other manner."[21]

These conventions appeared to be a direct threat at
Portuguese possession. Because of the fears of Portugal,
and possibly in the hope of outwitting Germany, Great
Britain in 1899 reaffirmed its ancient treaty alliance with
Portugal. If Portugal had tried to borrow during the subsequent years a most difficult case of conscience would have
presented itself to the British Government, even to the
skilful minds that phrased the original agreements. But
possibly Great Britain counted upon her ability to keep
Portugal out of the loan market.

The convention served to protect the colonies against
other powers, and to permit English and German influence to develop within the assigned spheres. The French
Government felt the exclusion strongly. While the negotiation of these conventions was under way the French
banks, with official encouragement, offered financial assistance to Portugal. Upon its being rumored that the
French lenders were asking a lien upon the Azores, the
British Government intervened.[22] The French Government desisted only after repeated attempts to favor and
support, in the words of the British Minister at Lisbon,
"every financial intrigue, with a view, no doubt, to further
entangling this Government in the toils of doubtful French
financiers and speculators."[23]

When finally in 1902 Portugal reached an agreement
with its foreign creditors, the most immediate danger of

21 *British Documents*, I, 71–72.
22 *Ibid.*, pp. 100–104.   23 *Ibid.*, pp. 112 *et seq.*

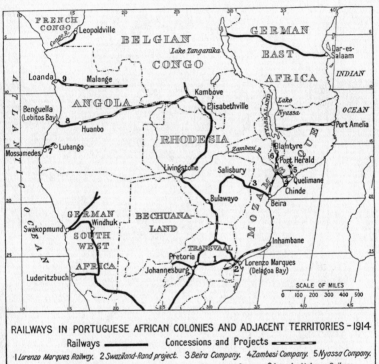

FRENCH CONGO · Leopoldville · BELGIAN · Lake Tanganïka · GERMAN · EAST · Dar-es-Salaam · INDIAN · CONGO · AFRICA · Loanda · 9 · Malange · Benguella (Lobitos Bay) · 8 · Huanbo · ANGOLA · Kambove · Elisabethville · Lake Nyassa · OCEAN · Port Amelia · Mossamedes · 7 · Lubango · RHODESIA · Zambesi R. · Blantyre · 6 · Port Herald · 5 · Quelimane · 4 · Chinde · Livingstone · Salisbury · 3 · Beira · Bulawayo · German · Windhuk · BECHUANA-LAND · Swakopmund · SOUTH · WEST · AFRICA · Inhambane · TRANSVAAL · Pretoria · 1 · Luderitzbuch · Johannesburg · 12 · Lorenzo Marques (Delagoa Bay)

SCALE OF MILES
0 100 200 300 400 500

RAILWAYS IN PORTUGUESE AFRICAN COLONIES AND ADJACENT TERRITORIES – 1914

Railways ———— Concessions and Projects ‑‑‑‑‑‑

1 Lorenzo Marques Railway. 2 Swaziland-Rand project. 3 Beira Company. 4 Zambesi Company. 5 Nyassa Company.
6 British Central Africa Company. 7 Mossamedes Company. 8 Benguella Company. 9 Loanda-Malange Railway.

having to cede control of her colonies in return for a loan, passed. From then on to 1914 Portugal by many difficult shifts managed to meet its external liabilities.

During these years British and German foreign capital undertook various railroads and trading ventures in the Portuguese colonies. In Mozambique, especially in the region of Delagoa Bay, Great Britain opposed the entry of enterprises other than British.[24] British capital was in control of the Delagoa Bay Development Corporation, which operated the waterworks, the telephone, and electrical tramway at Lorenzo Marques, and had a large interest in the electrical company and owned much land. Three companies, in all of which British capital was heavily interested, holding charters from the Portuguese Government, carried on virtually all of the trading and developmental work in Mozambique. Their charters conveyed mining, railroad construction rights, and a measure of sovereignty over the regions traversed. One of these chartered companies, the Mozambique Chartered Company, constructed the railroad from the port of Beira inland to Rhodesia, providing an excellent outlet for Rhodesian trade, and administered a large part of the Mozambique territory. This railway was transferred to the Beira Company, one of the constellation under the control of the British South Africa Company. The Zambesi Company (another of the chartered companies) built from a point further north on the Mozambique coast (Quilimane) inland, planning to run northward into Nyassaland. The Nyassa Company, the third of the chartered companies, held railway concessions running to Lake Nyassa. The British Central Africa Company which had already constructed a railroad from Port Herald on the Shire River to Blantyre in the Highlands of Nyassaland, held also a further concession for extensions up to Lake Nyassa. Thus there was being built up rapidly a system of British controlled roads connecting the British

[24] A. Marvaud, *Le Portugal et les Colonies* (Paris, 1912).

colonies of the interior and the north with the ports of
the Portuguese colonies. In addition to these undertakings, the British Government sought to have constructed
a road connecting Delagoa Bay to the Rand via Swazi-
land. Portugal refused Chamberlain the required concession.[25] But the railway was undertaken later. A final attempt, made in 1910, however, to have the Delagoa Bay
railway turned over to British control, failed. The British-
French chartered company in Mozambique, the Nyassa
Company, whose territories were in the sphere assigned
to Germany by the secret agreement, passed under the
control of German banks in 1914. This was possibly the
first step in the creation of a situation which might be
used to invoke the application of the Treaty of 1914.[26]

In Angola, the largest enterprise, the Mossamedes Company, was controlled by French capital. Belgian interests
were active in many fields on a smaller scale. But British
enterprise had important power and public utility concessions. It was besides a leading force in the most important of the four railroads (two were Portuguese-
owned). That railway had been undertaken by a British
syndicate under a concession secured in 1902 without official assistance. The original purpose of the project was
to provide the Katanga mining districts of Belgian Congo
with a direct outlet to the sea—at Lobitos Bay in Angola,
known as the finest harbor in West Africa. The concession
for this Benguella Railway and the controlling interest
was in the hands of the Tanganyika Concession Company,
Ltd., a British corporation, which possessed vast interests
in the Katanga mines. The enterprise worked in close cooperation with the Zambesia Exploring Company and

25 Worsfold, *op. cit.*, p. 120.

26 K. H. Lichnowsky, *Heading for the Abyss* (New York, 1928), pp.
274–275. The former German Ambassador to Great Britain wrote to
the Imperial Chancellor on January 17, 1913, "If we could gain influence
over the administration of substantial areas in Angola through the establishment of a Chartered Company or in Mozambique by acquiring the
majority in the Nyassa Company, it might perhaps be possible to apply
the paragraph about colonies or portions thereof becoming independent."

L'Union Minière du Haut Katanga.[27] In the course of development, however, British capital lost its majority interest. But difficulties were met in financing the project. The British Government did nothing to assist it and by 1912 only a third of the line had been built at an average cost of over $70,000 per mile. Agreements had been made to connect with the Belgian lines in the Congo and the Cape to Cairo railways. In 1913–14, while the new Anglo-German convention was under discussion, the German banks offered to finance the completion of the railway which traversed regions assigned to German influence in return for control. Mr. Williams, whose energy and skill had sustained the road throughout, declared that the offer was refused "although the bribe was immense."[28] But responsible students of African affairs reported at the time that the transaction was consummated.[29] The German Government was seeking at the same time to stimulate enterprise in Southern Angola. During the spring of 1914, a German-Portuguese group, backed by the large German banks and shipping companies, and possessing official consent, began the execution of a plan to join the railroads of German South Africa to the small railway running to the port of Mossamedes in Angola and to develop that port.[30] Thus the German Government was strengthening by economic enterprise the plan of ultimate

[27] The Zambesia Exploring Company was a financial trust with a large interest in the Benguella Railway, the Tanganyika Concessions, L'Union Minière and the Rhodesia railways.

[28] Quoted by G. L. Beer in *African Questions at the Peace Conference* (New York, 1923), pp. 108–109, from R. Williams in the *United Empire*, July, 1917. In a report on the subject made to the annual meeting of the Tanganyika Concessions, Ltd., July 22, 1914, Williams declared that control would not be given up, but that half control might be conceded on suitable terms.

[29] E.g., the *Norddeutscher Gazette,* June 1, 1914, and in the careful study of M. Salesses, *Géographie,* May 15, 1914.

[30] An English company, the Angola Exploration Company, however, held at the time an option on 100,000 shares of the Mossamedes Company.

political control for which arrangements were made in the Anglo-German convention of 1914.[31]

Germany had grown impatient of waiting for Portugal to pledge her colonies in return for a loan, or to cede them in the event of default. In fact Portuguese government finances were beginning to improve. Thus proposals were made for a revision of 1898 conventions which would provide greater opportunity for asserting control. British consent was secured and the secret draft treaty was initialed in 1914. The share assigned to Germany was enlarged, and extended to include the islands of San Thomé and Principe lying north of the equator. The conditions justifying intervention were so vaguely phrased as to permit almost any difficulty to be taken as a reason for intervention. So in effect wrote Lichnowsky, the German Ambassador in London:

> Cases had been specified which empowered us to take steps to guard our interests in the district assigned to us. They were couched in such vague terms that it was really left to us to decide when "vital" interests arose, so with Portugal entirely dependent upon England, it was only necessary to cultivate further good relations with England in order to carry out our joint intentions at a later date with English assent.[32]

From the same pen came the judgment that "it might also become easy to give practical application to the paragraph about the endangering of important interests through maladministration once we have proceeded with energy to the creation of economic interests, especially in railway matters."[33] From the opening of the negotiations

---

[31] Lichnowsky, *op. cit.*, p. 312, prints a letter from the German Minister at Lisbon which states that "there can be scarcely any doubt that the financial world was encouraged to make the investments because it was led to assume that the conclusion of the treaty with England could be regarded as certain.

[32] *Ibid.*, p. 60.   [33] *Ibid.*, pp. 274–275.

the German Government had proceeded to the creation of these interests with avid energy and purpose.

Great Britain by this agreement abandoned—at least seemed prepared to abandon—a small and defenseless ally. Sir Edward Grey probably conceived it as a means of promoting conciliation with Germany without sacrificing any essential British interest; in fact, the expected end would bring valuable territorial accessions to Great Britain. It might have appeared like weak and muddled sentiment to continue to support a colonial administration as inhumane and withering as the Portuguese. The recent conduct of that administration had roused the indignation of the world. The treaty was never ratified. Sir Edward Grey insisted upon publication as a condition of ratification. Germany was afraid that publication would make its plans more difficult. Perhaps Sir Edward Grey had counted upon that fact. The outbreak of the war ended the discussions. The whole course of financing of Portugal and the Portuguese territories indicated how, in an area which is the object of political ambitions and which is directed by a government incapable of undertaking its proper development, the movement of capital from outside is dominated by political considerations. The banks and investors played a secondary rôle in the shaping of events. But still, financial failures, which might have cost a state of more primitive civilization its independence, were permitted Portugal because of its historic place in the European world.

CHAPTER XII

THE FINANCING OF THE BALKAN STATES

FROM the time of their liberation from Turkish rule, the Balkan states—Greece, Roumania, Bulgaria, Serbia—were borrowers. All of them endeavored to build railways within their territories and to join these railways with the systems of neighboring countries. Because the location of these railways was sometimes decided by military considerations, not economic calculations, because complete national control of rate and traffic policy was desired, the governments put upon their state budgets the financial burdens of construction or of acquisition. Heavier than the cost of railways, however, were the costs of war preparation and war. These and, all too often, lax budget administration, made budget deficits the rule rather than the exception, and kept the finance ministers busy with the problem of securing loans.

The credit of all the governments was doubtful (excepting Roumanian before the Balkan wars) despite the incentive provided by the fact that a sound debtor could borrow more than a shaky one. Three of the Balkan states, either to avoid bankruptcy, or as a consequence of it, had to enter into arrangements whereby their creditors were given a measure of control over the revenues pledged to the payment of the bonds they held. Relatively little foreign capital entered into private industrial enterprise in these countries, despite their proximity; probably not as much as a billion francs of foreign capital was so invested in their domains. Germany and Austria-Hungary, whose trade activity throughout the region was great, were, up to the nineties, the chief source of capital for both government and private enterprises. But the losses experienced through defaults, and the doubts entertained about the political tendencies of the borrowers, caused German lending to governments to decline rather than increase. German investment in banks and industrial establishments, especially in Bulgaria and Roumania, continued to grow however. British investors continued to give support to Greek loans. But the French became the chief purchasers of the bonds of the Balkan governments, passively buying the offerings of their banks, and finding assurance in the revenue controls established and in the increasing political influence which their government and the Russian Government were acquiring. French financial syndicates took the lead also in most of the important new projects of railway construction under consideration before 1914.

Each of the Balkan states cherished enmities and ambitions from the day they were established as independent states. These dominated their thoughts and their financial actions. The governments of the lending countries watched each movement, each turn of relationship. Sometimes they sought to make use of these rivalries for their own political advantage; sometimes they tried to discover means of reconciliation, for each Balkan quarrel drew the greater powers near to war. Thus each lending state exercised supervision over the negotiations between its banks and the Balkan countries. The purposes of the supervision wavered with the intentions and calculations, the fears and the desires of each lending state. Now a veto was imposed upon loans to a government whose policies were deemed hostile; now permission was freely granted in return for economic or political concessions; now it was reluctantly given lest refusal cause the borrower to make concessions elsewhere; now hesitating banks were urged to make a loan as a means of binding an alliance. Each of the lending countries on the whole wished peace to prevail in the Balkans, but each had unrevealed desires somewhere in the strains of national hope, and each was suspicious of the others. Thus since they could never agree upon and enforce a permanent territorial scheme in the Balkans, and since the Balkan states shifted their friendship with cunning self-interest, the control over loans did not in the long run serve general beneficial and peaceful purposes.

Even when control was exercised for such purposes it was defeated. Thus France, both before and during the Balkan wars, was consistent in its refusal to grant official listing to the loans of any Balkan Government. But both before and during the first Balkan war the allies against Turkey found credit in France as well as in Germany, Austria, England, and Russia. Banks made advances to be repaid out of loans to be issued after the conflict was ended; armament firms took bonds in payment for their product. Turkey resorted to the same markets and the same firms. Besides she drew upon those institutions which were connected with her financial destinies. The Banque Impériale Ottomane, the National Bank of Turkey (controlled by British capital), the Bagdad Railway, the International Financial Commission, and the Turkish Tobacco Monopoly all found it prudent to respond to Turkish demands.[1] Again in March, 1913, Sir Edward Grey, when plans for the peace conference after the first Balkan war were being discussed, tentatively suggested that there should be an international agreement to withhold funds from all the belligerents until affairs were settled.[2] The French Government was obstructing all public loans but still some French banks had helped Serbia and Bulgaria. This fact the German Secretary of Foreign Affairs stressed while indicating sympathy with Grey's proposal.[3] But the German Government had not long before indicated to the Deutsche Bank, which was refusing all requests before peace was concluded, that it would not oppose an advance to Turkey because of the possibility of a military breakdown in that empire.[4] Under these circum-

---

[1] *Le Marché Financier*, 1913–14, p. 761.

[2] *Die Grosse Politik*, Vol. XXXIV, Nos. 12962–12963.

[3] *Ibid.*

[4] Von Wangenheim, German Ambassador in Constantinople, had held out the hope of an advance of half a million pounds in return for the concession for the local subways (The Métropolitain). The Turkish Gov-

stances agreement was impossible. The Balkan states continued to be able to secure credit throughout the second Balkan war.

Upon its conclusion Russia took the lead in trying to establish an international financial boycott against Turkey with a view of forcing her to quit Adrianople. The Tobacco Monopoly, however, continued to pay instalments under its contracts, under penalty of losing its concession if it refused. The Austro-Hungarian Government, to whom the Russian Government applied because Austro-German institutions held share control, shifted the burden of responsibility to France since the direction of the business was in French hands. Russian effort died in the face of the hesitation of the other governments. Turkey retained Adrianople.[5]

Peace was finally arranged in August and September, 1913. Sucking their wounds, counting their debts, all the participants turned to the continental money markets. Under the scanning eye of the Russian Ambassador, and the promptings of the armament firms, Serbia, Roumania, Greece, and Turkey made terms in Paris. The last two immediately turned part of what they could spare from the payment or neglect of old debts, to the purchase of equipment for a fresh test of force with each other. Bitter at defeat, Bulgaria decided to give her pledges in Berlin rather than in Paris, as a step in that alliance which was to bring her into the Great War on the side of the Central Powers.

The outside larger powers were adding to their military

ernment granted the concession, but the Deutsche Bank refused the advance, stating that it had promised such advance only after the conclusion of peace. The ambassador attributed the refusal to an agreement between French and German banks not to come to the aid of Turkey till peace was signed. *Österreich-Ungarns Aussenpolitik*, Vol. V, Nos. 5661, 5681, 5692.

[5] *Österreich-Ungarns Aussenpolitik*, Vol. VII, Nos. 8397, 8404, 8422, 8427, 8443, 8458, 8482, 8503. The Austro-Hungarian, German, and French governments alike declared themselves to be powerless. The last two feared the financial breakdown of Turkey and loss to their investors.

forces and straining their financial resources to do so.
They were divided by alliances for which new accessions
were eagerly sought. Their cries of hostility were being
borne off to make the future whirlwind. How was it possible then to create a general understanding regarding
loaning policy that might contribute to the maintenance
of peace in the Balkans? Some secret plans, it is true, were
being discussed which might contribute to that end—the
internationalization of control of the Balkan railways,
and the division of economic opportunity in Turkey. But
these also succumbed to the blight.

The Great War came. The financing of the Balkans
proved to be a disaster to the whole wide world. Peoples
had been too ready to hate, investors too shortsighted,
banks too intent on special gain, armament firms too
smirched by the nature of their business, governments too
unsure, fallible, and deceitful.

SERBIA IS ASSISTED TO RISE

SERBIA was born as an independent state as a result of
the Treaty of Berlin of 1878. When the infant state first
opened its eyes its glance fell upon the creditors assembled
about its cradle. The war of independence had been financed by two loans from Russia, a forced domestic loan,
and by requisitions still unpaid; in all, though, hardly ten
million francs. Within fifteen years the new state was to
exhaust its credit and enter into composition with its
creditors.

The early borrowing was done in Austria, Germany,
and France. The Austrian and German governments encouraged the recourse to their investors.[6] Serbia had in
1881 bound herself by a secret treaty of alliance of ten
years' duration with Austria-Hungary. The Treaty of
Berlin had provided for the construction of new railway
lines in Serbia to create a continuous line from Constantinople to Vienna. The necessary construction was financed

6 *Geschichte der Frankfurter Zeitung,* pp. 585–586.

by a loan which the Austrian Government aided Serbia to secure from the Länderbank and L'Union Générale.[7] Throughout the reign of King Milan, and up to 1901, the Vienna banks remained willing lenders to Serbia. The loan of 1890 was used to buy back the salt monopoly; that of 1893 to consolidate the floating debt. In the 1890 loan the French bank of Hoskier participated as well as the Austrian and German banks. In the 1893 loan the Banque Impériale Ottomane took a share. This borrowing outran the state's financial resources. The emission price of each new loan fell below that of the last, until the effective interest cost was over 8 per cent. For each loan some definite revenue was pledged or some railway property mortgaged. Under the terms of the loans contracted, it was arranged that various pledged revenues from railways, stamp, and liquor taxes should be paid directly into a special "caisse" which was controlled jointly by the representatives of the government and the bondholders. The Tobacco Monopoly was ceded to the Wiener Bankverein from which it was later repurchased at a handsome profit to the institution.

Even these loans did not suffice to meet deficits and a large floating debt accumulated. By 1895 bankruptcy impended. The inexperience and financial irresponsibility of the country had been evident from the beginning, yet the banks had taken the risks for profit and the investors had followed them. Any independent state can buy enough rope to hang itself, if it will pay enough. The German banks took the lead in demanding some measure of supervision. Between 1873 and 1895 Serbia had accumulated an indebtedness of over 350 million francs.

After some preliminary difficulty a loan was negotiated to convert almost all of the old debts into a new one carrying smaller interest charges, and to enable the treasury to meet its most urgent needs. The revenues pledged to the loan service were put under a separate administration in the direction of which creditors' representatives shared.

[7] G. Y. Devas, *La Nouvelle Serbie* (Paris, 1918), pp. 246–247.

From this experience Serbia was to go on, not in a more sober fashion but in a more expansive one. The increase which this control and economic development brought in ability to get credit, was not neglected. The task of extending the railways was undertaken with energy. More costly still were the ambitions for a greater Serbia, a larger and more powerful national state. The cost of defense or aggression in that belligerent Balkan world continued to outrun the budgetary resources. Foreign lenders continued to supply the balance, finding assurance, despite all the noise and rumor of strife, in the Serbian government promise, in their own government's power to protect them from loss, and in Serbia's conscientious application to her economic tasks. After the termination of the Balkan wars the Serbian Government owed its foreign creditors over 900 million francs, and the debt service took over 30 per cent of its public revenue.[8]

As Serbian policy had come into accord with Russia after 1903, French banking relations with Serbia had grown intimate and dominant. All the large loans of the later years were issued in France; Germany shared only in the largest of them in 1909. The loan of 1906 went to France after a struggle of influence. As first arranged, Austrian and German banks were to have taken part of this loan, but they withdrew. Inability to agree upon the distribution of armament orders was certainly one of the causes of this decision. That question had been one of the issues creating dissension between the Serbian and Austrian governments. The latter, believing its armament manufacturers were being unjustly treated, had demanded a share of all orders as the condition of a commercial treaty.[9] The Serbian refusal may have been in part de-

[8] The reports of the British Minister to Serbia on the finances of that country, published somewhat irregularly in the *British Consular and Diplomatic Reports,* are a useful running commentary on the situation; M. Simitch, *La Dette Publique de la Serbie* (Paris, 1925), is a good detailed history.

[9] *British Documents,* Vol. V, No. 130.

termined by the necessity of giving these orders to French firms as a condition of securing listing for the loan in Paris.[10] In the upshot both loan and armament orders were placed in France. This loan served to enable Serbia to resist Austrian commercial demands and to wage a tariff war, momentous in the antagonisms it aroused. Serbia fought to escape from economic dependence upon the Austro-Hungarian Empire.

In 1909 the Serbian Government borrowed again chiefly for the purchase of armaments and other war materials. The Austro-Hungarian Government was gravely disturbed at the prospect of financial strengthening of its small but determined neighbor, who was at the time clamoring to be compensated because the Dual Monarchy had annexed the provinces of Bosnia and Herzegovina. Repeatedly its diplomatic representative at Paris was instructed to make the French Government realize that the extension of a loan to Serbia without clear guaranties that the proceeds would not be used to augment Serbian military strength, would be regarded in Vienna as an unfriendly action. Caillaux endeavored to quiet Austrian fears by showing how little of the loan proceeds would be available for new munitions purchases, and by emphasizing the French financial interest in undisturbed peace.[11] The French Government did not find it inconsistent with these assurances, however, to urge its armament manufacturers to meet the terms offered by Krupp, in whose behalf the German Government had intervened.[12]

During the Balkan wars, though the French Government in accord with its express policy did not permit any public loan, French banking syndicates furnished Serbia

[10] A. Andréadès, "Les Finances Serbes," *Revue Économique Internationale*, 1909; *British Documents*, Vol. V, No. 140.

[11] *Österreich-Ungarns Aussenpolitik*, Vol. II, Nos. 1646, 1658, 1669, 1690. France was sincerely desirous of seeing Austria-Hungary and Serbia come to terms.

[12] *Rapport de la Commission du Budget, Affaires Étrangères*, Exercice, 1910.

short-time advances in return for the promise of a concession of part of the projected Danube-Adriatic railway
line.[13] Even after the termination of the Balkan wars the
French Government hesitated to permit new borrowing,
afraid that some Serbian action might start war anew.
The banks tended to support this policy but the armament
firms kept up their competition.[14]

Late in 1913 permission to contract a long-term loan
was finally given in response to Russian persuasion. But
the French Government still fearing the outbreak of another conflict conditioned its consent upon the evacuation
of Albania and the settlement of frontier difficulties. The
Russian Foreign Minister, Sazonoff, informed the Czar
in November, 1913, that he, Sazonoff, had induced the
French Minister of Foreign Affairs, Pichon, to get the
bankers to float the Serbian loan so that Serbia would be
stronger in the event of war.[15] The resources of the Paris
market were insufficient at the time to make the loans that
were being sought; every government of Eastern Europe
was waiting its turn to borrow. Russia stepped aside to
give Serbia preference lest that country be compelled to
default on its debt.[16] The loan was issued in January,
1914. It enabled the Serbian army to take the field again.

CREDITORS' CONTROL IN SERBIA

SERBIA, in return for the consolidation loan of 1895,
undertook to put under a special *régime* those of its
sources of revenues which were specially pledged to meet
the service of this loan. These, then, would not flow into
the treasury in the ordinary way and would not be at the
free disposition of the government. It might use the rest
of its budget receipts freely, overspend and accumulate
deficits, but the bondholders would receive payment nevertheless. This scheme was put into effect by the law of
1895 which created a Monopolies Administration. The

---

[13] *Livre Noir*, II, 49.　　　　　[14] *Economist*, October 4, 1913.
[15] *Livre Noir*, II, 117, 360 *et seq.*　　[16] *Ibid.*, p. 174.

establishment of this body was made the subject of official communications to the interested powers who took note thereof, thereby indicating that their protective eye followed their investors' welfare. The law creating the Administration, as Serbia acknowledged in a later communication to the French Government, partook of the character of an international act.

The Monopolies Administration was directed by a Council of Six, two Serbs appointed by the Serbian Minister of Finance, two representatives of the bondholders, and the president and vice-president of the Serbian National Bank. The bondholders' representatives were in fact appointed by the Banque Impériale Ottomane and the Berliner Handelsgesellschaft. The French member of this commission attained inside place in Serbian official circles and had an important part in shaping Serbian public policy. Under the direction of the Monopolies Administration there were put the tobacco, salt, and petrol monopolies. To it also were paid the liquor taxes, certain stamp taxes, and the pledged railway and customs revenues. It held the power to determine the general policy of the monopolies, their purchases and sales, their budget. Subordinate officials were appointed jointly by the administration and the Ministry of Finance. The presence of bondholders' representatives guarded against corruption and inefficiency. The Serbian Government feared little to put so large a part of its revenues under this control, not only because of its representation on the administration, but also because of the general powers of supervision it retained under the law. Government and administration adjusted their wishes amicably, though the bondholders' representatives must have witnessed the growth of the debt with some anxiety.

The net yield of the monopolies and pledged revenues grew, but no more rapidly than the claims upon them.[17]

17 Compiled from Simitch, *op. cit.*, and O. Wormser, *Les Fonds Serbes* (Paris, 1910), and the *British Consular and Diplomatic Reports.*

AMOUNT
(millions of francs)

Year	The public debt of Serbia	Net yield monopolies administration	Needed for debt service
1896	369.2	18.6	16.7
1900	422.4	25.7	17.3
1905	461.6	32.6	20.2
1910	672.2	39.0	30.7
1913	659.0	43.4	32.3
1914	903.0 (approx.)		45.0 (approx.)

As new loans were contracted, additional revenues were placed under the Council's control. There can be little doubt that in the light of the financial exigencies of the Serbian Government it was only the existence of the Monopolies Administration that prevented irregularities in the payment of the debt service. On the other hand, it was only its existence that enabled Serbia to find purchasers for its later loans. In 1909 and 1914 default was avoided by new borrowing. The administration after all could only manage its business of revenue collection; it could do nothing to smooth or constrain the political storms midst which it lived. That is the business of government, not of debt-safeguarding. Whether the course of world affairs would have been more advantageously served if no such institution had been created to augment Serbia's borrowing power, is a question without answer. Whatever answer might be given, it would be applicable to the whole financing of the Balkan region by outside capital. All was fuel for the campfires of antagonistic states.

THE DEVELOPMENT OF ROUMANIA

THE credit of the Roumanian Government stood higher before the war than that of any other Balkan Government although it applied with sufficient frequency to Berlin and Paris, and occasionally to London. Up to 1913 most of the proceeds of its borrowing were used for productive purposes, and the debt service was met with regularity. Well

over half the capital obtained was used for the repurchase
and construction of railways, much of the rest for roads,
docks, and agricultural credit. Austrian and German investors supplied most of the funds, though in the nineties
French participation became increasingly important. In
1899 the French Government imposed conditions upon a
projected loan in Paris which caused Roumania to have
recourse to Berlin contrary to its intention. But after the
Roumanian Government had agreed to submit to arbitration a dispute concerning the treatment of a French enterprise which had been engaged in port construction at
Constanza, French finance was permitted to participate
in the loan.[18] Beginning in 1912, when Roumanian policy
shaped itself toward Russian, German investors began to
dispose of their securities. Still, the large 1913 loan occasioned by military expenditures was issued mainly in
Berlin. At the outbreak of the Great War, Roumania's
external debt was about 1.7 billions of francs of which
it was estimated 52 per cent was held in Germany, 32 per
cent in France, 5 per cent in Belgium, and 11 per cent
in Roumania.[19] Virtually all the loans were contracted at
an effective interest cost of about 5 per cent. Such revenues as were designated as special loan guaranties remained under Roumanian control and were collected by
the treasury in the ordinary way.

Both German and French capitalists acquired extensive
private interests in Roumania, in some of which in fact
the two groups coöperated. German capital financed the
government purchase of railroads. It founded in 1895 the
Banca Generala Romana to handle the financing of commerce and the development of Roumanian industry. Aus-

[18] R. Pinon, *L'Europe et la Jeune Turquie* (Paris, 1911), p. 441.

[19] S. Radulesco, *La Politique Financière de la Roumanie* (Paris,
1923), p. 87. Estimates for earlier years, confirming the importance of
German holdings, are given by Xenopol, "La Richesse de la Roumanie,"
in *Le Mouvement Économique,* May 1, 1907. In April, 1907, the foreign
debt annual charge was about 92 million francs of which 42.8 were paid
in Berlin, 6 in Frankfort, 23 in Paris, and 9 in Roumania.

trian capital established the Banque de Crédit Roumain.
In the Banque Marmorosch Blank, Austrian, German,
and French capital shared, as they did also in the Banca
Commerciala Romana.[20] It was the first of these particularly which brought Roumanian securities to Berlin
through the two banks which were its parents, the Diskonto-Gesellschaft and Bleichröder. The Diskonto acquired the concession for the tobacco monopoly. German
finance led, too, in the development of the Roumanian
petroleum resources, holding shares and directorships in
the many companies which they united in 1907 in the
Allgemeine Petroleum Gesellschaft. Companies directed
from Berlin engaged in the lumber and textile industries,
built branch plants to manufacture locomotives and
electrical equipment. German mechanics, executives, and
engineers directed the daily operations of all these enterprises. French financial interests supported similar undertakings on a smaller scale. The Roumanians, looking
back, now tend to describe this activity of German capital
as an attempt at domination. That is a matter of phrase-
ology. The German lenders hoped to strengthen German
industry by sales to Roumania, by profits derived from
Roumanian undertakings and by the sources of raw material developed. Beyond that it was thought that the
growth of financial and business interest within Roumania
would bind that country to Germany in political affairs.
In the latter expectation Germany was disappointed. The
political ambitions of Roumania were better served by
another course, and the economic affiliation was cast aside.

The negotiations incident to the flotation of the government loan of 1913 illustrate the political considerations
which entered into such transactions in all the Balkan
states. For some years previous the Paris market had been
closed to Roumanian loans because of the secret alliance

20 D. Kastris, *Les Capitaux Étrangers dans la Finance Roumaine*
(Paris, 1921).

of that country to the Central Powers.[21] In January, 1913, when the Deutsche Bank offered the Comptoir D'Escompte a third of the loan it was then negotiating, the French Government induced that institution to reject the proposal, noting that the funds were to be used for military purposes.[22] The refusal was repeated in July, 1913, in accordance with French policy of not permitting public loans to the Balkan governments during the Balkan wars.[23] In September, 1913, the Roumanian delegate to the peace conferences assured M. Poincaré that Roumania would not be "in the enemy's camp."[24] What the exact force of the declaration was—assuming it was made, and whether it was taken by Poincaré as significant, or merely as a step in the loan negotiations—remains a matter of doubt. However that may be, the Roumanian Minister of Finance discussed terms with the French banks under the approving eye of the Prime Minister.[25] The French Government believed the business arranged. Then to its disagreeable surprise it was informed that the loan had been contracted for in Berlin largely because of the negotiating aptitude of the German Ambassador.[26] The current explanation was that the French banks would not contract for the full sum asked by Roumania. The Russian *chargé d'affaires* at Paris cast the blame upon the officiousness of one of the department heads in the French Ministry of Finance. M. Paleologue, in charge of the Political Bureau of the Foreign Office, whom the Russian *chargé d'affaires* reported to be perturbed by the incident, and regretful that he had no greater power over the banks, explained it by German exploitation of French cupidity.[27] But in the

[21] T. Jonescu, *Some Personal Impressions* (London, 1910), p. 9; *Livre Noir*, II, 157.

[22] *Ibid.*, II, 14.

[23] *Documents Diplomatiques, Affaires Balkaniques, 1912-14*, Vol. II, No. 369.

[24] Jonescu, *op. cit.*, p. 11.   [25] *Livre Noir*, II, 157.

[26] *Die Grosse Politik*, Vol. XXXIX, Nos. 15796 *et seq.*

[27] *Livre Noir*, II, 155-158.

opinion of the Russian official, the fault was really that of the press which he declared to be entirely in the pay of the banks. A week after the announcement that a contract had been signed in Berlin, the Roumanian Government proposed that the loan be divided between Paris and Berlin. But the French Government, being informed that the German market was in no condition to purchase the loan, refused the arrangement. Additional reasons for its decisions were that the loan would go in part to discharge short-time debt held by the German bankers and to pay for armaments bought in Germany. The loan was issued in Berlin, London, Brussels, and Amsterdam.

But despite this service of Berlin, the Roumanian Government continued to direct its actions in accord with Russia. When the war came, the activities of German capital within its borders were denounced. The financial and industrial connections with Germany did not shape Roumania's ultimate political decisions.

THE FINANCING OF BULGARIAN AMBITIONS

VIRTUALLY every loan which was made to the Bulgarian Government was the cause or occasion of intricate diplomatic negotiations; each was an item in the calculations of opposed alliances.

The Bulgarian state wrested autonomy from Turkey in 1878, and complete independence in 1908. The foreign government debt, contracted mainly in Vienna and Berlin, grew rapidly between 1886 and 1902. Of all available markets for Bulgarian securities during this period Vienna was on the whole most reliable. Berlin gave thought to Russian wishes in passing upon the Bulgarian requests. In 1889, for example, the Berlin Stock Exchange refused to list a Bulgarian loan then under consideration; Bismarck did not want to flout further Russian feeling. The loan was contracted in Vienna, though the Russian government issued a public circular charging that it was a breach of the Treaty of Berlin. The proceeds of the early borrowing for which an effective interest of over 7 per cent was paid, were used to acquire a railway system, to found and support agricultural banks, and to sustain a growing army. By 1901, credit exhausted and deficits continuing, the government sought a consolidation loan.

French bankers undertook the transaction and in 1902 a large loan was issued in Paris and London. Thereafter Paris became the first resort of the Bulgarian Government though other money markets were not spurned. Under the provisions of this 1902 loan the revenues pledged to the debt service were placed under the indirect control of the lenders. In 1904 and 1907 new loans were contracted through the same syndicate and the control arrangement was extended. These loans served to pay for military supplies, for railways, and for general government expenditure. In 1908–9 Bulgaria became indebted to the Russian Government. As indemnity to Turkey for seizure of the lines of the Oriental railway within Bulgarian territory, and for the Turkish state property in Roumelia which it annexed, and for various other purposes, 125 million francs were required. The investors of Western Europe were not eager to supply them. To the Russian Government, stirred up by the Austrian annexation of Bosnia and Herzegovina, the opportunity presented itself of proving itself friendly to Bulgaria. Turkey was under the obligation of making annual payments to Russia as a consequence of past defeats. Now Russia released Turkey from the payments and accepted Bulgaria as debtor instead. Bulgaria was enabled to defray the expenses of its assertion of national independence. But the attainment of this object was followed by an increase in government outlay, not a decline.

Bulgaria continued to augment its military establishment and extend its railway plans. Its budget continued in deficit; its floating debt widened in circulation. When long-time loans could not be arranged, short-time advances were secured from the State Bank of Bulgaria, from foreign armament firms and banking syndicates. The conflicts with Turkey and its Balkan neighbors were in the making. In the autumn of 1913 a disappointed Bulgaria faced bankruptcy unless it could secure a loan to meet the pressing creditors who held its maturing promises. A loan was arranged in Vienna and Berlin after a struggle of influences which divided political parties within the state and called into action the diplomatic powers of the competing alliances. War came again before it could be issued.

The Bulgarian Government debt in 1914 approximated 850 million francs.[28] Yet this total was not too great for the capacity of the country, given peace and the productive employment of the borrowed resources. But these conditions were not achieved. Investors underestimated their importance, passed them over till the final calamity came which destroyed vaster hopes and interests than their own. Their investment was a political transaction rather than an economic one, though only official circles fully recognized that fact.

Besides the purchase of government loans, foreign capital sought profitable opportunity in the foundation of banks and industries in Bulgaria, especially Austrian and German capital. But the amounts ventured remained small.[29] Anxieties regarding the political outlook constantly obstructed the activity of private financial enterprise and technical skill in Bulgaria.

[28] K. C. Popov, *La Bulgarie Économique* (Sofia, 1920); *Le Marché Financier*, 1913–14, p. 757. The increase in debt was approximately as follows:

Year	Millions of gold francs Total debt	Debt service	Per cent of government revenue
1887	26.4	2.1	4.0
1900	205.5	24.6	30.0
1905	359.7	31.3	25.0
1911	633.2	39.9	20.0
1914	850.0	52.0	30.0

[29] Popov, *op. cit.*, estimates that this investment in private enterprise totaled in 1911 only 41.6 million francs of which 15 million were invested in banks.

THE FRENCH GOVERNMENT VACILLATES

THE Bulgarian Consolidation Loan of 1902 was bought chiefly in Paris. The French became the leading creditors of Bulgaria. The Banque de Paris et Pays Bas, which negotiated the 1902 loan, was the power which exercised the control created in accordance with the terms of the loan. This French bank maintained intimate touch with the Bulgarian Government; it founded a subsidiary bank in Bulgaria and a mortgage bank. But the French Government stepped in to guard and check the course of Bulgarian borrowing. It wavered between distrust of Bulgarian leanings toward Germany, hope of weakening these leanings by extending financial favors, and fear of increasing them if it too steadily blocked Bulgarian borrowing. The wiles of the Bulgarian monarch kept French diplomats in a state of indecision as that monarch knocked first on one financial door, then on another. No gratitude certainly was to be gained from that too clever ruler of too turbulent a nation. The record is for France full of vexatious failure.

Of the 1904 and 1907 loans, Paris took the major share, being assured in each case that the war materials, for which much of them was spent, would be bought from Creusot. In 1909 when the Bulgarian Government sought to borrow without granting special guaranties in the form of control, the Banque de Paris et Pays Bas stepped aside. When the Crédit Mobilier came forward, the French Government checked its move by refusing to grant listing on the Paris Bourse. Political considerations may have entered the decision as well as prudential ones. Probably too the demand for orders for French industry was not satisfied. The loan was finally issued in Austria, England, Holland, Switzerland, and Belgium. It was admitted to listing in Vienna, but for the time being refused listing in Berlin.

In 1911 Bulgaria wished to borrow once more to consolidate floating debt, to meet the expenditures of military preparations, and to extend its railways. Negotiations begun in Paris again failed of success in much the same way and for much the same reasons as in 1909. The year after, Bulgaria was again back in the Paris market. This time, March–June, 1912, it had in its negotiations the support of the Russian Government, which had made advances through its state bank, and which stood sponsor for the secret Balkan Alliance, which had been signed. "You know," the Russian Minister of Paris wrote to his government on June 7, 1912, "he [M. Poincaré, Prime Minister and Foreign Secretary] said to me that the French Government is disposed to facilitate the Bulgarian loan in Paris only because the Russian Government declared to it that Bulgaria, after forming a secret agreement with Serbia, had firmly decided to ally itself with the Entente."[30] Poincaré, who formerly opposed the transaction and had intervened personally with the Banque de Paris et Pays Bas, switched his position and agreed in principle to the loans. But a few weeks later he returned to his original refusal.[31] King Ferdinand's visit to Berlin and Vienna, where he was received with conspicuous honors, roused French fears afresh, and it was suggested to the Russian Government that before Bulgaria was given aid, further assurance should be obtained of Bulgarian policy.

The French Government persisted in its stand throughout 1912. A full knowledge of the terms of the Serbian-Bulgarian Treaty led Poincaré to reaffirm his refusal. The agreement seemed to be but preparatory to the declaration of war against Turkey, and Poincaré wanted to maintain peace in the Balkans.[32] His judgment was correct; within a few weeks war was proclaimed. During the six months

[30] *Livre Noir,* I, 283.

[31] *Ibid.,* and E. Judet, *George Louis* (Paris, 1925), pp. 195–196; R. Poincaré, *Au Service de la France,* II, 200; *Die Grosse Politik,* Vol. XXXIII, No. 12059.

[32] *Die Grosse Politik,* Vol. XXXIII, No. 12251; *Documents Diplomatiques, Les Affaires Balkaniques, 1912–1914,* Vol. I, Nos. 74, 75, 107; *Österreich-Ungarns Aussenpolitik,* Vol. IV, Nos. 3735, 4028.

of conflict (October, 1912—May, 1913), the French Government refused to sanction the admission to official listing of any Bulgarian loans. But French banks made advances to pay for munitions purchased in France as did also the German and Russian banks.[33]

The conclusion of fighting in this first Balkan war found Bulgaria seeking in Paris further advances on a future loan while refusing to accede to the Russian judgment of the distribution of conquered Turkish territory among the Balkan allies.[34] The French Government would not permit the advances.[35] Upon the conclusion of the second Balkan war (July–August, 1913) a defeated Bulgaria resumed its attempts to borrow. Concealing the promises of a secret alliance which it was giving to Austria-Hungary, the new Radoslavoff Cabinet bargained with the Paris bankers.[36] But Poincaré and Pichon hesitated until they received definite proof of Bulgarian intentions.[37] Russia too began to worry at the course of Bulgarian policy and secured a promise from the French Government that no loan would be permitted without its consent.[38] London also refused a loan.[39]

Bulgaria turned to the Austro-Hungarian Government which showed a disposition to facilitate the desired borrowing. The Vienna banks made some advances. The French

[33] *Die Grosse Politik*, Vol. XXXIV, No. 12963.

[34] In March, 1913, Bulgaria, issuing victorious from the first conflict and hoping to gain possession of the whole shore of the Aegean and even Saloniki, entered into negotiations with the Crédit Mobilier to purchase the Jonction Saloniki Railway in its behalf under a secret agreement to be ratified by the Sobranje after the conclusion of peace. Bulgaria was to give the Crédit Mobilier government bonds in payment for share control. *Le Marché Financier*, 1913–14, pp. 804–805.

[35] *Livre Noir*, II, 96.

[36] *Österreich-Ungarns Aussenpolitik*, Vol. VII, No. 9080.

[37] *Ibid.*, Nos. 9095, 9422. According to these documents France asked as a condition that Bulgaria enter into a military convention with Russia.

[38] *Livre Noir*, II, 185.

[39] V. Radoslavoff, *Bulgarien und die Weltkrise* (Berlin, 1923), pp. 80–101. Radoslavoff was in charge of the negotiations.

Government, alarmed, shifted its position, declared itself willing to favor a French loan if the Radoslavoff Cabinet were displaced by one less favorable to Germany. It exerted itself to create opposition within Bulgaria against the conditions asked by Berlin. The Russian Government also switched its position in response to the appeal of its Ambassador to Bulgaria who emphasized the advantages to be obtained in return for the loan.[40] Excited moves were made by all the interested states. The German banks were asking that a tobacco export monopoly be formed under their control as security for their loan. This the Bulgarian Cabinet refused. By May, 1914, during a rupture of the negotiations with Austria and Germany, France was willing in return for the desired cabinet changes not only to sanction immediate new advances by the French banks of 80–90 million francs, but to defer already overdue payment on 75 million francs of Bulgarian Treasury bonds held by these banks.[41] Russia went further and agreed to yield in its wish for immediate cabinet changes.[42]

But the official efforts with the French banks which had hitherto floated Bulgarian loans met discouragement. The Banque de Paris et Pays Bas, and the Crédit Lyonnais refused to make required advances because of the state of the market. The French Government turned to other financial groups which had connections with Creusot and the Bulgarian Régie Générale.[43] These arrangements too encountered difficulty. In June, 1914, the Banque Perier was striving to conclude the loan working in coöperation with the Russian State Bank.[44] The Russian Minister strove with might and main, called French banking representatives to Sofia, offered loans without political conditions, and resorted to bribery of the press.[45] These measures

[40] A. Savinsky, *Recollections of a Russian Diplomat* (London, n.d.), p. 216.

[41] *Livre Noir,* II, 266.

[42] Savinsky, *op. cit.,* p. 216.   [43] *Livre Noir,* II, 269.

[44] B. De Seibert, *Entente Diplomacy and the World,* pp. 450–456.

[45] Savinsky, *op. cit.,* p. 217.

failing, both France and Russia demanded immediate repayment of all the uncovered bills and debts due their institutions. But the Bulgarian Cabinet stayed pledged to the Austro-German financiers, who had ceased to require the formation of the tobacco export monopoly. In July Parliament gave its consent to the cabinet's action in a tumultuous session in which the ministry was accused of dishonesty and trickery.

In the whole process of negotiation between French investors and the Bulgarian Government the economic aspects were submerged in the political. Loans, like men, were but an item in the diplomatic play; in the last act the French Government saw its influence fail and its fears realized.

THE GERMAN GOVERNMENT WINS

THE early Austro-German loans to Bulgaria were used mainly for the construction or purchase of railways on which their security rested; the 1889 loan was spent chiefly for armaments. But the defaults of other shaky borrowing governments so accentuated doubts, after 1900, as to Bulgarian solvency in the judgment of the Berlin financial community, that they played only a secondary part in the financing of Bulgaria until the years immediately preceding 1914. Besides, in 1896, following a reconciliation with the Czar of Russia, the Bulgarian King seemed to yield to Russian influence. The French bankers gave better terms than the German bankers would. Thus, the loans of 1902, 1904, and 1907 were contracted in Paris.

In 1909 after being refused in Paris the Bulgarian Government secured advances in Vienna preliminary to the flotation of a loan by the Wiener Bankverein, a loan listed in Vienna. From this loan the Austro-Hungarian Government expected a turn in the political plans of Bulgaria, favorable to itself. Turkish doubts it allayed by promises that Vienna would persuade Bulgaria to be conciliatory.

French and Russian disappointment it ignored.[46] The German Government advised the Deutsche Bank not to participate in this loan and it withdrew against original intention. Lack of specific guaranties and lack of orders were given as reasons. Circumstances suggest that many additional calculations entered into the official action.[47] There was in Germany at the time a vigorous opposition to foreign lending. This loan was to enable Bulgaria to discharge a debt to Russia and to continue with her railroad program. There was a belief that Bulgaria had signed a secret treaty with Russia directed against Germany. Bulgaria showed signs of obstinacy in commercial treaty negotiations. All of these facts were before the German Government when it made its decision. Despite the attitude of the German Government and the closing by official orders of the Berlin and Hamburg exchanges, a Hamburg Bank, Schroeder Gebrueder and Company, took over part of the loan. For the next two years, relations between Bulgaria and the banks of the Central Powers remained rather unfriendly, mainly because of the belief that King Ferdinand had fallen in with Russian designs.[48] But in November, 1911, the Hamburg Stock Exchange was asked to admit the 1909 loan to listing. No official opposition appeared and the admission was granted. The loan terms earlier criticized as not giving sufficient security were no longer held to be a cause for rejection. In the meanwhile the commercial treaty negotiations between the two countries had been brought to a satisfactory conclusion. Ger-

46 *Österreich-Ungarns Aussenpolitik,* Vol. II, Nos. 1858, 1862, 1890, 1944.

47 W. H. C. Laves, "German Governmental Influence on Foreign Investments, 1871–1915," *Political Science Quarterly,* December, 1928, pp. 514–515, summarizes the situation.

48 M. Nekludoff, Russian Minister to Bulgaria, relates in *Diplomatic Reminiscences* (London, 1910), pp. 59–61, that during the winter of 1911–12 King Ferdinand asked the Russian Government to assist him in meeting personal obligations due to the Länderbank of Vienna, which bank was asking mortgage security that he could not give. The Czar arranged the required advance through a private Russian Bank.

man banking enterprise extended their private foundations and activities during the subsequent years.

During the period of the Balkan wars, Bulgaria secured
in Berlin some advances to finance munition purchases
from German and Austrian plants. Upon the termination
of these wars, as has been related, the Bulgarian Government, its hopes deferred in Paris, entered into a loan agreement with Vienna banks which acted with the emphatic
approval of their government.[49] The Radoslavoff Cabinet
in power in Bulgaria was offering a secret alliance to the
Central Powers. The Austrian banks proved incapable of
handling the loan unassisted. The Austrian Government
asked the German Government to secure German aid.[50]
The German Government hesitated to press its banking
institutions. Roumania was protesting against any Bulgarian loan arrangements. Even after Von Jagow indicated that the Foreign Office was impressed by the
Austrian arguments, the Prussian Minister of Commerce
refused to give permission to list any foreign loans on the
Berlin Exchange—on financial grounds.[51] For a time Austria-Hungary thought to circumvent the difficulty by
grouping a consortium around a Hamburg private bank
and securing listing on the Frankfort Exchange. But this
banking combination appears to have decided that listing
in Berlin was necessary for success. Austria-Hungary
next tried to persuade the Italian Government to join its
entreaties.

At the instance of the German Minister in Sofia the
Diskonto-Gesellschaft was brought into the negotiations.
The German Government appears finally to have indicated
its agreement provided that the loan was sufficiently se-
cured and German industry was sufficiently favored. The
German banking syndicate asked that Bulgarian Govern-

---

[49] Radoslavoff, *op. cit.*, pp. 89 *et seq.*

[50] *Österreich-Ungarns Aussenpolitik,* Vol. VII, No. 9422.

[51] *Ibid.*, Nos. 9428, 9442, 9522, 9552 give the course of discussion,
though leaving serious gaps.

ment orders be placed in Germany; this was in accordance
with official demand. As security it was suggested that
Bulgaria form a tobacco export monopoly over which the
bondholders should have a measure of control. Counter-
proposals and warnings were coming from France and
Russia. In addition, the peasants were aroused against the
proposed tobacco monopoly. For a while the Radoslavoff
Ministry dropped the negotiations. But the French-Russian plans were meeting difficulties also. The Austro-Hungarian Government strove might and main to cause the
Kaiser to dictate to the banks.[52] Whether because of such
pressure or otherwise the banks modified their terms. They
granted further advances, which amounted ultimately to
120 million francs, to be paid out of the final loan when
the matter of security was finally settled. In the upshot,
the Bulgarian Cabinet closed with the German syndicate
and rushed the parliamentary measure through Parliament. In the loan terms the scheme for a tobacco export
monopoly was dropped, but the German banking syndicate
was given concessions for railroad construction, harbor
development, and coal mining. In addition, the Bulgarian
Government promised German and Austro-Hungarian industry orders to the extent of one-fifth of the total loan.[53]
Furthermore, the Bulgarian Government obligated itself
to make for fifty years all supplementary purchases of
materials for the ports and railways which were to be
financed out of the loan through the agency of the Diskonto-Gesellschaft. Approximately half of the loan was to
be used to pay off the advances made by German, Austrian,
French, and Russian banks, spent for the conduct of war
and for armaments bought from Krupp, Skoda, and
Creusot. The Bulgarian Government pledged itself to
contract no further external loan for two years with-

---

[52] *Österreich-Ungarns Aussenpolitik*, Vol. VII, Nos. 9676, 9739, 9862.

[53] *Economist*, July 25, 1914; H. Prost, *La Liquidation Financière de
la Guerre en Bulgarie* (Paris, 1925), pp. 35 *et seq.*, gives the substance
of the loan contract, as published by the Bulgarian Government.

out the consent of the Diskonto-Gesellschaft. The loan
strengthened the position of the Radoslavoff Cabinet and
enabled it to push ahead with its plans of alliance with
Germany. The war, which was to make it unnecessary for
the armament factories to look for orders, was close at hand
and prevented the flotation of the loan. These calculations
which later induced Bulgaria to join the Central Powers
in the war, shaped themselves in the negotiations for the
loan of 1914.

CREDITORS' CONTROL IN BULGARIA

FOR the service of the consolidation loan of 1902, the Bulgarian excise tax on tobacco was set aside as a primary
guaranty. Arrangements were made whereby the proceeds of this tax, up to the amount required for the loan
service, went directly into the hands of the creditors' representative, thereby removing them from the field of temp-
tation. The law required that "banderoles" be put on
tobacco sold to consumers. These banderoles the Bulgarian Government had to purchase from the bondholders'
representative in Bulgaria. The issuing banks acted for
the bondholders in selecting this official whose appointment was notified to the Bulgarian Government by the
French Government. This detail was designed to indicate
to all and sundry, but particularly to the Bulgarian Government, that the French Government stood ready to
protect the investors if need be and thereby make it easier
to sell the loan in the first place. It also was a way of giving the French Government another spokesman on the
ground in Bulgaria. The Bulgarian Government was
pledged not to modify the scheme or schedule of the
pledged revenues. In addition, it was obliged to promise
to maintain gold payment for bank notes, subject to suspension in war-time—a provision which tended to prevent
an extravagant use of the printing press to the destruction
of Bulgarian credit. Small as was the outside control imposed by the scheme, its introduction was disliked by the

people. Parliament twice rejected it; the King dissolved Parliament; the new Parliament passed the necessary law.

By accepting this arrangement Bulgaria was enabled to borrow at a lower interest rate than was paid for previous loans, at an effective cost of about 5.5 per cent as contrasted with 6.5 per cent and more. The service of the 1904 and 1907 loans was also put under this control. For the later loan not only was the surplus of the tobacco banderoles tax pledged, but also the stamp tax, and, in cases of need, a tax on tobacco manufacture. The bondholders' representative sold the stamps as he did the banderoles. In the 1909 and 1914 loan arrangements no special revenues were set aside or control provided, though the government must have realized that their sales value would have been enhanced thereby. It fought against extension of foreign limitations on its freedom. It was afraid that political control might follow in the train of financial. It did, however, create a special semiautonomous Debt Administration composed of Bulgarian officials.[54]

The bondholders' representative in Sofia played a beneficial part in Bulgarian finances and Bulgarian economic life and attained considerable influence. That Bulgaria used its improved credit for purposes that proved disastrous is not a criticism of the control arrangement, but of the passions which governed the times.

FINANCING GREECE'S NATIONAL CAREER

THE history of Greek borrowing is that of a small and industrious nation whose ardent will for development and expansion caused it to live constantly beyond its resources, especially since it lived with the conviction that the decaying Turkey from which it had won independence had not yet yielded its natural territorial heritage. In this sense the loans of foreign investors were more a participation in

[54] See the text of the law in the report of the *Association des Porteurs Français*, 1912, pp. 270 *et seq.*

a national career than an ordinary economic investment.
Between 1879 and 1893 Greece became indebted to foreign
investors for the sum of 630 million francs of which she
received but 459 millions. Of this about 120 million francs
were used for economic purposes and the rest for ordinary
budget needs and military expenditures.[55] England,
traditionally a friend of Greek aspirations, was the chief
purchaser of the loans. This debt burden was plainly beyond Greek capacity and Greek currency was falling in
value, but the banks, in return for large commissions and
extensive pledges, found loyal investors to furnish the
funds to pay interest on old debts.

By 1892, however, this aid came to an end. The debt
service required half of the total revenue. In that year the
Premier, Tricoupis, tried to arrange for a loan in London
with the British Government. Mr. Law was sent to Greece
to study the financial situation. France, mistrusting this
step, asked that a Frenchman share in the inquiry. The
request was granted. The opposition in Greece criticized
this action, fearing it as the prelude to foreign financial
control. Such control in the final outcome the bankers
did ask as a condition of another loan. The Greek Government hunted for another way out of its difficulty. An
agreement was signed with Hambros Bank in London
under which interest on outstanding loans was to have been
temporarily paid in bonds which were to be guaranteed by
the proceeds of various taxes to be deposited directly in
designated banks.[56] But in May, 1893, the Greek Govern-

[55] Andréadès, "Les Finances de la Grèce," *Journal des Économistes,*
April, 1915, p. 53. Greece owed a large part of the roads, railways, and
mines which were in operation in 1914 to this era of borrowing by
Premier Tricoupis who managed to inspire foreign investors with great
confidence by restraining Greece from political adventure. By 1892
Greece had 630 miles of railway; by 1914 only 400 more miles had been
added. Another 400 roughly were acquired with territory taken from
Turkey. S. Koronis, "Einige Betrachtungen über die Eisenbahnpolitik
Griechenlands," *Balkan Revue,* May, 1914.

[56] E. Driault et M. L'Héritier, *L'Histoire Diplomatique de la Grèce
de 1821 à Nos Jours* (Paris, 1926), IV, 297 *et seq.*

ment denounced that agreement and declared that pending further negotiations, it would pay only 30 per cent of the interest on its debt. At the same time it took over the pledged revenues for general budget purposes. Most of the debt was held in Great Britain and Germany. The default, coming shortly after those of Portugal and Argentina, created intense irritation. Despite the pressure of the injured parties, the governments of the creditors refused to take strong measures against the defaulting state.[57]

For four years the creditors' committees and the Greek Government engaged in stubborn negotiation without issue. The Greek people rejected all suggestions of bondholders' supervision of revenue. Once in fact the Greek Parliament overthrew a ministry which planned to give foreign interests a place in the national bank.

In 1898 when Greece despite the constraint of the Powers plunged into a war with Turkey over Crete and emerged defeated, the bondholders' demands for protection were made effective. Future Greek wars at any rate were not to be fought at the direct expense of her creditors, though the risk had been obvious when the loans were made. On the initiative of the German Government provisions were written into the preliminary terms of peace whereby Greece intrusted to an International Financial Commission appointed by the Powers the duty of controlling the revenues set aside for the debt service and the newly imposed war indemnity. Clémenceau wrote at the time that France had collaborated in an "infamous act" under the orders of Germany.[58] Greek opinion was pro-

57 Kebedgy, "Les Difficultés Financiers de la Grèce," *Revue Générale de Droit International Public,* 1894, p. 261. Germany did try to get Great Britain and France to take more vigorous action, but they refused. Driault et L'Héritier, *op. cit.,* IV, 303–305, and *Die Grosse Politik,* Vol. IX, No. 2161.

58 E. J. Tsuderos, *Le Relèvement Économique de la Grèce* (Paris, 1919), p. 9. The official reports bear out the German insistence. France, *Archives Diplomatiques,* 1898, III, 67. The British Government exerted

foundly hostile to the arrangement but the subsequent
results of its operation do not support Clémenceau's char-
acterization. The Greek Government was forced to accept
in order to free its territory of Turkish troops. In return
for this supervision, the interest rate on the debt was cut
to about a third of the original rate and the Powers gave
their guaranty to a new Greek loan which she was thereby
enabled to market at 2½ per cent. The sale of this loan
marked the low point to which interest rates fell in Europe during the nineties.

The subsequent record of Greek borrowing is a repetition of this earlier history. The French investors, favorable to government securities, instructed by their banks
which acquired railroad and banking interests in Greece,
and encouraged by their government, began to take a
large share of the new loans issued by Greece. The German
investors took virtually none. The British investors were
not as approachable as before, but remained the most important creditors.[59] Expenditures for military purposes,
ports, and railways produced fresh deficits and occasioned
new borrowing. The payment of outstanding floating debt
continued to be the signal for the contraction of new ones.
Greece continued to push against the limitations of her
size and wealth.

From the Balkan wars Greece emerged with a heavy
debt to its national bank, to foreign armament firms, to
the Comptoir National for short-time advances, with a
budget deficit and with newly acquired provinces to administer. The necessary aid, a loan of 500 million francs,
was found chiefly in Paris and London though parts of
the loan were also sold in Egypt, Athens, and New York.

itself to secure preferred treatment for the British banks who had
made the funding loan of 1893. Great Britain, *Greece (No. 2), 1898,* p.
19 *et seq.*

[59] Payments made by the International Commission in 1912 upon loans
under its supervision were 8.1 million drachmae in Great Britain, 4.6
million in France, 1.2 million in Germany, 2.7 in Greece. *Le Marché
Financier,* 1912–13, p. 745.

King Constantine at the time asked the German Government to secure German participation, indicating an inclination to join the Triple Alliance as soon as the loan business in Paris was settled.[60] The publication of the news of the conversations between that sovereign and the Kaiser made it more difficult for a time to conclude arrangements in Paris. But the difficulties were finally overcome. As the price of permission to list the loan in Paris, during the days when the Paris market was under strain, the French Government was able to report advantages obtained. Material orders for the Greek army, navy, and railroads were reserved for French firms, a French company was given the contract for construction of the junction line between the Greek and Turkish railways. The Greek Government agreed to take over part of the Turkish debt in view of the transfer to Greek sovereignty of former Turkish territory and to guarantee the debt service of the Saloniki-Constantinople Junction line (a French-owned company, a large part of whose line was in the transferred territory) until its disposition was finally settled.[61] The loan carrying an actual interest return of 5.85 per cent was heavily oversubscribed in Paris.

There was at the time a French military mission in Greece, a French general being in command of the First Army Corps. Another Frenchman was in charge of the organization of the military supplies to be purchased in France. The French Government was supporting Greece in the current dispute over islands claimed by both Greece and Turkey.[62] In the spring of 1914 the Turkish Government was also borrowing in Paris to restore her military forces so that she might win back the disputed islands. The Turkish purchase of a dreadnought stimulated similar action on the part of Greece. Funds that were intended for railroad construction were spent for cruisers bought from

60 *Österreich-Ungarns Aussenpolitik,* Vol. VII, Nos. 8572, 8603.
61 *Livre Noir,* II, 233.
62 Driault et L'Héritier, *op. cit.,* V, 153–157.

the American Government out of its current stock.[63] But the threatened conflict was deferred until after the Great War.

The total Greek government debt at the outbreak of the war approximated a billion and a quarter francs, about half again as large as it was upon the establishment of control.[64] But the debt funded in 1898 paid interest of less than 2½ per cent; the debt subsequently contracted required the payment of 5 per cent. The ordinary revenues increased but not with great rapidity and debt charges rose in 1914 almost to 35 per cent. Some of the debt, perhaps 20 per cent, was held in Greece. The direct productive result was small. Roads had been built, some port and drainage works had been completed and about 150 million francs had been devoted to railway construction. Still in 1914 Greece looked back at her augmented territories and was satisfied. The country proved able during the Great War to carry the burden of debt it had accumulated. The holders of Greek bonds fared better than most purchasers of European government bonds.

CREDITORS' CONTROL IN GREECE

THE Greek law of 1898 transferred to the control of an International Financial Commission the revenues which had been pledged to the defaulted loans.[65] The six members of this Commission were appointed directly by their governments. That the Russian, Austrian, and Italian governments were given representation as well as the Eng-

[63] Andréadès, *Journal des Économistes*, May, 1915. For an account of the transaction in Washington, see H. Morgenthau, *I Was Sent to Athens* (New York, 1929), pp. 18 *et seq.*

[64] For a running account of the situation, see the reports of the British delegate on the International Financial Commission, published in the annual series of *Diplomatic and Consular Reports*.

[65] For the terms of the Greek Law of Control and the statutes of the Régie, see Great Britain, *Greece (No. 1), 1898,* and *Greece (No. 2), 1898.* For later agreements, accords, etc., see *La Dette Publique de la Grèce, Histoire, Lois, Décrets, Conventions, etc.* (Athens, 1916).

lish, German, and French, must be attributed to political considerations, for their citizens held but minute parts of the Greek debt. The Commission was given the power to name its subordinates. The Greek Government retained the right to veto all major appointments. The original pledged revenues put under the control of the Commission were those derived from the state monopolies (salt, petroleum, matches, playing cards, cigarette paper, and Naxos emery), from stamp and tobacco taxes and from the customs duties of the port of Piraeus. The Commission did not administer the revenues directly. That task was put in the hands of a Société de Régie, under the control of the Commission which could annul its decisions and dismiss its employees. The Régie was Greek in personnel and its director and subdirector were elected by the shareholders subject to the veto of the Commission. The Régie managed the monopolies and collected the other assigned revenues. To it the Commission sold the banderoles used to pay the tobacco taxes. The Commission was given the further right to inspect all institutions which in addition to the Régie took part in the collection of pledged revenues, for example, the customs service.

In the law of control there were inserted provisions intended to keep public finances healthy. They were incomplete but as extensive as the Greek Government would accept even in return for a guaranteed loan. The state debt in the form of currency notes and short-time treasury bonds, it was provided, was to be converted into a funded internal debt. The government, without the Commission's permission, was not to borrow more than ten million drachmae through treasury bills; this was circumvented at a later date. The outstanding paper currency was to be reduced by two million drachmae a year; this provision was observed until 1908 to the great improvement of the exchanges; thereafter the government need grew too great. The government gave up the right to make "forced loans" without the Commission's consent until all the paper currency which the government had put into circulation at forced values was amortized. These restrictions constituted a rudimentary scheme of monetary reconstruction. The government chafed under them and in the later years cast some aside. But even their partial application contributed to the course of development which brought the drachma back to par. From that improvement in Greek exchange, the bondholders benefited in the form of an increase in the rate of interest payment.

The Commission applied itself to improve the administration of the monopolies and pledged revenues and to stop frauds and contrabands. The yield of the controlled income mounted slowly.

NET YIELD OF PLEDGED REVENUES
(millions of drachmae)[66]

1899	47.4	1908	53.2
1900	46.7	1910	55.6
1902	48.0	1912	54.6
1904	51.8	1913	54.0
1906	57.1	1914	79.1

The increased yield is in part accounted for by an increase in certain customs duties made in 1905–6. The big leap in 1914 is explained by the inclusion of important additional sources of revenue pledged to the 1914 loan. What genuine increase in yield there was before 1914 came wholly from the Piraeus customs. The monopolies, stamp and tobacco taxes, did not improve their return under international administration. The Commission found it difficult to change established ways and practices, despite the powers of assertion with which it was, on paper, endowed. The annual reports of the Commission often record the complaint that despite its effort and urging no "noteworthy steps have been taken towards introducing the various reforms which have frequently been suggested."[67] Though the 1898 arrangement obligated the

[66] Prepared from the *Annual Reports of the International Financial Commission.*

[67] See *Reports of the Council of Foreign Bondholders,* 1908, p. 209; 1911, p. 191.

Greek Government to make such outlay as might be necessary for the improvement of the customs service, it always put aside such demand. The Greek Government accepted the Commission but was always somewhat frightened lest its prerogatives grow. The Powers intervened from time to time to support the Commission in its efforts.[68] But since the assigned revenues produced not only a sum sufficient to meet the minimum debt service, but also to yield substantial "plus-values" which were shared with the bondholders, the Commission did not attempt to assert the limits of its authority. The Greek Government used the institution when it could not secure credit any other way. In 1911 investors proved willing to purchase a loan not secured by the Commission's guardianship. But the large loan of 1914 was obtained only by placing many new revenues under its control.

The existence of the Commission increased the borrowing power of Greece and enabled it to borrow more cheaply than it could have otherwise. It emboldened investors to risk their money in the Near Eastern conflict. Whether Greece and the rest of the world would have been better served by not improving the security for such loans (the same question arises in regard to Turkish, Serbian, and Bulgarian loans) is matter of political judgment. Certainly only the existence of the scheme of control enabled the investors in Greek loans to receive their full interest payment during the stormy years that both preceded and followed 1914.

[68] *Reports of the Council of Foreign Bondholders,* 1903–4, p. 157; 1913, p. 33.

CHAPTER XIII

THE FINANCING OF THE
BALKAN RAILWAYS

ACROSS THE TURKISH PROVINCES FROM CONSTANTINOPLE
TO VIENNA

THE railways which connected Central Europe with Constantinople traversed and branched into the territorial domains of six states—Austria-Hungary, Roumania, Bulgaria, Serbia, Greece, and Turkey. With the exception of the first, these states were poorly provided with railways. Between the lines which did exist connections were few. There was no direct connection between Roumania and Serbia, and the Greek system was not connected at all with the Central European system. Each state wanted to control the lines within its territory and each had plans for connections and new through lines which would serve commerce and make armies mobile. It proved impossible to unite the scattered lines into a satisfactory system or coöperative scheme for common advantage. Their history shows all the difficulty of developing international economic coöperation in a world of small and warring states. It demonstrates that in such a world even the laying of a mile of track is an action disputed in a dozen Foreign Offices. Under such circumstances foreign capital can find no straightforward task. It adapts itself as best it can by seeking government favor, forms rival international groups that ally themselves with political forces and seek opportunity by serving political ends. The existence of national boundaries biases every act and negotiation. Plans molder for a decade that could be executed in a year.

By concession of the Turkish Government three rail-

ways were planned in the European territories which were
under Turkish sovereignty when the concessions were first
given. The first undertaken was the most important; it
was intended to join Constantinople with Western Europe
and by its branches to penetrate the rest of the Turkish
domains. On its main line a continuous service was finally
established—though not all under the control of the companies possessing the Turkish concessions; a through express service was operated to and from the Golden Horn.
That so continuous a route could be organized, despite the
perpetual quarrels among the states, was more or less an
accident in Balkan history. The changing regularity of
operation of the Orient Express (with its Wagon Lits)
was in fact a fairly good index of the state of feeling between the neighbors.

The Turkish Government, still master of most of southeast Europe, in the sixties had built, through a British
syndicate, lines from Varna on the Black Sea to Rustchuk
on the Danube, and from Kustendil westward. These
the Grand Vizier planned to link with the railways of
Central Europe and to make into a network which would
extend from the Black Sea to the Austrian border, from
the Danube to the Aegean. In 1868–69 a concession for
this scheme of railways to be about 2,500 kilometers long
was given to Baron Hirsch who was influential in the
South Austrian railways. The main stem was to run from
Constantinople to Sarajevo and from it four lateral
branches were to extend. In 1870 Baron Hirsch formed
an Austro-French company to build and operate the lines.
Under the terms of his concession the company was promised a bond subsidy for construction of 14,000 francs per
kilometer and guaranteed gross annual receipts of 8,000
francs per kilometer in effective operation. In return the
Turkish Government shared in the total gross receipts
over a fixed amount. So that the funds required for construction might be immediately available, the Turkish

Government turned over 3 per cent lottery bonds which Baron Hirsch proceeded to market.[1]

Construction was begun in 1870. But the task began to frighten Baron Hirsch's company. It asked for and obtained a revision of its concession whereby it was required to build only 1,274 kilometers and these in different and disconnected sections. The Turkish Government undertook to construct the complementary lines. By 1875 the sections intrusted to the company were built; those left to the Turkish Government remained uncompleted. For a few years the line rested in three isolated sections.

By the Treaty of Berlin in 1878, Serbia was confirmed in her independence. The territory which forms Northern Bulgaria now was made into a substantially independent principality, while Southern Bulgaria, known as Eastern Roumelia, was constituted an autonomous Turkish province under a Christian governor appointed by the Porte. Through all these territories the newly built and projected railways were to take their course. Under the terms of the treaty the company owning and operating the sections built was confirmed in its previously acquired rights. But if the lines were ever to pay, the construction of the connecting stretches was essential. Thus the treaty provided in principle for the construction of these connections and the junction of the system with the other lines in Austria, Bulgaria, and Serbia. Delegates of these three countries and of Turkey met in 1883 and entered into a convention whereby each promised to construct the necessary connec-

[1] For the terms of the concession, this transaction, and later agreements, see G. Young, *Corps de Droit Ottoman* (Oxford, 1906), Vol. IV. These bonds Baron Hirsch took from the government at 128.5 francs each; he sold them to the Austro-French group at 150, who issued them at 170–180. They were of 400 francs' nominal value. Because of their lottery character, both the London and Paris Stock Exchange refused to list them, and they were sold chiefly in Vienna. In the subsequent Turkish bankruptcy they were given smaller consideration than the regular Turkish government bond issues.

tions within its territory.[2] The junction points were Sem-
lin on the Hungarian border, Sofia in Bulgaria, Nich in
Serbia. By 1888 the connections were built and Europe
had a through line from Constantinople to Vienna—1,686
kilometers. This was the period in which, it may be recalled, German and Austrian capitalists, with the favorable regard of their governments, were loaning freely to
the Bulgarian and Serbian governments so that they
might build railways. Each government had reserved the
right to control the exploitation of the new sections and
connections which it built. The operation of those sections
of the lines which had been built under the original
Turkish concessions was retained by the operating company to which Baron Hirsch's construction company had
transferred its rights.[3] Ultimately these were bought out
by the Oriental Railways Company (Die Betriebsgesell-
schaft der Orientalischen Eisenbahnen).[4] The Oriental

2 For a careful analysis of the project, see *Correspondence Relating
to Article XXXVIII of the Treaty of Berlin,* Great Britain, Parliamentary Papers, Commercial No. 33, 1883, and Commercial No. 16, 1884.

3 Thus there became concerned in the management of different sections of this line the following administrations, as constituted in 1888:
the Austro-Hungarian State Railways, the Hungarian State Railways,
the Serbian State Railways, the Bulgarian State Railways, the Society
of Turkish Railways (Baron Hirsch).

4 This was after many vicissitudes and transactions. The company
was incorporated as an Austrian company. In 1908 it was turned into
a Turkish company and headquarters were transferred to Constantinople. The share capital was in the hands of German, Austrian, and
Swiss banks, who lodged control in a holding company created at Zurich,
which in turn was controlled by the Deutsche Bank; the control of the
Saloniki-Monastir line was held by the same parties. The properties
operated by the company were until 1908:

(a)	The main line, Constantinople to Bellova via Adrianople, with branches to Dedeagatch and Jamboli,	816 kms.
(b)	Saloniki-Uskub-Mitrovitza,	363 kms.
(c)	Uskub to Ziberce, linking since 1888 with Serbian National Railways,	85 kms.
(d)	Line, Nova Zagora to Tchirpaville, built by Bulgarian Government,	80 kms.

Railways Company until 1909 had its headquarters in Vienna; thereafter in Constantinople. But the effective control remained until 1913 in the hands of German banks headed by the Deutsche Bank.

One important part of the original Turkish scheme and of the revised Hirsch concession, these new arrangements left unfulfilled. A through route from Vienna to Saloniki on the Aegean had been planned. But no agreement was reached among the states concerned. The Austrian section running south ended in Uvac in Bosnia, a Turkish province under Austrian control. The section running north from Saloniki ended at Mitrovitza in Macedonia. Serbia opposed this direct line between Austria and the Aegean. Serbia itself had a railway outlet to the Aegean in the line from Nich to Uskub where it linked up with the Saloniki line. The plan was regarded as an attempt to check Serbian development since the projected line would not have passed through Serbia. But Austria did not renounce the wish and it was to become active again in 1908.

After the line from Constantinople to Vienna was in operation, Turkey granted concessions for two other railways to traverse her European provinces. In 1890 the Deutsche Bank was authorized to construct a line running westward from Saloniki 219 kilometers into Macedonia to Monastir. The operation of this line was turned over to the Oriental Railways Company. A French group, of which the Banque Impériale Ottomane was a part, secured the concession for the other railway. It ran eastward from Saloniki 550 kilometers in the direction of the coast line

> and (e) The Saloniki-Monastir Line (under an operating contract and with separate organization and accounts),   219 kms.
>
> Under the agreements between the company and the Turkish Government, all annual gross receipts over 7,000 francs per kilometer were divided between them. The railway guaranteed the government a minimum annual payment of 1,500 francs per kilometer, of which most was paid directly to the Banque de Paris and Pays Bas to discharge the service of the 1894 loan. The concession was to expire in 1958.

and joined 'the Oriental Railways near Adrianople. Constructed and operated by a French company, the Saloniki-Constantinople Junction Railway enjoyed a guaranty of 15,500 francs gross annual receipts per kilometer, guaranteed by the tithes of the districts it traversed. Neither this line nor those of the Oriental railways connected with the railways of Greece, as Greek territories then were. Turkey steadily refused to give the necessary authorization to build the 70-mile connection through its Macedonian province. This refusal was a great source of Greek resentment.

THE ORIENTAL RAILWAYS LIVE AMID TROUBLE

THE Oriental Railways Company was not to operate in the midst of Balkan conflicts and territorial changes without serious difficulties. For one thing, it was commonly regarded as an agent of Austrian and German political purposes in the Near East. As Serbia and Bulgaria made progress with their own railway system, as they repurchased other privately built railways within their territories, they resented the independence of the lines of the Oriental Railways within their borders. For that company was run from Vienna, had rate schedules and regulations outside of their control and its higher personnel was foreign. The company was accused, justly or otherwise, of subordinating the interests of the countries which it traversed to its own financial interests and to Austro-German economic interests and of making no effort to develop local resources and industry.[5] Bulgaria and Serbia, assisted chiefly by French capital, proceeded with the acquisition or construction of other lines and bided their time to ac-

---

[5] G. Bousquet, *Les Chemins de fer Bulgares* (Paris, 1909), pp. 17 *et seq.* To judge the degree of validity in these opinions a careful analysis of a most intricate body of facts would have to be undertaken. I have not discovered any such study among the colored and controversial literature on the subject.

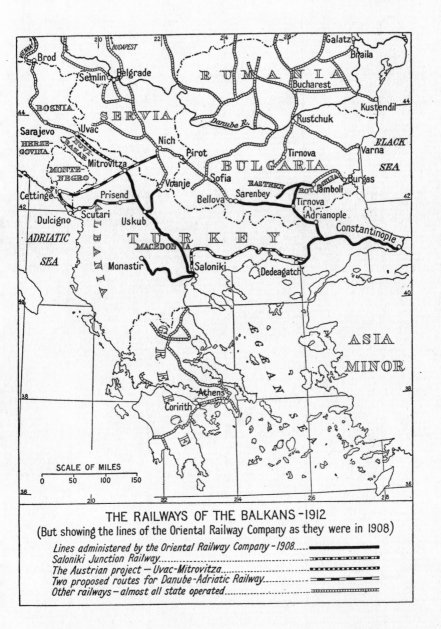

THE RAILWAYS OF THE BALKANS – 1912
(But showing the lines of the Oriental Railway Company as they were in 1908)

Lines administered by the Oriental Railway Company – 1908.....
Saloniki Junction Railway.................
The Austrian project – Uvac-Mitrovitza.................
Two proposed routes for Danube-Adriatic Railway.................
Other railways – almost all state operated.................

quire control of the properties operated by the Oriental
Railways.[6]

Bulgaria expressed its discontent by action. In 1896 it
undertook the construction of a parallel line as part of its
state system. The Oriental Railways Company protested
and was supported by the Austrian and German governments and banks which cut off credits to the Bulgarian
Government.[7] In 1898 the company offered the Bulgarian
Government the right to operate the 319 kilometers within
its territory for a reasonable compensation. The Bulgarian Parliament ratified the agreement but the Sultan
of Turkey opposed it and Bulgaria found it difficult to
borrow the necessary funds. Finally a new convention with
the company was signed in accordance with which the
parallel line was given up. At another time Bulgaria took
possession of one of the branch lines of the railroad and
kept it, paying an annual indemnity.

In January, 1908, a quarrel broke out which evoked
violent passion and drew in almost the whole of Europe.
Austria announced its intention to seek from the Turkish
Government a concession to join the railroads of Bosnia
to the line running north from Saloniki, to build the link
of 150 kilometers that had been left broken when the two
other sections were built, the link that would unite Vienna
to the Aegean at Saloniki via Sarajevo without traversing
Serbia. The connection was to be built across the then

[6] In 1881, the Austrian Länderbank in coöperation with L'Union
Générale had agreed with the Serbian Government to construct and
manage the important lines, Belgrade-Nich, Nich-Mitrovitza. Upon the
failure of the L'Union Générale other French interests were admitted.
The line to Mitrovitza was not built. In 1889 when the Comptoir D'Escompte failed, the Serbian Government took possession of the lines under
its control, those built to connect with the Oriental Railways and others.
The company asked not only payment for the physical property, but an
indemnity. The French Government stepped in and mediated an agreement. Serbia was enabled to issue a loan in Paris to pay for the railway and discharge floating debt; the loan was secured on the railway
receipts and other taxes.

[7] K. Helfferich, *Georg Von Siemens*, II, 11.

Turkish province of Novi-Bazar. Austria had delayed this action because of Hungarian opposition which now had diminished. Now its action was timed if not provoked by new initiative being shown by Serbia, Russia, and Italy in the plan for a railroad to run from the Danube to the Adriatic.[8] Austria asserted that the right to build the railroad to the Aegean had been conferred upon her by the Treaty of Berlin. This the other Powers disputed.[9] Plans for this road seem to have been formulated at least as early as 1900 and even in these early formulations stirred up fears abroad.[10] In its action Austria-Hungary sought to coöperate with Greece and at the time of the 1908 declaration Von Aehrenthal, Austro-Hungarian Secretary of Foreign Affairs, expressed the hope of effecting a junction between the Greek and Turkish roads at Saloniki and asserted that he was supporting Greek efforts at Constantinople.[11] The chief purpose of the Dual Monarchy in pushing forward this railway project was to establish clearly, against the possible smash-up of Turkey, its right to dominate the line to Saloniki. If Turkey retained possession of the Sandjak, the position of the line would remain unchanged, if it lost possession the Dual Monarchy would be in a

[8] This suggestion is made by the editors of the *British Documents,* Vol. V, No. 227, note; see also *Die Grosse Politik,* Vol. XXV, No. 8681, which relates the plan of the Anglo-French-Italian group for route, Dulcigno, Scutari, Prisend, Uskub, in October, 1906, and Nos. 8726, 8735, in which revival of this project with Russian support is discussed. The plan for the line to the Adriatic appears to have been first broached by Serbia in 1896. During 1901 a stubborn attempt had been made by Serbia, with Russian and Italian support, to get the necessary authorization from the Porte. The French Foreign Office had begun to favor the project; Italy put forward a joint Franco-Italian scheme; but when Delcassé was advised from Constantinople that Turkey opposed Italian participation, he evaded in the hope of the venture becoming wholly French. *Documents Diplomatiques Français* (1871–1914), 2d ser., Nos. 139, 182, 238, 247, 307, 308, 322.

[9] P. Crozier, "L'Autriche et L'Avant-Guerre," *Revue de France,* April 1, 1921, p. 302.

[10] C. Loiseau, *L'Équilibre Adriatique* (Paris, 1901), pp. 156 *et seq.*

[11] E. Driault et M. L'Héritier, *op. cit.,* IV, 562 *et seq.; British Documents,* Vol. V, Nos. 250, 256.

strong situation to bargain with the new masters over the disposition of the whole of the Oriental railways.[12] The authorization asked by Austria-Hungary was granted by Turkey in preliminary form. Its execution was deferred when the Dual Monarchy decided to annex Bosnia and Herzegovina later in the year.

There followed upon these Austrian actions fresh and aggressive retaliation on the part of the Balkan states and Russia. The first positive spectacular move was made by Bulgaria in September, 1908. On the occasion of a strike on the Oriental Railways which the Bulgarian Government fomented, that government took possession of 319 kilometers of company line in Roumelia (from the border to Bellova on the main line and the branch to Yamboli). After the strike ended the government declared its intention of retaining the line, asserting a willingness to indemnify the company, but not making clear where the necessary funds were to be found. Turkey appealed to the Powers for the restoration of the line to the company. The French and German governments refused to intervene. Finally, after the declaration of Bulgarian independence, agreements were signed between the company, the Bulgarian and Turkish governments by which the Bulgarian Government came into possession of the line and attached it to the state railways. The funds required to indemnify the company and Turkey for the seizure of the railway were furnished by the Russian Government.[13]

Serbia and Russia also responded vigorously to what they regarded as a serious violation by Austria of the *status quo* in the Balkans. This to them was not merely a railroad plan. It was an act of political aggression, an attempt to thwart the movement toward Slavic racial

[12] *Österreich-Ungarns Aussenpolitik,* Vol. I, Nos. 2, 3, 9, 32. Unfortunately most of the correspondence on the subject is omitted from the collection of documents, wherein it most clearly belongs. See footnote to Document No. 2.

[13] *British Documents,* V, 669 *et seq.,* and 792.

unity in the Balkans by dividing Serbia and Montenegro, a pretext for future intervention. The Russian Foreign Minister informed the British Ambassador that "he would not hesitate to take strong measures to prevent what he would consider to be an infringement of the Treaty of Berlin."[14] Italy also was stirred lest Austrian influence be strengthened in Northern Albania. Great Britain was indignant because of the belief that the necessary permission had been secured from Turkey in return for Austrian opposition to judicial reforms in Macedonia which the British Foreign Office had been trying to effect.

FROM THE DANUBE TO THE ADRIATIC

The opposition centered upon carrying through a plan to secure from the Turkish Government a concession for a railroad to run westward from the Danube to the Adriatic—uniting the Slavic peoples and connecting with the Roumanian and Russian railroads. This project which would cut across any Austro-German line running toward Saloniki had been broached as early as 1904 and was known as the Timok Valley Railroad.[15] During 1906–7 a number of competing plans and proposals had been in the field. For construction along various routes an Anglo-Serbian, an Anglo-French, and a German syndicate made offers to the Serbian Government asking for a government guaranty of interest. Montenegro endeavored to win over the Powers, especially Italy, to the support of an alternative road which would run to the port of Antivari in Montenegro. All required the consent of the Turkish Government and all presented serious physical obstacles which would make their cost exceed by much the amount that could be expected as immediate yield. Nevertheless, French

---

14 Report of Sir Charles Hardinge to Sir Edward Grey, June, 1906, in Viscount Grey's *Twenty-Five Years, 1892–1916* (London, 1927), pp. 206–207.

15 J. Aulneau, "La Querelle des Chemins de Fer Balkaniques," *Revue Politique et Parlementaire,* September, 1908.

financial interests, especially the Banque Impériale Ottomane and the Banque de Paris et Pays Bas, steadily encouraged the desires of the Serbian Government. Toward
all the British Government, and in a lesser measure the
Russian, had shown themselves till 1908 sympathetic but
noncommittal.

In 1908 the attitude of the Russian Government
changed.[16] It exerted itself to the utmost at Constantinople. Further it asked for the Austro-Hungarian diplomatic support in the Turkish capital, as the price of
Russian support to the Sandjak scheme. The Dual Monarchy permitted itself to express friendliness to the plan,
but refused positive help. Now moved to quick action in
March, 1908, Serbia sought the necessary authorization
from Turkey, having the promised aid of France, Russia,
and Italy.[17] The British Government expressed the view
that this concession should be granted to Serbia, or that
permission should be denied Austria to build across
Novi-Bazar. During the early discussions the Serbian
Government agreed to step aside in favor of the French-
owned Saloniki-Constantinople Junction Railway. The
Italian Government proposed that the venture be financed
by an international syndicate, 40 per cent of the capital
of which would be French, and the rest in equal amounts,
British, Russian, Serbian, Italian.[18] The Banque Impériale Ottomane and the Banque D'Italie entered into discussions and in June–July, 1908, an agreement concerning

[16] *British Documents*, Vol. V, No. 114; *Österreich-Ungarns Aussenpolitik,* Vol. I, Nos. 2, 3, 9, 32, 48, 412.

[17] *British Documents*, Vol. V, Nos. 244, 247, 248, 257; G. Giolitti, *op.
cit.,* p. 207.

[18] *British Documents*, Vol. V, No. 243; G. Y. Devas, *op. cit.,* p. 208,
gives slightly different proportions. Giolitti, *op. cit.,* p. 208, states that
by an agreement reached on June 3, 1908, the French were to provide
35 per cent of the capital and to appoint 5 directors, including the
president, the Italians were to provide 35 per cent and appoint 4 directors, the Russians were to provide 15 per cent and to appoint 2 directors, the Serbs were to provide 5 per cent and to appoint 1 director.
Of the capital of the Port Company the Italians were to provide 55 per
cent.

the company organization was reached. Efforts were renewed at Constantinople to secure the required grant for
the Saloniki-Constantinople Junction Railway.[19] The
Turkish Government at first refused the demands, especially since they were accompanied by the expectation that
a kilometric guaranty, such as other roads enjoyed, would
be given this one, and Turkey had no funds. In June,
1909, however, the Young Turk *régime*, friendly to
Anglo-French enterprise, accorded permission to make
preliminary studies. But the almost immediate shift in relations between Turkey, England, and France led to fresh
opposition on the part of the Turkish Government. Disputes about the route recurred and local authorities and
inhabitants blocked the efforts of the exploring missions.
The Turkish-Italian and Balkan wars ended all prospect
of immediate realization. The concessions obtained by
Austria to build across Novi-Bazar also remained unused.
Austria in March, 1909, had won over the Turkish Government to the idea that the construction of this line would
make the defense of the Sandjak easier, and promised financial and technical help.[20] But the Young Turk *régime*
dropped the discussions. Furthermore the Austro-Hungarian action in Bosnia had met such emphatic dissatisfaction in Serbia and Russia that it did not wish to make
hostility greater by pushing forward this railway plan.
Besides, Austrian finances from 1909 were taxed for other
needs.

THE BALKAN WARS BRING FRESH TROUBLES

THESE disputes over railroads contributed their not slight
part toward the antagonism that produced the Balkan
wars.[21] The territorial changes that followed these wars

[19] France, *Rapport de la Commission du Budget, Affaires Étrangères,*
Exercice, 1910, pp. 36–37.
[20] *Österreich-Ungarns Aussenpolitik,* Vol. II, Nos. 1105, 1217, 1244.
[21] G. Michon, *L'Alliance Franco-Russe,* p. 209, goes so far as to say
that this wish to get control of the railways was the chief cause of the

left new disputes about railroads and gave birth to new projects. These changes left far more than half of the line operated by the Oriental railways and most of the Saloniki-Monastir and Saloniki-Constantinople Junction railways in the territories transferred.[22] Serbia was unwilling to restore to the Oriental Railways Company the lines in the territory which passed to her possession (and these included a good part of the stretches which Austria had planned to include in the route from Vienna to Saloniki). Greece, which received the territory which included the city of Saloniki and sizable sections of all three of the railways running into Saloniki, was willing to restore to their previous owners part of their lines but not all of them. Bulgaria, chastened by defeat and its ambitions thwarted, was willing to turn back all the lines it had acquired.

Austria-Hungary demanded the return of all its lines to the Oriental Railways, and fearing that the enlargement of Serbia would block her plan of a direct route to Saloniki, had already sought from the company a lease on the line to Saloniki.[23] It had also entered into negotiations with Bulgaria early in 1913, when Bulgaria thought itself future master of Saloniki, for participation in the management of the railways and port of that important Aegean city, and its wishes had been listened to with good will.[24] The German Government supported Austria-Hungary against Serbia, justifying its protest by the German

war of the Balkan states against Turkey. To Serbia railway control seemed an essential preliminary to obtaining access to the Adriatic. See also F. Delaisi, "Une Guerre pour les Chemins de Fer," *La Grande Revue*, July 10, 1913.

[22] In the territory transferred to Serbia there were the extreme northern section of the Saloniki-Monastir Railway and 374 kilometers of the Macedonian line; in those transferred to Greece there were almost the whole of the Saloniki Monastir line, 78 kilometers of the line between Saloniki and Mitrovitza and 360 kilometers of the Jonction Saloniki-Constantinople Railway. In those transferred to Bulgaria there were 150 kilometers of the latter railway.

[23] *Livre Noir*, II, 331–332.

[24] *Österreich-Ungarns Aussenpolitik*, Vol. V, Nos. 5895, 6020, 6035, 6047.

capital investment in the lines.[25] Serbia refused the demand, promising an indemnity after the conclusion of peace. A dozen different plans and demands gave rise to as many intrigues.

The Austro-Hungarian Government entered negotiations with the owning German banks for the purchase of control of the Oriental Railways Company, fearing that such control might be sold to the Balkan governments assisted by French capital. The help of the German Government was enlisted in the negotiations. Finally in April, 1913, the transfer to an Austro-Hungarian banking consortium was arranged.

The Austrian Government stubbornly continued to ask for the return of the lines to the company, arguing that Austrian control was vital for the protection of its commerce which passed to the Aegean. The Serbian Government as stubbornly resisted the demands. Protracted direct negotiations between the Serbian and Austrian governments came to naught. Serbia would not return the lines and could not compensate Turkey and the company without outside help. The situation was difficult for Austria. Complete yielding to the Serbian position was deemed impossible. A show of force against Serbia might have provoked general conflict and probably would not have had German support.[26]

INTERNATIONAL OWNERSHIP IS PROPOSED

UNDER these circumstances, M. Pichon, anxious lest trouble arise and also alert to the chance to increase French influence in the Balkans, gave attention to a plan of internationalization as a solution.[27] Another scheme of

[25] *Die Grosse Politik,* Vol. XXXVII, Nos. 15115–15116.

[26] *Ibid.,* Nos. 15118–15119.

[27] A dispatch of Isvolsky's, November 23, 1913, indicates how important the question was considered, "in general, here, from the beginning of the crisis, it has been felt that the question of the Oriental Railways was most serious, and they (the French Foreign Office) feared the complications which Austrian stubbornness would create . . ." *Livre Noir,* II, 199.

internationalization—that for the Danube-Adriatic Railway—seemed at the time likely to eventuate. Now the French Government proposed, and the Austrian Government agreed, that in a similar plan might be found the way of reconciling Austrian and Serbian wishes, or at least of allaying their fears.[28]

In their early discussions of this idea, Serbia gave its consent and Italy and Russia were disposed to participate in the arrangement. Russian inclination was not entirely free or without special design. Isvolsky wrote to Sazonoff:

It would be very unwise to leave the French "en tête à tête" with the Austrians while questions so important for Serbia and Greece were being settled . . . , the presence of a Russian representative in the financial organizations which may become the agency of the international project would be a means of control and action in regard to (*par rapport aux*) the French financiers; furthermore if a peaceful solution of the grave question of the Eastern railways is to our interest, on the contrary too intimate a rapprochement between French and Austrian financiers would not be.[29]

Out of such rapprochement Russia feared not only a settlement of Balkan railway problems which might lessen its position of leadership, but even more so the reopening of the French money market to Austro-Hungarian loans. That the Austro-Hungarian Government hoped for such an outcome from these negotiations there can be no doubt. To prepare the way for friendly consideration in the Paris market, Austria was ready to show leniency in this matter of the lines controlled by the Oriental Railways Company to the extent of passing over to French financial groups a controlling interest.[30]

The French financial groups already had substantial

---

[28] *Die Grosse Politik*, Vol. XXXVII, No. 15126; *Livre Noir*, II, 95. The original suggestion and initiative may have come from Austrian financiers close to the Austrian Government, *Livre Noir*, II, 161–162.

[29] *Livre Noir*, II, 200.

[30] *Die Grosse Politik*, Vol. XXXVII, No. 15130.

interests in the Oriental Railways Company (its securities
were listed in Paris) and in the Serbian and Greek lines
which were to be connected with them, and in the Saloniki-
Constantinople Junction Railway, now largely in Greek
territory. Thus the groundwork for coöperation between
French and Austrian financial groups existed. The plan
as discussed between the banks and with the Greek and
Serbian governments toward the end of 1913 was to form
three companies, a financial parent company at Paris, and
two operating companies, one Greek and one Serbian, to
run the roads in their respective territories. In the Greek
operating company, the Greek Government was to have
one-third ownership; in the Serbian, the Serbian Government was to have an equal share; the other two-thirds in
each would be divided between the Austrian and French
groups. Greece and Serbia would be supplied the funds
necessary to take up their shares by bonds to be issued by
the holding company, and loaned to them. The plan also
provided for the building of important junction lines for
the Greek railways, by which the former would be joined
to the Central European systems. The French group
might give part of its share to Russia; the Austrian might
act the same way toward Italy and Germany. In its wish
to conciliate, the Austrian Government consented to a
French president for the parent company.[31]

Such was the general outline of the plan which, having
the favorable regard of both the Austrian and French
governments, seemed in January, 1914, to promise a solution of the situation.[32] The French and Austrian financial
groups had agreed on terms. But protests and difficulties
checked final action. Italy demanded a larger share than
France was willing to yield.[33] Russia was still ready to

[31] The French group included Count Vitali, who was connected with
the Banque Impériale Ottomane and M. Paul Doumer, former Minister
of Finance in France. The Société Générale was to handle the financial
arrangements. *Livre Noir,* II, 202.

[32] *Die Grosse Politik,* Vol. XXXVII, No. 15131.

[33] *Livre Noir,* II, 237-238.

oppose the admission of Austro-Hungarian securities to the French market and so to cheat Austrian hopes. The former German owners of the Oriental Railways Company, the Deutsche Bank and its associates, supported by the German Government, asked that the eastern network of those railways remaining in Turkish territory (248 kilometers, including the Adrianople-Constantinople line) be excluded from the scheme of internationalization.[34] The Germans in fact sought to repurchase the operating concession for this eastern network or to obtain guaranties, among which was representation on the board of directors, to insure that its policy would not be conducted in a way injurious to the German railway interests in Asiatic Turkey.[35] The German Government warned the Austrian against a growth of French influence in the Balkans. But the Austrian Government, still lured by the hope of admission to the French market and needing a settlement with Serbia, was most reluctant to yield to the German demand, which was not acceptable to the French bankers.[36] The French bankers tended to insist that if they were not given a share of control in this eastern network, neither should the Germans be given one; or if the Germans were given representation in control, the French representation should be equal.[37] It was not until March, 1914, that a satisfactory compromise was worked out between the Ger-

[34] *Die Grosse Politik,* Vol. XXXVII, Nos. 15132–15133. According to the statement of Helfferich of the Deutsche Bank, the agreement between the German and Austrian governments in April, 1913, whereby the control of the railways was sold to the Austrians, stipulated that after the company had settled the question of the western lines with Serbia and Greece and arranged for the operation of the lines within Bulgarian territory, the stock of the company, which would still possess operating rights on the section remaining Turkish, should be resold to the Germans. The Austro-Hungarian Government argued that this obligation was no longer binding, because the frontier changes that resulted from the second Balkan war left more of the line in Turkey than had been anticipated when the agreement was signed.

[35] *Ibid.*

[36] *Ibid.,* Nos. 15134–15135, 15137, 15138, 15140.

[37] *Ibid.,* Nos. 15132, 15137, 15139.

man and Austrian governments.[38] The mixture of doggedness and evasion by which the Austrian Government met
the most serious appeals and arguments of its ally is evidence of the importance it set upon the successful achievement of agreement with the French.[39]

Before the compromise was reached the Serbian Government, swung over by vigorous popular opposition,
would go no further with the idea of internationalization.
Its original consent was forced by dependence upon
French finance; the plan which gave Serbia only a minority control over the lines within its boundaries was
unsatisfactory.[40] Serbia returned to its original desire to
secure the lines by direct purchase. By May, 1914, the
plan of internationalization had disintegrated under the
tugs of opposed national wills.[41]

SARAJEVO—THE ORIGINAL TERMINUS OF THE LINE

Austria and Serbia now engaged in direct discussions
concerning the disposition of the disputed lines. In return
for the right to purchase the lines within its borders, the
Serbian Government offered the Austrian certain rights
of supervision over the surveys of any connecting railway
that might be built through the Sandjak of Novi-Bazar
to the Bosnian railway net, and offered to place orders
for railway materials within Austria.[42] The lack of agreement upon the purchase price was the only matter de-

[38] *Die Grosse Politik,* Vol. XXXVII, Nos. 15140–15142 give the terms
of the compromise.

[39] *Ibid.,* No. 15140. The whole of this correspondence leaves it unclear
whether the Austro-Hungarian Government had or had not originally
promised the French group to include the eastern network in the arrangement. In this note, conveyed by the Austro-Hungarian Ambassador
in Paris to the French Government, February 25, 1914, the assertion is
made that no such promise was given, but earlier communications indicate the contrary. The Austro-Hungarian Government, trying to snake
its way out of a difficult situation, was not always consistent in its
statements.

[40] *Ibid.,* Nos. 15136, 15143, 15145.

[41] *Ibid.,* No. 15147.   [42] *Ibid.,* Nos. 15148, 15149.

terring the settlement when the assassinations occurred at Sarajevo. The preliminary agreement was shown to be but a momentary pause in the strife between Serbia and the Dual Monarchy.

The same catastrophe finally terminated recurrent differences which were holding the other international project—the Danube-Adriatic line. No subject had caused more difficulties in those conferences of the Great Powers which met during and after the Balkan wars. Austria-Hungary had opposed all plans whereby Serbia would acquire territorial access to the Adriatic and a port upon that sea toward which Serbia reached in dreams. To the proposals of a railway giving economic access to that sea, the Dual Monarchy could no longer offer effective resistance. Over the details of the organization of the lines, the conferences dragged themselves out in tired controversy. Austria-Hungary refused final assent until it should be assured that the line would be built and operated by a private company, that in time of war Serbia would not be permitted to secure munitions through the neutral terminal port, that the policing system of the line could not be turned to Serbian advantage. Italy held strong preferences as to the route, which were not easily adjusted to the wishes of the other powers. The Albanian people resented all Serbian invasion. In June, 1913, the text of a declaration to Serbia was finally agreed upon. The six Great Powers, Serbia, and Albania were to guarantee interest on the bonds of an international company to be organized to build and operate the line under the concession of the Albanian Government.[43] But conflicting national desires continued to defeat all attempts to define the route. Local populations near the Adriatic drove away the representatives sent to make preliminary studies. Ac-

[43] For the course of discussion, see *Österreich-Ungarns Aussenpolitik*, Vol. IV, Nos. 4382, 4426; Vol. V, Nos. 4855, 4994, 5015, 5047, 5411, 5612. The draft of the plan prepared by Count Berchtold is in *Die Grosse Politik*, Vol. XXXIV, No. 12664.

cess to the Adriatic remained a matter to quarrel over among all the nations which could see it from their hills. The line between Constantinople and Vienna remained the only long route across national boundaries that capital could construct midst the din, and that was a relic of the time when the Sultan held sway throughout the Near East. The railways by which the Sultan hoped to unify his European domains had turned out to be one of the chief matters in dispute between him and his rebellious subjects.

The arguments which they engendered had kept perpetually astir all the national conflicts of pre-war Europe. No matter contributed more to produce the final nervous exhaustion and hostility which finally found vent in war. The rival projects of construction brought to an end the understanding by which Austria-Hungary and Russia had been guided in Balkan affairs and placed them in inimical positions. They roused Serbian envy and ambition and led her into the headlong agitation which the Dual Monarchy feared and tried to suppress by restricting all Serbian plans. The secret understandings of which they were made the subject tangled worse the confusion in which Europe groped. Each spike was made to mark a grave.

A closing note about the railways in Greece. In 1912 Greece had 1,520 kilometers of railway in operation. The Greek Government had not been idle since 1912 in its plans and barterings with foreign financial groups. Projects for unification of the lines in old and new Greece and their extension to Monastir and beyond were put before the Greek Parliament.[44] As one of the rewards for the loan granted to the Greek Government in Paris, a French company was authorized to construct a connecting line between the Greek railways and the European net. In that country, too, national plans, aided by French finance, superseded international; and in that country, too, their consummation was deferred by the coming of the war.

[44] *Le Marché Financier*, 1913–14, pp. 687–689, 696–699.

CHAPTER XIV

THE TURKISH EMPIRE AND EUROPEAN INVESTORS

BETWEEN WAR AND BANKRUPTCY

TURKEY of the nineteenth century, heir to the diminished domains of the Byzantine Empire, and to all the weaknesses displayed in its decline, owned no capital to equip itself with the instruments of modern life or industry. Nor did its rulers possess the necessary integrity and sense of responsibility to their subjects to utilize sparingly and well the capital offered by European investors. That Mohammedan state, politically decadent, fell victim to its rulers' passions and fantasies, to its people's helplessness and ignorance, to the greed of money-lenders, to the rebellion of its subjects, and the political pressure of the more purposeful and disciplined European states. The record of its public borrowings was but one element in the course of a general decline in the face of a more masterful civilization.

Between 1854 and 1875 Turkey contracted an external debt of about 200 million Turkish pounds (worth $4.40 at par) of which she received not much more than three-fifths. The borrowed sums went to meet the extravagance of the sovereign, the service of former loans, the military expense of an insurrection in Crete, and to repair damages of the Crimean wars. A bare 10 per cent was so used as to increase the country's economic strength. The borrowing country had no budget system. Its public accounts were elementary and made no separation between the financial affairs of the state and of the sovereign. No constitutional control existed over the borrowings of the sovereign or his use of the proceeds. The European states regarded the decomposition of the state as likely and speculated upon the outcome. Bankers, local and foreign,

matched their wits against circumstance. When one group
among them would not lend another would, provided the
return offered was high enough (a substantial part of the
debt bore an effective interest rate of over 10 per cent).
The chance of rapid escape or recovery of the loaned funds
even in the face of catastrophe was a reasonable one to
shrewd men who secured cover for themselves, and enough
profit from emissions to take care of incidental losses.
Besides, the Turkish Government, no matter how badly
managed and reckless its actual behavior was, always
continued to give investors the impression that it was
directing effort to the improvement of its affairs, that
right beyond the memory of the latest extravagance reform and order waited. By promises it managed to con-
ceal actualities—no less to its own expense than to the expense of others.[1]

In the late seventies the load of debt became wholly
beyond the capacity of the state—the debt service requiring over half of a total revenue which was in itself
inadequate. Turkey reduced debt payments in 1875 and
suspended in 1876. The expense of the war with Russia
which followed, the loss of rich European provinces as a
result of rebellion, the Russian demands for indemnity,
capped the financial disorganization of the country. The
European powers at the Council of Berlin set in motion
plans for international financial control. After failing
in other attempts to reach an agreement with its creditors,
Turkey decreed such control in 1881, securing a reduction
of debt. Its amount (with several preferred exceptions)
was cut roughly to the original amount paid Turkey for

[1] The literature on Turkish finance is enormous and much of it good.
Among the important sources are: C. Morawitz, *Les Finances de la Turquie* (Paris, 1902); A. Du Velay, *Essai sur l'Histoire Financière de la
Turquie* (Paris, 1903); A. Roumani, *Essai Historique et Technique sur
la Dette Publique Ottomane* (Paris, 1927). The terms of the loan contracts, etc., are to be found in *Recueil des Contrats d'Emprunts, etc.,
Conclus par le Gouvernement Impérial.* Vol. I (1905), and Vol. II
(1913), were published by the Banque Impériale Ottomane, Vol. III, by
the Public Debt Administration (1918).

each loan, plus 10 per cent for interest arrears. Principal and interest due on debts included in the conversion amounted to 252 million Turkish pounds. This was reduced to 117 million. The total Turkish debt, after the operation, approximated 140 million. On the converted debt, interest was reduced, to begin at 1 per cent, and to rise up to 4 per cent, if and as the revenues intrusted to creditors' control increased. The annual debt service had been about 15 million Turkish pounds; now its minimum was about 1.6 millions.

With reduced debt and a creditors' organization in charge of revenues pledged to lenders, Turkey undertook further conversions. Two of the loans not included in the Decree of Mouharrem, which paid 5 per cent and 4.5 per cent respectively, were in 1894 converted into a 3.5 per cent loan despite the protest of the French and English bondholders. A 1903 conversion of the Consolidated Debt which had been issued under the 1881 arrangement reduced the principal but increased the rate of interest. After this conversion the Turkish debt stood at about 98 million Turkish pounds. Between 1881 and 1903 the indebtedness of the Turkish Government did not increase, and even between 1903 and 1908 it did not increase immoderately. The system of pledged revenues enabled Turkey to borrow during this period at an effective interest rate of less than 5 per cent.

From 1908 to 1914 Turkish finance again fell into alarming arrears. Free revenues no longer sufficed to meet current expenses swollen by the cost of military preparation. War with Italy and two wars with the Balkan states had to be met entirely out of new loans. The first reliable budget published for Turkey, after the Young Turks' revolution, indicated revenue for 1909–10 of 25.1 million Turkish pounds, and expenditure of 32.1 millions, out of which about 11.0 millions were used for public debt.[2] The

[2] In a special report on the Ottoman public debt made in 1914 by the British representative, Sir Adam Block, the debt service is put at 11.3 million Turkish pounds out of a budget of 33 millions.

estimates for the following year showed no improvement. When Turkey could make no large public issue, she secured short-time advances from the French and German banks, armament firms, the Bagdad and Anatolian railways and the Tobacco Monopoly. Even so, salaries grew overdue, and claims and bills unpaid. M. Chas. Laurent said that when put in charge of financial accounts of the Turkish Empire in 1909, he could discover no record of the floating debt, and in the claims register which he opened, 560,000 separate claims were entered.[3] When debts and claims were funded by long-time borrowing, it resulted that the total long-time debt stood in 1914 in excess of 150 million Turkish pounds, an increase of over 50 million since 1903. About 5 million Turkish pounds of floating debt remained and the Turkish Government had in addition the duty of meeting various contingent guaranties.[4] The debt service required approximately one-third of the total revenue after making allowance for the imposition of new taxes.

During this period Turkey, under earlier agreements, had been amortizing old debts and contracting new ones on less favorable terms. Her territories had been reduced; the states which acquired the detached provinces made no contribution toward the debt service. Of the total debt, as it stood in 1914, about one-fifth had been put to productive use. Turkey had 5,252 kilometers of railroad, representing a nominal invested capital of approximately 45 million Turkish pounds; but at least a third of this mileage was built without expense to the government. War and the preparation therefor was the chief consumer of the rest. As security for the later loans, additional sources of reve-

[3] In his lecture on "La Réforme Financière en Turquie," in *La Politique Budgetaire en Europe* (Paris, 1910), p. 77.

[4] The *Report of the Council of Foreign Bondholders,* 1914, gives it as 149.5 million Turkish pounds, taking no account of railroad and other guaranties and the floating debt. A memorandum prepared by the British Treasury for the Peace Conference gives it as 152 million Turkish pounds.

nue were taken out of the general budget and placed under
the supervision of the creditors' organization. The list became more and more inclusive. Railway revenues, the tribute received from Egypt, the net income of the salt and
tobacco monopolies, stamp taxes, tithes, taxes on sheep and
cattle in some provinces, the customs duties of some ports
including Constantinople, wine and spirit duties, levies
on silk production and the catch of fish—these and others
were put under creditors' control. Only a long continuance
of peace could have saved the bondholders from a repetition of the suspension of 1875–76. But in 1914 war, not
peace, was on the horizon.

It was not only in response to government demands that
foreign capital moved into Turkey. All organized large-
scale enterprise was dependent upon it and owned by it.
The Turkish banking system was entirely foreign, and
foreign banks conducted the official business as well as
private business. The railroad system was financed almost
entirely from outside, as were irrigation works, ports and
bridge construction, mineral exploitation, and municipal
public utilities. The economic development of Turkey
rested in the hands of those who could amass large capital
sums and utilize the machine technique. With so incompetent a government, so unorganized a people, it was
almost inevitable that the political fate of Turkey should
rest in the same hands. This fact observers on the spot
recognized. Thus, the British representative on the Debt
Administration, in urging his government to promote more
actively the investment of British capital in Turkey, explained in 1907:

The national credit of Turkey, thanks to the Ottoman
Public Debt Administration, is still good; but, nevertheless,
swiftly and surely, the borrowing power of the Treasury is
becoming more and more impaired . . . It would appear today that when the moment arrives the powers interested will
in the defence of the holders of Turkish stock and of the rail-

ways they control, be obliged, whether they desire it or not, to take measures for creating order out of financial chaos in which the Turkish Government is inextricably involved. Apart from the fact that the English Houses have no share in the profits of these operations and undertakings, they will have no interest to speak of to protect in comparison with the French and Germans, who are laying an economic foundation on which they will later be able to build a political edifice.[5]

An aroused Turkish nationalism strove hard to keep control of its own affairs, but it did not fight the deepest real source of peril, its own shortcomings.

THE RÔLE OF THE POWERS—GERMANY

BECAUSE Turkey seemed close to dissolution and that event would affect their strategic and economic interests, because each loan to the Turkish Government or concession granted by it might lead to new events, the governments of the lending states regulated the actions of their capitalists.

The policy of Germany was consistent, and its interests concentrated. Up to 1882 there was virtually no German capital in Turkey. The German Government sought to create so dependable and numerous connections between the Turkish Government and itself that they would become actual political allies, and that the lead in the exploitation of Turkish resources would be granted to German finance and industry. The core of these connections was the Bagdad railway system. To the more ambitious and aggressive elements in Germany this railway was undoubtedly regarded as marking out a field of empire, a penetrative agent in foreign regions that would fall under German domination. Germany desired a strong Turkey and was willing to finance it.

Up to its limits of absorption the Berlin capital market

5 *British Documents,* Vol. V, No. 147.

was, beginning in 1888, opened to Turkish government securities, and the powerful German banks were pressed to accept risks and burdens before which they sometimes hesitated. In that year the Deutsche Bank, with the encouraging attention of the German Government, arranged a loan for the Sultan after the powerful French-English institution, the Banque Impériale Ottomane, had refused it. Thereby was earned the good will of the Sultan and the Anatolian railway concession.[6] In 1910, to select a later example, the Deutsche Bank was again called upon to furnish a loan which the French refused and, thereby, to regain Turkish favor, which had been inclined toward France and England. Throughout the period, it may be observed, the German banks were encouraged to seek the coöperation of French and English capitalist groups in order to be able to undertake ventures too great for them alone. Between banks and the government there was a partnership in thought and action in which sometimes one, sometimes the other, took the initiative. Despite continuously pressing domestic needs and the tendency of German investors to resell Turkish government bonds on the French market, the German-owned share of the growing Turkish government debt rose from about 5 to about 20 per cent between 1880 and 1914.[7]

German investment in industrial ventures in Turkey grew from virtually nothing in 1880 to independent importance before the war—from about 40 million marks to over 600 million marks. This investment was concentrated mainly in the Bagdad Railway, of which about 2,000

[6] K. Helfferich, *Georg Von Siemens,* III, 37.

[7] The estimates of K. Helfferich as given in C. A. Schafer, *Deutsch-Türkische Freundschaft* (Berlin, 1914), p. 12, were, omitting Turkish lottery bonds:

	Per cent French	Per cent German	Per cent English
End of 1881	38.9	4.7	28.9
End of 1898	44.9	12.1	10.0
End of 1912	58.5	19.3	....

kilometers had been constructed by 1914. The development of this enterprise was watched by the German people with the sense of imperial destiny asserting itself, and in its behalf the officials exerted themselves in tireless diplomatic negotiation.

THE RÔLE OF THE POWERS—FRANCE

THE French Government found it more difficult, impossible in fact, to formulate a fixed policy. As each episode arose, there had to be taken into account not only the varied interests of the investors and its own political purposes in Turkey, but the wishes of its Russian ally, and its stand and purposes in Balkan affairs. The French holdings of Turkish public debt and investment in Turkish enterprises exceeded that of any other country.[8] Of the twenty-six loan emissions of the Turkish Government between 1854 and 1914, French investors took a major share in sixteen. The French investment in railroads exceeded half a billion francs; vast further concessions secured in 1913–14 provided for 2,300 kilometers of new construction and still larger investment. French capital controlled the Banque Impériale Ottomane which, with its sixty-two branches, was Treasurer-General and fiscal agent for Turkey. This bank brought out most of the Turkish loans in Paris.[9] It shared control of the Turkish

[8] In a detailed study made by the Commission pour la Défense des Porteurs de Valeurs et de Fonds Ottomans (Paris, 1914), the French holdings of Turkish internal and external debt in 1914 were computed to be 2.4 billion francs, the German 0.9 billion francs, the British 0.6 billion. French investment in enterprises in Turkey are computed as 903 millions, German 553, English 230 millions. The figures probably exaggerate the French investment and understate the German.

[9] Though this bank had been given a Royal Charter by Great Britain in 1856, and English bankers were upon its Board, and its head was in 1913 English, the British generally regarded it as under the control of the French Foreign Office. The French Government, however, sometimes had difficulty in controlling its policy because of its connections with German banking institutions in the Bagdad railway loans. The Russian Government in 1913 thought to weaken these connections by fostering an *entente* between the Banque Impériale Ottomane and the

Tobacco Monopoly with an Austro-German group. Through interlocking directorates it was represented on all the important French railways in Turkey, and on the Bagdad Railway. The French port companies at Constantinople and Beirut, the companies which supplied water, street-car service, and electric light to Constantinople acknowledged its interest. Working in connection with this bank and other French banks, French companies held besides numerous contracts and ventures throughout the Empire—roads, ports, docks, tramways, irrigation works, lighting and power plants. Despite Turkish friendship for Germany, it was the French investor who above all financed economic change in Turkey.[10]

France struggled with Germany for ascendancy. Still French and German banks joined in many loan issues; and according to Sir Adam Block, British representative on the Debt Council, there was a permanent understanding between them. In a memorandum sent by him to the British Government, it is stated: ". . . it would seem that as far back as 1894 some agreement was come to between the French and Germans for a joint participation in the financial operations of this country . . . Whatever the date of the agreement may be, it is certain that an

Banque Russo-Asiatique. The founding of banks in the Near East was always a diplomatic affair. For an account of the policies and operations of the Banque Impériale Ottomane, see A. Billiotti, *La Banque Impériale Ottomane* (Paris, 1908), and G. Poulgi-Bey, *Annales des Écoles Libres de Sciences Politiques* (Paris, 1910). The provision in the 1875 Convention between the bank and the government whereby the bank was appointed Treasurer-General was mainly inoperative.

[10] In the terms of the report of the Commission pour la Défense des Porteurs de Valeurs et de Fonds Ottomans, pp. 102–103, French capital "directed public services through companies which concealed, under the legal mask imposed by the Turkish law, the French character of the funds which built them and the directors whom they obeyed. The network of these enterprises catches the whole economic life of the Turkish Empire; they write to our credit a mortgage which rests lightly on all parts of the Empire . . ." The plans of road building which certainly would have benefited Turkey were especially extensive. The Société Générale d'Entreprises dans l'Empire Ottoman had 12 branches spread throughout the land; when the war came it had 10,000 men at work.

agreement of some kind exists."[11] The main partners to
the agreement were the Deutsche Bank and the Banque
Impériale Ottomane.

In general the French Government favored the investment of French capital in Turkey. But before giving
official listing to the Turkish government loans, the government always imposed conditions or sought advantage.
It would not permit the listing of the Turkish lottery
bonds issued to finance the Oriental railways in the (then)
European provinces of Turkey. In 1894–97 it acted as
intermediary between Turkey and the Banque de Paris
et Pays Bas (which the French Government drew into the
affair) in arranging a loan for Crete—as part of a never
executed plan of governmental and administrative reform
drawn up by the Powers. The 1903 conversion loan was
delayed until Turkey settled to the satisfaction of the authorities the claims of the French railway company, agreed
to leave the control of the Constantinople docks in French
hands, and gave its orders for military supplies to French
factories.[12] This conversion was promoted by interests
concerned with the Bagdad Railway, who wanted to clear
a path for the bond issues by which the railway was financed. Official listing of the Turkish loan of 1905 was
deferred until the government was satisfied that French
armament concerns would receive a suitable share of the
orders which the loan was used to pay. In 1907, when the
Turkish Treasury was empty, the French Government
made assistance conditional upon the successful carrying
through of a plan, in which French capital was interested,
for the consolidation of the Heraclea coal fields.[13]

In 1910 the French Government attempted to impose
conditions which caused the Turkish Government to borrow in Germany against its original desire. The new

[11] *British Documents*, Vol. V, No. 147.
[12] France, *Rapport de la Commission du Budget, Ministère des Affaires Étrangères*, Exercice, 1906, p. 110.
[13] *British Documents*, V, 45–47.

Young Turk *régime*, regarding Germany as the supporter of the reactionary politics of the deposed Sultan, looked to France and Great Britain for sympathetic support in what had been hailed at the time of the revolution as an effort to create a constitutional and enlightened government. In 1909 the French and English banks had joined with the German in a loan issue, although the new Turkish *régime* would not consent to place the revenues assigned as specific pledge for the loan under the supervision of the Debt Administration. The habitual frown of the French and English governments seemed to have vanished. By July, 1910, however, when Djavid Bey, the Turkish Finance Minister, approached the British and French governments, their enthusiasm had changed to doubt and revulsion because of the massacres in Macedonia and Armenia.

Negotiations were, to review the course of this important loan episode briefly, undertaken with the Banque Impériale Ottomane despite the wish of the Young Turk *régime* to lessen Turkish dependence upon that institution. No agreement was reached, whether because of the terms asked by the bank, or because of the interference of the French Government, is not clearly established.[14] It is safe to surmise, however, that the French Government was already at this stage taking a hand in the negotiations, for it was interested in the effort to establish a budget and audit bureau in Turkey through the agency of the Banque Impériale Ottomane. A Frenchman, M. Laurent, was already engaged in this work as vice-president of the Commission of Financial Reform which drew up the first budget ever prepared in Turkey.[15]

[14] Contemporary accounts call attention to the hostility of the Young Turk *régime* to the Banque Impériale Ottomane. R. L. Pinon, *L'Europe et la Jeune Turquie*, pp. 138 *et seq.*, says that the bank merely turned aside the request stating that the diplomatic agreement with the French Government was an essential preliminary since official listing was indispensable.

[15] *Le Marché Financier*, 1909–10, p. 542. The Turkish Ministry of

A syndicate headed by the Crédit Mobilier was more agreeable, and in return for the pledge of the customs of the province of Constantinople undertook to issue a substantial loan. This loan pledge had been refused to the Banque Impériale Ottomane.[16] The French Government, when asked to grant official listing, put forward various conditions to its consent. Some time earlier the Russian Ambassador had suggested to his government that the opportunity be seized:

to profit by the lack of money in Constantinople to secure from Turkey obligations restricting Turkey's future military growth. From a military point of view the question of the Turkish railway constructions in the Caucasus and Northern Persia as well as the acquisition of men-of-war, is fraught with special importance.[17]

These objectives the French Government did not see its way clear to pursue directly. But in the conditions put forward might be discerned by the suspicious Turk hints of an attempt to achieve the same ends indirectly. The French Government asked first, that orders be reserved for French industry; not long before Turkey had purchased two battleships in Germany, the cost of which would be ultimately discharged out of the loan. Second, it sought a satisfactory settlement of disputes caused by the Turk-

Finance had previously set up a commission composed of one Frenchman, one Englishman, and one Italian, to study the reorganization of its financial system. This commission made its recommendations early in 1910 and the government had submitted various finance laws to Parliament. In 1909 European officials had also been engaged by the Ministry of Finance among whom were M. Joly, a Frenchman, who was in charge of the Tax Control Section, and M. Laurent, in charge of accounts. Before the loan was arranged, however, M. Laurent had fallen out with various members of the government because of his refusal to allow expenditures by the Minister of War not provided in the budget. For a picture of Turkish finances at the time, see his lecture in *La Politique Budgetaire en Europe* (Paris, 1910). On the controversy, see *Le Marché Financier,* 1910–11, pp. 492–493.

16 *Die Grosse Politik,* Vol. XXVII, No. 10043.

17 B. De Seibert, *Entente Diplomacy and the World,* p. 299.

ish treatment of the Tunisian and Algerian subjects of
France in the Turkish domains. Third, it sought a pledge
that Turkey would reorganize its system of management
of the public finances.[18] The exact range and nature of the
financial reorganization sought, is hard to determine because of the mist of motives which hung over the discussions. The main feature of the plan previously formulated by M. Laurent, in the brief period that he was in
charge of the Accounts Bureau of the Ministry of Finance,
was that the Banque Impériale Ottomane should be made
public Treasurer and given a visa power over public expenditure, to insure that it was in accord with the prepared budget.[19] In addition to this arrangement, the
French Government asked that French officials be installed as financial counselors, and in the Bureaus of Au-
diting and Accounts.[20]

These arrangements would certainly have benefited
Turkey; and they, or alternative arrangements of the
same import, were certainly necessary for the protection
of the bondholders. But the Turkish Government refused
to accept them in effective form.[21] Behind the proposals
it suspected an indirect attempt to limit its military preparations in behalf of Russia.[22] In this refusal the Turkish
Government may have been encouraged by German and
English influences. The Turkish and German governments were in touch during the negotiations. According,
further, to reports sent to Berlin by the German Ambassador in Constantinople, the Turkish Minister had been
moved to refuse by the advice of Sir Adam Block, the
English delegate on the Debt Council, and by the promises
of Sir Ernest Cassel.[23]

[18] *Ibid.;* Mahmud Moukthar Pacha, *La Turquie, L'Allemagne et L'Europe* (Paris, 1924), pp. 102–103.
[19] *Die Grosse Politik,* Vol. XXVII, No. 10046.
[20] *Ibid.,* No. 10052, and *Le Marché Financier,* 1910–11, p. 516.
[21] D. C. Blaisdell, *European Financial Control in the Ottoman Empire* (New York, 1929), pp. 216 *et seq.*
[22] *Die Grosse Politik,* Vol. XXVII, No. 10045.
[23] *Ibid.,* No. 10046.

At all events it was to Cassel, director of the National Bank of Turkey and rival (within measure) of the Banque Impériale Ottomane, that Djavid Bey now turned. Cassel was prepared to arrange the loan, seeking the coöperation of the Deutsche Bank. But the English Government, acting in response to an official French request, made energetic representations to Cassel, who thereupon dropped the matter.[24] In this action the British Government was probably moved, too, by popular disapproval of recent Turkish conduct, and the wish to withhold aid to Turkey until assured of satisfaction in Bagdad railway plans.[25]

Only Berlin remained, and negotiations were undertaken there. The German Government pressed the banks to arrange the loan. The Kaiser issued his order to the Chancellor, "We must help Turkey financially without condition, with the aid of Austria, so that she will not come permanently under Anglo-French domination. Speak to Von Gwinner about this."[26] The German banks wished at first to make only a six months' advance but the arguments of the Chancellor prevailed. The French Government appears at the last moment to have made a conciliatory gesture through the French representative on the Debt Council, but without effect.[27]

The extension of aid by Germany did much to restore the Germans in favor in Constantinople, to make them appear as the only dependable ally. They were more strongly established than under the old *régime*.[28] France paid for its effort to arrest Turkish financial disorder and

[24] De Seibert, *op. cit.*, p. 302; R. Recouly, *Revue Politique et Parlementaire*, October, 1910, pp. 158 *et seq.; Die Grosse Politik*, Vol. XXVII, Nos. 10045 *et seq.*

[25] Even the *Economist*, October, 1910, approved the action because of the necessity of reforming Turkish finance and limiting its military expenditure.

[26] *Die Grosse Politik*, Vol. XXVII, Nos. 10049, 10053, 10058, 10063-10067.

[27] *Ibid.*, Nos. 10057, 10062.

[28] K. Helfferich, *Die Deutsche Türkenpolitik* (Berlin, 1921), pp. 22-23.

military expenditure; its previous, actions and alliance with Russia made it suspect. Turkey chose the lender who permitted her to go to ruin in her own way, suspecting that in the plans of reform only another form of ruin was being prepared for her anyhow.

After this episode, as before, Turkish government borrowing continued to be the subject of prolonged negotiations with the governments of the lending states. The French Government refused to permit the listing of a new Turkish loan during the Balkan War.[29] But during the conflict, the initiative of banks and armament firms defeated official purposes.[30]

The Turkish Finance Minister in the autumn of 1913 took up his travels. In Berlin he was informed that the condition of the capital market would make a Turkish loan unsalable.[31] The French Government was next approached. It disliked the risk of strengthening Turkey, of perhaps making possible a new war. But in return for the loan and the cessation of French opposition to the Bagdad railway project, large industrial orders and railroad concessions were now obtainable. The French Government was willing to make the bargain. But in its way stood a treaty which gave Russia a veto over railways in the districts which the French lines were to traverse. Russia would lift the veto only if Turkey entered into a new accord, exchanging old privileges for new ones.[32]

While waiting for Turkey's need to assert itself decisively enough, the French Government was shocked by the

[29] *Livre Noir,* II, 562; France, *Documents Diplomatiques, Affaires Balkaniques, 1912–1914,* Vol. III, Nos. 13, 39, 120.

[30] Isvolsky, Ambassador in Paris, wrote to his government and explained the difficulties faced by it because of the limits of its control over the banks and tobacco monopoly, *Livre Noir,* II, 116, 118, 127–128, 137–138.

[31] Djemal Pasha, *Memoirs of a Turkish Statesman* (New York, 1922), p. 55.

[32] *Livre Noir,* II, 142–143, 231; *Documents Diplomatiques Français, 1871–1914,* 3d ser., Vol. I, No. 528. The demand of the Russian Government had stood throughout 1912 in the way of plans of the French banks.

extension in November, 1913, of a loan to Turkey by the
French banking house of Perier & Co., which was tempted
by a spread of fourteen points between purchase and pub-
lic sale prices.[33] Official listing was not asked and the
French Government was not informed in advance. Both
French plans and peace in the Balkans seemed menaced.
In Constantinople the ambassadors of France and Great
Britain expressed their indignation. In Paris the French
Minister of Finance reprimanded Perier, brought them
to renounce their option for the second part of the loan.
Belgian banks took up the option.[34] The loan was
ostensibly to pay back salaries of Turkish officials and sol-
diers. But part of it was spent for the purchase of a dreadnought and ammunition in Great Britain.[35] The negotiations were resumed, but twice they were held up by the
fears of the Russian Government. The Russian Government in January, 1914, urged that the loan be not permitted because of the appointment of the German Field
Marshal Liman Von Sanders to reorganize the Turkish
army.[36] The French Government did not venture to argue
this matter too strongly. In February a new war between
Greece and Turkey seemed imminent, and Russia was
afraid that the loan would stiffen Turkish purposes. The
French Government promised that it would make its realization contingent upon the pacific march of Balkan affairs, and pointed out that most of the part to be issued
immediately would be used to pay off outstanding debts
and that the Banque Impériale Ottomane would be in a
position to oversee its expenditure.[37] Again, the French
Government was unwilling to put forward too firm conditions. It knew in January, 1914, that Turkey would buy
the Moltke and the Goeben.[38]

[33] *Le Marché Financier,* 1913–14, p. 222.
[34] *Livre Noir,* II, 209–214; R. Poincaré, *Au Service de la France,* IV,
10.
[35] *Économist,* January 3, 1914.   [36] *Livre Noir,* II, 230–235.
[37] *Ibid.,* pp. 242–243; Poincaré, *op. cit.,* IV, 44.
[38] Poincaré, *op. cit.,* IV, 24.

The loan was finally issued in Paris in April, 1914, after Turkey had reached an agreement with Greece about the islands. In compensation for this aid and for withdrawing opposition to the Bagdad Railway, railroad concessions for 2,300 miles of line in Syria and Anatolia were secured. French companies were to be given rights to harbor works in three Mediterranean and two Black Sea ports. French officials were to be employed in the Turkish financial and public works services. M. Joly, a Frenchman, was made Inspector-General of Finance. The privileges of French institutions and schools, hospitals, and churches were confirmed and extended.[39]

What portion of this loan was not required to pay off previous advances of the French and German banks was mainly used for military preparation. Despite its agreement with Greece, Turkey cherished a resolution toward war in behalf of the islands ceded.[40] It ordered in France six destroyers, two submarines to be built by Creusot, mountain guns and seaplanes.[41] Part of the Greek loan issued in Paris the month before was similarly spent.[42] A French mission was strengthening the Greek army and fortifications; a German mission was doing the same in Turkey. A British naval mission was busy in Greece; another British naval mission was no less busy in Turkey.[43] English armament firms were modernizing the Turkish arsenals and building floating docks for newly purchased warships. Greece called on Serbia to carry out its military

[39] *Rapport de la Commission du Budget, Affaires Étrangères,* Exercice, 1914.

[40] E. Driault et M. L'Héritier, *op. cit.,* V, 156–157.

[41] Djemal Pasha, *op. cit.,* pp. 95, 102.

[42] Driault et L'Héritier, *op. cit.,* V, 153–157.

[43] *Economist,* January 3, 1914, and May 30, 1914, spoke of the dreadnought purchases made from the Perier loan as "the first fruits of our naval mission to Constantinople" and continued "fortunately for Greece by the beneficial foresight of Mr. Churchill, the Turkish Rear-Admiral Limpus will be opposed in the forthcoming war by Rear-Admiral Mark Kerr."

convention of June 1, 1913, but the latter hesitated. Such was the situation when the war came.

THE RÔLE OF THE POWERS—GREAT BRITAIN

BRITISH official policy up to the default of 1875 had rather encouraged the flotation of Turkish securities in London. The 1855 loan, incurred for the conduct of the Crimean War, the British Government joined with the French to guarantee. Despite the cold skepticism of many observers of Turkish affairs, it tended to continue to indicate such optimistic regard for Turkish effort as to encourage British investors to continue to buy Turkish loans. Coloring its attitude was the wish to maintain the integrity of the Turkish Empire as an obstacle to Russian ambitions. After the declaration of Turkish bankruptcy in 1876, and in the face of the weakening of the Turkish Empire, British policy became more complex.

Toward new public borrowing the British Government, warned by its experience, maintained a noncommittal attitude. British financiers fell in the way of consulting the government before entering into loan engagements. But whenever possible the government tried to avoid responsibility. Thus in 1908 when the Young Turk Cabinet asked Sir Edward Grey to intercede with the British bankers in their behalf, he passed on the request to Rothschild and Baring; but when these bankers decided that a Turkish loan could not be satisfactorily marketed, no attempt was made to reverse the decision.[44] Now and again, however, the government interposed itself or gave advice. In 1910, as has been related, the Foreign Office induced Sir Ernest Cassel to drop his loan arrangements. Again in 1912, when consulted by the National Bank of Turkey, it advised against the making of advances until Balkan disputes were settled.[45] But with these exceptions it permitted bankers and investors to reach their own deci-

[44] *British Documents*, Vol. V, No. 202.
[45] *Die Grosse Politik*, Vol. XXXIV, No. 24645.

sions. These took only a lesser part in Turkish government financing. Their preference ran to other fields. The spectacle of a government which put itself perpetually in debt to sustain a military effort, did not attract them. The government did not ask them to make loans against their judgment. It refused a responsibility undertaken by the governments of Germany and France.

But in the rivalry between its financial groups and those of other countries, the British Government began to display firmness and initiative after the entry of German enterprises. Persistently it was pushed forward along this course. Still Sir Edward affirmed in 1908:

I was distressed to find when I came into office how completely we had been ousted from commercial enterprises in Turkey and how apparently hopeless it was to get a footing. That is why I encouraged coöperation with the French; it seemed as if British enterprise in itself had no prospect. Since then I have been disappointed to find what a very poor set of financiers had got commercial enterprise in Turkey in their hands.[46]

Perhaps this statement explains why Sir Ernest Cassel was encouraged to found the National Bank of Turkey— to serve British enterprise in that land. From 1910 to 1914 when the breakdown of Turkey seemed imminent, the British Government interposed itself strongly against the neglect of British interests. In the series of settlements negotiated just before the outbreak of the war, it acquired for British enterprise the area of operation, the opportunities most desired. Though it might have preferred to see the financing of Turkey left entirely to the ordinary play of private interests, the British Government, like those of Germany and France, intervened in the process with all its diplomatic force—while the Turkish Government continued to borrow and spend with the laxity of despair.

[46] *British Documents,* Vol. V, No. 208.

TO PROTECT THE BONDHOLDERS—THE OTTOMAN PUBLIC DEBT ADMINISTRATION

WHEN after the disasters of 1876–78, the European Powers met at Berlin to settle Near Eastern affairs, they induced Russia to lessen its indemnity demands and sought to save for their bondholders something from the wreck of Turkish finances. The British and French governments had in indirect ways upheld the faith of their capitalists in the ultimate solvency of the Turkish Empire.[47] In the protocol of peace was inserted:

The powers represented at the Congress are of the opinion to recommend to the Sublime Porte, the establishment at Constantinople of a Financial Commission of specially qualified men named by their respective governments, and authorized to examine the claims of the holders of the Turkish debt and to propose the most effective means to give them satisfaction compatible with the financial situation of the Sublime Porte.

Turkey refused to accept the appointment of an official commission. But realizing that control probably would be imposed if all debt payment remained in default and all measures neglected, she entered negotiations with the representatives of the bondholders. The negotiations not going to her satisfaction, she attempted to settle the question by arbitrary action. The resistance of the bondholders and their supporting governments blocked all avenues of credit. The Turkish Government faced by a large volume of short-time obligations, held chiefly by local banks which pressed their claims vigorously, leased revenues to them. The foreign bondholders protested against the discrimination with their governments' support. In 1880–81 agreement was reached and embodied in a decree of the Sultan —the Decree of Mouharrem. Turkey, thereby, put into receivership under control of the creditors, certain of her

[47] Blaisdell, *op. cit.*, p. 54.

revenues. The decree can be considered as a bilateral contract. The creditors could resume their original rights in
event of its repeal or violation. The Powers took official
note of the arrangement.

For the service of the much reduced debt there was
placed under the creditors' control (a) the government
monopolies of salt and tobacco (not including the customs
duty on tobacco), (b) the stamp, spirits, and fishing
taxes, (c) the tax on raw silk production in certain districts, (d) any excess of customs that might result from
rate increases, (e) the annual tribute due from Bulgaria,
which was never paid and was replaced by a tithe on tobacco, and (f) other miscellaneous sources of income which
never grew important. Without the consent of the creditors the level of these taxes could not be changed to the
detriment of the bondholders. The decree provided that
four-fifths of the product of these revenues was to be used
in payment of interest, one-fifth for amortization. The fact
that the bondholders alone could profit from any increase
in their yield deprived the Turkish Government of any
direct incentive to coöperate in augmenting the yield.

For supervision of the administration and collection of
these revenues and their application to the debt service, an
international administration was established. This administration was empowered with "the administration, collection and direct encashment, for the account of the bondholders and by means of its agents, of the revenues and
other resources" put aside for the debt service. The seven
members of the Council of the Administration were named
by foreign banks or bondholders' groups, one each by the
French, German, Austrian, Italian, and Turkish, one by
the English and Dutch together, one by the holders of the
Privileged Debt (represented by the Banque Impériale
Ottomane). The presidency alternated between the French
and English representatives; the Director-General for
most of the period up to 1914 was French. The Council

acted by majority vote. Its members could not be withdrawn except by the appointing bodies, and could not hold
positions in the Turkish or foreign military or diplomatic
service. Its acts of administration had to be in conform-
ance with existing laws and the terms of the decree. Disputes with the Turkish Government were to be submitted
to arbitration. Though it appointed its subordinates, these
were Turkish officials; their promotion required the consent of the Turkish Government. In all the meetings of the
Council the Turkish Government had a representative
with advisory powers. Official Turkish controllers had access to all books and papers but could not intervene in the
work of the administration. The administration drew up
its own budget; the Turkish Government was obliged to
approve it as long as it was in accord with law and decree.

Such was the arrangement by which the foreign bondholders guarded their rights.[48] The Council administered
directly the Salt Monopoly, the stamp, fishing, spirits,
and silk taxes. The Tobacco Monopoly was farmed out to
a Régie (owned by French and Austrian-German capital)
for a fixed annuity and share in the profits.[49] The whole
arrangement worked with surprisingly little conflict. The
only dispute of importance between the Turkish Government and the Council which required arbitration arose in
1903 over the wish of the Council to make an extra interest distribution. From 1881 to 1903 the ceded revenues
yielded enough to meet the minimum interest obligation
of 1 per cent but little more. The net yield was virtually stationary—averaging annually about 2.1 million

[48] For a full list of the regular and special reports issued by the
Debt Administration, see Blaisdell, *op. cit.*, p. 109. For details of its
organization, legal status, etc., see G. Young, *op. cit.*, Vol. V, Chap.
LXXXV.

[49] Its operations and balance sheets are given in the annual Reports
of the Council of the Régie to the General Meeting of Shareholders,
1884-1913. After a period of deficits, which compelled a reduction of
capital, the Régie became profitable; in 1913-14 the shareholders received 13-14 per cent on their capital.

Turkish pounds for the period 1882–1902.[50] The reports of the Council affirm repeatedly that the Turkish Government coöperated only half-heartedly in action necessary for the development of the revenues because it had no direct interest in the result.[51] Improvement was made in the salt industry and an export trade developed. Silk cultivation was encouraged, instructed, and extended. The yield of the stamp tax was less than might have been hoped because of the virtual exemption of foreigners, the native habit of verbal bargaining, and the laxity of the Turkish authorities. The taxes on spirits favored importation rather than domestic production.

By 1903, about 22 per cent of the debt affected by the Decree of Mouharrem had been redeemed. But circumstances favored a debt conversion and revision of the arrangement. The bondholders had become impatient with their low return. The Turkish Government wished to increase its customs duties in order to pledge the increase for the payment of Bagdad Railway bonds, but under the 1881 decree such increase would go only to the holders of the previous bond issues. In France the Ministry of Finance was occupied by Rouvier, who not long before coming into office had participated in the formulation of conversion plans. A new agreement was successfully negotiated. The old debt was converted into a new one bearing higher interest but much reduced in principal. Thereafter three-quarters of any surplus in the yield of ceded revenues over the fixed annuities would be turned over to the

[50] The average annual yield of the revenues for 5-year periods were as follows in thousands of Turkish pounds:

Years	Yield	Years	Yield
1882–87	2,339	1897–1902	2,538
1887–92	2,328	1902–7	3,064
1892–97	2,503	1907–12	4,527 (Including new customs surtax)

[51] The description given by Laurent, *op. cit.*, shows that even after the 1903 conversion the situation left much to be desired.

Turkish Government; the remaining fourth was used for amortization.

From 1903 on, the yield of the ceded revenues increased more rapidly despite the disorder that prevailed within the Ottoman Empire. Between 1883 and 1913 the yield of the revenues administered directly by the administration doubled (after deduction of the yield of special surtaxes imposed in the later years). Including the returns from the increases in the customs duties and the additional revenues subsequently put under the administration's guardianship, the gross revenue received by the Commission was in 1913–14 almost 5.4 million Turkish pounds as against 3 millions in 1903–4.[52] This growth despite the obstacle of circumstance is to be attributed to the efforts of the international Debt Administration. The administration strove to improve commerce, agriculture, and industry. It regularized the application of the tax laws under its control, fought evasion and contraband. It encouraged, by technical help, the growth of silk production. Still in all these efforts it stopped short of entering too frequently into the ordinary life of the people; for that reason it left undone much that it recognized as needing doing. The administration of the farmed Tobacco Monopoly remained rather poorer than that of the Salt Monopoly which was under direct control. Some of the revenues under the administration's care it made no attempt to collect directly, leaving that task in the hands of the Treasury or other agents of the Turkish Government; it was aware of the danger of bringing the stranger into contact with the Mussulman population in the unpopular character of tax collector. The administration, itself, had on March 1, 1912, 8,931 employees, of whom two-thirds were permanent.

The establishment of the Debt Administration assured debt payments despite the recurrence of heavy budget deficits. As new debts were contracted after 1903, the

[52] Sir Adam Block, *Special Report on the Ottoman Public Debt,* 1914.

range of revenues put under the supervision of the Debt Administration was extended. Turkey, when it could, borrowed without going further in the direction of taking sources of revenue out of the hands of its General Treasury and setting them aside. Thus the Young Turk *régime* managed to secure large loans in 1909 and 1910 without assigning special revenue to the care of the administration. But when no other terms were possible, it yielded to necessity. The existence of the Debt Administration secured it trust that otherwise would have been denied, trust on interest terms lower than 5 per cent up to 1914. Lenders counted for their security upon the increase in yield that could be obtained from a source of revenue after it was transferred from the government to the administration. They believed, too, that the support of their governments would be given to the administration if trouble came. This speculative judgment overlooked the determining fact that in the long run, no matter what safeguards are taken, the security of an investment cannot be better than the political health of the country in which it is made. If that is weak and abused, security will fail, unless the power to borrow is checked or taken away. Without such provision international financial control cannot avoid a final crash.

Beginning in 1907 the Debt Administration was made by treaty the official agent of the European Powers in the collection of the 3 per cent customs surtax, most of which was to be devoted to Macedonian reforms. Its duties were limited to the verification of the records of collection and to encashment. This extension of its activities gave the administration a clearer claim than before upon the support of the Powers for the execution of its duties. But even previously it had become plain that the will of the governments as well as of the bondholders was represented in the Council.

Gradually there developed a large measure of common interest among the members of the Council and the foreign groups which held railway and industrial concessions in Turkey. The British, French, and German members encouraged the Turkish Government in its wish to build railways across its territories, thereby to increase the basis of revenue available for the public debt. The revenues pledged for the kilometric guaranties given were put under the guard of the Debt Administration. The chief revenue so pledged was derived from the tithes of the territories traversed. The representatives of the administration had an effective voice in the proceedings incident to the adjudication and encashment of these tithes, stepping in to prevent maladministration and diversion of receipts. Toward the Turkish Government they took the rôle as trustees of the railroad bondholders.

With these foreign-owned railroads, and with much of the rest of foreign enterprise in Turkey the members of the Council were personally connected.[53] For example, Sir Vincent Caillard, British member of the Council, shared with Herr Kaula of the Deutsche Bank the preliminary concessions in 1888 for the extension of the Haidar-Pasha-Ismidt Railway and later served on the Board of Directors of the Anatolian Railway. One of his successors, Sir Adam Block, was President of the British Chamber of Commerce in Constantinople, and a director of the National Bank of Turkey. He was also on the Board of Directors of the Imperial Ottoman Docks, Arsenals, and Naval Constructions Company, a Turco-British venture organized in 1914 by English armament firms to reconstruct the dockyards and arsenals of the Golden Horn, and to construct floating docks in the Gulf of Ismidt.[54] Commandant Berger, for many years French representative on the Council, was the dominating personality in the direction of three important French-owned railway lines, on the Board of Directors of the Anatolian Railway,

[53] Blaisdell, *op. cit.,* pp. 215–224, enumerates these connections in detail.

[54] *Economist,* December 6, 1913.

and vice-president of the Tobacco Monopoly. On the Board of Directors of the Bagdad Railway were the German, French, and Turkish members of the Council, as well as the Director-General of the Administration. The German member of the Council was on the Haidar-Pasha Port Company.

These positions in major industrial enterprises—of which the preceding is but an incomplete review—tended to pass with the succession to place on the Council. By virtue of their official duties, their personal interests, and their connections with the governments of the countries from which they came, the members of the Council became the advocates of foreign enterprise in Turkey.[55] Thus the Debt Administration became more than a protective body for the holders of Turkish government bonds. It developed into an agency whereby the enterprising capital of Western Europe sought profit midst the disorder and weakness of Turkey.

In the rivalry between the governments of the capital-lending countries for place in Turkey, the members of the Council were also involved. The representatives tended to act in defense and promotion of the financial groups of the countries from which they came. But much of the financing carried out in Turkey was undertaken by international combinations, as in the case of the Bagdad Railway, and the Banque Impériale Ottomane; and for the sake of mutual adjustment of interests, mutual aid and support were common.

The members of the Council, and the banking groups which appointed them, were aware that they needed the backing of their governments, and could not afford to cross them seriously. Most of the appointees were drawn from government service, and were

thoroughly conversant with the technique of granting official protection to special interests, or, on the other hand, equally

---

[55] Blaisdell, *op. cit.*, p. 224.

familiar with the most effective means of commanding such defense. At the same time it can be safely ventured that the larger interests of their respective governments would receive solicitous attention to the degree that each member was able to accord.[56]

Each member of the Council was in the habit of keeping in close touch with the ambassador of his country, and ordinarily in correspondence with his government. The German representative was nominated by the President of the Prussian State Bank, and elected by the Deutsche Bank and Bleichröder with the concurrence of the Foreign Office. On one occasion this concurrence was given only on the condition that the appointee should not be subject to the control of the house of Bleichröder.[57] The French and British appointments were made by groups accustomed to discern their government's preference. Because of the fact that the holders of the Privileged Bonds retained a place upon the Council even after the conversion of these securities, the French interests controlled two places. In 1913–14 Russia made efforts to secure a place, though Russian investment in Turkish securities was negligible.[58] The French Government for a time gave its support. But Germany demanded in return that a second German delegate be appointed, and that the presidency of the Council should be open to the representative of the German bondholders in rotation with the French and English. In the attempt to enforce its demand Russia withheld consent to an increase in the Turkish customs duties.[59]

Despite the connections with their governments, the individual members of the Council were, in their daily activities, primarily concerned with the interests of the bond-

[56] Blaisdell, *op. cit.*, p. 224.

[57] British Treasury, *Memorandum on the Ottoman Public Debt*, prepared for the Peace Conference.

[58] *Livre Noir*, II, 240 *et seq.*

[59] A. Lichnowsky, *Heading for the Abyss*, p. 32.

holders they represented, and the financial groups with which they worked. The methods of public business in Turkey they lamented but accepted. The Turkish Government and people wanted their support, and needed the groups behind them. As long as Turkey resorted continually to European investors, outside control was a primary condition of security demanded by the investors. But the security obtained was only superficial. The arrangements for international control could not, when calamity came, protect those who furnished capital to finance Turkey. It is even conceivable—but this is merely one of the threads of speculation which may be drawn out of the skein of pre-war history—that it made the calamity more certain by enabling Turkey to borrow.

CHAPTER XV

THE FINANCING OF RAILROADS IN ASIATIC TURKEY

THE Sultan Abdul Hamid found the task of governing his empire an anxious one.[1] His was a polyglot and rebellious people. The Arabs were often in revolt, the Armenians in protest and disorder, the Kurds against the law, the Slavs and Bulgars fighting for their freedom. His power to maintain unity and order was balked by mountains and distance. Foreign Powers threatened his sovereignty and independence. Foreign residents in Turkey lived under their own legal administration. His power to change customs duties was limited by treaty, and many of his other revenues were pledged to foreign creditors and under their supervision. Thus many were his difficulties and sorrows; and small seemed the sums furnished by his subjects.

His country had few roads, little organized trade, an unproductive agriculture despite much good soil; its mineral resources lay unextracted. If the country was to be preserved it was plain that political control and unity must be restored, the military power increased, and resources and trade developed. These were the vital ends that railways were to serve in Turkey.

THE RAILWAY PROGRESSES TOWARD BAGDAD

RAILROAD building in Turkey had begun in the sixties. French and English capitalists had built roads in Syria and Asia Minor, and one of the first acts of the Sultan

---

[1] The matters dealt with in this chapter have been studied in great detail by E. M. Earle, *Turkey, the Great Powers, and the Bagdad Railway* (New York, 1923). The general course of events is well portrayed by P. T. Moon, *Imperialism and World Politics* (New York, 1927). I have drawn on both these sources.

was to arrange for their extension. The through line from the Austro-Hungarian border to Constantinople had been opened in 1888 and gave access to the European domains. But the great dream of the Sultan was the construction of a trunk line through Turkey in Asia, which would with its branches unite Constantinople, Smyrna, Aleppo, Damascus, Beirut, Mosul, Bagdad, and end at the Persian Gulf. Then Turkish police and military power could be made effective from the Black Sea to the Persian Gulf, and from the Bosphorus to the Persian Gulf. Troops could be drawn from distant places. Rebellion could be suppressed, revenue increased, enemies met, and freedom rewon. The members of the international Debt Administration encouraged the plan. Sir Vincent Caillard, Chairman of the Administration, tried to form a British syndicate to finance the project, but failed.

The Germans accepted the opportunity. The British had built a railroad from Haidar-Pasha, across the straits from Constantinople, inland to Ismidt. This a German syndicate bought, and sought from the Sultan a concession to carry it on to Angora. The Sultan gave the company an annual subsidy per kilometer built. The Anatolian Railway Company was formed. Sir Vincent Caillard was elected to its board so that the support of the Debt Administration and of British capital would be assured. Ownership was vested in a holding company, the Bank für Orientalische Eisenbahnen, at Zurich—which held also the control of the Oriental railways. This concession was not secured without German official aid. The German Ambassador had taken the initiative of inducing German capital to seek it. But at the start the Deutsche Bank was hesitant because of the large capital needed. Bismarck, while offering no objection, made it clear that he accepted no responsibility for the protection of the company. He foresaw the struggle of influence which would rage about Turkish railroads. But once the German group had decided to finance the undertaking, the German Government gave its vigorous support in rivalry with other governments. Von Siemens of the Deutsche Bank gained favor by lending the Sultan 30 million marks wherewith to discharge a Russian debt. In October, 1888, the final concession was granted. The march of German enterprise and political influence in Turkey had begun.

The railroad reached Angora in 1893. The Sultan wished it carried to Konia, in the interior, at once. Inside and outside of Turkey obstacles had to be met. Many members of the Sultan's government, encouraged by the French, opposed the grant. The Deutsche Bank found the technical and financial difficulties serious. The Sultan appealed to the Kaiser for aid against the opposition and hesitation. They were, in the end, overcome. Construction was begun, and under the eager watchfulness of the monarchs, Konia was reached in 1896.

The French had not been left without compensation for this new grant to German capital. French capital had financed and French management controlled railways running north and east from Smyrna. They had bought the road from Smyrna to Cassaba from the British owners. They had begun to link towns and seaports in Syria. The mileage of these roads was greater than the Anatolian Railway. Now the Smyrna-Cassaba line was given a concession for extension further into the interior. The French strove to keep a predominant place in the operation of railroads in Asiatic Turkey, especially in Syria where other French economic interests were numerous and French clerical and cultural institutions firmly established.[2]

The original concession to the German group had carried a provision looking toward prolongation to the Persian Gulf. But this needed confirmation and definition;

[2] *Report of the Association Nationale des Porteurs Français, 1915–20,* contains a good series of detailed studies of the financial history of the French railways in Turkey. The British had also sought compensation at the time in the form of a railway concession to Angora; the German threat to oppose British policy in Egypt quickly brought a compromise.

and even when these were obtained the financial and political obstructions had to be met. The next section of the road had barren stretches to cross and mountains to pierce, and no great amount of capital was easily to be found in Berlin for this purpose. The Paris market had capital easier to be attracted, and the French bankers were, with strong diplomatic support, pushing forward with a plan for a railroad to run from the Mediterranean to the Persian Gulf, which would use the existing French railroads as nucleus. The German Ambassador at Constantinople was warning that if the German group did go forward with its concession, the French and English groups active in Constantinople would. But the Deutsche Bank was insisting upon the need of foreign assistance in order to reduce the burden and the risk, and reluctantly the German Government consented to the prospect of outside participation. In May, 1899, the German interests, the Deutsche Bank and Anatolian Railroad Company, and the Anglo-French interests, the Banque Impériale Ottomane, and the Smyrna-Cassaba Railway, reached an agreement.[3] The two main groups were to have equal participation in ownership and control of a new company to be formed to build from Konia to the Persian Gulf. Forty per cent of the capital was to be German, 40 per cent French (Anglo-French), and the remaining 20 per cent was to be offered to Turkish investors.[4] The Anatolian and Smyrna-Cassaba railways were to coöperate with the new road under a working agreement. Both banking groups were to endeavor to secure the united support of their governments in behalf of the claims of the Deutsche Bank to the concession. The French Ambassador gave his friendly aid to the German Ambassador. The British Government, informed by its representatives, seemed not op-

[3] K. Helfferich, *Georg Von Siemens*, III, 92 *et seq.*, gives details of the understanding.

[4] In an annex it was provided that a share should be reserved for possible British participants.

posed; it was occupied with affairs in South Africa. In November, 1899, the award of the concession for construction, clear to the Persian Gulf, was announced. In return, the Deutsche Bank was induced under the urgent pressure of the German Ambassador to grant a loan to the Sultan.

Routes were surveyed, and the award made definitive in January–March, 1902. Probably in deference to Russian opposition, a route more southerly than that originally proposed was selected. The road was to traverse high table-lands and mountains, and to connect with the Syrian railways; its terminus was to be at Basra, on the Turkish Gulf 500 miles beyond Bagdad. A branch was to extend to Khanikin on the Turkish-Persian border. In March, 1903, the Bagdad Railway Company was organized by the Deutsche Bank under Turkish law. To it was conveyed without right of cession, transfer or assignment, the concession for the construction and operation of the new railway beyond Konia.[5] The charter of the company provided for the subscription of 10 per cent of the capital by the Anatolian Railway Company. Three, at least, of the eleven members of the Board of Directors were to be appointed by the board of the Anatolian Railway Company, and at least three others were to be Turkish subjects. This, as Mr. Earle states, assured Turco-German control.[6]

[5] For the text of the convention between the Turkish Government and the company, the statutes of the company, and the various loan contracts it entered into, see Great Britain, *Bagdad Railway* (*No. 1*), *1911* (Cmd. 5635, 1911).

[6] Earle, *op. cit.*, p. 70. Mr. Earle is of the opinion (footnote 31, p. 88) that such control was not inconsistent with the 1899 agreement which "assured French interests 40 per cent of the shares of the Bagdad Railway." But it would appear to be plainly contrary to Clause 1 of that agreement which states that the German and French bankers were to be equally represented in ownership and control. Clause 1 may have been deliberately drawn in such a way to permit differing interpretations by different parties and at different times. The French bankers were eager to share in the business even though they might be in a minority position; Clause 1 might have been intended to satisfy their government.

Some of the main features of the agreement (March 5, 1903) between the company and the Turkish Government should be noted. To the company the Turkish Government was to give 4 per cent bonds at the rate of 275,000 francs, nominal value, per kilometer constructed, which the company would sell to finance the road. This bonded debt was to be a first mortgage on the road, and the revenues of the districts traversed were set aside for debt service, and put under the supervision of the international Debt Administration. The government guaranteed, further, to cover operating expenses up to 4,500 francs per kilometer, provided receipts did not do so. In return, the government was to share largely in any excess of gross receipts over that amount. The banks had to furnish little capital outside of that secured by the sale of the bonds. Similar guaranties had been given previously to other railway enterprises. The materials needed for the railroad construction and development of the road, and coal used in its operation, were to be free of domestic taxes and customs. The land required for right of way was to be conveyed free of charge to the company. Timber necessary for the construction and operation of the railway might be cut without compensation from the state forests.

This assistance was none too great, nor these terms none too burdensome for a railroad undertaking built in advance of traffic in the disturbed Turkish Empire. But certain of the other subsidiary rights granted went beyond the reckoning of wisdom. The railroad property and revenue were given perpetual tax exemption. The company was given the right to operate tile and brick works along the railway, and to establish hydroelectric plants to generate light and power—without sufficiently clear restriction as to the extension these enterprises might take, and with the same exemption from taxation as the railway enjoyed. And finally the company was given mining rights —but not monopolistic rights—within a zone twenty kilometers each side of the line. Considering the fact of government guaranties, there was little more to be given away; and yet the supporting banks and investors lost their money. If peace had prevailed, these privileges would have been unjust; when war came they proved unavailing, and war was the most evident danger.

In compensation, the convention provided that the railroad, free of debt, should become the property of the government in 99 years. The government was given the right to repurchase the road by paying an annual sum equal to 50 per cent of the average gross revenue receipts during the previous five years—in no event to be less than 12,000 francs per kilometer. It was agreed that disputes arising out of the convention should be settled in the competent Turkish courts. In a secret appendix the company promised not to encourage or locate foreign settlements in the vicinity of the railroad.

THE PROJECT OF INTERNATIONALIZATION FAILS

SUCH were the main terms of the convention under which capital drawn from France, England, and Germany was to unite and restore Turkey. The German group immediately began further negotiations with French and English groups for the disposition of the bonds to be issued to finance the first section. The governments watched, and in the outcome both French and English governments discouraged the participation of their citizens.

The Russian Government had shown unfriendliness to the project as early as 1889, fearing that a strengthened Turkey would be a menace to its position in Northern Asia Minor, and cherishing fitful ambitions to possess the straits. The abandonment of the more northerly route, and the pledge obtained from Turkey in 1900 that no concessions would be granted for railroad construction in Northern Anatolia or Armenia except to Russian nationals or syndicates having the approval of the Czar, had removed the strategic menace. For a short time thereafter the Russian opposition waned because of French financial

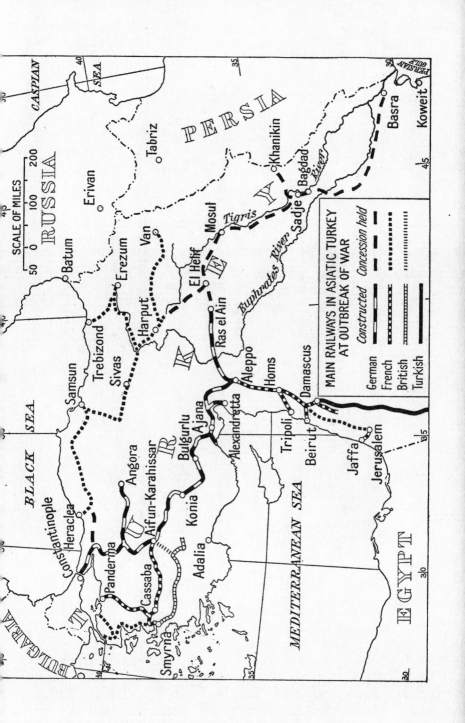

MAIN RAILWAYS IN ASIATIC TURKEY
AT OUTBREAK OF WAR

Constructed Concession held

German
French
British
Turkish

SCALE OF MILES
50 0 100 200

CASPIAN SEA

RUSSIA

PERSIA

BLACK SEA

Constantinople
Heraclea
Samsun
Trebizond
Batum
Erivan
Tabriz

Angora
Sivas
Erezum
Van
Harput
Mosul
Khanikin
Bagdad
Sadje
Basra
Koweit

Aifun-Karahissar
Bulgurlu
Ras el Ain
El Heif
Aleppo
Konia
Ajana
Alexandretta
Homs
Damascus

Panderma
Cassaba
Smyrna
Adalia

Tripoli
Beirut
Jaffa
Jerusalem

MEDITERRANEAN SEA

EGYPT

BULGARIA

Tigris
Euphrates River
River

PERSIAN GULF

persuasion and anticipation that Great Britain would share in the enterprise.[7] But thereafter the Russian Government again viewed the project with uneasiness. It preferred a Turkey impoverished and disunited to a Turkey developed and united, and feared it would give Germany preponderance in Asia Minor. These views were impressed upon the French Government. Besides, the commercial interests of Lyon and Marseilles were alarmed lest their trade with the Near East be injured by the new overland route. The clerical interests voiced their fear that France would lose its protectorate over the Catholics in the Near East. These combined anxieties found support in the French Parliament in 1902.[8] Besides, it is also probable that the French Government did not believe that in the final arrangements French interests would be given as large a share as the German in the actual determination of the policy of the company.[9] Thus, despite its earlier friendliness, in October, 1903, the French Government declared that it would refuse official listing to the Bagdad Railway bonds and admonished the bankers not to participate. The Banque Impériale Ottomane remained bound by its contract and took up its participation; the bonds remained in its portfolio and it had a minority representation on the board of the company.

The British Government had been openly friendly to the concession award to the Deutsche Bank while it was being negotiated. The official attitude had been that since the railway was to be built, it would be desirable to have British capitalists share in the venture.[10] This attitude had been sustained throughout 1901 and 1902. The government on several occasions exerted itself to induce Brit-

[7] *British Documents,* Vol. II, Nos. 202, 203, 217.

[8] *Débats Parl. Chambre de Députés,* March 24, 1902.

[9] This view the British Ambassador at Constantinople reported the French Ambassador to have expressed in July, 1903. *British Documents,* Vol. II, No. 223. See also E. Dubief, *Revue Économique Internationale,* April, 1912, pp. 32–37.

[10] *British Documents,* I, 334.

ish bankers to join in negotiations with the French and
Germans, and undertake the business.[11] The German
group needed not only the participation of the British
capital but the coöperation of the British Government.
They desired, first, that Great Britain should join effort
with Germany to get general consent to an increase of
customs duties, whereby Turkey would find it easier to
meet her interest guaranties; second, that Great Britain
send the Indian mails over the new railroad route, and pay
a subsidy for its carriage; third, that Great Britain aid
in securing a terminus for the railroad on the Persian
Gulf—in which region British dominance was admitted.
In February, 1903, the Foreign Secretary informed the
bankers, who by now had conditionally accepted a share in
the plan, that the British Government was willing to consider these proposals; its conditions were first, absolute
equality in participation and control; second, the inclusion
of the Anatolian Railway in the scheme.[12] These conditions Lansdowne, the Foreign Secretary, had from the
beginning made clear he would demand. Now he went so
far as to ask Baring Brothers to take over, so that it might
better succeed, the management of the British participation in the bond issues.[13]

On April 7, 1903, a statement of the government's intentions was made in the House of Commons, and there
they were vigorously attacked. A hostile press campaign
of increasing vigor swept the country. The cabinet decided

11 *British Documents*, I, 334.

12 *Ibid.*, Vol. II, No. 206. The advantages foreseen by Lord Lansdowne
were (a) the disappearance of the Anatolian Railway, a German enterprise which might acquire a line from sea to sea, and (b) a peaceful
settlement of the Persian Gulf Question. Lord Newton, *Lord Lansdowne*
(London, 1929), p. 252.

13 *Ibid.*, No. 208. The leaders in the previous discussions with the
German group had been Sir Clinton Dawkins of Morgan, Grenfell & Co.,
and Sir Ernest Cassel. The former was nervous, for his firm was at the
moment unpopular because it had fathered the transatlantic shipping
combine; the latter felt that as a naturalized British citizen of German
origin his position was delicate.

not to stand out against the opposition. On April 23, 1903, Mr. Balfour declared in the House of Commons that the government would not give support to the Bagdad Railway scheme. It had come to the conclusion, this declaration continued, that the proposals "do not give to this country sufficient security for the application of the principles" of genuine internationalization, of equality of commercial treatment, and of equality of control, construction, and management.[14] Mr. Earle writes that the British financiers concerned were chagrined at the sudden decision of their government.[15] A memorandum by the Foreign Secretary, written later, seems to indicate that they, the bankers, yielded to the public opposition before, at least, a part of the cabinet. In it he states that, "If it had not been for the scuttle of the financiers I should have been in favor of sticking to our position."[16]

It is difficult to be certain whether the German group offered effective equality in every respect to the English group, and whether the German Government ever accepted such an arrangement. The original company plan provided German-Turkish control. But the German group put forward amended plans in the later negotiations; these provided that 25 per cent of the capital should be German, 25 per cent French, 25 per cent English—the remaining quarter to be subscribed 10 per cent by the Anatolian Railway, and 15 per cent by neutral interests.[17] After much shuffling about and dispute it appears to have been decided that of the board of thirty directors, eight each were to be elected by the German, French, and English

[14] *Parl. Debates, House of Commons,* 5th ser., CXXI, 222.

[15] Earle, *op. cit.,* p. 185.

[16] *British Documents,* Vol. II, No. 224. This appears possible in the light of the position of Sir Clinton Dawkins and Sir Ernest Cassel.

[17] *Ibid.,* Nos. 212, 224. According to M. Constans, the French Ambassador to Turkey, the French group had only agreed to the 10 per cent allotment to the Anatolian Railway on condition that they would receive an equal sum out of the neutral participation which was to be under the control of a French bank. *Ibid.,* No. 210.

groups, three by the Anatolian Railroad, and three by the
Austrian and Swiss groups; each of the three main groups
was to have equal place in control upon the Construction
Committee.[18] Mr. Von Gwinner of the Deutsche Bank
stated that he had practically accepted all the conditions of
the British bankers, which were the conditions formulated
by the British Government.[19] It would appear as though
nothing in these terms would have prevented eventual
French-British domination of the line.[20] Still, there is
Balfour's declaration, there are the repeated statements
on the part of the German Government that the line must
not lose its German character, an opinion never clearly
renounced. About the affair there still remains, after close
examination, suspicion that though the German Government was willing to have the façade international, it held
to the intention of having the internal organization German.[21]

Among the statements of the opposition to which the
British Cabinet deferred, a hundred different strains of
feeling, argument, and interest appeared. Vested interests
—the British navigation companies which possessed a
monopoly of navigation rights on the Tigris, the shipping
companies that saw a possible loss of freight and mails,
the exporters to Turkey, the British-owned railroad in
Turkey—all these had their vigorous spokesmen. A general feeling of unfriendliness against Germany, whose
plans for an increased navy and whose African aspirations
were becoming more assertive, was common among the
masses; and the railroad, it was uneasily felt, might be a
prelude to a German-Turkish alliance. But most important of all probably in government and official circles was

---

[18] *British Documents,* Vol. II, No. 218.

[19] *Ibid.,* No. 224. Schwabach of Bleichröder made the same assertion.

[20] Earle, *op. cit.,* pp. 188–189.

[21] A telegram of Von Wangenheim, *Chargé d'Affaires* of the German
Legation, April 28, 1903, suggests that the façade could be made mod-
erately French provided that the internal organization remained German.
Die Grosse Politik, Vol. XVII, No. 5264.

the fear that the construction of the road might put India, the Persian Gulf, and the Suez Canal in danger, make them harder to defend if need be. These and other matters dictated the decision which was to stand as a source of anger between Germany and Great Britain till 1914, and to delay the construction of the railway in the face of German and Turkish effort.[22]

GERMAN CAPITAL GOES AS FAR AS IT CAN

FAILING French and British official consent, 10 per cent of the capital required for the first section was subscribed by the Anatolian Railway, 10 per cent by the Turkish Government, and the rest by an international syndicate dominated by the Deutsche Bank. The work went forward. The German Government patiently persisted in its efforts to remove the diplomatic and financial obstacles—determined to record success. The conversion of the Turkish public debt in 1903 aided the financiers by providing a surplus as security for the railway loans.[23] Within 19 months the first section of the new line—200 kilometers, Konia to Bulgurlu—was completed. Beyond this section lay high mountains and difficult construction. The Turkish Government was in no position to meet the service of additional bonds. Thus it was not until 1908 that the terms were settled for the construction of the next two sections of the line—850 kilometers; these were to bring the road to within 700 of its terminus on the Persian Gulf.

But the Young Turk Revolution delayed the construction of these sections. The new government insisted that the Deutsche Bank again seek English participation.

[22] A good review of British policy is A. Parker, *Quarterly Review,* October, 1917.

[23] This conversion the British Representative in the Debt Administration opposed because it would help Germany to go forward with the Bagdad Railway, and help France to collect claims, while it might weaken the security of the bondholders.

Again the matter was reopened with Sir Ernest Cassel and the British Cabinet; the same refusal stood.[24] But shortly thereafter German prestige and influence revived, nourished by the financial aid which the German banks extended the Young Turk government when France and Great Britain refused. The Young Turk movement turned into aggressive nationalism, of which Germany alone, of the Great Powers, had nothing to fear. Toward the end of 1909 construction was begun and the second and third series of Bagdad Railway bonds were underwritten by the same syndicate which had taken the first. As the line went forward from Bulgurlu toward El Helif, arrangements were made for the construction of a branch that would give the road a second sea terminal, at Alexandretta on the Mediterranean, with extensive and exclusive port and terminal facilities.

In 1911 a new convention was signed between the company and the Turkish Government which obligated the company to proceed with the third section of the road from El Helif to Bagdad, 600 kilometers; but for this section the state of Turkish finances made impossible the grant of such kilometric guaranties as had been given for previous sections. Traffic on the sections already in operation was increasing with encouraging rapidity; the payments required from the Turkish Government, as guaranties, were declining rapidly. By this convention, as a prelude to a new arrangement, the Bagdad Railway Com-

24 Intermittently from 1903 on the German Government had sought favorable diplomatic circumstances under which to strike a bargain. For example, the Kaiser raised the question with the British Government when the preliminary discussions were going on regarding the Anglo-Russian agreement. The Kaiser gave his consent to the British control of the section from Bagdad to the Persian Gulf. But the German Foreign Office was not entirely in accord with the Kaiser's offer. Besides Sir Edward Grey insisted that France and Russia be associated in the discussions and Germany thought she would fare better in separate negotiations. *British Documents,* IV, 263. In 1907–8 Germany was near agreement with Russia which sought in return relief from German rivalry in Persia.

pany returned its rights to the line beyond Bagdad and to the port at Basra to the Turkish Government—under condition that their construction, if and when undertaken, should be by a Turkish company internationally owned and administered. The way was again clearly open for international negotiations.

OPPORTUNITY IS DIVIDED BY SPHERES

THE time was, in Mr. Earle's phrase, propitious for "bargains to be struck." The section to Bagdad would be more costly than the preceding ones, and the waiting traffic smaller. The German capital market could hardly meet the new demands; the German banks dared hardly accept the risk. Russian opposition to the completion of the road was stilled in accordance with the agreement arrived at between Russia and Germany in November, 1910—the Potsdam Agreement. That agreement weakened the force of the British and French opposition. France tended to welcome the chance to change its position. Great Britain's consent was more difficult to obtain. Without it the road could not be brought to the Persian Gulf or the necessary increase in customs duties obtained. But even stubborn British opinion was growing weary. The progress of the line indicated that the opposition would fail in its object in the final event. The Foreign Secretary, Sir Edward Grey, alarmed at the tenseness of ill feeling between his country and Germany, grew willing to seek the way to bring to an end this subject of quarrel.

For almost three years bankers and governments sought the terms of settlement—bringing into numerous combinations those two principles of adjustment which always dominate the dealings of Great Powers in such matters— the principles of compromise and of compensation. The course of negotiations between France and Turkey became in their later stages connected with the attempt of Turkey to borrow in Paris for general government purposes. The

French Minister of Foreign Affairs declared as early as 1911:

> Circumstances are, therefore, very favorable for examining in agreement with the Turkish Government, the conditions of economic collaboration between the two countries. We desire that the Turkish Government be provided with resources . . . but on the doubtful condition that the higher interests of France in the Levant are safeguarded and that French commercial, industrial, and financial interests are treated in a fully satisfactory manner . . .[25]

In these 1911 negotiations with Turkey, Russia made itself felt, reminding the French ally that Russia still claimed a right under the 1900 Treaty with Turkey to veto all railroads built by foreign capital in northern Asia Minor (east of the line Samsun-Sivas-Diabekir-Mosul-Khanikin), and recalling the pledge of the French Government not to permit any loan for this purpose without Russian consent.[26] In return for permission Russia expected assurances from Turkey and compensation. During the summer of 1911 negotiations were renewed between the German and French financiers. The former were urging that French banking group which shared in the earlier Bagdad lines to aid in the new issues. This group was favorably disposed and Poincaré wished it to stay in the enterprise; but he was determined that the aid should be rewarded. When the Deutsche Bank proposed to this group that it would buy back all the bonds of the previous issues that rested unsold in their portfolio, on condition that the group would assume responsibility for the subsequent issues, the French Government brought pressure to insure refusal. The recompense was not sufficient. During the Balkan wars, negotiations ceased.

But during 1913 a whole series of agreements among the Powers, and between the Powers and Turkey, took

[25] *Débats Parl. Senat*, April 7, 1911.
[26] *Livre Noir*, I, 58–60.

form. The French Government used its power over the official market to cause Turkey to reach agreement with Russia. This was achieved.

The French and German financiers now could proceed to formulate the terms of apportionment of French and German railroad opportunity in Turkey. French enterprise had, since 1908, been pushing forward with extensions of the lines under its control. In 1913–14 a secret agreement was finally reached between the two financial groups.[27] France was given Northern Anatolia and Syria as a sphere of influence for railroad development; Germany was assigned the district traversed by the Anatolian and Bagdad railways. The German bankers took over from the French the Bagdad Railway bonds which they held, and also their share holdings in the company. The French bankers were relieved of the obligation of taking 35 per cent of the next issue. The Germans, on the other hand, sold to the French their holdings in the 1911 Turkish government loan. They received a promise that advances they had made to Turkey, 66 million francs, would be repaid out of the large Turkish reorganization loan to be issued in France. Out of that large loan, the first section of the French railway net in the Black Sea region was to be financed; any disposable sums left thereafter for public works were to be divided equally between French and German enterprises. The agreement was countersigned by officials of the French and German Foreign Offices. To secure that loan which she so urgently needed, the Turkish Government immediately confirmed the concessions to France of railroads in the Black Sea and Syrian regions.

British negotiations with Turkey and Germany likewise found their issue. Turkey recognized the special position of Great Britain in the Persian Gulf, agreed that the Bagdad Railway should not be carried further than Basra without British consent. The Turkish Government agreed

[27] Earle, *op. cit.*, pp. 246–250; Poincaré, *Au Service de la France,* IV, 13–14; *Livre Noir,* II, 143.

that two British citizens should be elected to the Board of
Directors of the Bagdad Railway. The existing rights of
British capitalists who had navigation privileges were re-
affirmed, and exclusive rights of navigation on the Tigris,
Euphrates, and Shatt-el-Arab were granted to a British-
Turkish company to be formed by Lord Inchcape of the
Peninsular and Oriental Navigation Company. This com-
pany was to have wide powers for the improvement and
regulation of all navigable streams in Mesopotamia, in co-
operation with a Turkish commission. In return Great
Britain consented to support an increase of 4 per cent in
the Turkish customs duties.

A series of Anglo-German agreements followed. The
newly formed navigation company and the Bagdad Railway reached an agreement upon shipping and navigation
matters; the signatures were witnessed by representatives
of the Foreign Offices. The same official cognizance was
taken of a draft agreement between the Bagdad Railway
Company and the British-owned Smyrna-Aidin Railway
Company, providing for the extension on the latter and
its junction with the Bagdad Railway. The two governments agreed to join their efforts to procure from the
Turkish Government exclusive rights of exploitation of
oil resources of the provinces of Mosul and Bagdad, which
had been solicited by the British Government as early as
1907. These were to be turned over to the Anglo-German
enterprise—the Turkish Petroleum Company which was
now constituted. In this company there were joined together the interests of the Royal Dutch Company, the
Anglo-Persian Oil Company, and the Deutsche Bank
group, all of which had claims entitling them to consideration. The German group consented to accept the minor
share and in addition recognized the exclusive right of the
Anglo-Persian Oil Company to the Southern and Central
Mesopotamian fields.[28] In June, 1914, the two govern-

[28] Earle, "The Turkish Petroleum Company," *Political Science Quarterly*, June, 1924. The agreement signed on March 19, 1914, at the

ments approached the Sultan in behalf of the company
and received a promise which had not yet been definitely
confirmed when the war broke out.

Then finally, all these adjustments of interests having
been made in June, 1914, Sir Edward Grey and the German Ambassador initiated a convention defining the German and British interests in Turkey. The British Government agreed to withdraw its opposition to the Bagdad
Railway and to support no competing lines. Its consent
to an increase in Turkish customs duties would make possible the extension of the line. The road was not to be
carried to the Persian Gulf without consent of the British
Government. The German Government recognized the recent Anglo-Turkish convention, and the rights conferred
therein upon British companies.

The half century of activity of foreign capital in Turkey began to provide that region with the equipment of
a modern industrial state and to improve the use of its
natural resources. But with the foreign capital came im-
pending foreign dominance. In 1913–14 before the war
the contestants reached an adjustment of their claims in
a virtual division of Asiatic Turkey in spheres of economic
influence. The Russian sphere was in Armenia and in the
region next the Russian border. The English in the regions near the Persian Gulf and along the line of the
Smyrna-Aidin Railway, the French in Syria and the
Black Sea region, the German in the territories traversed
by the Anatolian and Bagdad railways, Central and
Southern Anatolia and Northern Mesopotamia.

Whether these spheres would have been made the basis
of political division if war had not come in 1914 remains
a matter for speculation. In the months before the war

British Foreign Office had the signatures of Sir Ernest Cassel (National
Bank of Turkey), Sir Henry Deterding (Royal Dutch Company), Mr.
Walter Samuel (Shell Oil Company), Mr. Carl Bergman (Deutsche
Bank), Sir Charles Greenway and Mr. H. S. Barnes (Anglo-Persian Oil
Company), Sir Eyre Crowe (British Foreign Office), Baron Von Kuhl-
man (German Foreign Office).

Turkey was arming to win back lost territory in Europe; when war came Turkey entered in a gamble to win back lost strength and independence. The forces of the nineteenth century had pulled apart Turkish conquests of past centuries. The Ottoman Empire could not survive in its inherited form and boundaries within the world of newly strengthened nationalist European states. Foreign capital and modern industrial technique might have restored its power. They proved to be one of the forces which brought out all its inherent weakness. It requires an orderly and competent government and a healthy state to utilize them advantageously.

CHAPTER XVI

THE FINANCING OF PERSIA: BETWEEN TWO IMPERIAL AMBITIONS

FROM the time of its first entry the actions of foreign capital in Persia had political consequences, and were managed by outside governments for national purposes. Each outside power feared that other governments would turn any financial opportunities or pledges secured by their nationals to political advantage, and so intervened to control the action of the Persian state and to support their own interests. Under these circumstances, the political aspects of the relations between the Persian Government and foreign capital were always to the front, the economic aspects out of sight, except as they bore upon the political.

THE SHAH MORTGAGES HIS DOMAINS TO TRAVEL IN EUROPE

In 1872–73 while the British prestige in the Middle East was high, the Persian Government granted to a British subject, Baron Reuter, a concession conveying almost complete monopoly of the economic life of Persia. Of this concession which roused the fury of Europe, neither the British Government nor British investors took advantage. It remained unexecuted because of lack of adequate security, and was canceled without protest by the British Government. Several other concessions granted to English groups at about this time came to grief, causing losses to investors; as a result, Persian credit and enterprise were ranked as a bad risk in London.

Between 1888 and 1890, both the British and Russian governments became extremely active in the effort to introduce their capital and undertakings in Persia. In 1889–90 the aid of the British legation secured for Baron Reuter the right to establish the Imperial Bank of Persia.

This bank was given the exclusive right of note issue, and became the agency through which the British Government conducted its financial operations in Persia. The shares were issued in London, while the Shah was visiting there. "In order to facilitate the issue it was also incorporated under a Royal Charter."[1] The bank was given mining rights throughout the Empire, which were ceded to the Persian Bank Mining Rights Corporation. This venture in 1894 joined the list of the unfortunate British gambles in Persia. Another concession secured in this period almost produced the overthrow of the Persian monarchy. This concession, countersigned by the British Minister, conferred a monopoly of the sale of tobacco and tobacco products. The beneficiaries paid the Persian Government 15,000 pounds, and a 25 per cent participation in the profits; according to the prospectus they expected to earn 371,000 pounds annually on a capital of 650,000—not wholly paid up. The arrival of the officials produced a revolutionary movement and a boycott led by the clergy. Russia demanded cancellation of the grant. The British Government consented to its cancellation upon the payment of an indemnity of half a million pounds. The Imperial Bank loaned the Persian Government the necessary funds, obtaining an assignment of the customs revenues of certain of the South Persian ports of entry, as security. The French Government had offered to induce its banks to extend the loan, if the customs revenues and turquoise mines were assigned as security.[2] No one would lend the Persian Government without such security, and the government was not able so to manage its affairs as to dispense with outside aid.

The triumphs of the British Minister—another was the securing of navigation rights on the Karun River—moved the Russian Government to action.[3] After modulated

1 Sir H. D. Wolff, *Rambling Recollections* (London, 1908), II, 350.
2 J. B. Feuvrier, *Trois Ans à la Cour de Perse* (Paris, 1906), p. 309.
3 The Persian Government, by various regulations, prevented the use

coercion, the Persian Government acceded to a secret convention in 1899 under which it promised Russia that it would not construct any railroads for ten years, or permit others to construct them; the duration of the promise was subsequently prolonged. In 1891 the establishment of a Russian Bank was authorized—the Loan Bank of Persia. This bank was a branch of the Russian State Bank and entirely under the control of the Russian Cabinet. To Russia, also, were given concessions for fisheries on the Persian side of the Caspian Sea, monopolistic navigation privileges on that sea, and grants for the exploitation of mines, forest-lands, and telegraphs. The two governments, by obtaining these financial and economic privileges, installed themselves solidly in Persian affairs, and faced each other hostilely.

Both of the banks made advances to the Persian Shah. In 1898 the new Shah's purse was empty, and he wished to take his usual European tour. The British Government would not guarantee his loan, and the British bankers asked control of the customs as a condition of the loan. The Shah endeavored to solve his difficulties by hiring Belgians to take charge of the Customs Administration. But this did not meet his needs; the customs duties were limited to 5 per cent by treaty with Russia. The need continued, and the Boer War closed the London market. Lord Curzon in India proposed the exaction of harsh terms for British government aid, but the London Cabinet rejected his suggestions. Finally Russia in return for a most favorable commercial treaty lent 2.4 millions of pounds. Out of this loan it was provided that the British advance of 1892 be repaid, thus releasing the South Persian customs. On the other hand all Persian customs duties, save those received at Fars and the Persian Gulf ports, were pledged to the Russian loan—subject to Russian control in the

of this concession till 1894, and then handicapped it. The British Government showed itself conciliatory. See V. Chirol, *The Middle Eastern Question* (London, 1903), pp. 164–165.

event of default. Persia promised that no new foreign indebtedness would be contracted for ten years except with the consent of the Russian Government. In 1902 Russia made another loan in return for a railway concession from Teheran, the capital, to the Russian frontier, and tariff concessions. A prior effort had been made to negotiate the loan in Great Britain without success, the British Government taking no steps to aid it. The proceeds of this Russian lending were spent by a corrupt and voluptuous court without benefit to the country.

The strengthening of the Russian place in Persian affairs disturbed Great Britain. As early as July, 1900, the Persian Government had been reminded of the fact that it could grant no railway concessions in South Persia without consultation with the British Government.[4] To forestall any daring move, the British Government announced in 1903 that no country would be permitted to construct railroads or a naval base on the Persian Gulf, and that British dominance in that region must be maintained.[5] During 1903–4, to break the Russian monopoly, and despite pledges held by the Russian Government, the British Government authorized advances to the Persian Government through the Imperial Bank of Persia, obtaining as securities the revenues of the Caspian fisheries, of the posts and telegraphs and, if need be, of the customs collected at Fars and the Persian Gulf ports. During the same period the British Government put its support behind British projects of road building in South Persia, navigation of the Karun, the extension of the network of the Indo-European Telegraph Company, the establishment of provincial agencies by the Imperial Bank, and the D'Arcy Oil Concession from which the Anglo-Persian Oil Company was later built.[6]

[4] *British Documents*, IV, 365.   [5] *Ibid.*, p. 370.

[6] *Ibid.*, pp. 370–373, and Sir A. C. Hardinge, *A Diplomatist in the East* (London, 1928), pp. 328–329. The former Ambassador to Persia also relates in this volume of memoirs, pp. 278 *et seq.*, the circumstances under which the grant for the D'Arcy Oil concession was obtained. The

During the succeeding years the Russian-British rivalry remained tense not only in Persia but in Afghanistan and Tibet. The Persian financial administration grew poorer and more spendthrift rather than more careful as its burdens increased. There was no fixed budget, no system of public accounts, mismanagement of the farmed-out taxes, and dishonesty in the others. Corruption sat in every branch of a government which was both tyrannous and cowardly, and unable to keep order. Under these conditions the gradual extension of foreign intervention was inevitable. Throughout the country agitation spread against the mismanagement and the foreign control it invited.

LENDING IS CONTROLLED

In August, 1906, in response to the continued demand, a constitution was granted. A parliament (the Medjliss) was established under a system of group representation, with effective powers of control over finances, concessions, and foreign policy. The Shah and the Medjliss fell almost immediately into conflict over financial questions. The Medjliss was controlled by a Nationalist party, among whose leaders were a scattered few with a developed sense of European political standards. It desired to avoid the further foreign intervention that further financial improvidence would necessarily produce. Its first actions were to oppose a new loan which the Shah had negotiated with Great Britain and Russia, under conditions which conveyed control over public expenditure and further control of the customs. An abortive attempt was made to found

Grand Vizier was willing to grant it and advised Hardinge to draw it up in the Persian language for necessary submission to the Russian Embassy, in the knowledge that the Ambassador could not read Persian and that his secretary was absent from Teheran. This concession conveyed exclusive rights to exploit the oil resources of all of Persia except five provinces. Later the British Government bought controlling ownership in the company formed to exploit it, the Anglo-Persian Oil Company.

a National Bank, financed by the Persians, to enable the government to do without the aid of the British and Russian banks. The Belgian adviser who had been engaged in 1899 to supervise the administration of the customs, was dismissed. A limit was set upon the Shah's civil list. All these actions roused the antagonism of Russia, which disliked the Nationalist movement, and perhaps paid it the tribute of fear as an honest and real opposition.[7]

British official sympathy had been extended to the Nationalist movement throughout 1906 and 1907, to the point of giving offense to Russia. But the Russian enmity was costly and affairs on the continent were troubling. Rather than attempt to place faith and give continued support to a movement which might easily deteriorate and engender further Russian hostility, British policy turned to conciliation with Russia and protection to British interests thereby, no matter what the future consequences to the Persian state.[8]

RUSSIA AND GREAT BRITAIN DIVIDE THE FIELD

THE negotiations for this agreement were laborious and checkered. As early as 1899 the Secretary of State for India being of the opinion that a policy of joint Russian-British coöperation in Persian reform was out of the question since Russia was interested in the decay of Persia, not its reform, suggested a sphere of influence agreement for Persia.[9] This was the era in which China was being

---

[7] For the record of these events, see Great Britain, *Persia (No. 1), 1909* (Cmd. 4581, 1909).

[8] E. G. Browne, *The Persian Revolution of 1905–1909* (London, 1910), p. 193, explains the action of the British Government by (a) desire for peace with Russia, (b) the wish to avoid further responsibilities of Empire, (c) the wish to economize on military expenditure in India. The British diplomatic documents support this analysis, but also bring out the fact that the wish to check German action within Persia and growing hostility to the general political aims of Germany were also moving considerations in bringing Great Britain together with Russia on the Persian question.

[9] *British Documents,* IV, 359–362.

partitioned in spheres. From time to time the proposal had reappeared but Russia, living with the idea that the whole of Persia would fall under its influence, had avoided the suggestion.[10] Now the discussions between the two governments became connected with the loans which the Shah was trying to contract with both, and the loans which Russia wished to contract in Great Britain. Great Britain, sympathetic to the rising constitutional movement, was reluctant to provide the Shah with funds to combat it. But in September, 1906, impelled by fear of Germany, it agreed to join Russia in an advance. In return for this advance the British Government suggested the imposition of conditions which forecast the application of the spheres of influence idea. The contemporary internal and financial difficulties of Russia seemed to make a good opportunity to wrest its consent to the boundaries of division desired by Great Britain.[11] Russia was reluctant still so to divide place in Persia with Great Britain and feared besides that by connecting these conditions with an advance Persia might be driven to offer still stronger invitations to Germany.[12] During these months, September–November, 1906, the Russian Government was most seriously negotiating with Germany over the possibility of an agreement whereby Germany would avoid interference in North Persia in return for a cessation of Russian opposition to the Bagdad Railway. Finally in February, 1907, Great Britain gave in and the advance was made without seeking political recompense.[13] The negotiations between London and St. Petersburg were resumed. Russia was persuaded to compromise its desires and to run the risk of offending Germany. By February, 1907, the Anglo-Russian agreement was in sight.[14]

This agreement dealt with Persia, Afghanistan, and Tibet. It was negotiated without consultation with the

10 *Ibid.*, p. 270.   11 *Ibid.*, pp. 392–394, 397.
12 *Ibid.*, p. 391.   13 *Ibid.*, p. 427.
14 *Ibid.*, pp. 442–443.

Persian Government and was not recognized by that government despite the elaborate attempt of the signatories to prove that it would benefit Persia. Above all, it gives explicit recognition of the fact that in a country like Persia, foreign financial and economic enterprises have political consequences, when connected with a national policy of the lending states. The preamble of the agreement pledged the signatories "to respect the integrity and independence of Persia." The remainder of the agreement divided Persia into spheres of influence. In the northern of three indicated zones the British Government promised to seek no concessions for British subjects. The Russian Government gave the same pledge as regards the southern zone. The central zone was left open to the enterprise of both nations. A similar geographical division was established as regards the customs revenues which might be pledged for loans by the British and Russian banks, or put under control in the event of default. The British Government defended the agreement by arguing that the cessation of rivalry between Russia and Great Britain would lessen the necessity of an aggressive stand in Persia. This might have been the actual outcome if Russia had not had aggressive intentions on other accounts; but Russian policy being as it was, the agreement merely made the pursuit of Russian purposes easier, and caused Great Britain to subordinate its action to Russian action.

Fear of German action in Persia, as has already been indicated, played its part in bringing Great Britain and Russia together. Upon the first opportunity offered it to facilitate the entry of German enterprise in Persia—the offer in 1895 of a concession for a railroad from Teheran to Khanikin—the German Government had turned its back, not wishing to challenge Russia's treaty rights.[15] But the mere offer was sufficient to alarm the government of British India.[16] During the subsequent decade of Rus-

---

[15] *Die Grosse Politik*, Vol. XXV, No. 8567.
[16] *British Documents*, IV, 357.

sian and British penetration, Germany, occupied in Turkey, stood aside. In 1906 it began to take vigorous advantage of the openings which presented themselves. But probably from the very beginning it had no lasting intention of winning place in Persia for German enterprise. It was seeking rather to embarrass the progress of Russian understanding with Great Britain, to win from Russia consent for the Bagdad Railway plan, and to assure as large a measure of equality of treatment for German trade in Persia as might be possible.

In the late spring of 1906, the Shah in extreme need, for his extravagance grew no less as his position grew weaker, hoped to secure from Germany the financial aid which was being refused by Russia and Great Britain. He encouraged the establishment of a German steamship line to Persian ports, and the establishment of a German bank in Teheran. The steamship line was started. The bank concession was granted in July, 1906, the German Government refusing to date back the concession, as asked by the Persian Government, to make it appear to antedate the current loan discussions with Russia. To the Russian and British governments, the German sought to give assurance that it was executing this bank concession solely for commercial reasons and that it would pursue no political aims in Persia.[17] In fulfilment of these assurances the Foreign Office turned aside from the enthusiastic schemes presented by its representative at Teheran, dealing with railway, tariff, and other advantages to be obtained through the bank.[18] In September, 1906, it refused the Persian Government's loan requests.[19] Doubtful of its ability to secure any real place in Persian affairs, it did not wish to provoke the two other rivals to any decisive action. It would show itself willing to step out when compensation

[17] *Die Grosse Politik,* Vol. XXV, Nos. 8571–8572, 8576–8578, and *British Documents,* IV, 396.

[18] *Die Grosse Politik,* Vol. XXV, No. 8573, and *British Documents,* IV, 413.

[19] *Die Grosse Politik,* Vol. XXV, No. 8576.

was accorded. Meanwhile enough activity was maintained to show that it had to be taken into account.

During the closing months of 1906 and the early months of 1907 the German Government induced the Deutsche Orient Bank to take up the Persian bank concession, while renewing its previous assurances in London, and emphasizing the fact that the bank would be operated as a private bank, not a state bank. Finally in April, 1907, the Deutsche Orient Bank negotiated an agreement with the Persian Government which gave the bank the right to issue silver money, and left the way open for further negotiation with the Persian Government for concessions for mining rights and waterworks at Teheran, if these were granted to foreigners.[20] This agreement the German Government censored to bring it in accord with the promises given to M. Isvolsky in October, 1906. It erased clauses whereby the bank promised to share in advances to the Persian Government on guarantees left to future determination, and others by which the bank acquired the right to share in loans and railway concessions.[21] For the German negotiations with Russia at the time seemed likely to produce agreement, a draft of terms having been prepared in February, 1907.[22]

But the strategic position of Great Britain proved stronger than that of Germany, it having the financial power Russia so eagerly courted. While the discussions between Great Britain and Russia marched to definite accord in March–July, 1907, those between Germany and Russia lagged. Attempts to connect the two sets of discussions were made by the French banker, Count Vitali, and the Banque Impériale Ottomane, which wished to end the ban of the French Government on Bagdad railway

---

[20] *Die Grosse Politik,* Vol. XXV, No. 8578, note.

[21] *Ibid.,* No. 8589.

[22] *Ibid.,* No. 8580. For an interesting and detailed analysis of German purposes as seen by the Russian Government, see the "Protocol of Deliberations of the Russian Ministerial Council" of February 1, 1907, printed in *British Documents,* IV, 270–271.

loans, but they failed.[23] Russia became more demanding and Germany reluctantly gave up hope of immediate accord. At about the same time the Deutsche Orient Bank decided not to make use of the Persian concession.[24]

After the 1907 agreement the Russian and British governments took for granted their right to veto concessions which were not to their interest, and to demand that their consent be obtained in important financial operations. The Medjliss was, during the next few years, almost constantly in dispute with Russia. Russian help was given the reactionary Shah in his attack upon the Medjliss. At this juncture the British policy was hesitant and hard to analyze. Faced with the Russian wish to give financial support to the Shah, it wavered, seeking assurance that the Shah would remain faithful to the constitution; at the same time it used the occasion to secure pledges that Persia would not borrow elsewhere, and would have sought railway concessions, had it not been for Russian disfavor.[25] Despite Russian support, the Shah was overthrown in 1909. Thereupon Russia again fomented civil war. There was chaos in the capital, tribal revolt throughout the provinces, and an empty treasury.

The possibility of German interference was eliminated in 1910. The German Government had continued to maintain a stubborn front against the Anglo-Russian assertion of dominance in Persia. It did not recognize the Anglo-Russian agreement, and tried to insist upon the open door for German commerce and finance. When it was proposed that French financial advisers be appointed in Persia, German objections were vigorously heard.[26] To show that it was still a factor to be reckoned with, the German Government gave support to an expedition sent by the

23 *Die Grosse Politik,* Vol. XXV, No. 8580.

24 *Ibid.,* No. 8597 and footnote.

25 *British Documents,* V, 241. For the details, see also Great Britain, *Persia (No. 1), 1909,* and *Persia (No. 2), 1909.*

26 B. De Seibert, *Entente Diplomacy and the World,* pp. 67, 75; *Die Grosse Politik,* Vol. XXVII, Nos. 10090–10091.

Deutsche Bank to study railroad possibilities. The expedition was designed in part to make "Isvolski amenable to our desires in the Bagdad question."[27] Thus was the campaign carried on in the form of support for private enterprise. Finally in March, 1910, the German Government warned the Russian Government that this support would take a more vigorous form.[28] Still it refrained from responding to the appeal of the Persian Government that it should, under a treaty of 1873, use its good offices to settle Persia's disputes with Russia and Great Britain. The German policy gained its end when in November, 1910, Russia promised to put no future obstacles in the way of the completion of the Bagdad Railway, and to construct, as the first railway in Persia, a line to connect with the Bagdad Railway at Khanikin. In return Germany renounced all claim to railway and public works concessions in the Russian zone of influence in Persia. German enterprise had shown little eagerness to enter it.

Persian financial need after the overthrow of the Shah was extreme. The means of maintaining internal peace and order were lacking. The Medjliss showed little capacity to master the difficulties by which it was beset. The financial administration and tax system were still so dishonest and disorganized that it was doubtful whether any further borrowing would have any durable result beyond adding to the government's burdens. Russia and Great Britain insisted that any further loans should be contracted through them. There was solid reason for asking for a reform of Persian financial administration and supervision of the expenditure of proceeds, as conditions of

[27] *Die Grosse Politik,* Vol. XXVII, Nos. 10013, 10102, 10108.

[28] For the details of German policy, see *ibid.,* Vol. XXV, especially Nos. 8566-8603, and Vol. XXVII, Nos. 10090, 10091, 10094, 10095, 10102, 10105, 10108, 10113. How badly it had the British Government worried even up to 1912 is indicated by the fact that Sir Edward Grey proposed to the Czar, September, 1912, that they should join to secure railroad concessions in the neutral zone, to remove them from German reach. *Livre Noir,* II, 351.

further loans. But the demand of reform as coming from
the two dominating governments smacked of guile, for it
was to their policy, especially Russian policy, that much
of the internal disorder and financial distress of Persia was
to be traced. Besides, the demands of reform and control,
when made, went beyond the necessities of the case. In
March, 1910, the two governments asked as the conditions
of financial aid (a) that the borrowed funds be spent in
accordance with an approved program, under the supervision of a commission of six members, of whom two were
to be Europeans; (b) that seven French be engaged to
occupy various executive posts in the Ministry of Finance;
(c) that Great Britain and Russia be assured a prior right
to construct railroads within their zones; (d) that Russia
be given a monopoly of navigation on Lake Ourmiah; (e)
that a police force be organized under foreign officers.[29]
Upon these terms the Medjliss would not borrow, despite
the unveiled pressure of both governments.

These in retaliation prevented recourse to sources beyond their control. Thus, when, just as the Anglo-Russian conditions were being put forward, Sir Edward Grey
heard that a British firm had been offered an option to
make a loan in Persia by the International Oriental Syndicate (presumably German, for the Potsdam agreement
had not yet been reached), he took swift action to prevent
Persia from proceeding with the negotiations.[30] Again in
April, 1910, an individual understood to represent a
French syndicate tried to arrange for the issue of a loan
in Paris, having received an option pledged on the revenues of the Customs and Telegraph Services. Both governments protested and the French Government refused to
sanction the loan.[31] As early as 1907 the French Government, eager to foster the progress of the Anglo-Russian

[29] M. Sauvé, "La Situation en Perse," *Questions Diplomatiques et
Coloniales,* July 16, 1909, and Great Britain, *Persia (No. 1), 1911.*

[30] Great Britain, *Persia (No. 1), 1911,* No. 37.

[31] G. L. Dickinson, *The International Anarchy* (New York, 1926),
pp. 262–263; De Seibert, *op. cit.,* p. 85.

agreement, had shown itself willing to use its control of the
Paris market to prevent financial transactions which might
interfere with their joint plans in Persia.[32] During the
latter part of 1910 Seligman Brothers of London arranged to loan 1,250,000 pounds to be spent for designated
purposes under supervision; 700,000 were to be used to
pay off an advance made by the Imperial Bank of Persia,
and so remove their lien upon the customs of Southern
Persia, freeing them for the larger loan. The British
Foreign Office appears to have induced or compelled Seligman to retire from the transaction on the ground that it
would be detrimental to the Imperial Bank.[33] By that time
some willingness to compromise was being shown by the
Persian Medjliss and Great Britain did not want its position weakened, or concessions taken out of its hands, despite its genuine desire to see order established in Persia.
In January, 1911, a convention was reached between the
Persian Government and the Russian bank which consolidated all but two of the previous Russian advances
into a 7 per cent debt pledged on all Persian customs save
those of Fars and the Persian Gulf. And the following
month Great Britain authorized some small advances pending a larger loan, to enable Persia to maintain a police
force. The larger loan was arranged in May. It paid only
5 per cent, and bore no conditions except the pledge of
the Persian Gulf customs. Because the British Government
had not wished to go to the extreme of actually occupying
Persia, the will of the Medjliss in a large measure prevailed.[34]

Even after receiving this aid Persia continued to be in
want of funds to maintain a police force, security on roads,
and to establish the authority of the Central Government
in the provinces. Thinking to improve its credit and to

[32] *British Documents,* IV, 443.

[33] See letter signed "Jus" in the *Economist,* November 12, 1910, p.
976, also *Economist,* November 26, 1910, p. 1081.

[34] Great Britain, *Persia (No. 3), 1912,* Nos. 91, 97.

escape conditions that gravely limited its independence, the Persian Government in May, 1911, engaged Mr. Morgan Shuster, an American, and a group of assistants, giving him full power to control and centralize the collection of all Persian revenues, and audit government expenditures. Mr. Shuster undertook his work in a vigorous, systematic, and downright fashion—setting aside both the traditional privileges of certain parasitic Persian office-holders and nobles, and the arrangements entered into between Great Britain and Russia as regards Persian affairs. Within three months he was the center of a dispute in which the Medjliss backed him dramatically against both internal opposition and Russian and British pressure. Despite Russian opposition his will that the Belgian customs officials be under his authority prevailed. He set about to organize a Treasury Police to enforce the collection of legal taxes. But his plans of fiscal reorganization were soon brought to a halt.

Russian plans left no place for the presence of such an official as Mr. Shuster, who took seriously the Persian stand of independence, and who might have, besides, so improved the Persian Government that all foreign domination might have been thrown off. One of the things feared was that the Medjliss would give Shuster control of the granting of railway concessions, in the exercise of which he would not show sufficient consideration to Russia. The Russian Government created new difficulties for the smaller country by aiding an attempt of the ex-Shah to return to power. It multiplied ground of complaint against Mr. Shuster's actions. Sir Edward Grey bent his decisions to Russian wishes. Mr. Shuster sought to save himself by an appeal to British opinion, through the British press, but his obstinacy was of no avail.[35] Finally in November, 1911,

[35] For a full account of the various episodes which brought Shuster into conflict with Russia, see Great Britain, *Persia (No. 3), 1912; Persia (No. 4), 1912, Persia (No. 5), 1912;* M. Shuster, *The Strangling of Persia* (New York, 1912).

Russia delivered an ultimatum demanding, among other matters, the dismissal of Shuster, and the appointment of no foreigners to the Persian government service without Russian and British approval. The Medjliss at first refused unanimously. But under the threat of an immediate Russian march upon Teheran, a cabinet which accepted the demands took power and dismissed the Medjliss (December, 1911). The attempt of Persia to reform its own financial affairs was prematurely killed; with it went for a decade the attempt at democratic control. Thenceforward, to the outbreak of the war, Persia was to exist only by the sufferance of the Powers and their occasional advances.

The negotiations over these advances fill the record of the years 1912–14. The British Government took the lead in proposing and making them. For anarchy had gone so far in the country, largely as a result of Russian interference, that British trade could not be conducted in safety. They were a substitute for the costs of an expeditionary force. In January, 1912, Great Britain was willing to make advances without conditions, but Russia insisted upon the contrary course. A joint advance was made in February, 1912; its expenditure was put under control.[36] As part of the price of receiving it, the staggering Persian Government undertook to observe the principles of the Anglo-Russian Convention of 1907. Russia had her way. In return for further advances, Russia asked now for the concession of a railroad to traverse Persia, now for a revision of an old concession to construct a short road from its border into North Persia. Great Britain, though anxious to restore order and to keep out of power the reactionary group which Russia was favoring, asked the concession of a railroad in the neutral zone from Khoramabad to Mohammerah.[37] The British Govern-

[36] Apparently after the failure of the Russian Government to organize a British-French banking syndicate under the leadership of the Banque de Paris et Pays Bas. *Livre Noir,* I, 187–188, 194–195.

[37] Great Britain, *Persia (No. 1), 1913,* Nos. 276, 305, 333, 341, 392.

ment appears to have been moved to make this demand largely through its fear that Russia would admit German capital to participate in its concession. Then, too, it sought this Mohammerah-Khoramabad concession so that it might be able to dictate the terms of any project for extending the Russian lines southward.

The railway concession to Russia—North Persian border to Tabriz—was granted. It carried with it the right to work the coal and oil deposits for forty miles on each side of the line. Russia obtained at the same time preference on equal terms for another railroad in its zone —Kazvin to Tabriz.[38] But the Persian Government and the British syndicate found it difficult to come to terms upon the railway of the neutral zone, despite the attention of Sir Edward Grey to every feature of the negotiations. An option was finally arranged in March, 1913.[39] Then further advances were made. For those made by Great Britain, there were pledged the customs revenues of South Persia, the opium receipts, and the spirits excise tax. The English syndicate to whose direction the acquired option was turned over united all the business and financial groups which had been sustaining British trade and concessions in Persia. Among them were the Imperial Bank of Persia, the Anglo-Persian Oil Company, and the Ellerman line. The list of original stockholders included Lord Strathcona, Lord Lamington, Lord Cowdray, Lord Inchcape, Sir John Ellerman, Mr. Lynch, and Mr. D'Arcy.[40] Their spokesman in Parliament had kept after the Secretary of State for Foreign Affairs. English engineers were

[38] *Ibid.*, and *L'Asie Française*, February, 1913, p. 11. The contract gave mining and oil rights within 60 versts of the line. The company to which this concession was conveyed was given an Imperial Charter. All the shares were to be held by the Russian Government, who would appoint the higher officials. For the terms of the contract and charter, see *L'Asie Française*, April, 1913, p. 191, June, 1913, p. 285.

[39] Great Britain, *Persia (No. 1), 1914*, Nos. 14, 15, 25; *Parl. Debates, House of Commons*, 5th ser., Vol. LXIV, pp. 1388–1389.

[40] *L'Asie Française*, June, 1913.

sent to survey the route. Meanwhile efforts were being
made to arrange a large long-time loan in connection with
a Trans-Persian railway project.

By 1914 there was some promise of permanent order in
Persia. With the help of the foreign officers paid out of
the advances, order was being reëstablished in the provinces. The customs revenues were increasing, and the financial administration was improving. The foreign loan
obligations were not beyond the capacity of the country,
if it was left in peace. They approximated, as of June 30,
1913, 6.5 millions of pounds for the service of which about
25 per cent of the public revenue was required.[41] Virtually
the whole of this debt was to the British and Russian official institutions in Persia. It is obvious that Persian financial fate was within their hands. The Russian troops
were still in occupation, and the Russian hold on the
northern provinces was almost complete. The resistance to
this aggression was at its low ebb; all of the former parliamentary leaders were either dead or in hiding, and their
means of assertion were gone. The financing of Persia had
brought it under dominance, not because of the pressure
of outside financial interests, but because its territory lay
in the path of ambition of stronger powers. The Persian
people continued to endure the lack of conveniences, of the
orderly ways and means, the sanitation of industrial Europe. They could not organize themselves to use the new
technique or equipment of industry to build roads, towns,
better houses; nor could they by maintaining order and
steadiness of purpose, induce outside groups to place their
investment in the hands of the Persian Government and
people. The weakness and incompetence of the country
attracted only those who wished to dominate, not those
who might have coöperated.

[41] Memorandum by H. L. MacLean, Great Britain, *Persia* (*No. 1*),
1914, No. 295.

THE TRANS-PERSIAN RAILWAY PROJECT

THE project of a railroad to traverse Persia, to run from
the Caspian Sea to the Persian Gulf, to connect the Russian railways with British India, had been seriously discussed in Great Britain as early as 1872–73, when Baron
Reuter was in possession of a concession which would have
permitted the construction of such a line. At various later
times it was the subject of earnest discussion between the
British Foreign Office and its diplomatic representatives.
But the British Government had repeatedly reaffirmed its
traditional policy of maintaining buffer states between
Russia and British India, and of not encouraging any
railroad building headed toward the Indian frontier. In
1908 the British Government would go no farther than to
"approve of a line passing through Persia to the Persian
Gulf at Mohammerah, from which place a British road
concession as far as the Russian zone of Khoramabad already exists."[42]

But in 1910–12, while England was unhappily trailing
Russia in its Persian policy, the plan received serious
diplomatic and financial backing. A French-Russian financial group was formed which in turn founded a "Société d'Études" in which British participation was invited,
to make surveys, to secure the necessary concession from
the Persian Government and to win over the other governments. The support of the Russian Government was
willingly granted, as Russia saw the project as an opportunity to offset the influence acquired by Germany
through the Bagdad Railway. In November, 1911, Isvolsky, Russian Minister at Paris, wrote to the Russian
Secretary for Foreign Affairs:

I would make that expulsion (of Shuster) our first demand.
Then after that lesson to the Persian Government, do you
not think the time has come to busy ourselves with the con-

[42] *British Documents*, V, 242.

struction of the Persian railroads, especially the through
line of the Trans-Persian? Here the preparatory financial
work has made material progress recently . . . But as far
as I know the diplomatic preparation of that affair has not
gone far, and without that foundation no financial combination is possible . . .[43]

The Russian Government attempted to make the grant of
a concession for such a line a condition of advances to the
Persian Government.

The British Government appeared to favor the plan
until opposition appeared. Lord Morley in July, 1912,
asserted that only negative aid had been extended, adding
that the plans had been studied by the General Staff in
India, who had advised against it.[44] The Foreign Secretary informed the House of Commons not long thereafter
that it would not receive the assent of the British Government until a satisfactory agreement had been reached with
Russia regarding the construction of branch lines, the
control of the road within the British zone in Persia, and
the equality of treatment of British trade. The British
Government permitted the British participants in the Société d'Études to proceed with the effort to obtain an option on the whole line, on condition that its consent be
secured before the line was extended into the British
sphere.[45] It also took the precaution, as has been observed,
of seeking for itself alone a concession in the neutral zone
so as to be able to block any project which it disliked.

The effort was eagerly carried along by the Russian

[43] *Livre Noir*, I, 165; *Documents Diplomatiques Français, 1871–1914*,
3d ser., Vol. I, No. 422. This company had 24 directors of which at least
8 were to be Russian and at least 8 French; included in the French
group was an influential member of the Chamber of Deputies, M. Bluy-
sen, and M. Raindre, former Director of Political Affairs in the Foreign
Office.

[44] *Parl. Debates, House of Lords*, 5th ser., XII, 471–479; E. Cam-
maerts, "Le Transpersan et la Question Persane," *Revue Économique
Internationale*, April, 1912.

[45] Great Britain, *Persia (No. 1), 1913*, No. 341.

Government. It held already the right to build the first
section of the line to Teheran. The scheme was connected,
at any rate for a time, with the granting of a long-
time loan to the Persian Government. The Russian
Ministry of Foreign Affairs discussed financial ways and
means with the English and French financiers, and with
the French Government which gave its favoring aid.[46] But
the British and Russian governments could reach no
agreement as regards the route. The Russian Government
desired that the trunk line run from Resht (on the Caspian Sea) through Teheran, thence in a southeasterly
direction through Baluchistan to the Indian frontier. The
British Government, doubtful as to whether any road at
all should be built, was willing only to consider a more
southerly course that would connect the Persian Gulf with
the northern trade centers, thereby aiding British commerce and coming largely into the zone of British influence. On that difference of purpose, on British doubt, on
Persian opposition which made the prospects of adequate
financial guaranties slight, the whole project faltered.
Russia was preparing to start construction on a shorter
line when the war broke out. In 1914 there were no railways in Persia except one tiny local line.

[46] *Livre Noir,* II, 349–350. Report of Sazonoff to the Czar.

CHAPTER XVII

FINANCE AND FATE IN NORTH AFRICA

1. THE FINANCING OF EGYPT

EGYPT, nominally a province of the Turkish Empire, was granted the right to borrow on its own account in 1841. Many separate races lived within the land. Of them, the Turkish upper class approached in status and privilege the European residents. Almost all the other people strained throughout long days to get a bare subsistence from the soil. As in all other states of the North African littoral, the will of the ruler was the sole rule, and the improvidence of the ruler was a heavy scourge. No administrative system capable of carrying on the proper tasks of government existed. In the political outlook of two important European countries, Egypt held a major place. France nourished old ambitions, spectacularly acted upon by Napoleon. Great Britain maintained a firm determination that Egypt, as the land of passage to India and the Far East, should not be dominated by any third Power. These were the vital facts and circumstances which shaped the course of events after Egypt began to borrow abroad.[1]

[1] The literature on Egyptian finance is enormous. Among the sources of special importance, besides the volumes of diplomatic correspondence issued by the British and French governments, the following may be mentioned: *Annual Reports of the Financial Adviser to the Khedive* reproduced in the *Reports of the Council of Foreign Bondholders; Annual Reports by His Majesty's Agent and Consul General on the Finances, etc., of Egypt,* published as Parliamentary Documents; Lord Milner, *England and Egypt* (11th ed., London, 1914); Lord Cromer, *Modern Egypt* (London, 1908); C. L. Freycinet, *La Question de l'Égypte* (Paris, 190?); R. G. Levy, "Les Finances Égyptiennes," *Revue des Deux Mondes,* February 1, 1899; M. H. Haekel, *La Dette Publique Égyptienne* (Paris, 1912); A. Andréadès, *Les Contrôles Financiers Internationaux* (Paris, 1925).

THE KHEDIVE GOES BANKRUPT

WHEN Ismail Pasha became Khedive of Egypt in 1863, he inherited a substantial debt, contracted in part for the construction of the Suez Canal, from which Egypt derived little obvious benefit. During his reign, which lasted until 1879, the debt rose from 367 to 1,712 million francs. His subjects, almost entirely peasants, with nothing beyond their huts and daily food, numbered less than eight millions. Ismail Pasha, once engaged in borrowing, lost all sense of its significance and prescience of its ultimate outcome. His mind and spirit surrendered to the taste of novel grandeur, to wish-inspired notions of Egypt's wealth, to fantastic dreams of glory and plans of imitating western civilization. In part, he was a dupe of his friends and advisers, Egyptian and European, who turned his good nature, his ambitious purposes, his generosity, to their own ends. He built a road system, tried to model Cairo after Paris, built an opera house to hear "Aïda" sung, attempted to operate factories, and extended his property until it included one-fifth of the country's arable land. Always, until bankruptcy loomed as inevitable, he found some European lenders to extend him credit. The ordinary investor did not realize the financial state of the country. Banks were willing to take the risk of loss for large return and special pledges, matching their powers and calculations against his profligacy. When one banking group retired, another entered the field. For foreign loans from 7 per cent upward was paid on nominal sums of which he received four-fifths, two-thirds, or less. On some of the issues, short-time treasury bonds, the interest soared to 30 per cent. With the growth of the debt burden, taxes were increased. These taxes had no fixed base and there was no official register. With the intensification of need, the revenue collection became a system of tribute rather than of taxation. If the docile peasants could not pay, their possessions were confiscated.

The borrowing continued as long as new loans could be procured to pay old interest. By 1875 no new sources of revenue could be found, no new pledges or inducements could be arranged. Despite the collection of taxes in advance, the issue of a forced loan, and the sale of government shares in the Suez Canal, interest payments could not be met. Upon the creditors, M. Freycinet has passed just judgment.

The simple enumeration (of debts) indicated the bottomless pit into which the capitalists were tossing their savings. If they complain it must be remarked that the risk was patent and ought to have enlightened. The sympathy they awaken would be much keener if they had not voluntarily taken such great risks to increase their profits inordinately.[2]

But from this time on, foreign governments intervened in support of the bondholders' committees which were formed. Among the most important of the creditors was the Crédit Foncier over which the French Government exercised supervision. The necessity of safeguarding the interests of this institution was among the moving considerations of French policy.[3]

THE CREDITORS TAKE CONTROL

GIVING in to his creditors and desiring to forestall foreign governmental intervention, Ismail established in 1876 a receivership—the Caisse de la Dette. Under the control of the representatives of the creditors were put the long list of revenues which had been assigned as security for the loans: the provincial government taxes, the local customs duties of Cairo and Alexandria, the foreign customs of main Egyptian ports, the salt and tobacco taxes, among others. The Caisse or Commission was composed of four representatives appointed by the Khedive on the separate

2 Freycinet, *op. cit.*, p. 154.
3 Lord Newton, *Life of Lord Lyons*, II, 175.

recommendation of the French, English, Austrian, and Italian governments. They were to have the status of Egyptian officials, not recallable by their government without khedival consent. The Egyptian Government pledged itself not to modify the assigned revenues without the consent of the Caisse, and not to borrow without its permission. Upon the establishment of the Caisse, various types of existing debts were unified into one 7 per cent debt (this being less than the average rate due). The old debt was exchanged for the new at rates ranging from 80 per cent of new debt for 100 per cent of old debt, to parity. Outside of the conversion were left (a) the loans of 1864, 1865, and 1867, bearing 7 and 9 per cent, (b) the preference stock which had been secured on port and railway revenues, (c) the Daira-Sanieh debt (pledged on the Khedive's lands, mainly in upper Egypt, planted in sugar cane). This Daira debt was the subject of a special settlement in 1877 after the bondholders had obtained a verdict in the Egyptian Mixed Tribunals, *pro tanto*, setting aside the 1876 agreements and authorizing them to foreclose. As part of the settlement, these pledged domains were put under the management of two representatives of the creditors.

Another khedival decree named two European controllers, one French and one English, to watch over the state finances. The one was to direct the collection of the revenue, the other to control the accounts of the Treasury. It created also a separate commission of three, one Frenchman, one Englishman, one Egyptian, to manage the railways whose revenues were pledged to the Preference Debt, and the port of Alexandria. But this commission had only limited executive powers. Thus Egyptian finances and economic life, as a result of bankruptcy, were put under the supervision of four international bodies—the Caisse, the Controllers, the Daira-Sanieh Administration, the Railway and Port Commission. It is interesting in view of Great Britain's later stand that its government at the time refused to make nominations for the posts assigned to Englishmen. Lord Derby declared that "Her Majesty's Government cannot accept any responsibility for these nominations, but however, makes no objection to them."

The total government debt, after these settlements, approximated 91 million pounds; the debt service was over 8 million pounds; the total government revenue did not exceed 9 million pounds. The new arrangements quickly revealed their defects. The revenues were not sufficient for the debt service and the elementary needs of government though the peasants were coerced and taxes were collected with the whip. The two European controllers were powerless before the confusion of Egyptian public accounts and the demoralization of the financial administration. Despite the criticisms of the bondholders and the warnings of the French, English, and other governments, the sovereign did not meet his obligations. In response to a joint protest of the governments, he created in January, 1878, an expert Commission of Inquiry to study the means of improving the situation.

The commission reported that among the important causes of Egypt's difficulties were the arbitrariness of the tax system, the lack of a budget system, the absoluteness of the Khedive's power, the concentration of so large a part of the lands of the country in his inefficient hands. The Khedive accepted, or appeared to accept, the conclusions of the committee. A constitutional government was ordained, in the cabinet of which an Englishman was made Minister of Finance and a Frenchman was appointed Minister of Public Works (in place of the system of controllers established in 1876). In the same year the Egyptian Government was enabled to borrow again from the Rothschilds to meet its deficits and pay its floating debt. The property pledged to this loan (khedival property transferred to the state) was put under a Dominial Commission of three—one native, one Frenchman, one Englishman, named by their respective governments.

Thus a fifth agency of international financial control was established in Egypt.

It is doubtful whether the Khedive had any genuine intention of parting with his personal power in accepting the first set of recommendations of the Committee of Inquiry. The reform offered the chance to place upon the Foreign Ministers the onus of increasing taxation and reducing expenditure if repudiation were to be avoided, or of repudiation if that became inevitable. The Khedive did not try to help the Foreign Ministers and they excluded him from their counsels. The British officials tended to be of the opinion that debt reduction must precede reconstruction and there was strong support for such a step in the British Parliament; but the French bondholders and government did not share the opinion.[4] The newly formulated plans for improving the financial situation of the government required the taxation of the Egyptian upper classes and the dismissal of army officers. The Khedive fostered the resistance of both these groups and gave indirect support to antichristian agitation. Finally, in 1879, he refused to accept the final recommendations of the commission which would have further curtailed his power. He dismissed the cabinet of which the European officials were members, and created an all-native cabinet. The Europeans were asked to resume their posts as controllers.

The Powers protested and demanded that the Khedive abdicate.[5] The French and British governments feared

[4] Thus Lord Salisbury, commenting upon the situation brought about shortly thereafter by the Khedive's dismissal of the European cabinet ministers, wrote to Lord Lyons, April 10, 1879, "Egypt can never prosper as long as some 25 per cent of her revenues goes in paying interest on her debt." Lord Newton, *op. cit.*, II, 175.

[5] Various authors attribute this action to the initiative of Rothschild and Bismarck, who became anxious lest all debt obligations be renounced. Their initiative, it is said, forced Great Britain to act lest Germany obtain some advantage. See W. Blunt, *Secret History of the Occupation* (London, 1907), p. 65, and T. Rothstein, *Egypt's Ruin* (London, 1910), for assertions along this line. G. Young, *Modern Egypt* (London, 1927), p. 95, also credits this explanation.

that he planned to seize again absolute power, with all of his faulty use of it. With him in control they decided political reform was impossible. Neither wished to assume direct responsibility for the government of Egypt; neither was willing to permit the other to assume it. Yet the bond-holders' interests and the Canal required a stable and well-governed Egypt. By decree of the Sultan of Turkey, June, 1879, Ismail was deposed and Tewfik Pasha was put in his place. Anglo-French control of finances was established again by the appointment of two Controllers-General with an advisory voice in the cabinet. They were given powers of "inquiry, control, and surveillance" and charged with the duty of reorganizing Egyptian finances.

It was admitted, at last, that the burden of debt resting upon the Egyptian Government had to be reduced. The first report of the newly appointed Controllers-General announced the fact. After investigations by an international committee and prolonged discussion among the governments of Europe, the financial obligations of Egypt were modified in the Liquidation Law of 1880. The principal of the debts was increased slightly by new loans to help Egypt meet the existing emergency, but the interest of most of the debt was reduced to 4 per cent. However, a heavy amortization program was arranged at the same time. The five international institutions or arrangements were left in existence. The powers of the Caisse were extended and defined. It was made into an international body in law as in fact and its subordinates were freed from the authority of the Egyptian Government. The Egyptian Government could issue no long-term loans without its consent. The administrative expenses of the Egyptian Government were limited to 4.9 million pounds, and its power to contract short-term indebtedness on current account was limited to 2 million pounds.

The liquidation arrangements and the change in ruler did not meet the requirements of the situation. The bond-holders, supported by their governments, had continued to insist on more than the Egyptian Government could pay and carry out its functions effectively. Lord Milner wrote afterward:

The arrangements embodied in the Law of Liquidation, the work of able and conscientious men who had made themselves masters of the subject, was based on just and reasonable ideas, but it left no margin for contingencies. We can see now, looking back upon it, that it was a mistake to make at that time any immediate provision for a Sinking Fund. The institution was excellent, but Egypt was not yet in a position in which she could afford to begin to reduce her liabilities. . . . It was good—indeed, it was essential—to check administrative waste; but the Law of Liquidation went further. It not only suppressed the extravagances, but it touched upon the necessaries of government. By reducing too rapidly the expenditure on public services, and especially on the army, it contributed in some degree to that revolutionary movement which was destined to upset the financial equilibrium of Egypt almost as soon as it had been re-established.[6]

Disputes arose immediately between the foreign controllers and the Egyptian Assembly over financial questions. Great Britain was willing to compromise the matters at issue but yielded to France's opposition, probably because a French-English commercial treaty was under negotiation at the time.[7] Thus can utterly unrelated situations determine the fate of a debtor nation. The two governments sent a strong note upholding the position of the controllers. This note, wrote Lord Cromer, made intervention an almost unavoidable necessity.[8] The controllers further recommended dismissal of many army officers and the curtailment of other state activities. Discontent grew in all corners of the land, in the Assembly against the

6 Lord Milner, *op. cit.*, pp. 182–183.
7 Young, *op. cit.*, pp. 113–115, and Lord Cromer, *op. cit.*, p. 221.
8 Lord Cromer, *op. cit.*, p. 385.

checks to which it was subject, in the army because of its treatment, among the merchants and overtaxed peasants, among the officials accustomed to prey upon the Treasury. It acquired a religious fervor and awakened a sense of national unity; it assumed an anti-European character. A leader came forward—a Colonel Ahmed Arabi, Egyptian, of peasant origin. By 1881 he was virtual ruler of the land and government. Grave disorders ensued. Bondholders took fright, and European governments grew anxious about the safety of their residents.

Upon the murder of Europeans in Alexandria and the fortification of the town, the English forces occupied Egypt. France had been invited to join in the act of intervention; but preoccupied with continental affairs and afraid of new adventures, it abstained. Gladstone had been gradually pushed into an action which he did not like. Mr. Moon is probably right in regarding Ireland, bonds, and the Suez Canal as the three underlying considerations and circumstances that led to the final decision.[9] The British occupation was the result of twenty years of corruption and extravagance on one side, of ambition and greed on the other. Between Great Britain and France it created antipathy for over twenty years. French opposition exhausted itself in a series of sterile efforts to hinder and end the occupation.

THE BRITISH TAKE CHARGE

WITHIN a few months after the British took charge, the Anglo-French Dual Control of 1879 was abolished. The French controller was dismissed. The British Consul-General was given authority over all the English advisers that were placed in the Egyptian ministries. From 1883 to 1907 Lord Cromer (then Sir Evelyn Baring) held this place, and under the Egyptian Constitution of 1883 was the real governing power of Egypt. The Khedive was de-

[9] P. T. Moon, *Imperialism and World Politics*, p. 228.

pendent upon him. The Egyptian representative bodies could advise and criticize the executive branch of the government but could not directly oppose it. Their consent was necessary to the imposition of new taxes, but not to the disposition of the income of the existing ones. The most important of the other English advisers was the financial adviser who had a seat in the Council of Ministers. Though he possessed no vote, the British Government enforced the rule that "no financial decision should be taken without his consent," which gave him an extensive power over all government operations.[10]

But his power to modify Egyptian financial affairs was restricted by the previous agreements with the bondholders, and by the powers of the Caisse. The French still held two-thirds of the government debt. They and their government refused to permit any reduction in the authority of the Caisse, hindering as the insistence was.

The revolution and occupation had put still new burdens on the Egyptian finances. An indemnity of 100 million francs was imposed for the victims of the violence in Alexandria. Operations carried on by Great Britain in the Soudan were costly. The budget was in deficit, the government without means for public undertakings. Upon the advice of the British representative, the debt service was temporarily suspended. The dissatisfied bondholders' representatives on the Caisse challenged this action in the Egyptian Mixed Tribunal and had it annulled. There was no longer any alternative to a further resort to foreign lenders. England, anxious in the knowledge that fresh bankruptcy would offer an occasion for demanding a further extension of international control, summoned a conference which met in London in June, 1884. After a month of sterile bickering, it failed. The French held that Great Britain should bear the special budget expenses since hers

[10] For an excellent brief summary of the arrangements and methods by which the British authority was exercised, see G. L. Beer, *African Questions at the Peace Conference*, pp. 334–338.

was to be the benefit. Bismarck at the time was dissatisfied with the British response to his colonial plans and proved obdurate. By a variety of emergency measures, the British administration managed to keep the government running while the London Cabinet continued its negotiations.

Finally in February, 1885, an agreement was reached which enabled it to go ahead with its plans. The British Government took the initiative in arranging a loan and in so modifying the international engagements of Egypt that some, though still inadequate, funds were put at the administration's disposal. A new loan of 9.4 million pounds, paying 3 per cent, was issued with the guaranty of the six Powers who were represented on the Caisse (Germany and Russia being given place, thus bringing the total to six). The amortization program for some of the older loans was suspended. The maximum limit of the administrative expenses of the government was raised from 4.9 to 5.2 million pounds, and the government was given a share in any surpluses of pledged revenues which might appear, such surpluses having been hitherto assigned wholly to amortization. Sinking fund payments were suspended. The British Treasury shouldered some of the special expenses. Thus acknowledgment, still somewhat meager, was made of the too great strictness of previous arrangements made in the bondholders' favor.

The Caisse was kept in existence with undiminished powers. A virtually steady quarrel, thereafter, prevailed between the British advisers and the majority of the Caisse, led by France, because of Great Britain's desire to use funds accumulated by the Caisse for badly needed public works, irrigation, and drainage undertakings, railroad rolling stock and the like. The majority of the Caisse restrained this expenditure so that amortization payments should be more amply protected and carried out. The opposed purposes of the two Powers became sharply manifest when in 1896 Great Britain wished to draw upon the reserve to finance an expedition to conquer the Soudan. The

Caisse, over the strong opposing votes of the French and Russian members, authorized an advance of 500,000 pounds. The French representative, asserting that unanimous consent was necessary for such action, appealed to the Mixed Tribunal, which sustained his argument. The advance was repaid to the Caisse by the government.

This was but one phase of the conflict of British and French purposes which centered upon the financial rehabilitation of Egypt. As Egyptian credit improved, the British administration wished to convert the debt. The French bondholders refused to sanction any conversion and their government upheld them. A partial conversion was arranged in 1890–93; Germany joined France in restricting its scope.[11] Immediately thereafter dispute followed over the disposition of the savings resulting from conversion. France refused to permit their expenditure, even to substitute paid labor for forced labor on irrigation works, until recompense was secured in the form of improved pay and position for French officials in the Egyptian service.[12]

The English rule slowly restored strength to Egyptian finances. The total debt remained in the neighborhood of 100 million pounds, but the burden grew lighter. More important still, the public revenues increased from 9.1 million pounds in 1882 to 12.7 million pounds in 1903. Under the guidance of the English officials, per capita taxes were reduced, especially the taxes on land, salt, sheep, and cattle. Out of the limited budget surpluses, roads, railroads, irrigation works, and drainage canals were built. The area of cultivatable land was extended. Hospitals and courthouses were constructed, maps and a census were completed. Private foreign capital, especially French capital, began to enter in large volume. In 1898, by favor of the British Government, the National Bank of Egypt

[11] *Die Grosse Politik,* Vol. VII, No. 1543; Vol. VIII, Nos. 1777, 1779, 1791, 1848, 1849.
[12] Lord Milner, *op. cit.,* pp. 195–198.

was established with the exclusive privilege of note issue. The appointments for president and vice-president were made subject to the approval of the Egyptian Government. The system of public accounts was revised, the treasury control of expenditure enforced, and the system of tax collection regularized. The market valuation of Egyptian bonds began to rank among the most secure. The place of the British Government in Egypt, and its determination to remain, became plainer. French opinion came to recognize the ineffectiveness of its opposition and to ponder the possibilities of securing some compensating advantage for giving up the remaining restraints it possessed upon British action in Egypt.

In 1903 the British desire to convert further the outstanding debt and to lessen the control exercised by international administrations led to discussions between the two governments.[13] It was only by winning over the French Government that the British Government hoped to persuade the French bondholders to permit their obligations to be paid off or made exchangeable for a security bearing a lower rate of interest.[14] The discussion of conversion merged with negotiations of broader range by which a settlement of many outstanding differences between the two countries was sought. In their final outcome, Great Britain was given freedom in Egypt in return for freedom granted to France in Morocco.

The Anglo-French Declaration of April 8, 1904, dealing with Egypt, provided that France "will not obstruct the action of Great Britain in that country by asking that a limit of time be fixed for the British occupation or in any other matter."[15] The Khedival Decree which accompanied the Declaration changed the financial management

---

[13] See *British Documents*, Vol. II, Nos. 378 *et seq.* for the discussions.

[14] *Report Association Nationale des Porteurs Français*, 1902–3, pp. 31–38.

[15] N. Politis, "La Declaration Concernant L'Égypte," *Revue Générale de Droit International Public*, November–December, 1904, is a good study of this document.

of Egypt. 1. For the many sources of revenue pledged to the three main types of debt, one tax was substituted—the net revenue of the property tax. As a result of this change the international body in control of the railways, telegraphs, and port of Alexandria was abolished. 2. The competence of the Caisse was reduced to merely the receiving and paying out of the pledged revenue. It was provided that its consent was no longer necessary for the emission of government loans. 3. The reserve funds which had been accumulated by the Caisse were entirely freed and all limitations on the administrative expenditures of the government were removed. 4. The holders of the two types of debt that had been guaranteed by landed property, the Daira-Sanieh and Dominial Debt, were protected against conversion until 1905. The holders of the Privileged Debt were protected until 1910, of the Unified Debt till 1912.

These arrangements restored to Egypt, or rather to the English financial administration, the liberty that was lost by the bankruptcy of 1876. The international administration of the Daira-Sanieh property was brought to an end in 1905 when this part of the debt was extinguished. The administration in charge of the Domains property was likewise ended in 1913 when that debt was paid off. The record of the international bodies in charge of these properties was a striking contrast between western purpose and order, and eastern ignorance and carelessness. When the Domains administration, by way of illustration, took over its bankrupt properties in 1885, it was highly doubtful whether their value was as great as the principal of the debt to which they were pledged. But as a result of their improvement and sale, the administration paid off the interest and principal of the loan and in 1913 turned back to the government a substantial part of the original property.[16]

[16] A. D'Anthouard, "La Dette Dominiale Égyptienne," *Revue Politique et Parlementaire,* October, 1915.

The merits of the Caisse cannot be accorded such unstinted praise. Its part in Egyptian financial affairs between 1876, the year of its establishment, and 1885, was blackened by the fact that it had to execute arrangements which imposed upon Egypt too heavy an obligation—so heavy an obligation as to produce the cruel oppression and outright misery of the taxpayer. Thereafter, up to the 1904 arrangement, it hindered rather than helped the development of Egypt because it was made to serve political purposes by the Powers who were represented upon it. The French Government made use of it, first, to try to force Great Britain to evacuate Egypt, later to create such difficulties for the administration that Great Britain would buy off French interference. Other governments used their places for a similar purpose from time to time. Thus Viscount Grey has recorded the fact that Germany used its place to force Great Britain to moderate its competition for railway concessions in Turkey, by threatening to withdraw its support.

Instructions in this sense were actually sent without delay to the German representative at Cairo, and the German ultimatum was followed, almost accomplished, by a despairing telegram from Lord Cromer pointing out that it would be impossible to carry on his work in Egypt without German support in face of French and Russian opposition.[17]

The existence of the Caisse, it is true, brought benefit to the bondholders by increasing their security and preventing earlier conversion of their loans. Its powers of control over Egyptian expenditure would have been valuable if they had been less strictly and more impartially exercised. As used, they almost threw Egypt back into financial ruin.

After the 1904 agreement Egyptian finances were put in excellent shape and Egyptian government credit entirely restored. During the thirty years of British administration up to 1913, the Egyptian external debt was

17 Viscount Grey, *Twenty-Five Years, 1892–1916,* II, 9–10.

reduced from about 102 million pounds to 94 million pounds (of which 5.4 million was held by Caisse and the government in reserve funds), despite the financing of numerous important public works and the reduction of taxation. The government revenue was increased from 9.1 million pounds to 17.8 million. In its financial aspects at least the British Administration succeeded extraordinarily well. It relieved Egypt of a crushing receivership, of an overbearing burden of debt. It attracted foreign capital to agricultural and commercial enterprise. Whether as a result of the example and instruction of this administration Egypt would retain some measure of the same competence in the event of British withdrawal, the event alone can decide. The reëstablishment of Egyptian independence would afford an interesting opportunity to measure how much the world has changed since Ismail Pasha borrowed at 10 per cent to turn Cairo into a second Paris.

2. THE FINANCING OF MOROCCO

As in Tunis, so in the larger Mohammedan state of Morocco, the borrowings of the government ended in bankruptcy, the advent of foreign capital brought conflict. The vision presented to the ruler when the purse strings were opened was too large for his incompetent and reckless character; when the purse strings closed, Morocco was within the purse.

The Sultan held only a loose and uncertain authority over the tribes of the interior. Commerce was scanty and hazardous, roads poor, currency mixed and fluctuating. The taxes were mostly direct, collected by tribal authorities who used whatever means were necessary. The principal tax was the "achour" imposed upon landowners —one-tenth of the harvest or flocks in money or in kind. The public expenditures were small and highly variable, going mainly for the support of the Sultan's civil list and the army. The judicial system was complex, corrupt, and accustomed to administer a law far different from that

of European countries. Under it foreign commerce and
business felt insecure and soon discovered that economic
advantage was to be obtained by personal favor or the
support of their governments. Such was the country which
put itself in debt.

Morocco, it will be recalled, adjoins Algeria, France's
earliest North African possession. The French lenders and
French Government steadily asserted a predominant interest in Moroccan affairs. From the time of the acquisition of Algeria the extension of French power over
Morocco was indicated, but the idea did not assume com-
pulsive force until economic and financial activities turned
the country into a center of dispute. No natural frontiers
exist between Algeria and Morocco and the inhabitants
of the two states shared the same race, religion, and customs. It was difficult to exercise authority over the tribes
in one while the tribes outside were free. The wish to constrain the Moroccan tribes, the advantages of extending
the colonial domain, the fear that other Powers would obtain strong vested interests therein, the insecurity faced
by foreign enterprise—these combined to give gradual
strength to the French purpose. The disorder and back-
wardness of the country made the idea of control inviting
and justifiable; the colonial ambitions of France made it
alluring; the claims of enterprise and finance made it
actual. That its execution was so long delayed, that the
process was so halting and devious, are not to be traced to
the recuperative or restraining powers of the Moroccan
Government, but to the mutual fears of European governments. Before the assertion of control was completed Europe was brought twice to the verge of war.

In 1902 the Sultan had miscellaneous debts to local and
European bankers, and no adequate means of paying
them. Tribes were in rebellion, and their rebellion interrupted commerce between Morocco and Algiers. The Sultan desired to increase taxes and change their administration. He wished, too, to end the tax exemption of the

numerous subjects and *protégés* of the European powers
who lived in Morocco. For the contemplated changes the
permission of these Powers, especially of France, was not
immediately forthcoming.[18] The Sultan turned to European bankers. Three loans were contracted by a French
bank, an English bank, and a Spanish syndicate. They
paid 6 per cent, were secured by a special assignment of
the customs duties, and were purchased by the bankers at
62 per cent of their nominal value; in other words, their
effective interest cost was about 10 per cent, as high as the
Sultan's credit was doubtful.[19] This did not improve after
the European governments gave consent to part of his
plan of tax reform. The state expenditure still outran the
state income. The tribes refused to pay the new taxes
despite the pressure of the Kaids. Nor did the deliberate
debasement of the currency prove a more effective way of
meeting too large a need. By the end of 1903 suspension
of the debt service was again imminent. Assistance at such
a time, under such circumstances, inevitably carried its
price. Lenders would provide no more unless their loans
were given protection. The French Government had prepared by a series of understandings with other European
governments to assume direction of affairs in the foreshadowed crisis.

FRANCE BARGAINS FOR A FREE HAND

In April, 1902, an accord had been signed with the Sultan
under which French support was promised to consolidate
his authority over the tribes. Arrangements had been made
also for the establishment of customs posts, markets, and
guards along the frontier. Economic, military, and fiscal
collaboration was encouraged. But the accord had not
worked well, and was always under suspicion by the other
Powers who feared that it would result in French domi-

---

[18] *British Documents*, Vol. II, No. 325.
[19] France, *Documents Diplomatiques, Affaires du Maroc, 1901–1905*,
Nos. 32, 56, 108.

nance. France engaged in discussion with Italy, Spain, and Great Britain as to the action "they might be constrained to take in the event of Morocco passing into liquidation."[20] Italy was granted freedom of action in the Turkish provinces of Tripoli and Cyrenaica to step out of the situation. With Spain a tentative agreement was reached defining spheres of influence.

English official policy was hesitant but traditionally opposed to French aggrandizement, though relatively indifferent to Moroccan trade. But the interested British groups feared that the establishment of a French protectorate would shut Morocco to English trade and investment, as the French Congo had been shut. The English representative in Morocco, Kaid MacLean, was eager to extend British interests and gave a lead to his government. That representative counseled the Sultan against further reliance on France, and enjoined him not to go farther into debt.[21] He appears to have persuaded the Sultan, in fact, to intrust him with financial control, and appeared in London in October, 1902, charged with the duty of arranging a loan and the privilege of granting railroad concessions. "The Sultan," the British Foreign Secretary informed the French Ambassador, "was prepared to divide both the loan and concessions between France, Germany, and England." The French Ambassador observed in reply "that if, in his opinion, Kaid MacLean were to go to Paris for the purpose of borrowing there, the French Government would endeavor to dissuade him from borrowing."[22] The British banks were probably not willing to make a loan, and the English Government was willing to renounce any part in Moroccan affairs for advantages elsewhere. Lord Lansdowne persuaded King Edward, whom Kaid MacLean had approached, to treat him with reserve for Lansdowne wished an understanding

---

[20] *British Documents,* Vol. II, No. 322.
[21] *Ibid.*   [22] *Ibid.,* No. 325.

with France.[23] In the face of Germany's growing strength and expansion, amity with France appeared newly desirable.

The two countries adjusted their interests in a joint declaration of April 8, 1904. In return for freedom of action in Egypt, Great Britain stepped aside in Morocco. The British Government recognized "that it appertains to France as bordering power to keep order in Morocco, to lend its assistance in administrative, economic and financial reforms." France pledged itself not to discriminate as regards tariffs, taxes, and railroad rates, while reserving a right to see that concessions for roads and ports were made under conditions that would leave the authority of the state over these great enterprises of general interest intact. The language of the provision concerning concessions is here paraphrased, but the curious concealment and obscurity are in the original language. It is not to be wondered that the German Ambassador at London asked for its interpretation, stating that his government was not sure that they could depend upon fair treatment in regard to concessions and industrial enterprises.[24] In the Anglo-French declaration as published at the time, France repudiated any intention of changing Morocco's political status. But the treaty had secret clauses, published only seven years thereafter, which provided that when the Sultan ceased to exercise sovereignty over Morocco, the northern part should come within the sphere of influence of Spain, the rest under French influence. Yet the British Secretary of State for Foreign Affairs wrote, not long after the publication of the declaration, "The policy of the French was to avoid a partition of the country and to render the process of peaceful penetration either under

[23] Sir Sidney Lee, *King Edward VII*, II, 220–221.

[24] *British Documents*, Vol. II, No. 62. As a matter of fact in the secret treaty between France and Spain in 1904, the two governments agreed that enterprises for public works in Morocco should be undertaken by French and Spanish groups whom the two governments pledge themselves to favor.

the Spanish or French side as gradual and unobtrusive as possible."[25] If the British Secretary of State for Foreign Affairs could crowd so many contradictory thoughts into one sentence, outside opinion, especially in Germany, took a more definite view of the situation. As enveloped in imprecision as the language of much of the declaration was, as positive as the formula of repudiation was, this opinion took the English-French agreement to indicate that Morocco would come under French political control.

While the French Government was executing these agreements with Italy, Spain, and Great Britain, a French banking group headed by the Banque de Paris et Pays Bas was discussing with the Sultan terms of the loan essential to the financial and military reorganization of Morocco. The group had already made short-time advances at the instance of the French Government. A representative of the French Government, under instructions from the Foreign Office, participated in the discussion of loan terms.[26] The loan as arranged was of nominal total of 62.5 million francs, sold to the bankers at 80 and to the public at 96.[27] The customs revenues were pledged as guaranty. These revenues were placed under the supervision of the bondholders, whose representative was given the right to appoint an assistant in each port to watch over the collection. The representative was appointed by a procedure intended to give his nomination an official character, if the French Government cared to make use of that fact, but to leave it in the background otherwise. He was selected by the contracting banks, but the nomination was passed on to the Moroccan Government by the French Government. For this post the French Government detached M. Regnault, Consul-General at Geneva. Most of his assistants were drawn from the consular or

25 *British Documents*, Vol. III, No. 54.
26 *Affaires du Maroc, 1901–1905*, Nos. 138, 140, 170, 184.
27 H. Collas, La Banque de Paris et de Pays Bas (Paris, 1908), p. 179; also statement by M. Gustave Rouanet, *Débats Parl. Chambre de Députés*, February 7, 1907.

Tunisian colonial service; all were considered to be "on mission."[28] Finally the loan provided that the contracting banks should have "priority on equal terms for all future Moroccan Government loans." The customs control was undoubtedly necessary if purchasers were to be found for the loan, though the concurrent negotiations in which France engaged gave it a political significance. Such control was inevitable unless France and the other Powers were willing to let the debtors of Morocco swallow their losses and let the Moroccan Government struggle along as well or badly as it could. But the state of European politics prevented that alternative policy from receiving serious attention. For the priority in Moroccan public borrowing conferred upon the contracting banks, no adequate justification can be found; a clause prohibiting further borrowing would have been harsher but more useful. The provision was a special favor conferred upon the contracting banks and afterward supported strongly by the French Government.

The flotation of this loan was but one element in the program of financial change inaugurated after the Anglo-French declaration of 1904. Moroccan currency had been debased; this disturbed commerce and reduced public revenues. There was need for a central bank of issue to improve the currency and regulate monetary policy. The French bankers asked the Sultan for a concession for the creation of a State Bank. Its formation was delayed by the French Government until its wishes were clarified by events. It was only after agreement with Spain that the French Government entered into discussion with the Sultan, as to the composition, form, and powers of the State Bank, which was to be public treasurer for the state.[29] The arrangements drawn up tended to put virtual control of

---

[28] *Bulletin du Comité de L'Afrique Française,* July, 1904, p. 238.

[29] *Affaires du Maroc, 1901–1905,* Nos. 170, 203, 208, 209, 220, 228, and P. Bonnet, *La Banque d'État du Maroc et du Problème Marocain* (Paris, 1913), p. 136.

the financial actions of Morocco in the hands of the French Government, a control that could check even if it could not command.

GERMANY DEMANDS INTERNATIONAL CONTROL

THIS prospect of financial control (combined with that provision of the Anglo-French Declaration that seemed to imply control over concessions) was undoubtedly among the matters which moved the German Government to intervene, and thus to make the financing of Morocco an issue of grave international concern.[30] German business and financial circles were stirred by the conviction that opportunity in Morocco was being foreclosed. As early as 1880 Germany had insisted upon the open door in that country. When a change in the status of the country seemed likely, the government apparently decided at first to put the best possible face on the event. The German Chancellor upon being informed of the Anglo-French Declaration asserted "that the interests of Germany in Morocco were mainly of an economic order . . . Germany had no reason to fear that her economic interests in Morocco will be injured by any other power."[31] But behind this assertion there was some disappointed hope and displeasure. The government, apparently on the suggestion of its representative in Morocco, tried to induce the German banks to compete for the 1904 loan, but they refused. An attempt had also been made to have the concession for the State Bank given to a German firm. German displeasure grew as the complaints of German enterprise were heard and the scope of French plans became clear. Besides, the German Government, despite its public statement, probably felt cheated on political grounds. Great

[30] Certainly the instructions of the German delegation at the Algeciras Conference emphasized the importance of internationalizing the bank. *Die Grosse Politik*, Vol. XXI, No. 6922. See also *Affaires du Maroc, 1901–1905*, No. 271.

[31] *Bulletin du Comité de l'Afrique Française*, July, 1904, p. 238.

Britain, Spain, and Italy had all been consulted and had
received some political compensation for standing aside
in Morocco; Germany had been passed over in these re-
spects. The Foreign Office proposed a naval demonstra-
tion but this the Kaiser opposed. Instead, after grave
hesitance, he landed in March, 1905, at Tangier and in
two speeches affirmed the independence of the Sultan and
warned him against the acceptance of the French plans
of reforms. The move immediately checked their application.

The Sultan, after rejecting the French plans, then proposed that they be submitted to an international conference, and Germany made the same demand. For France
the choice seemed to be one between war and consent. Russia was still weakened by war with Japan. French consent
was given in July, 1905, and the conference of Algeciras
was arranged. The task of the conference was to determine
what reforms were necessary for Morocco and the proper
means and agents for executing them. Public finance and
currency, public administration, especially the police and
military branches, all obviously required attention and
new plans. Before the deliberations began, the German
representative in Morocco, Count Tattenbach, secured
concessions for German enterprise to build port works.
This action the French Government asserted to be in contravention of an agreement that no concessions would be
sought until the conference ended. French firms were
charged by Germany with similar violations. The German
banks made a short-time advance to the Sultan which, it
was asserted, violated the priority privilege of the French
banks.[32] Only after protracted days of conciliatory efforts
were these matters patched up in compromise, and the conference enabled to begin its anxious course.

In the outcome of the conference (January to April,
1906) German expectations were poorly met, and France

[32] For an account of these difficulties, see *Affaires du Maroc, 1901–
1905,* Nos. 289–298.

was able to a substantial degree to work its will. The
Powers with which she had alliances and those which had
benefited by treaties dealing with Morocco brought the
necessary support. Still Germany succeeded in submitting
the process of economic and political penetration of Morocco to a certain measure of international control. The
General Act of Algeciras, which issued from the conference
(April 7, 1906), in laying down a political *régime* for
Morocco, recognized its independence. The State Bank
was made into an elaborate international institution in
which the distribution of influence was decided only after
intense diplomatic effort.[33] Its ownership was lodged in
the hands of banking syndicates of twelve countries, each
nominated by the government of its own country.[34] Its
capital was divided into fourteen parts. Twelve were for
the owning banks, two for the French banking syndicate
which had issued the 1904 loan and held a priority over
Moroccan government loans, which they now renounced.
This French banking group accepted the arrangement
only because of the pleas and pressure of the French Government. The new State Bank was made Agent-General
and Treasurer-General of the Empire and given the sole
right of note issue and of the negotiations of treasury
bonds. This last provision was intended to restrain the
government from accumulating a floating debt, but as
such was ineffective. This was as far as the Powers could
agree to go in limiting Moroccan borrowing. By virtue of
the three French votes and of more or less formally
pledged aid of friends and allies, French influence was
preponderant in the bank's operations. Morocco had been

[33] See A. Tardieu, *Le Mystère d'Agadir* (Paris, 1912); Bonnet, *op.
cit.*, pp. 156 *et seq.*, and *Die Grosse Politik,* Vol. XXI, Nos. 7031-7040,
7048, 7055, 7070, 7072, 7078-7079, 7129, 7278, for details of the controversy. The French and Germans brought in competing projects. The
main points of the controversy were distribution of capital ownership, of
representation on the governing board, on the importance of the priority
privileges claimed by the French banks, and over the power of the new
bank to make loans.

[34] The United States did not accept its part.

granted a share in the administration of the bank with the provision that the Sultan could designate a private bank to exercise the subscription right for the Moroccan Government. Germany endeavored to persuade the Sultan to give the privilege to a German bank but the French Government opposed the transaction.[35] The establishment of this internationally owned bank was an attempt, grudgingly accepted, to take, partly at least, the question of Moroccan financial affairs out of the area of international competition.

A similar purpose led to the formulation of imperfect rules to regulate the awarding of concessions for public works, rules which required public and competitive bidding. These were poorly drawn and inadequate for their purpose. Whatever effectiveness might have been in the idea was spoiled by the complicated character of the procedure provided and the weakness of the Moroccan Government. The nature of the efforts of private groups and governments to secure concessions was little changed by their enactment.

FRANCE PUSHES AHEAD

THE notions of international control of Moroccan affairs (of which only some have been given), expressed in the Act of Algeciras, were soon to fail of effect, and the state of Morocco to grow more disturbed than before. During 1906–7 the disorder among the tribesmen grew chronic and widespread and the Sultan's government grew less able to subdue it. The revolt was, in part, induced by the opposition to the measures of European control which had been accepted. In 1907 the Sultan was forced to yield to his brother, Moulay-Hafid. This tumult of revolt had reduced the finances of the former Sultan to the last extremity and made him dependent once again upon French financial aid. Three times before his overthrow the French

[35] *Die Grosse Politik,* Vol. XXI, Nos. 7278–7282.

Government had persuaded the French banks to grant him advances.[36] The State Bank of Morocco had loaned him almost all its capital. The new ruler had no funds to conduct his operations. Large claims for damages faced him. The French Government assessed the throne with the cost of a military expedition undertaken after the murder of five Frenchmen by tribes excited by a rumor that a railroad was to be run through a Moslem cemetery at Casablanca. The Spanish Government presented a similar demand. Due debts and claims of all sorts at the beginning of 1909 totaled about 150 million francs.[37] The new Sultan had a total disposable revenue of about 9 million francs. Obviously the whole structure of government and reform had gone to pieces before the internal and external difficulties.

The promulgation of the Algeciras Act had not helped the government's finances. The provisions of that act concerning the creation of new revenues (Chapter IV) had not been carried out because they required negotiations on the part of the Sultan which were too difficult for the elementary structure of his government.[38] The customs revenue, it is true, showed a distinct improvement in yield under foreign supervision, increasing from 6 million francs in 1907 to 13 million francs in 1910. The claims and loans of private institutions made up between 70–80 million francs of the government's obligations, all acquired since 1904. The French and Spanish governments in demanding the expenses of their military expeditions denied any intention of oppressing Morocco. France asserted its willingness to accept an annual remittance at a low rate of interest and its intention of aiding Morocco to secure a new loan.[39] Spain followed the same line of policy. No matter what the intention may have been, the

---

[36] *Affaires du Maroc, 1906–1907,* Nos. 435, 441, 445, 502; *ibid., 1907–1908,* Nos. 139, 140, 152, 156, 157, 162.

[37] Bonnet, *op. cit.,* p. 304.   [38] *Ibid.,* pp. 299–300.

[39] M. Pichon, Secretary of Foreign Affairs, *Débats Parl. Sénat,* December 28, 1909.

event proved that the addition of these claims to Morocco's other obligations made the burden of the government an unbearable one, even when aided over the crisis by a new loan.

The new Sultan, Moulay-Hafid, was made to face the debts and claims. The only means by which this could be done even temporarily was by contracting another large external loan which was certain to be conditioned upon an extension of the creditors' control over his revenues and actions. If this firmer control had been imposed earlier when the debt burden was smaller, it might have worked to the ultimate advantage of the country, but combined with too large a debt, it inevitably meant future difficulties. The Sultan endeavored to evade his responsibilities and for a time refused to accept the proffered loan terms. But a French ultimatum ended his resistance. M. Pichon, the Minister of Foreign Affairs, declared:

The response needed most urgently (from Morocco) is that concerning the loan. It interests foreign governments as much as our own. It would be dangerous for the Sultan to delay the matter and exhaust the patience of the powers; already their nationals protest vehemently and claim vigorously the repayment of sums long due them. The English, German, and Italian press indicate that they share the views of the French Government and approve measures that we will be led to take to protect our interests in Morocco.[40]

French evacuation was delayed until the loan was arranged. The French Government appears to have forced the issue partly out of fear that German firms, with the support of the German Government, might resort to direct seizure of Moroccan property. These fears centered upon the firm of Renschausen to whom the Sultan was indebted for port construction work at Tangier, for which debt seacoast property had been pledged under terms which gave the creditors power to sell it. The French Government

[40] *Débats Parl. Chambre de Députés,* November 23, 1909.

feared too that the creditors might suggest another international conference thus taking the lead again out of French hands. The French ultimatum was effective. The loan contract was signed. The private claims were submitted to an arbitral commission upon which the Moroccan representative was in reality nominated by France. Thus, the new sovereign was forced to meet the expenses of his climb to power, and thereby prepared his fall from power.

The loan contract was signed with the same group of banks that had secured the 1904 loan. It was accompanied by accords between the two governments which provided for French evacuation, the appointment of a French engineer as adviser on public works to the Finance Minister, and the use of French instructors in the Moroccan army which was to be reorganized along with the police. These were constructive arrangéments which at the same time increased French power. The German Government in disarming the criticism of their terms that arose in Germany indicated that it had asked the German banks to consider the loan business, but that they had not been disposed to do it. At the time the two governments were pledged to a measure of joint economic activity in Morocco, and the German Government was agreeable to the loan and convinced of its necessity. The loan was for 107 million francs and bore 5 per cent interest. It was sold to the bankers at 89, and to the public at 97. To its service and to the annuity due the French Government there was pledged most of the still disposable revenue of the Sultan. The creditors' control of customs was turned into a general debt control. Their powers of supervision of customs revenues had been incomplete and unsatisfactory. Now they were made effective by being extended to the actual work of collection. The new ceded revenues—the remainder of the customs, the net product of the tobacco taxes, of the tax on landed property in port areas, of the urban tax, and others—were put under their direct administration. An increase of 2.5 per cent in customs duties was permitted and this revenue was left outside the loan pledges. It was reserved for public works under a plan formulated in collaboration with the Powers and controlled by a special international committee.

The French Government of the day held the view that these obligations were within the capacity of the Sultan, and that these plans would pave the way to peace and foster economic development. The State Bank had stabilized currency; the control would increase revenues, the public works plan would stimulate economic activity, the new loan funds would permit the reorganization of the army and thereby assure order. But events immediately disproved these conclusions, if they were genuinely held. The Sultan's expenditures soon outran the disposable revenue. This was but little over 3 million francs in 1910. Out of a total revenue of 24 million francs, approximately 16.5 millions were required to meet the annuities of the debt service and war cost payments to the French and Spanish governments. It was on the evidence of these facts that M. Jaures remarked of the 1910 loan that it took away from the Sultan all financial autonomy, all military strength, and all moral authority.[41] It was almost inevitable that some responsible power should step in to assume charge of events; anarchy could not indefinitely continue.

The Sultan within a few months was without resources. An attempt to borrow further in Paris did not succeed because of the lack of further security to offer. The French Government remitted part of the annual payment due to it. The Sultan tried to impose new taxes and increase existing ones. The Powers still opposed the taxation of their subjects and the growing number of their *protégés*, arguing that the administration could not be trusted to be just. The new taxes were imposed upon the tribes that remained loyal, and the tax rights were sold to chiefs who

---

[41] *Débats Parl. Chambre de Députés,* March 24, 1911. See also the debate of December 19, 1911. His powerful address had no effect upon government policy, however. The Ministers in power continued to assert that the Sultan could manage.

sought to increase their yield by the use of force and cruelty. When the Sultan tried to turn some of the taxes payable in kind into a money tax and create a register of taxable people, both the chiefs and the religious orders opposed, and aroused the tribes. Tax receipts fell rather than rose. The tax gatherers resorted to pillage. The French commander of the expedition that ushered in the French protectorate declared, "It is to the crying abuses and shameful exactions that the revolt of the tribes must be attributed."[42]

Before the spreading revolt, the bankrupt Sultan was helpless. On March 13, 1911, to keep himself in power he offered France a complete and intimate understanding to inaugurate a *régime* of general reform.[43] The tribes around Fez joined in revolt and threatened the Sultan, the city, and its European colony. The French Government, asserting that Europeans were in danger and promising to evacuate when the danger was ended, dispatched an expeditionary army of 10,000 men which occupied Fez. The course of bankruptcy and borrowing, the anarchy, had come to its inevitable end.

ON THE VERGE OF WAR

THE German Government did not accept the argument or the promise given. Before the expedition was sent, it expressed distrust; when it was sent it declared that the Act of Algeciras was violated. It nourished the determination that the crisis should not be turned to French account unless national advantage were secured as compensation. Under a pretext generally recognized as thin, a German gunboat was dispatched to a Moroccan port—there to remain as a sign of German power until German interests were satisfied. Its ambassador explained to the French Government that the German Government considered that

---

[42] Cited by Tardieu, *op. cit.*, p. 376.
[43] Rapport Gaillard, *Bulletin de l'Afrique Française, Supplement*, 1911, p. 261.

the Act of Algeciras had failed of its purpose and that the
situation required fresh discussion. Over the territory of
a chaotic Morocco, the whole European continent was
brought to the verge of war.

The German action was not the result of a sudden impulse. It indicated the complete failure of a formal attempt on the part of France and Germany to adjust their
purposes in Morocco. From the record of that attempt it
becomes clear that international economic coöperation in
backward areas is not possible without candor, trust, and
singleness of purpose. It indicates also how well-nigh impossible it is for the banking and business groups of two
hostile countries to avoid the influence of that hostility,
and in the end not to enter into it, and augment it.

The Act of Algeciras, though confirming Moroccan independence and planning international coöperation in
Morocco, had been regarded with resentment in France
and distrust in Germany. Each scrutinized the action of
the other with quick suspicion. The French interventions
of 1907–8 were regarded in Germany with great uneasiness, and out of the trifling incidents which arose from
time to time, national feeling created exciting issues. German enterprise had pushed its way forward in Morocco
with the support of the government. German merchants
were active in every trade center. German steamship lines
called at Moroccan ports, mining prospectors marked out
claims, and banking syndicates sought and acquired concessions for public works with the vigorous aid of their
government.

But beginning in 1908 Germany inclined to ease her
effort to check the measures of France to secure order and
internal peace in Morocco, even though these measures
might infringe on Morocco's independence. She inclined to
come to terms with France in the hope that the lessening
of French antagonism might facilitate German policy
elsewhere. German preoccupations in the Balkans and
Near East were growing serious and the sterility and in-

effectiveness of obstruction in Morocco were becoming manifest. The change was indicated in the handling of a dispute which arose from the Mannesman concessions. This powerful band of German brothers had obtained in October, 1906, with the aid of the German Minister at Tangier, an oral promise of important mineral concessions, after two years of skilful negotiation.[44] Morocco had no mining laws—a code was being considered during 1906-7. The promises to Mannesman were kept secret and confirmation was delayed until a mining law should be drafted and put into effect. The two governments vied with each other to get a mining law suitable to their respective interests. The proposals made during 1907-8 under French influence would have handicapped the projected concession. The German Government threw its weight into the scales to secure an immediate confirmation of the concession. The French Government opposed. So did an international syndicate that had been formed to work Morocco's mineral resources—L'Union Minière. In this syndicate a French group owned 50 per cent of the capital, a German group 20 per cent. Creusot was represented in the French group, Krupp in the German. The L'Union Minière was willing to negotiate with the Mannesman group but they, fearing poor terms and having official backing, refused. Up to the summer of 1908 the German Government supported the Mannesman group, but thereafter changed its attitude and urged conciliation and an agreement between the groups. Conciliation fitted in better with its changing intentions.[45] Other financial groups were giving proof of

44 L. Pohl, "Morokko und Mannesman," *Zeitschrift für Politik,* 1912.
45 See W. E. Von Schoen, *Memoirs of an Ambassador* (London, 1922), pp. 115-120. The history of the subsequent negotiations between the two syndicates and their governments is too much a matter of detail and too involved to be given here. There was a French interest in the Mannesman syndicate—and there were numerous internal disputes within each. In 1911 a fusion was finally arranged. The Kaiser intervened in the negotiations (through Herr Rathenau) to try and persuade the French Government to press the other group to accept proposed terms, and also to bring the groups together. In the later negotiations he prob-

willingness to enter into coöperation. French and German
interests joined together in the State Bank, the tobacco
monopoly, enterprises for public works—in all of which
the French held preponderance. Still the program of joint
enterprise did not flourish.

Its basis was formally defined in an accord reached between the two governments in February, 1909. The accord read:

The Government of the French Republic, being completely
devoted to the maintenance of the integrity and independence
of the Cherifien empire, resolved to safeguard economic opportunity there, and consequently not to hinder the German
commercial and industrial interests there,

And the Imperial German government, pursuing only economic aims in Morocco, and recognizing on the other hand
that the special political interests of France are closely
linked with the establishment of internal peace and order,
and determined not to hinder these interests,

Declare they will not pursue or encourage any measure of
a kind which creates in their favor or in the favor of any
power whatsoever, an economic privilege and that they will
endeavor to associate their nationals in enterprises which
they are authorized to undertake.

This agreement, it may be reasonably argued, violated,
beneath its phrases, the letter of the Act of Algeciras
(though not perhaps the expectation of the signatories
of that Act) politically in favor of France and economically in favor of Germany. It proved not to fit the needs
of the Moroccan situation, the proper handling of which
needed both greater authority than it, or the Act of Al-

ably wished to coerce Mannesman but did not have the power, and furthermore German public opinion tended to support the Mannesman
claims. The difficulties encountered in the formulation of the mining
law also make a prolonged and intricate tale. For an account of the
situation and the defense of the German Government for ceasing to support the Mannesman Claims, see *London Times,* January 18, 19, 20, 1910.

geciras, gave, and greater singleness of purpose than either party showed. The last clause could not be turned into actuality. For true admission of vigorous German enterprise into partnership in the economic development of Morocco, under the troubled political circumstances, would almost certainly have led to a limitation of French political influence; and France would never accept that prospect. When the significance of such partnership became plain France drew back, and the idea of joint undertakings faltered and weakened.

Germany urged at once that this accord be promptly turned into account as the basis of an extensive program of public works. It was undoubtedly the prospect of sharing in an economic program after Moroccan financial affairs were put in order which induced Germany not only to accept but to facilitate the arrangements for the large liquidation loan of 1910. From 1909 to 1911, discussions between the two governments and two sets of financial groups were intermittently carried on. The full extent of German hopes and claims became evident. The German Government in general urged that in order to avoid "sterile and injurious competition," bids for public works should be limited to groups designated by the two governments, although the Act of Algeciras provided for open and competitive bidding.[46] It also at first claimed a half share in such projects as might be undertaken; any parts given to British or Spanish groups were to be part of the other half share.[47] This desire it appears later to have

[46] Bonnet, *op. cit.*, p. 314; P. Albin, *Le Coup d'Agadir* (Paris, 1912), pp. 33 *et seq.*

[47] Tardieu, *op. cit.*, p. 29. It is asserted by certain French writers, e.g., Mermeix (pseud.), *La Chronique de l'An 1911* (Paris, 1912), p. 14, and supported by certain circumstantial episodes which occurred during the special French parliamentary investigation of Moroccan affairs, that the 1909 accord was accompanied by an exchange of letters between M. Cambon and Herr Von Schoen which formed a secret understanding to the effect that Germany acknowledged that the French economic interest in Morocco was greater than the German interest, and that Germans should not seek places in the public services in Morocco.

completely relinquished, approving and supporting international groups in which the German interests held only a minority part.

But mutual distrust and the differences of purpose continued to block every attempt to carry forward joint enterprise. For the execution of public works the two governments had encouraged in October, 1909, the formation of an international syndicate to build and operate them. In this "Société Marocaine des Travaux Publiques," French interests held 50 per cent of the capital, and elected six out of the twelve directors. German interests held 30 per cent of the capital and elected four directors. The remainder of the capital and representation was distributed among Spanish, British, Belgian, and Swedish interests. The same proportions were to be observed in the distribution of public works, an arrangement which was difficult to interpret and even more difficult to apply, except by creating spheres of influence. To this syndicate the German Government had wished to turn over all public works construction in Morocco, including railway construction and operation. But the maintenance of such a monopoly the French Government opposed. Its refusal was supported by reference to the terms of the Act of Algeciras, but the real reason was probably a dislike of giving German enterprise any real foothold in Morocco through this condominium. Monopolistic support of this syndicate would have meant constant discussion with Wilhelmstrasse and a loss of freedom which the French Government wished to retain. In certain enterprises it was judged desirable that Germany should have no participation. Thus, despite many meetings and the consideration of many projects, the syndicate never commenced actual operations. The project nearest realization, one for lighthouse construction, had been opposed by the British Government because the share given to its nationals was so small; that government had demanded that open competitive bids be asked in accordance with the terms of the Act of Algeciras.[48]

Similar conflicts and difficulties had beset the plans for the coöperation in railroad undertakings. The desires of the German Government turned out to be substantially different from those of the French. The former urged that all railway concessions be given to the Société Marocaine des Travaux Publiques. The latter wished to keep open the possibility of carrying through projects through its own services (it had already built two short military roads), or to submit them to open bidding. Even upon these schemes which it was agreed might be granted to the Société Marocaine, differences arose upon essential details such as the distribution of orders and the positions to be held by German personnel. In addition, the British Government would not promise to discourage British competition. The discussions were long and fruitless. The disagreement was marked shortly before the Fez expedition was dispatched. The outcome was inevitable as long as France feared that the German Government would use every vestige of German interest as the basis of a claim in case of the ultimate downfall of the Moroccan Government, as long as Germany believed that France wished, by skilful negotiation, to shut German enterprise out of Morocco completely so that it might have freedom in disposing of the country. The wish for reconciliation between France and Germany, shared by a few statesmen and bankers of each country, could find no effective realization under the circumstances. Indeed, these persons were suspected of trying to serve a private purpose in contravention of their country's interest.

[48] That act provided, as stated in the text, that concessions for public works be offered by public tender, after submission of the project to the Diplomatic Corps which was to draw up regulations in coöperation with the Moroccan Government. There, also, was created a special 2.5 per cent customs tax for public works, which was not collected, however, until 1910. The first undertaking to be paid out of this tax was contracted only in 1910.

The negotiations just reviewed had become curiously entangled with a joint French-German project in the French Congo. This situation arose out of the claims of one of the French concessionary companies in the Congo, the N'Goko Sangha Company, against the French Government for alleged violation of its lands by German traders. The French Government, in order to settle the border troubles and to cut short court action taken by the N'Goko Sangha Company against the German traders (and against British traders who had been compensated by the French Government for dispossession), had lent its active attention to plans for a joint consortium which would operate on both sides of the frontier. There was a hope that this project might partly compensate Germany for the checks suffered in Morocco. The original demands of the company were presented by André Tardieu who was then political correspondent for the *Temps*. When the consortium idea came under attention, M. Tardieu also took a leading rôle in its formation. The N'Goko Sangha Company agreed to enter the consortium if the French Government admitted in principle responsibility for past damages. An arbitration was arranged to decide their amount. This condition had been accepted and discussions had been undertaken with the German Government. The status of the company had been approved at the Quai D'Orsay and accepted by the Germans. But parliamentary opposition in France led to the rejection of the plan after negotiations had been virtually completed. The opponents of the concession system had opposed this renewal of it. In many quarters doubt had been entertained as to the justice of the company's claim and as to the legality of the arbitration in which its amount had been decided. The honesty of the participants had been brought into question. Fears grew that the proposed arrangements would give Germany preponderance. These and socialist opposition made any arrangement impossible.[49]

49 *Débats Parl. Chambre de Députés*, April 6, 1911; *Sénat*, June 30,

The Monis Cabinet in 1911 had renounced the idea of
the German-French consortium. An attempt had then been
made by Caillaux, Minister of Finance, and Messimy,
Minister of the Colonies, working with the German Ambassador, to find some other scheme which might satisfy
German hopes.[50] A plan had been formulated for the joint
construction of a railway to join the German colony of
Cameroons and the French Congo. One aim of the plan
was certainly to satisfy the outcries of the German colonial groups which were led by the German Deputy Semler.
The French ministers were cautious, however, in their
promises, and in the final outcome the scheme was buried
in the vortex of French political controversy. France suspected double design in Germany. Besides, a stale odor of
personal and financial intrigue was scented by the popular nose when the negotiations were exposed.

With the dispatch on July 1, 1911, of the *Panther* to
Agadir the long course of controversy over the financing
and economic penetration of Morocco came to its final
stage. The governments had attempted to bargain through
their banks and enterprises; now they bargained directly
with each other. The results of the bargaining were embodied in the treaty of November, 1911. If Germany had
hoped to secure political authority over part of Morocco,
as was widely believed in France, the hope was disappointed. France received unimpeded right to take Moroccan affairs in charge. There was no alternative save
genuine international administration and the Powers had
not developed for that alternative either a political attitude, or a technique. Germany received compensation by

1911. For two opposed accounts of the negotiations, see, also, a book by
M. Viollette, *La N'Goko-Sangha* (Paris, 1914), and the book by Tardieu,
op. cit.

[50] Later, when Moroccan affairs were under investigation it was
charged that these ministers had acted without the knowledge of their
colleagues, and that they had made unauthorized promises. The incident
caused a storm and contributed to the fall of Caillaux, who had succeeded Monis as Prime Minister.

the transfer of some territory in Central Africa. The rights of the signatory powers of the Act of Algeciras to equality of economic treatment were protected in the new treaty; their chances of equality in obtaining concessions for public works and highways were guarded by rather vague phrases (Article 6).[51] The 1909 Franco-German accord was abrogated; but France promised that there should be no export tax on minerals, nor special tax on mineral production, and that mineral enterprises would be permitted to build connections to main lines and ports (Articles 5 and 7). The constitution of the State Bank was left intact. For years previous it had been under the effective control of the French Government and the Banque de Paris et Pays Bas.

A treaty of 1912 with Spain divided Morocco into zones of influence, a small fractional part being assigned to Spain. A French protectorate was declared, and the effort to subdue the will of the tribes to French rule, a task costly in human life, was begun. Morocco became part of the European state system.

[51] The first paragraph of this article provides that public works construction and materials should be distributed by "the rules of adjudication." The third paragraph provides that the exploitation of these works will be reserved to the Moroccan state or ceded by it to third parties who would furnish the necessary capital.

CHAPTER XVIII

JAPAN IS HELPED TO BECOME A GREAT POWER

JAPAN in 1870 was a small feudal island empire, making the grim beginning of the political and economic adjustments necessary to sustain itself as an independent force among a world of Great Powers. By 1914 it had become one of the Great Powers, and was ambitiously extending its hold and economic connections throughout the Far East. In this transition foreign capital rendered vital aid. Japan had need of it to provide itself with armament and to conduct war, to unify its railways under an effective national administration, to foster large-scale industry, to acquire and develop Korea and Manchuria, to equip its cities with public services. For all these purposes Japan borrowed abroad. About half its total public debt in the years before the war was foreign debt. The technical knowledge and equipment of the world were drawn upon, but the capital came mainly from Great Britain. By virtue of that capital no less than through its political allegiance Great Britain may be said to have made a great power of Japan.

Japan's two earliest foreign loans, the railway loans of 1870, and the pension loan of 1873, were both issued in London. So was the larger loan of 1897 by which the expenses of the war with China were defrayed. It is of interest to observe that while 9 per cent was paid for the first loan, and 7 per cent for the second, the loan after victory was disposed of at 5 per cent. In 1899 the first of the 4 per cent Sterling Loans was issued.

In the years following its victory over China, Japan felt a need both for foreign allies and foreign financial aid. The coalition of Powers which forced her to renounce territorial conquest in China had brought home her isolation. The sense of isolation was accentuated by the hastily devised agreements into which the European Powers were entering to safeguard or increase their place in China. Foreign loans were needed to meet expenditure for armaments and railways beyond the capacity of the budget. The financial discussions which were commenced became entwined with the political discussions.

Japan entered into loan negotiations in all of the chief capital markets in 1901. In Paris the negotiations dragged. The Russian Government in July offered to use its influence in Paris to assist them. Japan refused, presumably because of the concessions it would have been called upon to make.[1] Without Russian mediation Japan found the Paris market closed. The French bankers entertained fear of war between Russia and Japan over affairs in Korea and Manchuria. The French Government conveyed the intimation that it would permit no loan that might be used against its ally.[2] It counseled that Japan seek assurances from Russia to satisfy the bankers and itself.[3] Japan undertook to discuss the situation with Russia, but no headway was made toward an understanding.

At the same time the British market and government were also being sounded, and a more accommodating spirit met. Great Britain had reason to watch Japanese ambitions in China, but these were not difficult to reconcile with its own. In the first loan discussions with the British Government, in July or August, 1901, conditions appear to have been put forward which Japan found unacceptable.[4] Just what these conditions were, the documents do not clearly state. The Japanese had apparently first wished that the British Government guarantee a loan pledged on Chinese indemnity bonds, which proposal the British Secretary for Foreign Affairs, Lord Lansdowne, found

[1] Baron Von Eckardstein, *Lebenserinnerungen und Politischen Denkwürdigkeiten* (Leipzig, 1920), II, 262; *Die Grosse Politik*, Vol. XVII, No. 5040.

[2] *Die Grosse Politik*, Vol. XVII, No. 5042.

[3] *British Documents*, II, 57.

[4] *Die Grosse Politik*, Vol. XVII, No. 5023.

impracticable.[5] But that Minister was eager that Japan receive the aid it sought.[6] Negotiations were begun with the British banking houses, which asked German banks to participate. The German banks refused.[7] While these financial discussions were under way, the British and Japanese governments were giving thought to a project of alliance.[8] The political arrangements succeeded before the financial. In January, 1902, the Anglo-Japanese agreement was signed. Loan arrangements were concluded immediately thereafter. In the course of 1902 British investors bought not only a large Japanese government loan, but various municipal and industrial loans. Between the two sets of arrangements there was a natural coördination of interests. It is unlikely that the British Government had to interfere with the course of financial discussions. The British bankers and investors had standing faith in Japanese securities. The elaboration of the political agreement extinguished fears that political circumstances might endanger the investment. In Japan, the knowledge that such would be the result of an alliance undoubtedly stimulated the desire for it.

During the war with Russia, British capital staunchly stood by Japan. Before the outbreak of war, Japan sought direct aid from the British Government in the form of a government loan or loan guaranty.[9] But Great Britain feared that such action would be judged unneutral.[10] It proved unnecessary. British investors readily purchased the series of loans issued in 1904 and 1905, as did American investors.[11] In one of the 1905 loans German bankers

[5] *British Documents*, II, 58.

[6] *Ibid.*, and Von Eckardstein, *op. cit.*, II, 370.

[7] *Ibid.*, p. 363.

[8] *British Documents*, II, 114. These hung in the balance up to almost the last week. The Japanese discussions with Russia were not dropped until December, 1901.

[9] *Ibid.*, pp. 227–230.   [10] *Ibid.*

[11] An indication of the benevolent attitude taken by the British Government is to be found in the appreciations indirectly conveyed by King Edward to the American banker Schiff for his initiation in selling

took a share, urged by the Kaiser.[12] The British and American financial aid was undoubtedly essential to the Japanese victory. It followed upon numerous issues of Japanese industrial loans in London which enabled that country to build up its economic organization; it was to be followed by numerous further loans which served to enable Japan to solidify the strength obtained through victory.

Throughout the war the French official market had remained closed to Japanese loans. It was the cheapest and most receptive to government loans. By 1907, Japanese anxiety as to securing the means of refunding obligations maturing abroad, on the one hand, and the curtailed assurance of Russia on the other hand, prepared the way for a new three-party understanding whereby French financial resources could be drawn upon for the further upbuilding of Japan. Enmity between Germany and the allies was becoming pointed and ominous; the Anglo-Russian agreement was in the making. To the French Government the inclusion of Japan in the system of alliance was a natural step; if it could be arranged, Russia would no longer be menaced in the East in the event of war with Germany. French diplomacy labored to reach an understanding with Japan, and to foster a second understanding between Japan and Russia. Negotiations were begun early in 1907. Before much headway had been made Japan broached its financial needs. The French Minister at Tokio informed the Japanese Government that "according to my instructions . . . the inclinations of the French market and Government are clear, and that they could count upon our help as soon as negotiations between St. Petersburg and Tokio come to a clear issue, and that an accord should follow immediately that between Japan

Japanese securities in New York. *Jacob H. Schiff—Life and Letters,* I, 216.

[12] *Ibid.,* p. 224.

and France."[13] The British financial groups whose interests were engaged in the refunding loan were asking similar assurance.[14] By March, 1907, Japan reached accords
in principle with both France and Russia. The accord
with Russia provided for mutual support of each other's
claims in China.[15] American initiative in Manchuria was
at the time disturbing both countries, and stimulated their
combination. Now the path was cleared for Japanese borrowing. The French Government immediately gave its authorization. The French Ambassador described the action
as "the first augury and gage of the new relations, political as well as financial, between Japan, France and
through France's agency, Russia."[16] After the flotation of
the loan, negotiations with France and Russia passed from
the stage of formula to precision. The accord with France
was signed in June, 1907, that with Russia in July, 1907.
Certainly one of the chief benefits which the Japanese
hoped therefrom was regular communication with the
Paris market.[17]

To facilitate the investment of French capital, Count
Hayashi, who had negotiated the loan agreement, proposed
the foundation of a Japanese-French bank. The French
Government looked with favor on the project and a banking mission headed by an executive of the Banque de Paris
et Pays Bas was dispatched to Tokio, where it was received
by Japanese bankers and government officials. The discussions were halted by the difficulty of adjusting already
existing contracts with British banks to French desires,
and then interrupted by the panic. Only in 1912 were the
discussions renewed and successfully concluded.[18] The
bank was opened in July, 1912. Almost at once it under-

[13] A. Gérard, *Ma Mission au Japon, 1907–1914* (Paris, 1919), pp. 7, 12.
[14] *Die Grosse Politik*, Vol. XXV, No. 8527.
[15] Gérard, *op. cit.*, p. 13, and *British Documents*, IV, 430.
[16] Gérard, *op. cit.*, p. 13.
[17] *Ibid.*, p. 14, and *The Secret Memoirs of Count Hayashi* (New York, 1915), p. 218.
[18] *Le Marché Financier*, 1911–12, pp. 566–567.

took the emission in Paris of a Japanese loan for coloniza-
tion purposes.

Japan had continued to resort to the Paris market in
the meantime. The French bought a large share of the conversion loan of 1910; the French Government extended
the privilege of official listing not only to the share
originally sold in Paris, but to the whole issue.[19] In 1913
Japan sold treasury bonds in Paris to convert part of its
internal debt. Between 1907 and 1913 France loaned or
invested almost a billion and a half francs in Japan.[20] The
alliance was working smoothly. Japan and Russia had
found strong common ground in their resistance to American plans and loan proposals. France was assured of
Japanese friendship in the event of world conflict.

Still London remained the chief financing center for the
Japanese Government and Japanese industry. It continued to hold the largest share of the Japanese external
debt, which rose in total from 779 million yen in 1905
to about double that amount in 1914.[21] In London, too,
the capital was chiefly found to develop those agencies
through which the Japanese Government exerted itself to
create a strong modern industrial system.

The government had early determined that its support,
organizing power, and command over national will were required for that task. It subsidized ironworks, smelters,
navigation companies, banks, telephone companies, among
other forms of enterprise. It has early perceived also that
foreign capital would have to be solicited. On the one hand
that capital would require security; on the other hand the
government wished assurance that its employment would
be in accordance with Japanese desires and under Japanese direction. To meet these various requirements there
were established a series of semigovernmental organizations to which were turned over the main tasks of industrial

[19] Gérard, *op. cit.*, p. 132.   [20] *Ibid.*, p. 327.
[21] *The Financial and Economic Annual of Japan*, 1912, estimates the
total outstanding, as of March 31, 1912, 1,437.5 million yen.

development and national expansion. Over all of them
the Japanese Government exercised effective supervision.
These were the agencies through which much of the Japanese investment in industrial enterprise in China was chan-
neled. Some of them secured funds by borrowing abroad
in their own name, with or without the guaranty of the
government; others did not borrow abroad but were assisted with part of the proceeds of the government's foreign borrowings. Outside of the fields allotted to them the
range of opportunity open to foreign capital was limited.
The railways were nationalized. Foreign rights of ownership in land and mining properties were limited by law.[22]

Notable among these semiofficial agencies was the
South Manchuria Railway Company, to which were
turned over the properties and privileges in Manchuria
which were won from Russia. Later, too, the railways of
Korea were unified with this enterprise. In London, before
1914, the South Manchuria Railway was enabled to borrow 14 million pounds to extend its lines, develop its ports,
and build its workshops. The Yokohama Specie Bank,
which was the agency through which the government
assured participation in the general and railway loans of
China, did not borrow abroad. But funds secured abroad
by the government made easier the large government
participation in its ownership. The Industrial Bank of
Japan, organized to finance industry in Japan and Manchuria, did borrow abroad; this bank helped to finance
the South Manchuria Railway and Hokkaido Colliery
among other ventures.[23] In similar fashion the Oriental

[22] The land and mining laws prohibited ownership by foreign individuals or companies. They permitted, however, foreign participation
in companies formed under Japanese law, and long leases of surface
property. See *Foreign Relations of the United States,* 1911, p. 236. When
Japan annexed Korea it was feared that the same restrictions would be
applied there. Great Britain took the lead in safeguarding acquired
rights. Great Britain, *Japan (No. 2), 1911* (Cmd. 5717).

[23] The Industrial Bank, which was under close government supervision, was authorized to issue bonds to the amount of ten times its
capital stock.

Development Company sold its bonds in foreign markets. This company was organized in 1908 to operate especially in Manchuria, but it soon extended its field to other parts of China.

Japan, of all the countries of the Orient, proved itself capable of using to good advantage the capital of Europe. Its government succeeded in the threefold task of promoting internal industrial development, extending and reinforcing Japanese economic interests in Korea and China, and adjusting its plans to the political rivalries of the European continent. All three were connected with each other. Western Europe financed its armaments, its wars, and its economic development, drawing it in to its system of alliances. The growing strength obtained from the use of that capital made Japan a better credit risk for investors and a more important ally. By 1914 the small island empire had become a great power in its own right and might. During the war in Europe it was to try to use its newly acquired might to obtain a position of dominance throughout the Orient.

CHAPTER XIX

THE FINANCING OF THE CHINESE
GOVERNMENT

THE vast and fertile territories of China, and the hardly to be numbered millions of its industrious population with none of the technical equipment of contemporary economic life, lay open to foreign enterprise and capital. The record of the pre-war movement of that enterprise and capital into China leaves a need of explaining not so much why it sought opportunity there, but rather why the loans and investments in that land were not much greater, why the government's financial capacity was so low, why foreign enterprise grew so slowly. The explanation is to be found in the condition of the people, the traditions of Chinese economic life, the character of the government, and the rivalries of the foreign Powers. The poverty of the people, their ignorance of industrial technique, their attachment to their ancient ways of life and labor, created an indifference—often a hostility—to large-scale industry of machines, steam, and electricity. The weakness of the central government, its incompetence in tasks requiring disciplined organization, its revenue system designed to do little more than support a court, all contributed to limit government credit and capacity.

The record of the borrowing and lending relations between China and European lenders cannot be understood apart from the course of Chinese political relations with the Great Powers.

THE CHINESE GOVERNMENT AND THE POWERS

THE warships of the European Powers caused the Imperial Government at Peking to open the country to foreign commerce and merchants, overcoming the determined isolation which the country had sought to maintain. A uniform customs tariff was installed in place of the many local charges and imposts previously paid by foreign merchants. Though this tariff was but 5 per cent, at the time it was fixed it brought a clear fiscal gain for China. Later, however, the limitation increased the Chinese need to borrow. The Powers obtained extraterritorial rights for their subjects and cessions of land in various Chinese cities which were put under the government of their citizens.

Step by step parts of the sprawling, loosely connected Chinese Empire were detached; first the outlying sections, bound loosely by past conquest or heritage to China, but hardly integral parts of it; later, parts of its central domains. In 1842 Great Britain acquired the island and port of Hong Kong. In the fifties the territory that became the maritime provinces of Siberia was attached to Russia. In the eighties France added Annam and Tonkin provinces to its Indo-Chinese colony, and Great Britain put Burma under its Indian administration. Thereafter the struggle grew more tense. During the last five years of the nineteenth century, the demands of foreign countries beat like hammers upon the seams of the ancient empire. To Japan the Island of Formosa was ceded, and Korea was given independence—the obvious object of Japan's further ambitions. Russia, as a reward for frustrating the Japanese demand for possession of the end of the Liaotung Peninsula (the southern end and ocean access to Manchuria), acquired possession itself, in addition to the right to construct railways across Manchuria. France contented itself with a lease of the territory in Southern China, around the Bay of Kuang-Chow-Wan, and exclusive economic privileges in the three southern provinces bordering Tonkin. Germany secured a lease of Kiachow Bay in the center of the Chinese coast, and economic control of the province of Shantung. Lest it fall behind in this reach for dominion, Great Britain insisted upon leases of territory along the coast near Hong Kong, and of Wei-Hai-Wei, on the northern coast of Shantung;

in addition a prior claim was established over the Yangtse Valley.

The investment of foreign capital in China was at the time small, as were the foreign loans to the Chinese Government. The movement of division of China had been carried out by aims and forces far beyond those which participated in the few financial transactions that had occurred. Without the push of governments these transactions might have occurred without unusual consequences. But the strivings for empire, for greater economic and financial advantages, ruled the Foreign Offices. To each government it seemed clear that economic or financial opportunity extended to the citizens of other Powers must result in political domination; thus each stepped in to assure its share in advance. In 1899 the lines of future division seemed clear. The Yangtse Valley region would fall to Great Britain; Shantung to Germany; the three southern provinces to France; Korea to Japan; Manchuria and the territory north of the Great Wall to Russia. This was not as a consequence of the entry of foreign capital and enterprise, but rather as a preparation for it.

But strikingly enough, the division of China now came to a pause. An Italian attempt to secure leased territory was successfully resisted. The Dowager Empress fostered agitation against foreign methods, ideas, and aims. The Chinese people rose in a fanatical attempt to kill or expel all foreigners and thrust out their influence. Though the Boxer Rebellion was crushed, though it left China with heavy financial obligations, it awakened European understanding to the difficulty of subduing the Chinese national state. Great Britain had already leaned away from this idea, seeking to keep the whole of China unified and open to British commerce. During the Boxer Rebellion, Great Britain and Germany joined, with American support, in a declaration upholding the integrity of China and agreeing not to use the complications of the time to obtain territorial advantage. The same position was affirmed in the Anglo-Japanese Treaty of 1902. The Russo-Japanese War halted for a time the Russian efforts to secure possession of Manchuria and other parts of Northern China. As a consequence of victory, Japan acquired the leased territories held by Russia in South Manchuria; a few years later she annexed Korea.

The years between the Russian-Japanese war and 1914 were a period of uncertainty and confusion, of awakening to the necessity of reform along western lines, of attempts to recover Chinese ownership of railroads and other concessions, and finally of revolution. Within China the elements that believed that the country would be benefited by developing its industrial resources, and had confidence that China could control the forces thus introduced into its life, clashed with those who feared political change and the growth of foreign interests. The revolution of 1911 rose from the mounting antagonism against the Manchu Dynasty, the irritated humiliation caused by their incompetence and submission to Foreign Powers, and from the force of the republican ideas brought back from the west. Into its making went many memories, many theories, many personal interests. The immediate provocation was the insistence of the Imperial Government that railway construction and finance should be under its control. Provincial interests, which nourished illusions of their capacity to build with their own resources and which suffered financial loss because of the imperial policy, organized an opposition which turned into a revolutionary tide.

The Republic was born in poverty, in confusion and dissension. Despite the financial aid of the Powers, the president, Yuan-Shih-Kai, could restore neither order nor unity. Because of the suspicion that he was aiming to restore the empire, and because of the concessions he made to secure foreign financial assistance the representatives of the people put themselves in opposition to him. In 1914 an impoverished Central Government at Peking exercised doubtful power over some central provinces. Numerous resistant provincial governments of a semimilitary order ruled their sections. A broad line of antagonistic purpose and allegiance divided North and South China.

In the course of internal difficulty, the Powers had resumed their march. Japan strengthened its interests and claims in Manchuria. In 1913 Russia compelled China to recognize Outer Mongolia as an autonomous province; Great Britain took the same action as regards Thibet. The debt of the Chinese Government to foreign lenders had greatly increased. Virtually all the surplus revenue that could be secured in the divided land by a broken government was pledged to the indebtedness.

Such was the tumultuous course of change, the cracking of old forms, the molding of new political sovereignties midst which foreign capital carried on its negotiations to finance the government and put forward its proposals to introduce the equipment of western industrial life. The Chinese mind, its ruler and its people, hesitated between recognition of the fact that, without this aid, strength could not be built to meet the pressing outside world, mingled contempt and admiration for the achieved strength of this outside world, and fear lest the capital and enterprise that entered to aid would be made the means of ruling. It swung from philosophy and submission to resistance. To the governments of Great Britain, Germany, France, the movement of capital and enterprise in China represented a healthy and irresistible push forward of their economic vigor, promising financial and commercial benefit. In the face of a shattered empire which might fall to the control of outside Powers, the undertakings of their capitalists conferred means and grounds of asserting political control when and as any issues affecting the political destiny of China arose. In addition each was convinced that without political support, economic and financial opportunity would be shut to it by rival Powers. Hence these governments sought place for their capital and enterprise by official action, supported them, often directed them. Their desire to establish a *régime* in which such action might be diminished, by which coöperation could in some measure supplant distrust, led them to support the arrangements for an international financial consortium which took form in 1910–13. To Russia, its loans to China, its railroad ventures, were primarily a means of extending political dominion over the regions bordering its already vast territories. To Japan they were the substance of plans by which its discipline and power, proven in the wars with China and Russia, might build a greater Japan on the Asian mainland.

The financing groups invoked their governments' help because they could hope for no equal consideration without it, and because special profits might be found in special concessions. But beyond these aspects of the situation was the further one that loans and investments in China could not be secure, unless some measure of control were exerted over their expenditure and some special pledges were granted and put under their care. In the rivalry of financial groups, and in the disturbed and suspicious condition of China, such guaranties were not easily secured or protected. The financial groups looked to their governments for protection against these risks and for support of advantages obtained.

THE FINANCING OF GOVERNMENT NEEDS[1]

BEFORE the war with Japan in 1894–95, the Chinese Government contracted almost no debt. The Imperial Court spent little either for the administrative, economic, or military activities that require most of the revenue of western governments. For the maintenance of the court, the ancient system of taxation, intrusted mainly to the pro-

---

[1] For the terms of the loan contracts, agreements, treaties, etc., referred to in the chapter I have relied on W. W. Rockhill, *Treaties and Conventions Concerning China and Korea, 1894–1904* (Washington, 1904), and W. W. Willoughby, *Foreign Rights and Interests in China* (Baltimore, 1927).

vincial authorities, had supplied enough. When the government sought to borrow, only foreign lenders came forward. An attempt to sell a domestic loan during the Japanese war failed. A second attempt, made in 1898 when the terms offered by foreign groups were judged dangerous to the independence of the government, likewise found insufficient support. The wealthy Chinese merchants did not trust their government, and had no recourse against it. The government had no organized system of selling its securities. Later during the revolutionary period, both the Yuan-Shih-Kai Cabinet at Peking and the Nanking Government appealed to their followers to support them by purchasing loans, all to no end. During the era before 1914, the Chinese Government was entirely dependent upon foreign lenders for the means of meeting new and special burdens.

Most of these burdens before the revolutionary period arose as a consequence of indemnities imposed upon China after defeat in war and antiforeign uprisings. During the war with Japan, the Hong Kong and Shanghai Bank (the official financial representative of Great Britain in the Far East) issued two loans, secured on the customs. The terms of peace imposed an indemnity of 230 million Kuping taels (about 170 million dollars), payable in instalments running over seven years. The French, Russian, and German governments had joined to force Japan to renounce the territorial conquests demanded by Japan as a condition of peace. Their success in this action gave France and Russia up to 1898 an ascendancy in Chinese political circles which they used to secure economic advantages and political claims for themselves. The first step in the program was the arrangement of a loan whereby China was enabled to pay off the first instalment of its indemnity to Japan. The British and German governments had also moved to extend the required aid, aware of the political advantages to be gained thereby.[2] But the British independent effort

2 *British Documents*, I, 1–3.

failed against the wiles of Count Witte, the Russian Finance Minister, and the compliance of the French bankers. The German banks had wished to participate in the transaction, but this wish was balked by Russian-French opposition.[3] The first indemnity loan was guaranteed by the revenue of the Maritime Customs (to be supplemented if necessary). In addition, the Russian Government gave its guaranty. In return it secured, among other advantages, the pledge that China would not grant any foreign power any right or privilege concerning the administration of its revenues, but in the event of such right or privilege being granted, it was to be shared with Russia. The French Government secured, in return for its aid, promises of railway and mining concessions in China which were soon after realized. It also secured the promise that French membership in the Chinese Customs Service would be increased.[4]

In 1895 the main British and German banking groups made an agreement to share Chinese business. For the next two decades the agreement held in regard to loans for general governmental purposes; it was gradually given up in the field of railroad and industrial financing. The German interests were represented by the Deutsche-Asiatische Bank in which all the large German banks including the Prussian State Bank, the Seehandlung, held shares. In the establishment of the Deutsche-Asiatische Bank, the German Government had been active, and to this institution was intrusted later the task of developing the German leased area and German railroad and mining rights in Shantung.[5] The Anglo-German group bid with the support of their governments for the loan needed in

[3] Despite earlier promises to the contrary. The Russian Government attributed the action to the French Government, which denied it. *Die Grosse Politik*, Vol. IX, Nos. 2280–2283, 2297.

[4] A. Gérard, *Ma Mission en Chine, 1893–1897* (Paris, 1919), pp. 68–73.

[5] See testimony of Mr. Max Schinckel, Director of the Diskonto-Gesellschaft, *German Bank Inquiry, 1908, Stenographic Reports* (National Monetary Commission, Washington, 1910), III, 16.

1897 to pay the second instalment of the indemnity due to Japan. The loan terms offered were much less favorable than those of the first indemnity loan. China sought other lenders.[6] The French Government with Russian support offered easier terms for a loan it would guarantee, if it were given in return control of the Customs Administration and various special privileges in three of the Chinese provinces. The Anglo-German group modified its terms. The French Government could find no French group willing to surpass them. The loan was sold in England and Germany, a 5 per cent loan at 94, secured by the surplus of the customs and some internal tariff duties (*likin* taxes). Included in the loan conditions was the provision that for thirty-six years the loan should not be redeemable and that during its currency no change should be made in the Imperial Maritime Customs. Thus the bond buyers were protected against the vacillations of the Chinese Government.

In 1898 the Chinese Government moved to pay off the remaining instalments of the Japanese indemnity in order to free territory in Japanese possession, and to save interest. Again the necessary credit was to be obtained only abroad. The Russian Government offered it in return for the privilege of "financing, construction and control of all railways in Manchuria and North China and on condition that a Russian should be appointed Inspector-General of Customs when the post became vacant."[7] China turned to the Anglo-German group. To the loan the British Government attached conditions also deemed harsh. These included control of special revenues, the extension of British railway rights throughout the Yangtse Valley, and the pledge that territory in that region would not be alienated to any other Power. Great Britain, despairing of the attempt to prevent other governments from securing exclusive fields of economic opportunity in China, had set

[6] *China Year Book*, 1914, Chap. XVI; Gérard, *op. cit.*, pp. 127–128.
[7] Great Britain, *China (No. 1), 1898*, p. 1.

its mind upon obtaining the Yangtse Valley as its sphere. Upon receipt of news that the Russian Government was prepared to guarantee another loan on easy financial terms, but with conditions affecting British vested or claimed interests, the British Government put forward easier terms.[8] It appears to have been prepared even to guarantee the loan for the Chinese Government.[9] The Russian Government in turn protested against the possible change in the balance of power, and, supported by France, threatened China with force. The contending governments were angry, and the presence of British ships at Port Arthur set rumors of war in currency.[10]

China deferred its borrowing in the hope that Japan might postpone payment of the maturing indemnity instalment. Great Britain, put off by this attitude and fearing Russian action, which was materializing itself with the seizure of the end of the Liaotung Peninsula and the extension of the Chinese Eastern Railway, exacted in February, 1898, from the Chinese Government promises that (a) it would not alienate the Yangtse Valley to any other Power, (b) that the Inspector-General of the Maritime Customs Administration should continue to be British as long as British trade with China exceeded that of any other Power. Upon being further disappointed in its approach to Japan, China contracted the necessary loan with the Anglo-German group. It was guaranteed by the surplus of customs, the salt taxes of some provinces and certain *likin* revenues. These were put under the supervision of the Maritime Customs Administration. Upon the return of the territory of Wei-Hai-Wei from Japan shortly thereafter, China was forced to yield it to British control, to be held as long as Port Arthur remained in Russian hands.

The loans required to pay the Japanese indemnity had

8 Memorandum by J. A. C. Tilley, *British Documents*, I, 1 *et seq.*
9 Great Britain, *China (No. 1), 1898*, p. 16.
10 Memorandum by J. A. C. Tilley, *British Documents*, I, 1 *et seq.*

thus hurried the mortgaging of the Chinese Empire. They exposed China to necessities which were made the occasion of claims to territory and privileges. They took from other possibilities of use the most certain and easily collected of Chinese revenues. The Central Government was left more dependent upon taxes collected by the provincial authorities, and by ordering these to be increased, contributed to the antiforeign feeling that broke forth in the Boxer Rebellion. When the wild and bloody course of this rebellion was run, when foreign troops controlled Peking, China had to face its costs. By the Treaty of 1901, China was made to compensate states, companies, and private individuals whom the rebellion had injured. The indemnity totaled 450 million taels (about 335 million dollars). For the service of this indemnity, which was payable over forty years, various sources of revenue were pledged. To assist it in meeting this new annuity, China was permitted to revise its customs duties so that they might represent an effective 5 per cent, for the course of price change had reduced them far below this level since first they were set. Now the Maritime Customs were burdened almost to their limit, the salt tax largely so in the absence of improvement of its administration, and even the arbitrary and hindering *likin* taxes confirmed in existence, and partly absorbed. Not much was left to finance railroad or industrial construction, even though the will might exist.

For the next decade Chinese loans were contracted only for railroad and industrial undertakings; these were mainly financed from the proceeds of the railways themselves. In 1908 the Chinese Government determined to go forward with plans for reforming its currency and taxation system, thereby hoping to allay discontent in the provinces. Throughout China a variety of silver coins, all of fluctuating value in terms of gold, were in use. The system burdened commerce and increased the difficulties of the Chinese Government whose external indebtedness was payable in gold. Seeking to avoid the concession of further control to European groups, the Chinese Government asked the American Department of State to arrange a loan with American banks. Besides the wish for currency and tax reform, funds were wanted to construct the Chinchow-Aigun railway and for industrial enterprises in Manchuria, for which objects American private interests had been vigorously pressing. A preliminary loan agreement was signed in October, 1910. By that time the Manchurian railroad project had been dropped and the field of effort of the American banking groups had shifted, owing to the opposition of the Russian and Japanese governments. The American banks decided that the plan required the participation of European groups, and out of their discussions a four-power consortium was formed. The French banks had joined the Anglo-German agreement in March, 1909.

The Chinese Government disliked the formation of this four-power consortium as limiting its borrowing opportunities. Despite the difficulties of the negotiations and the wish of the Chinese Government, the consortium maintained unity, though at times the British and German groups were lukewarm. The American group, urged by the State Department, asked as a condition of the loan that an American adviser be appointed to supervise the expenditure of the loan proceeds and the execution of the reform program. Because of this condition and the contemplated use of part of the funds for the promotion of industry in Manchuria, the Russian and Japanese governments tried by all measures to prevent agreement from being reached. In the activity of the American group they saw an intention of thwarting their ambitions in China. Despite the opposition, the loan contract was signed in April, 1911. The loan was to pay 5 per cent and to be issued at 95. The consortium had carried the search for special security into the internal taxes. The taxes on wine and tobacco, various production and consumption taxes in the Manchurian provinces, and a new surtax on salt were assigned to its service. In the event of default the administration of these taxes was to be turned over to the Maritime Customs Administration. The consortium was to be given preference on such further loans as might be required to complete the operations contemplated in the agreement. The contract provided for a neutral adviser to be nominated by the banks. The American banks yielded in their desire for an American adviser in the hope of allaying the fears of the Russian Government.[11] This adviser was given no actual executive power. The loan proceeds were to be spent in accordance with plans drawn in advance and approved by the consortium; the adviser might guide and check their execution. The Chinese Government was required to report to the consortium when drawing upon the loan funds, and periodically to the National Assembly or Senate. The Manchu Government had made as many concessions as it dared in the face of a public opinion hostile to the increase of the foreign debt, and the private interests opposed to the reform. Still it is doubtful whether the control provisions would have proven effective; such was the disorganization of the government and the wavering intentions of some of its officials.[12] The loan was never issued. For in June, 1911, the revolutionary movement began to take possession of the country.

The revolution brought into power as Provisional President at the head of a constitutional *régime*, Yuan-Shih-Kai. Called by the emperor to serve against the revolutionaries, he had entered into a friendly agreement with them, whereby the emperor was to be dethroned. The support given him by the revolutionaries of the South began to wane shortly after his accession to power. Yuan-Shih-Kai turned to the consortium for financial aid. The negotiations that followed became the focus of fierce national purposes, occupied the continuous attention of the For-

11 *Die Grosse Politik*, Vol. XXXII, No. 11747.
12 *Economist*, May 27, 1911, pp. 1128–1129.

eign Offices of seven Great Powers and more strikingly than ever before led governments to compel banks to be obedient to their will. To be weighed, the record must be related in some detail.

The loan was known as the "Reorganization Loan." It was to enable China to pay off claims and accumulated unfunded debt, to facilitate troop disbandment, to finance industrial enterprise, especially in Manchuria, and to provide the means of improving the governmental system. As a condition of advances made in February–March, 1912, Yuan-Shih-Kai had promised to give preference on equal terms to the four-power consortium. The consortium had made the advances out of fear of losing the larger loan and of possible Japanese action.[13] Difficulties had come into sight even before the option was obtained.

Russian opposition had become clear as early as October, 1911, for Russia feared that its exclusive claims in Manchuria and Mongolia might be brought into question. It sought, by most insistent demands, to break up the consortium by having the French group withdrawn by the order of the French Government.[14] But neither the Banque de L'Indo-Chine nor the Comptoir National would consent to that action, and Caillaux did not attempt to force them, wherefore, Isvolsky declared him to be under their influence and was aggrieved.[15] Failing in the effort the Russian Government next attempted to have the uses of the loan limited. The Russian Ambassador at Paris wrote in December, 1911, "We desire to break up the syndicate by urging the French group to withdraw and we should only be willing to enter the syndicate were this latter so transformed that a privileged position would be granted us in enterprises north of the Great Wall."[16] The bankers re-

[13] *Far Eastern Review*, VIII, 374.

[14] *Documents Diplomatiques Français, 1871–1914*, 3d ser., Vol. I, No. 448; *Livre Noir*, I, pp. 152, 175 *et seq.*

[15] R. Poincaré, *Au Service de la France*, I, 347 *et seq.*, II, 107; *Livre Noir*, I, 185–190.

[16] B. De Seibert, *Entente Diplomacy and the World*, p. 39.

fused to insert these conditions though the French Government supported its ally. The French Government served notice to the bankers and the governments concerned that it would not grant official listing to the Chinese loan unless the objectionable Article 16, dealing with Manchuria, were suppressed, and gave support to Russian claims in Manchuria, Mongolia, and Turkestan.[17] The British Government could not be induced to coerce the British banking interests; but it also sought to soften Russian anxiety by promising support in future contingencies.[18] In the Russian documents there appear many expressions of mistrust of the leading part assumed by the American group in the negotiations.[19] As a way of gaining its end the Russian Government next bent its energies to the formation of a Russian-Belgian-French-British syndicate (headed by the Banque Russo-Asiatique—its official institution) to divide Chinese loans with the consortium.[20] But the consortium banks would not share the business.

In March, 1912, the syndicate fostered by the Russian Government, or at least certain of the banks that had come together in that connection, loaned Yuan-Shih-Kai a million pounds. The British participants acted against the expressed wish of Sir Edward Grey.[21] Yuan-Shih-Kai had been seeking escape from the control arrangements asked by the consortium, which was refusing further advances till their terms were met. It was currently believed that this advance was needed to enable Yuan-Shih-Kai to buy off his political opposition.[22] Certainly he was pressed to supply funds to the provincial authorities. In return the prior option on equal terms for the Reorganization Loan was transferred to this new group of creditors.[23] Though

[17] Poincaré, *op. cit.*, I, 347 *et seq.; Documents Diplomatiques Français, 1871–1914, op. cit.*

[18] *Livre Noir*, II, 487.   [19] *Ibid.*, I, 232–234.

[20] *Ibid.*, I, 206–215; II, 491 *et seq.*

[21] Great Britain, *China (No. 2), 1912*, No. 14; *Livre Noir*, II, 353.

[22] *Economist*, June 29, 1912, p. 1450.

[23] *China Year Book*, 1913, pp. 350–353.

it was hardly likely that this group had the financial strength required for the larger operation, the members of the consortium besieged their own and the Chinese Government in protest. To their account stood the previous Chinese promise, and the fact that their governments had given official approval to the earlier advances made to strengthen the *de facto* Chinese Government.[24] The American and German governments gave direct support to the arguments of the consortium; they did not have to reckon with the purposes of an ally or the claims of rival banking groups for a free field. The British Government refused to permit itself to be committed fully to a program of exclusive support for the consortium. But it instructed its ambassador in China to refuse to receive the customary notification of the loan. On the other hand, it urged the Hong Kong and Shanghai Bank to admit into the British group some of the competing institutions.[25] When the Hong Kong and Shanghai Bank took no move in this direction, the matter was allowed to drop, and in the next crisis in negotiations government support was vigorously extended. In thus standing behind the consortium, the governments were moved by various considerations. A succession of small advances, made by outside banking groups and quickly dissipated, would absorb the special securities that were available for the larger loan and leave the Chinese Government no firmer or more effective than before. Without some measure of supervision over the expenditures of the proceeds, they might be diverted for private or party purposes. Without some arrangements for improving the revenue system, the debt would prove to be a heavy weight and insecure. And lastly, the Chinese Government might sign away to other Powers, under some secret pressure or panicky need, rights of political consequence.

Shortly thereafter, the Russian and Japanese govern-

24 Great Britain, *China (No. 2), 1912*, Nos. 5, 6.
25 *Ibid.*, No. 6.

ments were, through the influence of the French Government, invited to join the consortium.[26] Both, it was true, were borrowers in foreign money markets. But the French Government, in particular, was eager to soothe the irritation displayed by the Russian ally at the unwillingness of the French banks to withdraw from the consortium. Both Russia and Japan, particularly the former, put forward conditions that the German and British banks and governments found unacceptable. Russia planned to dispose of any part of the Reorganization Loan which it might take through British banks which were not included in the consortium. This prospect of competition displeased the Hong Kong and Shanghai Bank.[27] Besides, Russia and Japan both continued to try to limit the field of activity open to the consortium. Their aims were forcibly described by Mr. J. O. P. Bland at the time.

Russia and Japan having decided upon a common policy for the dismemberment of Northern and Northwestern China, have availed themselves of the activities and proclivities of international finance, and of its influence in the counsels of commercial powers, to secure official recognition of their political schemes in Manchuria and Mongolia.[28]

But during the weary negotiations that ensued, the banking groups would not yield to this demand, and no precise restrictions were imposed upon the consortium's activity.[29] Russia had to be content with various vague formulas in the *procès-verbal* and the assurance of the French Government that it would refuse official listing to any loan judged injurious to Russian interests.[30] It joined as the only means of maintaining watch and control over the use of funds loaned to China. So did Japan. The four-power

---

26 Poincaré, *op. cit.*, I, 347 *et seq.*; II, 107; *Documents Diplomatiques Français, 1871–1914, op. cit.*, No. 448.

27 The Russian share of the loan was finally handled through a group of French, English, and Russian banks.

28 *Economist*, April 27, 1912.

29 *Livre Noir*, II, 510–516.　　　　30 *Ibid.*, pp. 510–519.

consortium became the Sextuple Group in April–June, 1912.

During these months of dispute over the admission of Russia and Japan, and over the terms of the loan, advances were withheld from the Chinese ruler, who was suffering from the delay. The Sextuple Group, as a condition of reopening negotiations, secured a cancellation of the loan option given to the other syndicate. In return for the loan the consortium now asked first, that the uses of the loan be carefully specified in advance; second, that an audit system, headed by their representatives, be created to supervise the expenditure in accordance with the specifications; third, that the specially designated revenues, of which the salt tax was most important, be put under the administration of foreigners; fourth, that China appoint an agent of the syndicate to assist during five years in the work of financial reorganization; and lastly, that the group be given an option on future loans.[31] All the governments concerned were insistent upon the establishment of this measure of control. The British, French, and Russian governments endeavored to obtain their immediate acceptance. No agreement had been reached among them, however, as to the nationality of the foreign officials to be appointed, and in their individual reflections this left not a little concern. Yuan-Shih-Kai's financial need grew more acute with the passing days, yet these terms meant a sacrifice of independence for which he was not prepared. Strong elements in Chinese opinion, more or less hostile to him, were strongly opposed to any further foreign borrowing.[32]

An independent British syndicate proved willing to take greater risks than the consortium, and willing to

[31] For these terms and the details of the negotiations, see *Foreign Relations of the United States,* 1912, and H. D. Croly, *Willard Straight* (New York, 1924).

[32] The many abortive borrowing efforts by Yuan-Shih-Kai and the revolutionaries are traced in an informed fashion by P. Reclus, *Revue Économique Internationale,* February, 1913.

gamble that Chinese affairs would be put into order without foreign supervision, and eager to contest the privileges of the consortium. In the view that the British Government had no right to give exclusive support to any one financial group, most of the City stood behind this independent syndicate (known as the Crisp Syndicate and made up of three or four large banks and a few stock exchange houses). A general feeling prevailed moreover that the Sextuple Group was being made the servant of Russian and Japanese political purpose. The Crisp Syndicate agreed in August, 1912, to make the required loan. According to the contract, China was to be loaned 10 million pounds, secured by the salt tax. The syndicate was given a preference on equal terms for future loans. Sir Edward Grey made his disapproval known and tried in vain to stop the execution of the contract.[33] The British Ambassador in China was instructed, "You should accordingly warn the Chinese Government in the most serious manner of the unwisdom of their persisting with the loan at this juncture . . ."[34] All British claims outstanding against the Chinese Government were presented for immediate payment. Other governments took similar action. But the first half of the loan was issued in September. According to the *Economist* 60 per cent of it was left in the underwriters' hands.[35] The second half was never issued, though this may be attributable to the serious Balkan crisis which held the financial world in anxiety at the time. The incident shook the consortium's position for a time, but in the final outcome it remained as strong as ever. Yuan-Shih-Kai was in a chastened mood, though searching in every possible quarter for funds. Torpedo boats and destroyers were bought from an Austrian syndicate not so much because they were greatly desired, but because the loan thereby secured yielded a small amount of ready cash.

Before the consortium consented to resume negotiations,

[33] Great Britain, *China* (*No. 2*), *1912*, Nos. 22, 23, 29.
[34] *Ibid.*, No. 35.   [35] October 5, 1912.

it demanded and obtained a cancellation of the option given to the Crisp Syndicate. That cost China 150,000 pounds. Fresh causes of difference delayed the conclusion of an agreement—first, the Balkan wars, then dispute among the participants as to the nationality of the officials to be appointed. Mutual suspicion caused these places to be regarded as opportunities to serve the political interests of the governments concerned. The first set of appointments which were made brought French and Russian protests. After long bargaining, the division of places was finally agreed upon in February, 1913.[36] Almost immediately thereafter the American group retired from the consortium. President Wilson had refused to renew the request of the Taft administration that the American bankers participate.[37] He gave as reasons that the conditions of the loan caused the imposition of antiquated taxes, touched the independence of China, and might lead to intervention in its political affairs.[38]

The five remaining participants signed the loan contract on April 26, 1913, having already begun to make advances. The terms asked by the syndicate for this loan of 25 million pounds were substantially met. The securities paid 5 per cent and were to be sold to the bankers at 84 and the public at 90. One-half the proceeds was presumably to be used for paying off the standing debts and claims (costs of the revolution). The other half was to serve to aid troop disbandment, to reorganize the administration of the salt tax and for other governmental purposes. As security, the proceeds of the salt tax, the surplus of the customs, and certain internal provincial

[36] For details, see *China Year Book,* 1914, p. 382.

[37] The preceding haggling created in the mind of the American State Department mistrust of the situation created by the Consortium loan even before Wilson entered office. See *Foreign Relations of the United States,* 1913, pp. 164 *et seq.*

[38] See *American Journal of International Law,* 1913, pp. 335–341, for the statements of the President and the American banking group; *Foreign Relations of the United States,* 1913, p. 170.

revenues were set aside. In the event of default, the salt
tax was to be put under the management of the Maritime
Customs Administration. The Chinese Government undertook to reorganize the administration of the system of collection of the salt revenues in accordance with a plan out-
lined in the loan agreement. To the bankers was given a
preference, on equal terms, on any future loans that were
secured on the salt tax, or devoted to the same purpose
as this loan. A German was appointed director of the
Loan Bureau, with the duty of assuring jointly with a
Chinese director that the funds were used for the designated purposes. An Englishman was installed as associate
chief inspector and foreign adviser of the salt tax, with
powers of advice, inquiry, and audit. French and Russian
advisers were introduced into the Audit Bureau.

The Chinese Government made an official declaration
to the five interested Powers, accepting the obligations of
this loan; they in turn "took cognizance" of this obligation. Of this exchange the *Economist* commented, " . . . a
term which, though it might not get much money from a
banker on a private account, is accepted as an 'endorse-
ment' in the case of a national loan almost amounting to
guarantee."[39]

These loan arrangements were ill conceived. The system of supervision of expenditure and reforms introduced
was not sufficiently prepared or sufficiently firm to pull
the Chinese Government out of its disorganized state, to
compel it against wavering will to follow a wise path.
More extensive and stronger control arrangements could
not be obtained in the existing state of Chinese opinion.
But those established were sufficient to restrain to some
extent, to represent an interference that could be cast off
without too much difficulty. They therefore would have
been almost certain, had the war not come, to lead to further political intervention. Some of the loan proceeds were
almost immediately turned from their purposes, and signs

[39] *Economist*, May, 1913, p. 1278.

of altercation began to appear almost as soon as the loan was issued. This was what President Wilson foresaw. The alternative possibility of more thoroughgoing control was, however, at the time both impracticable and undesirable. The Chinese officials were not prepared to accept further outside checks and guidance—partly because of a belief in Chinese unity and steadiness which the outside world did not share, partly because it seemed likely that the political ambitions of competing states would shape the terms of such control. It was not till after the war that the example was given of international financial control freed from political design.

Still other reasons exist for expressing doubt concerning the transaction. China was divided when it was concluded. Southern China and the elements dominating the National Assembly under Sun-Yat-Sen were opposed to the loan. According to the newly promulgated constitution, parliamentary sanction was required, but neither the Chinese Senate nor Assembly was consulted. The contract was signed in strain and panic.[40] The Chinese opposition feared to see the loan used to crush Parliament and finance civil war. Directly or indirectly it served these purposes. Furthermore, in view of the state of Chinese politics and of the further fact that at the same time the Chinese Government was contracting indebtedness lavishly from groups outside the consortium and was accumulating new unfunded debts, it was highly doubtful whether this loan was sufficient for reorganization purposes.[41] The likelihood was that this loan would be followed by others

[40] *Foreign Relations of the United States,* 1913, pp. 123 *et seq.; China Year Book,* 1914; *Economist,* May, 1913. All describe the circumstances as suspect.

[41] The current budget deficits were very large, a great amount of poorly secured paper money was in circulation. The costs of demobilization were sure to be great. Only thoroughgoing reforms and economy could have made the sum suffice. For one thing almost one-tenth of it was needed to pay advances already made on the loan. E. Rottach, "Les Finances de la République Chinoise," *Revue Politique et Parlementaire,* June, 1913.

till the last special pledge had been assigned, the last item of security put aside. Events were taking that direction. In badly governed countries the course of borrowing on pledges of particular resources has usually ended by depriving them of the means of meeting current expenses. To avoid this outcome China needed a stable government in which Parliament controlled finances, thoroughgoing tax reform, and industrial development. Neither the contemporary internal situation, nor the provisions embodied in the loan permitted serious hopes of the immediate achievement of these conditions. Failing them, if the European war had not occurred, further intervention in China could hardly have been avoided. That outcome might not have been entirely unwelcome, especially to Russia and Japan.

Still, the loan was oversubscribed. Investors looked merely at the private credit aspects of the situation. The issuing houses possessed authority and prestige. A general sense prevailed that European governments would not permit default; the special pledges would be put under the Maritime Customs Administration, if the need should arise. On these considerations the ordinary purchaser, with correctness, relied. Moreover, the lenders were impressed by the fact that the service of previous loans was being met despite the revolutionary troubles. That this had been made possible only by virtue of fresh borrowing was not perhaps sufficiently realized.

During the negotiations with the consortium, and after, the Chinese Government found lenders outside. German-Austrian groups loaned 3.7 million pounds, most of which was designated for the purchase of armaments and munitions from Austrian shipyards. It was reported that these securities were resold in London. The Japanese banks made various advances for railway and construction projects. The French and British banks made railway and other loans. But above all, a new institution, the Banque Industrielle de Chine, came into the field with elaborate

The Financing of the Chinese Government 453

hopes and a willingness to finance projects from which more conservative institutions stepped aside. The creation of this bank was encouraged by Yuan-Shih-Kai's government to avoid the restrictions of the consortium. The Chinese Government contributed part of its capital and gave it valuable railway concessions and the right of note issue. Control of the institution rested in France. In 1914 it issued a Chinese loan for 100 million francs for public works and general governmental purposes. As security there were pledged, though not put under control, the municipal taxes of Peking, the tobacco and wine taxes in various provinces, and the revenues derived from the works to be undertaken. The issue of the loan in France was characterized by an interesting incident. In the prospectus prepared there was reprinted a letter of the French Minister of Foreign Affairs which gave the illusion of an official guaranty. Parliamentary protest led to the withdrawal of the letter. The emission was reputed not to have met with much success. But not long thereafter the same bank signed a contract for a vastly greater loan—600 million francs. This was never issued.[42]

It is impossible, unfortunately, to make any precise estimate of the foreign indebtedness of the Chinese Government in 1914. No complete and reliable official record exists, especially of the short-time loans and advances made by or for the various departments of the government. But the total long-term direct government debt approximated 600 million dollars. Substantially equal parts of the total had been incurred to meet, first, war and indemnity burdens; second, railroad construction; third, general governmental purposes. A short-time scattered indebtedness perhaps came to as much as 50 million dollars. In addition, the country was under the obligation of paying almost 15 million dollars a year upon the Boxer

[42] The bank in fact went into bankruptcy in 1920. For an account of its early activity and rivalry with the consortium, see F. Farjenel, *Revue Politique et Parlementaire*, June, 1914.

indemnity. For a country of the population and dimensions of China, the sum total of this indebtedness was singularly small. Yet it was sufficient to require a substantial part (approximately one-half, before the reorganization of the Salt Gabelle) of the two most dependable sources of revenue of the Central Government, even when allowance is made for the fact that most of the interest on the railroad debt was paid out of railway revenues.[43] The land tax, alone of China's important sources of revenue, remained untouched. The foreign obligations were payable in gold. The revenues were paid in silver currency which varied in value in terms of gold. Therefore, only approximate calculation is possible. Besides, most of the revenues of the Central Government varied according to the state of peace and relations with the provincial authorities. The expenditure was subject to even greater uncertainties. Budget-making in any country undergoing vital change is a baffling problem; in China in the years before 1914 it was little more than a blind game of chance. The revenue of the customs had slowly but steadily grown under foreign administration. The salt tax showed an immediate and great increase in yield after the reforms which were introduced in accordance with the Loan Contract of 1913.

The price and condition of further Chinese Government foreign borrowing would have been, had the war not come, a continued making over of its governmental and financial administration, independently, or by gradual extension of outside control of Chinese financial affairs. The first flush period of easy and unfruitful borrowing was past. Capital and enterprise require a political and

[43] These calculations are of necessity rough and drawn from a variety of sources. The most careful compilation of Chinese loans known to me is that in F. E. Lee, *Currency, Banking and Finance in China* (United States, Bureau of Foreign and Domestic Commerce, Trade Promotion Series, No. 27, Washington, 1926). The *China Year Books* are also a useful source. In the *Economist,* September 21, 1912, pp. 518–519, an independent estimate was made which is in general accord with my estimate.

social life fitted to their operation. Those who seek to command them are either induced to reshape their life in conformity with the necessary standard, or have their life reshaped against their will by the slow movement of events. Such were the alternatives presented to China in 1914; such they remain.

A NOTE ON THE CONSORTIUM

THE four-power consortium for Chinese loans arose out of the negotiations for the financing of the Hukuang railways in 1909–11. It took firmer form in the arrangements for the Currency Reform Loan of 1911. In the following year Japan and Russia were admitted; in 1913 the American group withdrew.

Under the arrangements the banking interests of each country which was in the consortium left the lead in the negotiation of loans to one, or two, of their number. The Japanese, Russian, French, and German banks that held this leading place had direct official connections with their government. The British bank was not bound by any formal official tie, but its executives were in intimate touch with the British Government and with the Bank of England. It was the backbone of almost all British enterprise in China. Some of the national groups in the consortium were subject to competition from other banking interests in their own country; others were not. No competition came from outside Russian or Japanese banks because of official supervision and the lack of capital in these countries. The competition of outside German banks was scattering, and, as far as large loan projects were concerned, unimportant because all of the powerful banks were members of the consortium.[44] Virtually none came from

[44] Certain Austrian firms, Karberg & Co., Carlowitz & Co., did make provincial loans despite their indirect connection with the consortium; the former was reputed to be an agent of Krupps. Diederichsen & Co., a German firm, did the same. See Great Britain, *House of Commons, Parl. Debates,* 5th ser., LIII, 434–442.

outside American banks because they were not, at the
time, interested in Chinese finance. French banks, not represented in the consortium from time to time entered into
competing syndicates—usually in combination with Belgian, Russian, and British interests. The Banque Industrielle de Chine, the creation of which in 1912–13 was
encouraged by the French Government, was prepared to
compete for all Chinese loans, and issued one large one.
Outside British banks resented the position given to the
Hong Kong and Shanghai Bank, which refused to widen
British membership in the consortium. With independence
they attempted to compete for Chinese loan business.
Belgian financial interests, directed by Leopold II, were
active in all parts of the Chinese loan field in competition
with the consortium.

Thus the consortium held, in this pre-war period, an
insecure position. Considering the competition and the
often divergent aims of the interested governments, it
is rather remarkable that any permanence at all was
achieved. But in the main the original founders of the
consortium gave it their support as a means of adjusting
their interests and of safeguarding the capital of their
investors by obtaining satisfactory loan agreements.

When first the four-power banking agreement was
made, it was probably intended to extend to government
loans for railroad and industrial purposes. Such seems to
have been the intention of the tripartite agreement of
1909, and the quadruple agreement of June, 1910. In
fact, the first issue made by the consortium was employed
in railroad construction. When, shortly afterward, the
French banker, Cottu, negotiated a loan by which Creusot
was to be given a bridge-building order, the French Government seems to have intervened.[45] When in August,
1912, the German firm of Diederichsen received a concession for the Peking tramways in return for an advance, the
Russian and French governments argued that this trans-

45 Reclus, *op. cit.*

action violated the spirit of the consortium.[46] The German Government replied that the consortium agreement did not extend to loans for industrial purposes. This view came to prevail. The Japanese Government was eager to have freedom of action in the industrial field. Japanese banks were making a series of loans to the Chinese Government for railways and public utilities, especially in Manchuria.[47] As late as September, 1912, however, protests were entered by the governments of the consortium Powers against loans made by a Franco-Belgian group (Compagnie Générale de Chemins de Fer en Chine) in return for a railroad concession.[48] But in January, 1913, Belgian, French, and Japanese banks multiplied their activity in loaning to the central and provincial authorities in return for advantages acquired or promised. The financial unity of China, as well as of the banking interests in the lending companies, broke down. Therefore, it was formally agreed between the governments that railway and industrial loans be excluded from the consortium arrangement. The interested financial groups had reached this decision first, on the understanding that the governments concerned be asked not to aid nationals who offered loans without requiring protection for the investors by some form of control over loan expenditure. In March, 1913, the British Government asked complete freedom of action, since the Belgian and American governments were bound by no agreements. The other governments consented. From the Chinese Government, challenged by revolution, but anxious to promote the economic strengthening of the country, diverse financial groups of half a dozen countries secured in 1913–14 railroad concessions to be financed through Chinese loans.

It would have been impossible, even if desirable, to have

[46] *Livre Noir,* II, 539–540.

[47] *The Consortium; the official text of the four-power agreement* (New York, 1921), p. 6, letter from the British Secretary for Foreign Affairs.

[48] "Le Consortium et les Emprunts Industriels Chinois," *L'Asie Française,* November, 1913, p. 408; *Livre Noir,* II, 561–563.

maintained the other position. In fact the whole consortium agreement had little vitality after the issue of the Reorganization Loan of 1913. China was divided by civil conflict. Its main field of operation—the general government financing—was, for the time being, gone. The short experience had shown the unsatisfactory features of the consortium plan. The loan terms proposed had to be sufficiently favorable to permit the weakest of the national groups to hope for a profit. Single groups attempted to deflect for their own purposes the policies of the whole consortium. Government support was vitally needed to shelter it against competition; but such support necessarily curtailed the independence of the members and gave their actions an official stamp. Japan and Russia were admitted as members not because they had capital to serve China's need, but because they wanted to stand guard over the actions of the consortium in behalf of their special claims and plans. The repeated quarrels among the members over the nationality of the agents to be employed in China increased the suspicion with which it was regarded among the Chinese.

Despite these revealed faults and difficulties the course of events proved clearly that international banking cooperation was essential to avoid reckless overborrowing on unsatisfactory terms, and incessant struggle for private and national advantage. Such international coöperation as the consortium was originally formed to undertake should make it easier for constructive and generally beneficial policies to prevail. If the public credit of a country is so poor that it must accept some measure of financial control in order to secure capital, it is preferable that the control be in the hands of an international group rather than in the hands of a single national group. But the control should be limited to the necessities of the case, and used solely for the purposes of the case. The success of the League of Nations (if I may step outside of the time limits of this study) in its financial reconstruction work suggests that such a body is a better instrument of control than bankers' groups. But the circumstances of each case will obviously require separate consideration. No single type of arrangement can be declared the best for all cases that may arise.

A NOTE ON THE MARITIME CUSTOMS ADMINISTRATION[49]

THE foreign-staffed customs service of the Chinese Empire originated during the Taiping Rebellion of 1853. The foreign merchants at Shanghai paid their duties to their consuls, then, by later arrangement, to foreigners appointed by the Chinese. In time the system was extended to the other treaty ports. A centrally controlled administration was developed, responsible to the Peking government to train the personnel and coördinate the work. At its head a foreigner served as Inspector-General. This executive, under the laws, had undivided authority over his subordinates and the work of revenue collection. After collection the revenues were paid into Chinese banks. The Chinese Government favored the institution during these early years because of its success in augmenting the yield of the customs, and its utility in enabling China to borrow abroad.

Under the Customs Administration was put, as the result of successive loan agreements, the Maritime Customs in the "treaty" ports and "leased areas," the Native Customs within sixteen miles of the treaty ports (since 1911), the tonnage dues and transit duties, and in some provinces the *likin* and salt taxes. The terms of several loan contracts provided, besides, that, in the event of default, revenues other than those just named should be put in its care. The revenues it collected were in 1914 pledged to the service of nine foreign loans and the Boxer Indemnity. As an

[49] For an account of its origins, see Willoughby, *op. cit.* For an account of its development, see S. F. Wright, *The Collection and Disposal of the Maritime and Native Customs Revenue Since the Revolution of 1911* (Shanghai and London, 1927).

increasing part of the revenues collected by the administration were required to meet the service of foreign loans
the liking of the Chinese for the institution waned. Mr.
Morse has described the change:

The loans of 1895, 1896, and 1898 to provide for the Japanese war indemnity were secured on the customs revenue, and
the official class now realised that their foreign customs service existed chiefly as a collecting agent for foreign creditors,
and no longer fulfilled the purpose which was the foundation
of its continued existence—collecting efficiently and honestly
a gratifying amount of revenue for the use of the Imperial
Government. Moreover, the service had grasped the junk
trade with Hong-Kong and Macao—a mandarinal (even
more, a Manchu) preserve; had been injected into supervision of a part of the Chinese internal revenue collection,
and directed and operated the growing postal service. Now
in the hour of China's humiliation, it was made the master
of its master through several of the stipulations of the final
protocol of 1901 and the commercial treaties of 1902 and
1903; it was now the foreign interest which was now concerned to magnify its importance, and no longer the Chinese;
and losing the favor of the Chinese, it lost also much of its
importance.[50]

The administration had been created by the voluntary
action of the Chinese. But when the revenues which it collected were pledged to the service of foreign loans, the
Chinese Government gave up its right to modify or ex-
tinguish it. By the loan contract signed with the Anglo-
German banking groups in 1896, the Chinese acknowledged the fact, promising that the administration would
be maintained as long as any of the loan remained unpaid.
In crises the Powers showed that they were ready to use
force to sustain the administration. Considering the suspicion with which every foreign appointment in China was

[50] H. B. Morse, *International Relations of the Chinese Empire* (London, 1918), II, 404–405.

scrutinized by alert rival Powers, the selection of staff for the administration caused comparatively little trouble. The British Government secured in 1898 the promise that the Inspector-General would be of British nationality as long as British commerce with China remained greater than that of any other country. The officials appointed to ports within the "leased areas" were usually of the nationality of the controlling Powers, or of alternative nationality acceptable to them. Few of the higher personnel were Chinese; that the administration did not train Chinese for the higher posts was one of the standing criticisms of it.

The administration vastly improved the system of revenue collection, making it more equitable, honest, just, and productive. Commerce benefited from the more regular examination of cargo, appraisal of values, and the prevention of smuggling. In the *likin* and salt taxes intrusted to it little improvement was made, however. There can be no doubt that the existence of the administration alone secured regular interest payments to the foreign bondholders during the period of divided authority and revolution. Thus it strengthened Chinese credit and enabled the government to borrow on easier terms than would otherwise have been obtainable. It also increased the amount that China was able to borrow—but not by much, certainly not by more than the increase in the yield of the customs. China's early borrowing was compulsory, a means of paying indemnities imposed upon her. The borrowing for railway construction would have been arranged even though there had been no foreign-staffed Customs Administration. Only the loans of the revolutionary period remain in question. Those set back the movement toward Chinese unity rather than the contrary. But Yuan-Shih-Kai would certainly have found some revenue to mortgage, and some lender to take the longer risk for a larger promised return. Of all the controls established over

Chinese economic life, of all the limitations imposed upon the Chinese Government, the Customs Administration brought the greatest benefit. Nevertheless many Chinese tended to regard it as a suppressive force.

CONCLUDING OBSERVATIONS—BY WAY OF
APOSTROPHE

OF the international capital movements between 1870–1914, what must be remarked is their volume and extension, their anonymity, their close alliance with the technical forces of industry, and their adjustment to political circumstance.

In volume and in the area over which they scattered, the capital movements of this period far surpassed similar movements in the past. What had been previously the special and infrequent venture of a bold group, or a draft upon a few private fortunes, became an extensive and ordinary trade. Foreign securities entered into the possession of thousands or millions of people. This change was the natural counterpart of other changes—of the broader spread of liquid and spared wealth, the increased familiarity with the corporate form of enterprise and "paper evidences of debt or ownership," of the increased speed of travel and communication and the increased faith in the safety of property rights. The growth in volume was no more marked than the extension of the lending-borrowing area. That included by 1914 regions which a half century before had been but remote outposts of European trade or dominion. In 1870 the eyes of China watched only the slow movement of native junks down inland rivers; the tired traveler was jounced in stagecoaches from the fever-stricken coast to the plateau on which Mexico City stands; the rushlights or candles of antiquity still burned in the houses along the Bosphorus Straits. In 1914, the locomotive speeded on heavy rails to the Siberian coast and into the heart of China; four railways entered Mexico City; power plants sent the electric light that was reflected in the Straits; all had been provided by foreign capital. The circumference of capitalist activity restlessly expanded to include the outermost regions.

All this movement of capital acquired, through the com-
plexity of modern industrial organization, a sort of anonymity. Only those who spent their days in the inner court
of financial circles knew its details. When the "Council
established at Plymouth in the County of Devon for the
Planting, Ruling, Ordering and Governing of New England in America" was established in 1620, the gentlemen
whose names were on its subscription list were known to
each other and to everyone else. The investment was an
enterprise of familiars. The New York, New Haven &
Hartford Railway, which now runs into Plymouth, Mas-
sachusetts, likewise drew capital from Europe. But its
securities changed hands daily, unremarked midst the multitude of similar transactions. The investment had become
large-scale, and anonymous. Thousands of individuals unknown to each other joined to support a company of
whose existence a periodical report would be their most
direct proof. History was being made without a signature.

This large-scale anonymous investment carried European industrial civilization with it, because it paid for
European industrial equipment. The provision of capital
to finance a royal extravagance or to equip an army was
not always without consequence; ten million pounds might
change a boundary line. The provision of the same sum
to found banks or buy power machinery, to be utilized
under the direction of executives and engineers trained in
modern industry, was sufficient to change a civilization.
In the escort of the capital that traveled from western
Europe went the business practices, the technical ways of
western Europe. Where it went, old economic habits and
relationships vanished, new ones formed. The civilization
of large commercial centers, distant exchanges, specializa-
tion, roundabout production took as its own the areas
where its capital was employed. Of all the consequences of
the capital movement, this was the most permanent and
the most fertile of future consequence.

One simple economic outcome was the change produced

in the distribution of economic effort within and between lands. Inside the countries of western Europe more and more of the population were drawn close to the walls of the office buildings, foundries, machine shops, power plants, and coal mines by which were made the equipment that western capital was providing. Elsewhere peoples were turned to supply the expanded wants of that machine-equipped civilization by planting wheat or sugar, tending sheep or cattle, mining tin or copper in lands made newly traversable. All the economic histories document the shift with batteries of statistics.

The persistent underlying consequences of the capital movement worked their way heedless of the nationality of those who supplied the capital and those who used it. But that the political structure and state of the world influenced the course of capital movement needs no fresh emphasis. The uses which the spared capital of western Europe found were often determined by political circumstance rather than by economic or financial calculation. The traditional theory of capital movements given in the economic texts, wherein capital is portrayed as a fluid agent of production put at the service of those who paid or promised most, is inadequate to account for the direction capital took before the war. In the lending countries international financial transactions were supervised in accord with calculations of national advantage, which were often unrelated to the direct financial inducement offered the owners of capital. Peoples and governments exerted themselves to direct the capital to those purposes which were judged likely to strengthen the national state, especially in time of war, or increase the chances of extended dominion. Capital was called upon to abstain from investment in the lands of potential enemies. It was urged or commanded into the services of allies. It was encouraged to develop the areas that were within the political system of the country where it accumulated. It was upheld in ventures which sustained a national political ambition or hope. In France and Germany, and within the alliances which they headed it came to be commonly regarded as a servant of national purposes rather than an ordinary private possession to be disposed of in accordance with the private judgment and on the private risk of the owner. Within Great Britain this attitude was much less common, yet not without influence upon the course of British investment. True, in none of these countries did capital completely lose its theoretical character of cosmopolitan, free agent, setting itself to opportunities wherever they emerged. But this character was subdued and checked almost out of recognition. The capital had not a free, a peaceful and settled world to move in. It adapted itself to the unrest and unsettlement; it became an important instrument in the struggle between national states.

The countries which borrowed showed themselves alertly conscious of the nationality of the ownership of the capital which they used. Those countries within or near the system of alliances were called upon to give political pledges, especially if their credit was weak. Toward the foreign capital which entered their state coffers or their borders many peoples displayed sensitiveness, arising sometimes from fear, sometimes from dislike, sometimes from their own national ambition. The responsibilities which must rest on all borrowers were often found irksome. To borrow without too serious obligation, to spend without too serious heed to the consequences, to be able to waste or blunder in the cause of national greatness—these were the desires which often made the reality distasteful. Therefore one and all looked forward to the time when foreign capital with the restraints it imposed would no longer be needed. Each country wanted to buy back its public securities, to redeem its railways from foreign ownership, to withdraw from foreign lenders all share in the making of national policy. Some countries advanced toward this goal, the United States, the British Dominions, Japan, and Italy, for example; some slid further and further away from it, as did China and Turkey. In short, borrowers wanted to nationalize the capital which was active in their domains, to assure themselves that this capital was subordinate to the national powers. It became clear that debts are not the kind of bond which can unite the world.

The preceding observations bear upon the matter of peace and war. To them others of similar bearing may be joined. The international movements of capital and of the financial groups who negotiate these movements are by some regarded as a leading cause of war, by others as a strong force for maintaining peace. During the period 1870–1914 they worked their effects in both directions, though seldom determining events in either. In some situations, in Tunis and the Transvaal for example, it was the calculations and activities of profit-seeking groups which kept antagonism alive and provoked war. In their efforts to secure political and social conditions under which they could operate satisfactorily, foreign financial interests hauled the political and military power of their governments behind them. Such was one way in which international capital movements sometimes brought nations into war.

Still another arose out of the disputes over the same opportunity in which the financial groups of different countries engaged. The chance to make loans to the Chinese Government, to build railways in Turkey, to acquire mining concessions in Morocco, were examples of such controversy. Because of the readiness with which national spirit and organization magnified the importance of the stake, because of the way in which each item of advantage may be made to fit in with every other in a broad program of national ambition, these disputes were taken up as national causes. Becoming public frictions as well as private ones, they became thereby harder to settle. Few were the important banking groups which at some time or place did not figure into these contests which ultimately called upon the national will. They were natural episodes

in the business of international finance, which the groups
could not avoid even if they would. And sometimes it is
probable that the groups concerned were not without the
feeling of pride or power that came from playing an important part in determining national destiny. Bankers
are subject to the forces of national feeling as are their
fellow men. Because of these facts it must be recognized
that international financial activity provided fuel for international controversy.

Yet even while the banking groups, and the investors
who bought the foreign securities they issued, sometimes
provoked international hostility, their interests in general
disposed them toward peaceful arrangements. For the financial groups a war between the Great Powers was certain to shatter important connections, to harm some of
their clients, to decrease the value of some of the securities which they had sold, to bring unpredictable dangers
which would outweigh any immediate gains from domestic
financing. Thus the great banking houses of Europe
showed themselves inclined to fall into coöperation or compromise with each other when the situation demanded, and
public opinion sanctioned. True, none of them willingly
shared exclusive, or renounced profitable business because
it might make peace firmer. That, they reasoned, was not
their responsibility; and competition among different
groups in each country seemed to make such renunciation
meaningless. Still, when the outcome of rivalry became
obviously menacing as in the financing of Turkey, the
Balkans, and China, important houses proved themselves
capable of compromise. In times of crisis their weight was
usually behind peaceful statesmanship. They could and
sometimes did lift themselves above the clamor of national
feeling.

The course of events in the pre-war period would appear to indicate that the international activities of capital,
of the groups which direct it or the millions who share in
it, cannot be expected to contribute much to the support

of international peace—unless the temper of the important national states change. Great international conflicts prepare themselves slowly; loans are made chiefly to friends or potential friends; the financial interest in peace declines in the face of long existing possibility of war. Official action intervenes to assure itself that national feeling is respected.

Before the international activities of capital can become a strong support for peace and strengthen the conditions of peace, the world in which the activities go on must be transformed in two directions. Governments of borrowing countries must improve in their art so that injustice, disorder, and waste do not invite external conquest. The peoples of the wealthy Powers must deeply care for international peace and direct their acts accordingly. If these conditions prevail the international movement of capital will record itself merely as an instrument of a mutually beneficial process of development. Capital which moves abroad will not carry with it the power of an organized national state, nor will it be forced to serve the political purposes of the state. International political machinery will adjust the difficulties that are incident to its ventures. The annals of the next epoch will relate fewer disturbances, greater creations.